Geocriticism and Spatial Literary Studies

Series Editor
Robert T. Tally Jr.
Texas State University
San Marcos, TX, USA

D1711217

Geocriticism and Spatial Literary Studies is a new book series focusing on the dynamic relations among space, place, and literature. The spatial turn in the humanities and social sciences has occasioned an explosion of innovative, multidisciplinary scholarship in recent years, and geocriticism, broadly conceived, has been among the more promising developments in spatially oriented literary studies. Whether focused on literary geography, cartography, geopoetics, or the spatial humanities more generally, geocritical approaches enable readers to reflect upon the representation of space and place, both in imaginary universes and in those zones where fiction meets reality. Titles in the series include both monographs and collections of essays devoted to literary criticism, theory, and history, often in association with other arts and sciences. Drawing on diverse critical and theoretical traditions, books in the Geocriticism and Spatial Literary Studies series disclose, analyze, and explore the significance of space, place, and mapping in literature and in the world.

More information about this series at
http://www.palgrave.com/gp/series/15002

Philip Edward Phillips
Editor

Poe and Place

palgrave
macmillan

Editor
Philip Edward Phillips
Middle Tennessee State University
Murfreesboro, TN, USA

Geocriticism and Spatial Literary Studies
ISBN 978-3-030-07251-3   ISBN 978-3-319-96788-2   (eBook)
https://doi.org/10.1007/978-3-319-96788-2

Library of Congress Control Number: 2018951030

Cover credit: THEPALMER/Getty

This Palgrave Macmillan imprint is published by the registered company Springer Nature
Switzerland AG
The registered company address is: Gewerbestrasse 11, 6330 Cham, Switzerland

For Bhanu Patel—
You who [were] more than mother unto me
Edgar A. Poe, "To My Mother," 1849

Series Editor's Preface

The spatial turn in the humanities and social sciences has occasioned an explosion of innovative, multidisciplinary scholarship. Spatially oriented literary studies, whether operating under the banner of literary geography, literary cartography, geophilosophy, geopoetics, geocriticism, or the spatial humanities more generally, have helped to reframe or to transform contemporary criticism by focusing attention, in various ways, on the dynamic relations among space, place, and literature. Reflecting upon the representation of space and place, whether in the real world, in imaginary universes, or in those hybrid zones where fiction meets reality, scholars and critics working in spatial literary studies are helping to reorient literary criticism, history, and theory. *Geocriticism and Spatial Literary Studies* is a book series presenting new research in this burgeoning field of inquiry.

In exploring such matters as the representation of place in literary works, the relations between literature and geography, the historical transformation of literary and cartographic practices, and the role of space in critical theory, among many others, geocriticism and spatial literary studies have also developed interdisciplinary or transdisciplinary methods and practices, frequently making productive connections to architecture, art history, geography, history, philosophy, politics, social theory, and urban studies, to name but a few. Spatial criticism is not limited to the spaces of the so-called real world, and it sometimes calls into question any too facile distinction between real and imaginary places, as it frequently investigates what Edward Soja has referred to as the "real-and-imagined" places we experience in literature as in life. Indeed, although a great deal of important research has been devoted to the literary representation of certain identifiable and well known places (e.g., Dickens's London, Baudelaire's Paris, or Joyce's Dublin), spatial critics have also explored the otherworldly spaces of literature, such as those to be found in myth, fantasy, science fiction, video games, and cyberspace. Similarly, such criticism is interested in the relationship between spatiality and such different media or genres as film or television, music, comics, computer programs, and other forms that may supplement, compete with, and potentially problematize literary representation. Titles in the *Geocriticism and Spatial Literary Studies* series include both monographs and collections of essays devoted to literary criticism, theory, and history, often in association with other arts and sciences. Drawing on diverse critical and theoretical traditions, books in the series reveal, analyze, and explore the significance of space, place, and mapping in literature and in the world.

The concepts, practices, or theories implied by the title of this series are to be understood expansively. Although geocriticism and spatial literary studies represent a relatively new area of critical and scholarly investigation, the historical roots of spatial criticism extend well beyond the recent past, informing present and future work. Thanks to a growing critical awareness of spatiality, innovative research into the literary geography of real and imaginary places has helped to shape historical and cultural studies in ancient, medieval, early modern, and modernist literature, while a discourse of spatiality undergirds much of what is still understood as the postmodern condition. The suppression of distance by modern technology, transportation, and telecommunications has only enhanced the sense of place, and of displacement, in the age of globalization. Spatial criticism examines literary representations not only of places themselves, but of the experience of place and of displacement, while exploring the interrelations between lived experience and a more abstract or unrepresentable spatial network that subtly or directly shapes it. In sum, the work being done in geocriticism and spatial literary studies, broadly conceived, is diverse and far reaching. Each volume in this series takes seriously the mutually impressive effects of space or place and artistic representation, particularly as these effects manifest themselves in works of literature. By bringing the spatial and geographical concerns to bear on their scholarship, books in the *Geocriticism and Spatial Literary Studies* series seek to make possible different ways of seeing literary and cultural texts, to pose novel questions for criticism and theory, and to offer alternative approaches to literary and cultural studies. In short, the series aims to open up new spaces for critical inquiry.

San Marcos, USA   Robert T. Tally Jr.

Preface: Poe, Place, and Space

> The land undulated very remarkably; and my path, for the last hour, had wound about and about so confusedly, in its effort to keep in the valleys, that I no longer knew in what direction lay the sweet village of B——, where I had determined to stop for the night.
> —Edgar Allan Poe, "Landor's Cottage," 1849 (M3: 1328)

This collection of fifteen original essays and one original poem explores the theme of "place" in the works, life, and—to some extent—the afterlife of Edgar A. Poe (1809–1849). *Poe and Place* seeks to demonstrate that "place" is an important critical category through which to understand this classic American author in new and interesting ways. The geographical "places" examined in this volume include the cities—most of them major publishing centers—in which Poe lived and worked, specific locales included in his fictional works, imaginary places featured in his writings, the places and spaces from which he departed and those to which he sought to return, both physically and imaginatively, and even some places he claimed to have gone or places that have embraced and continue to embrace him as their own.

The project traces its origins to two events focusing on the theme of Poe and "place" held at Middle Tennessee State University. First, I invited Scott Peeples to deliver a lecture on "Poe Places" as part of the Fall 2014 Honors Lecture Series on *The Power of Place*. In his presentation, Peeples discussed Poe as a "nowhere man," whose peregrinations—which included such cities as Richmond, London, Charlottesville,

Boston, Sullivan's Island, Baltimore, Philadelphia, and New York—reveal a pattern of seeking the idea of "home sweet home," ideas that are more fully developed in Chapter 1 of this collection. Second, I organized a *SymPOEsium on PLACE* in Spring 2015, sponsored by the University Honors College, which featured two panels. In "Poe in Europe," Alexandra Urakova discussed St. Petersburg, a place that Poe never visited but one that continues to embrace his legacy in literature and art. Sonya Isaak, who explored not a place, but an idea—the gothic—associated with Germany, a country Poe mentions but never experienced. And I discussed Poe's reception in France, a place where Poe set his Dupin mysteries but never visited personally, and the dissemination of Poe's works throughout Europe through Baudelaire's masterful translations. In "Angelic Places in Poe's Works," William E. Engel called the audience's attention to some of the imaginary places in Poe's works, those inhabited by angels, whether "good" or "ill," and the ambiguous meaning of absence. Harry Lee Poe brought the series full circle by considering Poe as an "everywhere man," rather than a "nowhere man," concerned with the material world and the divine volition behind the expansion and contraction of the universe. The lectures were followed by a special exhibition, *Selections from the Harry Lee Poe Collection* (with additional items from the George Poe Collection) that was held in MTSU's James E. Walker Library.

Building upon the work presented at those special events and comprised of invited chapters written by well-established as well as emerging Poe scholars, *Poe and Place* aspires to contribute to Poe studies by participating in an ongoing spatial trend in literary scholarship to "map" literary relations with the aim of revealing hitherto unknown connections and ideological or cultural relationships. Poe is an appropriate figure for geocritical consideration because of his enormous versatility as a writer of reviews, cryptograms, hoaxes, satires, detective tales, science fiction, poetry, tales, literary theory, and a prose poem on the material universe, who struggled as an author and an editor to earn a living and achieve a name for himself in the U.S. literary marketplace and its "culture of reprinting."[1] While much nineteenth- and twentieth-century criticism characterized and considered Poe as an artist disengaged from the material world, "Out of Space—out of Time" (M1: 345),[2] more recently, early twenty-first criticism increasingly has examined Poe as a serious writer, deeply engaged in his world, a "magazinist" whose imaginative writings and aesthetic theories responded to and capitalized effectively upon the demands of the print culture of his time.[3] In addition to considering Poe within the context of antebellum America, *Poe and Place* attempts to contribute to the ongoing examination of Poe's trans-Atlantic affinities, global influence, and international appeal by exploring his associations with place and arguing for his global significance as a world author.[4]

Whether in overt or subtle ways, each chapter in this volume participates in the interdisciplinary project of "human geography" that studies the importance of "place" and "space." While these terms are related, they are not interchangeable. Without wanting to insist on overly pedantic distinctions, it is useful for the purposes of this collection to explain the broad outline of how they differ and, to some extent, overlap. In the Western intellectual tradition, as Edward S. Casey has shown, the Pythagorean philosopher Archytas "declared that place 'is the first of all beings, since everything that exists is in a place and cannot exist without a place."[5] Further, in his *Physics*, Aristotle "adds that 'if such a thing is true, the power of place will be a remarkable one, and prior to all things."[6] Basically, place is active and independent in its being; it is also likened by Aristotle to a vessel, yet coincident with the thing, insofar as boundaries are coincident with the bounded. Space concerns more the idea or extension of the idea of place (remembering that place, as such, has its own distinctive dimension, thus constituting what can be termed "regions"), the extending of place, within and through which things are said to happen—whether in the world or the imagination.

And so, throughout, this volume asserts the centrality of "place" in Poe's creative imagination and life journey by intentionally offering a range of new scholarly directions for future exploration. Moreover, as is made clear in a variety of ways, "place," especially as regards the life and work of Poe, implies far more than what traditionally is called "the setting," and it concerns much more than what usually is comprehended by the rhetorical tropes of *topographia* (literally, the vivid description of a place) and *chorographia* (the device designating a written description of a particular district or region, foreign city, or even country). Such traditional approaches to the literary understanding of place, of course, figure into many of these chapters; and yet, the wider issue at stake is why—and in what ways—place matters.

The volume thereby contributes to Poe studies (critical, literary historical, biographical, and comparative) and to the emerging field of "geocriticism," with its sustained interest in space and place. It is in this respect that comparativist concerns come into play in the volume with the aim of providing critical insight into geocriticism and, thereby, opening up a way to address global literary phenomena more generally. As Bernard Westphal has clarified, "geocriticism" is an approach that seeks "to explore some of the interstices that until recent times were blank spaces for literary studies" and tends to be "affiliated with those theories that unleash spatial perception and representation in a nomadic perspective."[7]

Immediately following this preface, the poem by Charles Cantalupo imaginatively engages with a city of particular significance to Poe from his childhood to his final days. Set in the present, "Poe in Richmond"[8] invokes the times he lived there and juxtaposes then and now in a continuum of poet, place, and people. The focus is on moments in the history of the place and the life of the poet as well as on specific locations in the city where Poe's biographers "place" him. Yet the poem's American variation of English and classical heroic hexameter blurs the line between history and fiction, biography and literature, real and imaginary. The poem provides what Westphal terms a "polysensuous approach to places," in this case Richmond, with its diverse "sounds, smells, tastes, and textures"[9] related to the present and past of this place. In a unique way, then, this poem provides various pathways into the themes of "place" and "space" throughout the volume.

The book, as a whole, follows a deliberately chiastic design in which two parts consider different modes of comprehending the idea of place, framing a central nest of chapters all foregrounding Poe's imaginative "spaces." It is followed by two more parts in which place is interrogated further, thereby establishing an itinerary, or "mapping," for the reader's journey suited to the thematics of place and space on display in this volume. Just as the chapters can be read sequentially, each one of them can be read individually, on its own, according to a reader's interests. In the latter case, the chapters speak for themselves and treat the themes of place and space in new, diverse, and nuanced ways.

Part I, *A Sense of Place*, serves as an introduction to the chapters that follow by providing a context in which to consider Poe's engagement with different geographical places and imaginative spaces. This part features Chapter 1, "'No Direction Home': The Itinerant Life of Edgar Poe," in which Scott Peeples takes a broad view of Poe places and suggests that Poe's itinerancy might well be the key to understanding his tumultuous life and, to a great extent, his work. In childhood and adolescence, Poe had little or no choice in the matter of relocations; as an adult, he was motivated primarily by poverty, literary ambition, and concern for his wife's health. Drawing on geographer Yi-Fu Tuan's axes of "cosmos" and "hearth,"[10] this introductory chapter posits Poe as a cosmopolitan less by choice than by lifelong circumstance and points out that Poe's tales, when they depict "home" at all, often counter popular antebellum ideals of domestic tranquility.

Part II, *Geographical Places*, features chapters devoted to Boston, Richmond, London, Baltimore, Philadelphia, and New York City, cities that were important to Poe and to the American publishing industry. In Chapter 2, "Poe and Boston," Katherine J. Kim examines Poe's complex and often tumultuous relationship with Boston, the city of his birth, from his grandmother's and parents' theatrical performances to his efforts to return as a young poet, as a speaker on the lyceum circuit, and as an author published in such periodicals as *The Flag of Our Union*. The chapter examines key episodes in Poe's life related to Boston—the publication of his first volume of poetry, his enlistment in the U.S. Army, his verbal rows with the Boston literati, including the 1845 Boston Lyceum appearance, and his romantic/literary relationships as well as his failed suicide attempt in Boston. It also considers places and spaces in Boston related to his professional life, perceptions of Poe by Bostonians, and his reception today in Boston with the installation of Stefanie Rocknak's statue, *Poe Returning to Boston*.

In Chapter 3, "Poe's Richmond and Richmond's Poe," Christopher P. Semtner follows the trail of Poe through Richmond, Virginia, from his childhood in the early nineteenth century to his lingering presence in the twenty-first. The chapter examines the ways antebellum Richmond shaped Poe's life and literature as well the ways Poe influenced the evolution of the city to the present day.

In Chapter 4, "The Realm of Dream and Memory: Poe's England," J. Gerald Kennedy examines place imagery in four tales—"Ligeia," "Usher," "William Wilson," and "The Man of the Crowd"—as fantastic projections of an imaginary England pieced together in part from recollections of Poe's childhood years, 1815–1820, a time spent in or near London with visits to Scotland. Kennedy examines the cultural history and makes use of period maps to note correlations, like the proximity of the British Museum to John Allan's residences. He elucidates the problem of "place" as articulated via the crucial sites and scenes envisioned in the principal tales. These works seem particularly provocative, suggesting that Poe wished to invest remembered places with something like the complex architecture of the unconscious.

In Chapter 5, "Poe and Baltimore: Crossroads and Redemption," Jeffrey A. Savoye discusses the role of Baltimore, its cultural milieu, and the likely effect on Poe's writings. It is the story of Poe finding an enduring family, a new career, and a tragic fate. Following his death in 1849, Poe's reputation suffered greatly at the hands of his literary executor, Rufus Wilmot Griswold, and the legion of professional scribblers who felt that Poe had personally abused them in his criticisms. The movement to erect a monument over his grave in Baltimore began quietly, but quickly became a rallying call to reconsider America's misunderstood genius. The final result was a renewed interest in Poe's life and writings, and a lasting place in the American literary pantheon.

In Chapter 6, "Poe in Philadelphia," Amy Branam Armiento explores Poe's life and productive literary career in Philadelphia, the place he lived the longest except for his childhood in Richmond. She also examines the many ways in which the city shaped Poe's tales, examines Poe's intention to found *Penn Magazine*, and discusses his early aspirations to become the owner and editor of a major literary magazine.

The part concludes with Chapter 7, "Outside Looking In: Poe and New York City," in which John Gruesser discusses the hopes and disappointments and the high and low points of Poe's New York years (early 1837 to early 1838 and April 1844 to October 1849). He also examines two sets of articles that reflect Poe's anomalous position in relationship to the metropolis: "Doings in Gotham" (1844), a travelogue by an outsider who shares what he has learned about the city with provincial readers, and "The Literati of New York City" (1846), a mix of gossipy portraits and glib assessments of New York writers from the perspective of a purported insider. He also analyzes Poe's most famous story about an outsider and an insider, "The Cask of Amontillado" (1846).

Part III, *Imaginative Spaces*, occupies the central place within this volume as it deals with various manifestations of the "fantastic" or "unknown." In Chapter 8, "Fantastic Places, Angelic Spaces," William E. Engel examines the implications of angelic spaces in the larger literary and ontological framework of Poe's thought and work. Angels in Poe are not traditional Judeo-Christian sweet-singing seraphs; there are no harps and no hosannas. Instead they create (and destroy) worlds through words; they guard and they goad; they sigh—and they mature over time. An amalgam of Neoplatonic, Gnostic, and Islamic attributes, angels bespeak an essential and fundamental place of cosmic wonder rooted squarely at the core of poe's poetic imagination.

In Chapter 9, "Re-ordering Place in Poe's *Arthur Gordon Pym*," Richard Kopley presents chronologically, first, the places in Poe's life, from Boston to New York City, suggested by the novel, and, second, the places in the Bible, from Jerusalem to the New Jerusalem, suggested by the novel. This "recomposition" seeks to highlight and to explore the underlying autobiographical and biblical allegories in the work.

In Chapter 10, "Poe's German Soulscape: Influenced by Angst or Anxiety of Influence?," Sonya Isaak discusses Poe's ambivalent relationship with German literary influences. In her chapter, Isaak explores a puzzling dilemma: Poe's familiarity with and use of German sources countered by his reluctance to be affiliated with the German Gothic tradition.

Part IV, *Imagining Spaces*, includes chapters dedicated to places that Poe claimed to have gone, spaces imagined by Poe that he incorporated into his writings, places that Poe never visited that nevertheless claim him as one of their own. In Chapter 11, "'Demon of Space': Poe in St. Petersburg," Alexandra Urakova focuses on one of Poe's imaginary destinations—St. Petersburg, Russia. In the first part, she describes the growth and the persistence of the autobiographical myth in the United States, France, and particularly in Russia from the early biographical records in mid-nineteenth century magazines to the Soviet time. She argues that Poe's Russian adepts almost tangibly felt Poe's "ghostly" presence in St. Petersburg while the story of his alleged visit to the Russian capital circulated as both a legend and fictional plot. In the second part, she highlights typological parallels and affinities between Poe and his kindred spirits and literary doubles, Gogol and Dostoevsky.

In Chapter 12, "Poe, Egypt, and 'Egyptomania'," Emily James Hansen examines Poe's interest in Ancient Egypt and "Egyptomania"—the nineteenth-century fascination with Ancient Egypt that influenced art, literature, architecture, fashion. Poe's incorporation of Egypt and "Egyptomania" in many works—including some of his most famous tales, "Ligeia" and "The Fall of the House of Usher"—not only reveals his deep awareness of popular culture but also hints at an attempt to preserve this place, Egypt, in literature.

In Chapter 13, In "Poe, Paris, and 'The Murders in the Rue Morgue,'" Philip Edward Phillips and George Poe explore how a cultural understanding of France, and of Paris, came to Poe, and in what ways it influenced his writings. The chapter discusses the ways in which Poe, as seen through the eyes of Charles Baudelaire, exerted such a profound influence in France. It also offers fresh perspectives on the relationship between Poe and France by considering Poe's Paris—as featured in "The Murders in the Rue Morgue"—and by examining specific Parisian places (some real, some imaginary) mentioned in the first of his Dupin mysteries, usually credited for inaugurating the genre of detective fiction.[11]

The section concludes with Chapter 14, "'Un muerto vivo': Poe and Argentina," in which Emron Esplin examines Poe's literary relevance in Argentina, including his influence on Leopoldo Lugones, Horacio Quiroga, Jorge Luis Borges, and Julio Cortázar. Poe's influence on and affinities with these major figures demonstrate his long-lasting presence in a place he never visited and about which he never wrote. In the place-oriented terminology of geographer Edward Relph, Poe's Argentine advocates have moved him from a position of oblivious "outsideness" to one of "existential insideness."[12] In short, while Argentina appears to be a non-place for Poe, it is a place that adopts, proliferates, responds to, and tweaks Poe like few others do.

The volume concludes with Part V, *Coda: Space as Place*, comprised of Chapter 15, "'Finding His Way Home': Tracing Poe's Solutions in *Eureka*," by Harry Lee Poe, which reflects on the idea of space as place. The universe, or "everywhere," signifies to Poe both our end and our beginning, according to his imagined cosmology. It is the ultimate space from which creativity itself emanates and eventually is reabsorbed, a cycle that repeats itself *ad infinitum*. In this concluding chapter, Poe explores the places of which, in which, and from which Edgar A. Poe devised his conception of the physical and spiritual universe from its beginning as a primordial particle until its end. The chapter maps the development of Western scientific thought from Athens to the major centers of thought in 1848 while exploring the universe from operations of the yet unknown sub-atomic world to the expansive universe of galaxies. In *Eureka*, Poe intuited what science would come later to understand about the universe before science had the vocabulary, methodology, or technology to examine it empirically. Without the necessary tools of science available to him to couch his discussion in scientific terms or formulae, Poe was left to refer to *Eureka* cryptically as a prose poem.

Collectively and individually, the chapters in *Poe and Place* argue that "place" is central to an understanding of Poe in relation to the geographical places he knew during his lifetime, the uniquely imaginary spaces that he conveyed in his works, and the imagined spaces claimed by Poe or places that claimed Poe as their own. The geo-critical and geo-spatial perspectives in the volume offer fresh, new readings of Poe. The poem, critical essays, and selected bibliography provide readers new vantage points from which to approach Poe's life, literary works, aesthetic concerns, and cultural afterlife. This volume, then, suggestively and instructively can be compared to Poe's "sweet village of B——," for it is the contributors' hope that their efforts will have supplied a place for the traveler to rest for now, until others come along to take up this itinerary once more in earnest.

Murfreesboro, USA   Philip Edward Phillips

NOTES

1. See Meredith L. McGill, *American Literature and the Culture of Reprinting, 1834–1853* (Philadelphia: University of Pennsylvania Press, 2003).
2. According to T. O. Mabbott, this oft-quoted phrase from "Dream-Land," line 8, is "sometimes applied with partial justice to Poe's poetry" (M1: 345, note 8).
3. Recent collections of essays on Poe that challenge previous characterizations of Poe as a figure on the margins of American literature and culture, arguing instead for a more nuanced consideration of Poe within a wide array of literary and cultural contexts. These include: James M. Hutchinsson, ed., *Edgar Allan Poe: Beyond Gothicism* (Newark: University of Delaware Press, 2011); J. Gerald Kennedy and Jerome McGann, eds., *Poe and the Remapping of Antebellum Print Culture* (Baton Rouge: Louisiana State University Press, 2012); Alexandra Urakova, ed., *Deciphering Poe: Subtexts, Contexts, Subversive Meanings* (Bethlehem, PA: Lehigh University Press, 2013); Kevin J. Hayes, ed., *Edgar Allan Poe in Context* (Cambridge: Cambridge University Press, 2013); and, forthcoming, J. Gerald Kennedy and Scott Peeples, eds., *The Oxford Handbook of Edgar A. Poe* (Oxford: Oxford University Press, 2019).
4. Recent collections of essays that argue for Poe's international significance and call for his reconsideration in respect to global concerns include: Lois Davis Vines, ed., *Poe Abroad: Influence, Reputation, Affinities* (Iowa City: University of Iowa Press, 1999); Barbara Cantalupo, ed., *Poe's Pervasive Influence* (Bethlehem, PA: Lehigh University Press, 2012); and Emron Esplin and Margarida Vale de Gato, eds., *Translated Poe* (Bethlehem, PA: Lehigh University Press, 2014).
5. Edward S. Casey, *Remembering: A Phenomenological Perspective* (Bloomington and Indianapolis: Indiana University Press, 1987), 184.

xx   PREFACE: POE, PLACE, AND SPACE

6. Ibid.
7. Bertrand Westphal, "Foreword," in *Geocritical Explorations: Space, Place, and Mapping in Literary and Cultural Studies*, ed. Robert T. Tally, Jr. (New York: Palgrave Macmillan, 2011), xiii.
8. Charles Cantalupo's "Poe in Richmond," is one of five poems in a series, "Poe in Place." The other four poems focus on Poe's extant residences in the United States—in Baltimore, Philadelphia, and the Bronx (or Fordham, as it was known in Poe's day)—and on one imagined location, the ruins of the winter palace of the Ethiopian emperor, Haile Salassie, in Massawa, Eritrea, where Cantalupo encountered a raven on a marble cornice. See Charles Cantalupo, "Poe in Place," in *Poe's Pervasive Influence*, 109–116, which includes the poems "Poe in Massawa," "Poe in Philadelphia," "Poe in Fordham," and "Poe in Baltimore."
9. Westphal, xiv.
10. Yi-Fu Tuan, *Cosmos & Hearth: A Cosmopolite's Viewpoint* (Minneapolis: University of Minnesota Press, 1996), 2.
11. For an authoritative treatment of the Dupin tales and their role in the development of the genre of detective fiction, see Richard Kopley, *Edgar Allan Poe and the Dupin Mysteries* (New York: Palgrave Macmillan, 2008). Kopley concludes his Introduction, "It is true, as Borges has noted, that Poe invented the genre that 'conquered the...world'; we should add that through this genre—especially the Dupin tales—Poe also taught the world" (5).
12. Relph theorizes that "[t]he major components of the identity of place do not apply solely to place, but are to be found in some forms in all geographies, landscapes, cities, and homes. The essence of place lies not so much in these as in the experience of an 'inside' that is distinct from an 'outside'. [...] To be inside a place is to belong to it and to identify with it, and the more profoundly inside you are the stronger is the identity with the place." See Edward Relph, *Place and Placelessness* (London: Pion Limited, 1976), 49.

Acknowledgements

It gives me great pleasure to recognize everyone who contributed to the creation and publication of *Poe and Place*, a volume that was several years in the making.

I am especially indebted to Richard Kopley, Penn State—Dubois, for his advice and support in the earliest stages of this project; Harry Lee Poe, Union University, who gave me full access to his extensive Poe collection and supplied many of the figures included in this volume; and William E. Engel, The University of the South: Sewanee, who contributed significantly to both the conceptualization and realization of this book.

I must give special thanks to my doctoral research assistant, Amy A. Harris-Aber, Middle Tennessee State University, for helping me most reliably with all aspects of the pre-publication process, from checking format and collecting author permission forms to copyediting text and creating the index.

Several chapters of this book trace their origins to two special events hosted by the University Honors College at Middle Tennessee State University. First, I would like to thank Scott Peeples for giving a presentation on "Poe Places" as part of the Fall 2014 Honors Lecture Series on "The Power of Place." Second, I would like to thank Alexandra Urakova, Sonya Isaak, William E. Engel, Harry Lee Poe, and George Poe for joining me in giving presentations at the Spring 2015 *SymPOEsium on PLACE*. I am grateful to everyone who attended and participated in those events, especially Arlo Hall and Mo Li, who served as moderators at the *SymPOEsium*.

I am grateful for the permission to use materials in this volume from the Harry Lee Poe Collection, Susan Jaffe Tane Collection, and the Edgar Allan Poe Museum, Richmond, Virginia. I am also grateful for the use of materials from the W. T. Bandy Center for Baudelaire and Modern French Studies, Vanderbilt University; the Boston Athenaeum; and the James E. Walker Library, Middle Tennessee State University. Special thanks to librarians Yvonne Boyer (Bandy Center) and Carolle Morini (Boston Athenaeum) for their kind assistance.

I would like to thank former Provosts Kaylene Gebert and Brad Bartel, current Provost Mark Byrnes, and Honors Dean John R. Vile for their generous support of my leadership roles in the Poe Studies Association and my various Poe-related trips to Boston, Baltimore, Philadelphia, Richmond, Charlottesville, and New York.

I am also grateful to Susan Lyons, Marsha Powers, Megan Donelson, and Erica Rodgers for their various contributions to this volume.

I owe special thanks to Series Editor Robert T. Talley, Jr., Literature Editor Allie Troyanos, Editorial Assistant Rachel Jacobe, Production Manager Meera Mithran, and the anonymous readers at Palgrave Macmillan for their professionalism, attention to detail, and enthusiastic support of this project from proposal to published book.

Finally, I would like to thank my wife, Sharmila Patel, and our son, Edward Phillips, who have supported and encouraged my interest in the life, works, and global influence of Poe throughout the years.

PRAISE FOR *POE AND PLACE*

"Bringing together a company of established and rising scholars, Philip Edward Phillips gives us a valuable collection of essays on a subject not previously explored with such concentrated attention—and the richly varied results bear out the choice of focus. That Poe's relations to place, whether in life or in text, whether geographical or imaginative, have a special tendency to tease and elude us makes for a provocative project."
>
> —Jana Argersinger, *Coeditor of* Poe Studies: History, Theory, Interpretation

"The essays here show how Poe was shaped by the cities he lived in—including Boston, Richmond, London, Charlottesville, Baltimore, Philadelphia, and New York—and how places, real and fantastic, figure in his works. In *Poe and Place*, scholars, teachers, and fans will find both historical specificity and new insights into the imagination that carried Poe, as he put it in 'Dream-Land' (1844), 'out of space [and] out of time.'"
>
> —Paul Lewis, *Professor of English, Boston College, USA*

"Although born in Boston, Poe has long been considered a genteel Southern writer whose works display a fascination with foreign countries and fantastical places. However, he spent the majority of his literary career working in the northeastern publishing centers of Baltimore, Philadelphia, and New York City. Is Poe a literary 'nowhere man,' an all-American writer, or a prophet of world literature? This collection of insightful essays is a critical mystery tour to the center of Poe's wonderful planet."

—Takayuki Tatsumi, *Professor of English, Keio University, Japan*

CONTENTS

Part V   Coda: Space as Place

Notes on Contributors

Amy Branam Armiento is Associate Professor of English at Frostburg State University and the current President of the Poe Studies Association. Her publications on Poe appear in *Edgar Allan Poe: Beyond Gothicism*, edited by James Hutchisson (2011), *Edgar Allan Poe in Context* (2012), edited by Kevin J. Hayes (2012), *Deciphering Poe: Subtexts, Contexts, and Subversive Meanings*, edited by Alexandra Urakova (2013), as well as various journals and literary encyclopediae. She has served on the Poe Studies Association executive committee since 2011.

Charles Cantalupo is Distinguished Professor of English, Comparative Literature, and African Studies at Penn State. "Poe in Richmond" is the last of a series of five poems called "Poe in Place," on cities where Poe lived. Previous sections appear in *Poe's Pervasive Influence* (Bethlehem: Lehigh University Press/Rowman & Littlefield, 2012: 109–116). Cantalupo has published three collections of poetry: *Where War Was* (Mkuki na Nyota, 2016), *Light the Lights* (Red Sea Press, 2004), and *Anima/l Woman and Other Spirits* (Spectacular Diseases, 1996). He has also published three books of translations of Eritrean poetry. His memoir, *Joining Africa–From Anthills to Asmara* (Michigan State University Press, 2012), a story of poets and poetry in Africa, won the Next Generation Indie Book Award in 2012. His scholarly publications also include books on Thomas Hobbes, Ngugi wa Thiong'o, and Eritrean poetry.

William E. Engel is the Nick B. Williams Professor of English at Sewanee, The University of the South. He is the author of five books of literary history, including *Early Modern Poetics in Melville and Poe: Memory, Melancholy, and the Emblematic Tradition* (a Yankee Book Peddler Literary Essentials Title for 2013; reprinted in paperback with Routledge, 2016) and, most recently, *The Memory Arts in Renaissance England: A Critical Anthology* (co-edited with Rory Loughnane and Grant Williams) for Cambridge University Press. He served on the Executive Committee of the Poe Studies Association, and is on the Editorial Board of *Renaissance Quarterly*.

Emron Esplin teaches U.S. literature and inter-American literary studies in the English Department at Brigham Young University. He received the 2013 James W. Gargano Award from the Poe Studies Association for his essay, "Borges's Philosophy of Poe's Composition," published in *Comparative Literature Studies*. He is the editor, with Margarida Vale de Gato, of *Translated Poe* (2014) and the author of *Borges's Poe: The Influence and Reinvention of Edgar Allan Poe in Spanish America* (2016).

John Gruesser Senior Research Scholar at Sam Houston State University in Huntsville, Texas, is the author of five books and the editor of five others, most recently a scholarly edition of Sutton E. Griggs's 1905 novel *The Hindered Hand; Or, the Reign of the Repressionist* (2017), co-edited with Hanna Wallinger. His monograph *Edgar Allan Poe and His Nineteenth-Century American Counterparts* will be published in early 2019. He is a Past President of the Poe Studies Association.

Emily James Hansen earned her M.A. in English from Middle Tennessee State University, where she taught Research and Argumentative Writing and wrote her thesis, "Love, Loss, Death, and Hope: The Egyptian Voice of Edgar Allan Poe" (2011), under the direction of Philip Edward Phillips. She was an associate curator (with Erica I. Rodgers) of the permanent online exhibition, "Baudelaire's Poe: Selections from the W.T. Bandy Collection" (curated by Philip Edward Phillips, 2015), at the W.T. Bandy Center for Baudelaire and Modern French Studies, Jean and Alexander Heard Library, Vanderbilt University. She lives in Nashville, TN with her husband and two dogs.

Sonya Isaak teaches English at the University of Heidelberg in Germany, where she recently completed her dissertation on Edgar Allan

Poe and Charles Baudelaire. She has also taught French, English, and German language and literature at other universities, including Fordham University, Manhattanville College, Pace University and Mannheim University. She was a W.T. Bandy Fellow at the W.T. Bandy Center for Baudelaire and Modern French Studies, Jean and Alexander Heard Library, Vanderbilt University.

J. Gerald Kennedy is Boyd Professor of English at Louisiana State University and the author or editor of several books on Poe, including *Poe, Death, and the Life of Writing*, the *Historical Guide to Edgar Allan Poe*, and the *Penguin Portable Poe*. With Leland S. Person, he co-edited *The American Novel to 1870* for the Oxford History of the Novel in English, and his principal contribution to American Studies is the recent volume, *Strange Nation: Literary Nationalism and Cultural Conflict in the Age of Poe*, for which he received the Patrick F. Quinn Award from the Poe Studies Association in 2016. He is also a Past President and an Honorary Member of the Poe Studies Association.

Katherine J. Kim received her Ph.D. from Boston College where, as a doctoral candidate, she conceived of and co-organized the two-day Poe Bicentennial Celebration in January 2009. She was a collaborator on the Boston Public Library exhibit *The Raven in the Frog Pond* and a member of the Edgar Allan Poe Foundation of Boston, which oversaw the installation of Stefanie Rocknak's statue, *Poe Returning to Boston*, in Boston on October 5, 2014. Among other projects, she has written a chapter on Poe and folklore (for Kevin J. Hayes's *Edgar Allan Poe in Context*) and an article on Charlotte Brontë's *Villette*, Joseph Sheridan LeFanu's "Schalken the Painter," and the fairy tale "Bluebeard" (appearing in *Studies in the Novel*). She currently teaches English and interdisciplinary studies courses at Boston College, Berklee College of Music, and Emerson College.

Richard Kopley Distinguished Professor of English, Emeritus, from Penn State DuBois, is the author of *Edgar Allan Poe and the Dupin Mysteries* and *The Threads of "The Scarlet Letter"*; the editor of *Poe's Pym: Critical Explorations*, *The Narrative of Arthur Gordon Pym*, and *The Salem Belle: A Tale of 1692*; and a co-editor of *Poe Writing/Writing Poe*, *Edgar Allan Poe in 20 Objects*, and the journal *Resources for American Literary Study*. He is an editor-in-chief of the American literature module of the Oxford Bibliographies Online; he received the first J. Lasley

Dameron Award from the Poe Studies Association for his annotated Poe bibliography in that module. He is a Past President and an Honorary Member of the Poe Studies Association. He has also published several short stories and children's picture-books.

Scott Peeples Professor of English at the College of Charleston, has published extensively on Poe, including the books *Edgar Allan Poe Revisited* (1998), *The Afterlife of Edgar Allan Poe* (2004), for which he received the Patrick F. Quinn Award from the Poe Studies Association, and *The Oxford Handbook of Edgar A. Poe*, co-edited with J. Gerald Kennedy (2019). He served as President of the Poe Studies Association from 2004–2007 and co-edited the journal *Poe Studies* from 2008–2013.

Philip Edward Phillips is Professor of English and Associate Dean of the University Honors College at Middle Tennessee State University. His work on Poe appears in *Approaches to Teaching Poe's Prose and Poetry* (2008), *Edgar Allan Poe in Context* (2013), *Deciphering Poe: Subtexts, Contexts, Subversive Meanings* (2013), *Edgar Allan Poe in 20 Objects* (2016), *The Oxford Handbook to Edgar Allan Poe* (2018), *The Edgar Allan Poe Review*, and *Poe Studies*. He was a Mary Catherine Mooney Research Fellow at the Boston Athenaeum and served as a member of the Edgar Allan Poe Foundation of Boston. He was a W.T. Bandy Fellow at Vanderbilt University, where he curated the permanent online exhibition, "Baudelaire's Poe: Selections from the W.T. Bandy Collection" (2015). He is a Past President of the Poe Studies Association.

George Poe is Professor of French & French Studies and Class of 1961 Chair of the College *Emeritus* at The University of the South (Sewanee), having been recognized in 2006 as the Carnegie Foundation and CASE Professor of the Year for the state of Tennessee. He has published books, articles, and reviews both in the United States and in France, and he won the Robert B. Heilman Prize "for excellence in book reviewing in *The Sewanee Review* in 2014." He is a current member of the Board of Trustees of the Poe Museum in Richmond, VA, and has enjoyed acquiring a full collection of French first editions of Charles Baudelaire and Stéphane Mallarmé's translations of Edgar Allan Poe's prose and poetry.

Harry Lee Poe is Charles Colson Professor of Faith and Culture at Union University in Jackson, Tennessee. He is the author of *Edgar Allan Poe: An Illustrated Companion to his Tell-Tale Stories*, for which he won the Edgar Award in 2009, *Evermore: Edgar Allan Poe and the Mystery* *of the Universe*, and thirteen other books on theology and culture. He served for ten years as president of the Poe Museum of Richmond, and his collection of Poe first editions, ephemera, and artifacts has been on exhibit at a number of libraries and universities.

Jeffrey A. Savoye is an Independent Scholar, long and closely associated with the Edgar Allan Poe Society of Baltimore. He is also an Honorary Member of the Poe Studies Association. As the co-editor of *The Collected Letters of Edgar Allan Poe* (2008), the standard edition of Poe's correspondence, and the author of dozens of articles, published chiefly in *The Edgar Allan Poe Review* and *Poe Studies/Dark Romanticism*, he has deeply explored various aspects of Poe's life and writings. He is also the driving force behind the website of the Poe Society: http://www.eapoe.org.

Christopher P. Semtner is the curator of the Edgar Allan Poe Museum in Richmond and the author of books, including *Edgar Allan Poe's Richmond*, *The Raven Illustrations of James Carling*, and *The Poe Shrine: Building the World's Finest Edgar Allan Poe Collection*. He has also written articles and chapters for Biography.com, *Crime Writers' Chronicle*, *Resources for American Literary Studies*, and other publications. In addition to many exhibits he has staged for the Poe Museum over the past eighteen years, Semtner also served as curator for the Library of Virginia's major 2009 exhibit *Poe: Man, Myth, or Monster*, which the *New York Times* called "provocative" and "a playful, robust exhibit."

Alexandra Urakova is a Senior Researcher at the A.M. Gorky Institute of World Literature of the Russian Academy of Sciences and Associate Professor at the Department of Comparative Literature and Linguistics, St. Petersburg School of Social Sciences and Humanities of the National Research University Higher School of Economics. She is the author of *The Poetics of the Body in the Short Fiction of Edgar Allan Poe* (2009, in Russian), the editor of *Deciphering Poe: Subtexts, Contexts, Subversive Meanings* (2013), and the co-editor of *Poe, Baudelaire, Dostoevsky: The Splendors and Miseries of a National Genius* (2017, in Russian). She has published articles on Poe and nineteenth-century American literature in journals including *Nineteenth Century Literature*, *The Edgar Allan Poe Review*, and *New England Quarterly*.

ABBREVIATIONS

Abbreviations for the following standard editions and works will be cited parenthetically throughout the volume. Letter(s) and volume numbers (if relevant) will be followed by a colon and the page number(s). Citations of other works will appear in the notes following each chapter.

ER   *Essays and Reviews.* Edited by G. R. Thompson. New York: Library of America, 1984.

H   *Complete Works of Edgar Allan Poe.* Edited by James A. Harrison. 17 vols. New York: T. Y. Crowell, 1902; New York: AMS Press, 1965.

L1   *Eureka.* Edited by Stuart Levine and Susan F. Levine. Urbana: University of Illinois Press, 2004.

L2   *Critical Theory: The Major Documents.* Edited by Stuart Levine and Susan F. Levine. Urbana: University of Illinois Press, 2009.

M   *Collected Works of Edgar Allan Poe*: vol. 1, *Poems*; vol. 2, *Tales and Sketches, 1831–1842*; and vol. 3, *Tales and Sketches, 1843–1849.* Edited by Thomas Ollive Mabbott. Cambridge, MA: Belknap Press of Harvard University, 1969, 1978; rpt. Urbana, IL: University of Illinois Press, 2000.

O   *The Collected Letters of Edgar Allan Poe*, 3rd ed. Edited by John Ward Ostrom; revised, corrected, and expanded by Burton R. Pollin and Jeffrey A. Savoye. 2 vols. New York: Gordian Press, 2008.

P   *Collected Writings of Edgar Allan*, Poe: vol. 1, *The Imaginary Voyages.* Boston: Twayne, 1981; revised and corrected, New York: Gordian, 1994; vol. 2, *The Brevities*; vol. 3, *The Broadway Journal: Text*; vol. 4, *The Broadway Journal: Annotations*; vol. 5, *The Southern Literary Messenger.* Edited by Burton R. Pollin and (for vol. 5) Joseph V. Ridgely. New York: Gordian Press, 1985–1997.

PL   *The Poe Log: A Documentary Life of Edgar Allan Poe, 1809–1849.* Edited by Dwight Thomas and David K. Jackson. New York: G. K. Hall & Co., 1987.

PT   *Poetry and Tales.* Edited by Patrick F. Quinn. New York: Library of America, 1984.

LIST OF FIGURES

POE IN RICHMOND

Charles Cantalupo

Cary Street, 3 a.m., what's that clacking, ratchet in 4/4?
Blues riffs on washboard or *guiro, pua, rapido,* and drunks
Laughing like crazy below our window, each one's grinding tune
Waking me over and over? "I heard nothing and slept well....
Only a dream," you say next day when I tell you at breakfast.
Clickerty, clackerty, click clack, clack click, clackerty click rack....
Only a dream? It feels real as now, today, and yesterday's

Glittering water's determined trickle into old brick and
Cobble stone streets where a black man still takes care of the ashes
Somewhere between Richmond's tallest building – brutish, erected
Over a parking garage, facing 95 – and some floor boards
Two hundred sixty years old or going one hundred fifty
More back to Powhatan, who's named Wahunsenacawh at birth,
And Pocahontas: the chief, his daughter; dealing with John Smith
And the first colonists to the point of marrying John Rolfe?
Better the British and Christianity weren't invented?
Who has done nothing to feel ashamed? The little bright islands,
Tree clumps, and rocks in the James? Why not let there be Rome again,
Built on these hills and a temple not mere brick but marble faced –
First in the new world and fitting a republic to thrive at
Home in the liberty of its own words: buried exactly
Where they are written and spoken; rooted in the same ground; at

Home in the markets: tobacco, iron, cotton, grain, and slaves?
Also at home in the *clack crack, click crick, clankerty* drunks' song?

Or is that too much a letdown? Crazy dream within a dream
Vying with history? In between and hopelessly small scale
If not invisible, yet like sunlight playing in the leaves
If we look up in the trees, is that not Mordecai leaving
Synagogue? Samuel, tell me. VA DMV seems to
Dominate everything. Can I really see you and dirt streets,
Three-story houses the highest, mostly two and not the brick
Still to be found up and down these hills but wooden without paint?
No more than drunks grinding crazy music, in my dreams or not;
No more than ten thousand others of your fellow Richmondites;
Freed men and Indians; all the way down to the many more
Thousands of slaves to and from their market next to their graveyard
(Talk about lost in the *clank clank, rack clack, crackerty*) down from
Where we are sleeping on Cary: Shockoe Bottom, not quite the
Flowering gardens behind most of those old Richmond houses.

"Bottom" I get but the "Shockoe?" "Shockoe?" Saying it I peer
Into a church like a little Pantheon but plain and gray:
Couple of columns and funeral embellishments of urns,
Wrought iron spikes, and half open shells, but really a mass tomb,
So says the plaque on it, where a local blue blood packed theater
Burns down the night after Christmas, when my reason to be here
Almost aged two could have burned up with them: or should I say
"burned"
Once and for all since he burned before and after not only
Up and down Shockoe and any other places that claimed him,
He barely wanting or able to claim any; Virginia,
Nevertheless, making the best case for his being its...son?
That's what I'm seeing in Richmond? Maybe, yet not forgetting
"Want of parental affection" is, in his words, his worst pain.
Two weeks before Richmond's aristocracy incinerates,
Poe's mother dies of tuberculosis: she who, in his words,
"Looks with contempt on the mediocrity...of a king," or
Poe does at least in comparing her work as an actor who
Consecrates herself to beauty; thus does he "from child-hood's hour...
Not see... / [a]s others" see "in" his "childhood," barely aware of
Anything but his new middle name or brand of pain: "Allan."

Out of or into the fire, it burns, but not so directly
Into his flesh and more slowly, cooler: colder with more death,
Seemingly warm at first with a word; the *clackerty crack crick*
Spelling the syllables of "established" as if they could be
Anything more than some scintillations in a long poem –
Something that doesn't exist; a simple, flat contradiction.
Orphan of actors and brought to worship right where the theater
Burns itself into a tomb called Monumental Church; *"finis"* –
History shouts at the actors – *clank clack, clinkerty* be damned?
Not that things looked quite as bad at first: the delicate oval
Portraits gold framed and the state star woven into the bedding;
Endless white violets, lover's seats, and classical verse at
Ease in the orris root air with pillars, porticoed temples,
Whether in church or at home, and clear views down to the river,
Surging with "Come to me," power, and, "Jump in. Swim, swim,
swim, swim...."
Who would have thought every dollar, book, and comfort would be
lost,
Coming back home, and the slaves not even caring who he was,
Playing their *clickerty, click clack* – master boy nothing to them;
Iron, tobacco, and cotton with their flesh going to market?

Not the whole story but scintillations, that word again, and
Not merely bio but what the place, in this case it's Richmond,
More or less randomly adds to make this kind of pilgrimage
Minor heroic in form, with one more way to find the Poe:
Clickerty, clank click, "a dream within a dream," you said to me.
Was it facetiously even though I claimed the dream was real?
Somehow the words, if they're words, the *"Clack, clink, clickerty,
clank, crank"*
Intimate something about Poe here, not only rational,
Scattered all over the surface, deeper, deeper, and deeper;
Some kind of music I never would have followed until now:
Driving itself into what I say and *the* way to say it;
Structure subverted by losing where it thinks it should follow,
Conscious designs notwithstanding, so that spontaneity
Dominates thinking and tone however paradoxically:
Clackenting ratchets in drunken 4/4, breaking the same way;
Dactyls and trochees to match the sub- or unconscious demands –

Making it or should I say returning to the oral first,
If unexpectedly, real and/or imagined, or in dreams,
Conjuring metrically with remains of place and the poet?

Thus, I see Poe reappear, aged twenty-six, establishing
Manly and writer's credentials – if such words may be allowed;
"Poe" and "establishing" still an oxymoron, at least in
His time though nevermore now. A term like "normalcy" also
Could be applied to his coming back to Richmond and making
Writing itself the most sane and steady, rational, constant
Part of his being despite the horror stories more famous
Both in his art and his life; his writing; melody, meter,
Narrative, character, image, language, and intelligence:
Even his penmanship – perfect! The best place he'd never leave:
Found when he moves back to Richmond, in the summer when it's
hot,
And that he keeps, thank God, even though he leaves by twenty-eight,
Till the penultimate moments of his life, when he comes back,
Twelve years elapsed and all written out but welcomed once again.

"[All] is right.... I have success," Poe writes in 1836.
Good health and money, Canova-looking wife, the Capital
Never too far out of sight, his "reputation...extending,"
Richmond "friends...open arms" – bring on Roman legions surrounded,
Marching through walls of flames to the gates of hell. Why not feel
this,
Being the editor of a great new journal and knowing
He has a vision of southern writing culture to match his
New England rivals and all their self-important novelties?
Make way: the SLM, *Southern Literary Messenger* –
"Literature...Every Department...and...Fine Arts" its devotion.
All the years of his transcribing lines from Shakespeare and Milton,
Classical prosody, and his hard work come to fruition.
Why not tell poets they stink worse than their paper, and they should
Grab a gun if there's a chance to end their misery? Why not
Walk with the gorgeous Virginia Clemm up Shockoe Hill streets and
See Allan dead in his grave? And then go back to editing:
All for himself but for other writers, too; countless letters –
Raising the SLM's circulation high as anyone's,
British included; the manuscripts and money rolling in....

Why not a story? It scintillates – its *clankerty crank grank*:
Someone reports in a recent *Christian Sentinel* how he
Helped a drunk get off the street. He reaches into his pocket,
Opens a box and says, "Take one. My dead beautiful wife's teeth."
Mordecai's version is: Poe went walking near Shockoe market,
Where a slave rattles a gourd to which more slaves sing *"click, clack, click."*
Poe asks the master, "What that?" He's drunk and laughs, "It's your wife's teeth."
Mabbott and nobody else reports on any other source.

Act three of Richmond in Poe, excuse me, that's "Poe in Richmond" –
Richmond not Allan would be a better middle name for him –
Opens with Poe writing, "It's no use to reason with me now."
He wants to go home to die: Virginia dead and *Eureka*
"Done," he says. He can "accomplish nothing more" than feel "depressed."
That's on July 19, '49, but forty days later
He could sing, can "It...be" me "on / whom thy tempests fell all night?"
"Nothing but praise" from the papers, rave reviews, and gratitude
For the "nativity" of the boy from Richmond now famous –
All for his writing. He's even known in France, the ... *Whig* reports.
"Nothing but kindness," distinguished invitations, and love is
Paving the way to his being absolutely established.
"After so many deaths, I live...write.... / And relish versing. Oh,
[M]y only light...." Can he really be imagined singing this?
Clickerty, clackerty, click clack, clack click, clackerty click rack....
Forty days later he's dead, found derelict in Baltimore.
Classical tragedy? After all, he's recognized as great.
Or is it tabloid? "The papers here are praising me to death."
In his last letter to Clemm, Poe writes this without irony.

What does this place seem to answer? Nowhere can evoke him more:
Come out of iron and slaves; tobacco-fed to be pounded
Into fine grain; to be spun like cotton down the mighty James;
Classical columns provide the frame and stage for re-entrance.
Enter he does and more totally abstracted than ever,
Says his best translator, Baudelaire; yet like the tallest pine
Blasted by lightning and wind, to topple powerlessly on

Monte altissimo, where it grows (see Horace, *Odes* 2.10).
Long little scrolls of the works he wants to read fill his pockets.
Raven black clothes melt to dove white in the Richmond summer heat.
Mothers and children run out to greet him walking Richmond's streets.
Lectures unfold like an orris root perfume: "The Poetic
Principle" out to "The Raven" – unforgettable, "graceful,"
"Musical," "full of strong sense," and "clear" – the voice one gorgeous flow.
He sees Elmira, his lost love, sitting now in the front row.
Later he's climbing the hill up to her home and meets backers
For his new journal, the highest glory, christened the *Stylus*,
Jesus to *SLM*'s John…. Now see him lecturing the crowd
Gathered in wonder at the esteemed Exchange Hotel. See him
Reading to friends out at Talavera's farm, the first yellows
Tingeing September's full leaves; and that idyllic Norfolk scene:
Moonlight and ocean and Poe on the veranda reciting
"Annabel Lee" and "The Raven," with an "Ulalume" encore.
Pretty young women in formal gowns surrounding him love it.

Who can say what goes wrong? No pretending. Spare the simplistic.
Drinking or temperance? Mother, father – gone? Eurydice
Lost as *Eureka*? The scintillations versus established?
Grankety, clackerty, imp of the perverse? *Clink, grack, clack, crack?*

Plenty of details here complicate a much better story:
Far more than I can provide, including ugly skyscrapers,
DMVs, who empties ashes out of what. Still here's a few:
Views of the river now blocked by corporate offices and cars;
Columns and portico where the boy grew up now disappeared;
Even the building replacing it condemned, and graffiti:
"Ion. Fuck cops" on the peeling turquoise bricks once rich brown red
Still making much of the downtown, older buildings so pretty.
SLM offices? Same fate, but the bricks are painted white.
Grave of Elmira? It's fetishized with smooth James River stones.
Maybe I've fetishized Poe in Richmond much in the same way?
Visiting Hollywood Cemetery, where he used to play:
Cliffs overlooking the river, in his day called Harvey's Woods,

Jefferson Davis's tomb all dignified just up the way.
What can I say of the blood stained banners, thousands and thousands
Buried there, haunting today? They might just as well have been
slaves?

Or should I run away, taking refuge, like Richard Crashaw
Making Loreto's Shrine of Our Lady home in his old age,
Only the shrine is to Poe and filled with all kinds of relics,
Many of which I note in this poem – yet so many more:
SLM building beams; bricks from Greenwich Village where he lived
Almost as famously as he did in Richmond at the end;
Gentle black cat to make school girls scream if they read the story;
Quinn's bust of Poe or at least a copy with lipstick kisses.
Poe priest Chris Semtner is the best one to tell all the rest.
Listen to him and the *clank grank, grock clink, clackerty clack click*....

PART I

A Sense of Place

CHAPTER 1

"No Direction Home": The Itinerant Life of Edgar Poe

Scott Peeples

If, until recently, little has been written about Poe and place, we can probably blame Poe himself: he never made it easy to connect the dots between his lived experience and the places he wrote about. Poe fabricated stories of foreign adventure in Greece and Russia in biographical sketches, covering up the less glamorous reality of serving in the US Army in Massachusetts, South Carolina, and Virginia.[1] Then there is the sense of placelessness that characterizes his most famous tales; where exactly *is* the House of Usher? In what "kingdom by what sea" did Annabel Lee perish? What city's police officers hear the shrieking confession of the narrator in "The Tell-Tale Heart," and what kind of accent do we hear when we listen to him calmly tell us the whole story? The three Dupin tales foreground their Parisian setting, but the author of those tales never set foot in France; the same is true of Venice, the setting for "The Assignation," and Toledo, where "The Pit and the Pendulum" takes place. When Poe sets stories in locations where he did spend time, he exhibits little sensitivity to place beyond what he might just as well have gleaned from other writers. He was many years

S. Peeples (✉)
College of Charleston, Charleston, SC, USA

© The Author(s) 2018
P. E. Phillips (ed.), *Poe and Place*,
Geocriticism and Spatial Literary Studies,
https://doi.org/10.1007/978-3-319-96788-2_1

removed from his boyhood sojourn in suburban London when he wrote "The Man of the Crowd," and the same can be said of his writing "A Tale of the Ragged Mountains" and "The Gold-Bug" long after his time in Charlottesville, VA, and Sullivan's Island, SC. If I were not writing an essay for a volume entitled *Poe and Place*, I might be tempted to think that "place" didn't really matter to Poe.

In fact, it was the critical consensus through the mid-twentieth century that Poe's domain was a land of dreams, with only coincidental resemblance to earthly locales. "There is no place," wrote W. H. Auden in an introduction to a 1950 edition of Poe, "in any of [his stories] for the human individual as he actually exists in space and time."[2] In his lecture "The House of Poe," Richard Wilbur would go one better, arguing that Poe "sees the poetic soul as *at war with the mundane physical world*; and that warfare is Poe's fundamental subject."[3] As late as 1988, Galway Kinnell, in an interview for the *Voices and Visions* film devoted to Walt Whitman, declared that Poe (in contrast to Whitman) "was absolutely blind...Poe's poetry was the poetry of a blind man, a man who was imagining some realm somewhere else." He is followed in the film by Allen Ginsberg, who adds that Poe was "a philosophical dreamer who had phantoms that he described in detail."[4]

The New Historicism of the 1980s and 1990s would largely dismantle the traditional view of Poe the blind dreamer, replacing it with a fully sighted writer enmeshed in American culture and politics. And yet, even as his antebellum "American face" became easier to discern, the Poe of late twentieth-century scholarship remained strangely unattached to the more specific places on the map of his life. There have been exceptions, of course, including essays by Elise Lemire on "Rue Morgue" and "amalgamation discourses" in 1830s Philadelphia, J. Gerald Kennedy on Poe, Frederick Douglass, and Baltimore in the early 1830s, and David Leverenz on Poe and Gentry Virginia. But even these outstanding examples demonstrate how hard it is to pin Poe down to a place: Lemire reads a story set in Paris through what Poe would have experienced in Philadelphia; Kennedy explores Poe's and Douglass's Baltimore partly to set up a reading of *Pym*, which takes place on Nantucket, the high seas, and the mysterious island of Tsalal; and the stories Leverenz discusses in relation to Poe's Virginia upbringing are not set in Virginia or even in the American South.[5]

Yet, as of this writing, interest in Poe and place is clearly on the rise, inspired not only by the "spatial turn" in literary studies but also by the 2009 bicentennial of Poe's birth, which prompted various cities to stake their claims to Poe's literary and, at one point, literal remains. In the run-up to the bicentennial, literary historian Edward Pettit jokingly (I think) urged fellow Philadelphians to "hop in our cars, drive down I-95 and appropriate a body from a certain Baltimore cemetery."[6] "Philadelphia can keep its broken bell and its cheese steak, but Poe's body isn't going anywhere," countered Jeff Jerome, then curator of the Baltimore Poe House. The *New York Times* article reporting on the controversy observed that "The one city that probably will never claim Poe is Boston."[7] And yet, on January 13, 2009, Paul Lewis, leading a crusade for Boston to honor Poe publicly, joined Pettit and Jerome in the "Great Poe Debate" over which city was truly Poe's home.[8] Lewis's efforts resulted in a mayoral proclamation, a Poe exhibit at the Boston Public Library, a "Poe's Boston" walking tour, and, finally, Stefanie Rocknak's life-sized Poe statue at Boylston and Charles Streets. (See Chapter 2 for a full account of the statue selection, installation, and celebration; also see Fig. 2.1 "Poe Returning to Boston," bronze, by Stefanie Rocknak.) The premise, and much of the rhetoric, of the Great Poe Debate—however good-natured—implied that Poe could have only one home, one place that defined him, whether it was Boston, his birthplace and the city he loved to hate, or Philadelphia, where he reached his creative peak as a short story writer, or Baltimore, where his career really began and his life ended. Richmond and New York, though they stayed on the sidelines of the debate, surely have their own answers to the question, "Where is Poe's home?"

In fact, the answer given by Richmond Poe Museum Curator Chris Semtner at the time was that "Poe belongs to the world."[9] He certainly does, but that gracious sentiment has more to do with Poe's reception than with trying to locate the geographical and biographical place that he would have called home. My answer, developed throughout this essay, is that Poe lived in many places but never found a home. Rather than insist that Poe was rooted in any particular place, we might, *should*, think of him as itinerant—not because he was "blind" or did not care about place but because he did not put down roots. Many places were important to him, but no place was essential, and his relationships with not only the cities but the neighborhoods, forts, academies, and houses in which he lived were strained by the fact that he knew they were only temporary; each was the latest in a succession of places to move to, and then move from.

A Moving Biography

Most of this book's readers will have a firm knowledge of Poe's biography, but I would like to retell the story, briefly, emphasizing the extent to which he stayed on the move.[10] Poe's parents, Eliza and David Poe, were actors living in Boston when he was born on January 19, 1809; when Poe was about five weeks old, they left him with his paternal grandparents in Baltimore for about six months (PL 6). While it is possible that Edgar spent still more time in Baltimore as an infant, he probably moved with his parents to New York City, where they were hired for a theatrical season in 1809–1810. At that point, David Poe's days as a professional actor, as well as his days with the family, were numbered, but Eliza joined the Placide and Green Company in 1810, performing in Richmond, Norfolk, Charleston, SC, and possibly other Southeastern cities (PL 10–11). Thus Poe, by age two, would have spent significant time in at least six different cities; one can only guess how many different houses and rented rooms he inhabited. This rootlessness, compounded by the disappearance of his father sometime in early to mid-1811, was the norm for Edgar as an infant and toddler. His mother's death in December of that year removed what little stability he had known in his first three years. Being fostered by Frances and John Allan would restore some regularity and provide something like a home town: for three and a half years, ages three to six, he lived in the same house at Thirteenth and Main Streets in Richmond. Then, in the summer of 1815, the Allans brought Edgar with them to England, settling in London after a short time in Scotland. Enrolled in London boarding schools, Poe probably saw his foster parents only on weekends for most of the five years they spent abroad.

The family returned to Richmond in 1820 after John Allan's London business failed. While the Allans were hardly destitute—thanks mainly to the support of John's wealthy uncle William Galt—the family was less financially secure than before and lived in at least three different houses in Richmond over the next five years. When they first returned, they lived with the family of Charles Ellis, Allan's business partner, then moved before the end of 1820 to a house on Shockoe Hill, where they stayed for about a year and a half, at which point they moved to Fourteenth Street and Tobacco Alley, not far from the state capitol.[11] Poe came to know Richmond well as a teenager, but he knew it from a series of residences that crisscrossed the walking city. And his sense of belonging, his place in Richmond society, was surely undermined by his status as an orphan, fostered but not adopted. When William Galt died in March 1825, John Allan inherited a tremendous fortune and purchased a mansion, Moldavia, near the James River in Southwest Richmond. Moldavia typically plays the role of Poe's Richmond residence in the popular and scholarly imagination—it is nearly always mentioned by name in biographies, which often include a photograph of the house taken in the early twentieth century—but it was only the last in a series of Allan family homes, and he spent only a short time there. In February 1826, only half a year after the family moved into their mansion, he left Richmond for Charlottesville and the University of Virginia for most of that year, then spent just a few more months back in Richmond in early 1827. A tumultuous year at the university and the resulting acrimony between Poe and his foster father led him to declare his independence, "to leave [Allan's] house and indeavor [sic] to find some place in this wide world, where I will be treated—not as you have treated me" (O 1:10).

At the age of 18, then, Poe was for the first time able to make his own move. He spent about a month in Baltimore and then ventured to Boston, far from the Allans and far from the upper South of his youth. As if realigning himself with the city of his birth, Poe identified himself (only) as "A Bostonian" on the title page of *Tamerlane and Other Poems* (see Fig. 2.5 *Tamerlane and Other Poems. By a Bostonian*. Boston: Calvin F. S. Thomas, 1827. Susan Jaffe Tane Collection), the slim volume of poems he published there in 1827. Having exercised his self-determination in coming to Boston, he almost immediately surrendered it by enlisting in the US Army, and after five months at Fort Independence in Boston Harbor, he and his company were transferred to Fort Moultrie, on Sullivan's Island, SC. Thirteen months later, he was back in Virginia, having been transferred to Fort Monroe, where he was granted a discharge in April 1829. Following Frances Allan's death, Poe temporarily reconciled with his foster father but moved to Baltimore upon his discharge from the Army. Over the next several months, Poe traveled to Philadelphia to get his second book of poems published; at one point, he walked from Baltimore to Washington and back to try to secure an appointment to West Point.[12] He entered the US Military Academy in June 1830 but was dismissed in March 1831. Poe then tried living in New York City, where he managed to publish a third book of poetry, but after several weeks made his way back to Baltimore, where he shared cramped quarters with his aunt Maria Clemm, her daughter Virginia, and other family members for the next four years.

Most biographers attribute Poe's self-sabotage and the resulting court-martial at West Point to John Allan's marriage in October 1830, which signaled a final break between the two and the loss of any chance of an inheritance for Poe.[13] Poe had now lost not only the semblance of a hometown but also a second set of parents, and he had not found a substitute for family in the military, as an enlisted man or as a cadet. Instead, he made a new family with Maria and Virginia Clemm. In Baltimore, he began experimenting with fiction, eventually contributing to a new Richmond magazine, the *Southern Literary Messenger*. He moved to Richmond in August 1835 to edit that publication, then about a month later either lost the job or quit and returned to Baltimore, before being reinstated and moving back to Richmond, this time with his aunt and cousin, in early October. Over the next year, Poe became a versatile fiction writer and a caustic literary critic at the *Messenger*; he also married Virginia, who was 13 at the time. Yet mainly because of conflicts with the magazine's patriarchal owner, Thomas White, Poe again uprooted the family and ventured to New York City in early 1837. We know little of Poe's activity and whereabouts for the next year, the dearth of documentary evidence suggesting hard times amid the national financial panic; but by early 1838 he, Maria, and Virginia had settled in Philadelphia.

The next six years in Philadelphia were a relatively stable period for Poe as well as his creative peak as a fiction writer. In fact, he probably lived in the same house, not far from Rittenhouse Square, for about three and a half years. Even so, the family lived in at least five different locations over this six-year period in Philadelphia, while Poe experienced the usual calamities of his professional life: a bitter parting with another boss after a year editing *Burton's Gentleman's Magazine*; a failed attempt to launch his own *Penn Magazine*; then a year-long stint as editor of *Graham's Magazine*. After leaving *Graham's*, Poe freelanced in Philadelphia for another two years before moving, for the third time, to New York City in April 1844.

In New York, Poe, Maria, and Virginia lived at five or six different addresses over two years before moving to a small cottage in Fordham in mid-1846. By the time of this move, Poe had achieved the height of his fame as the author of "The Raven" but had failed to turn that success into a lucrative editorial position or any other reliable source of income.

Virginia had been suffering from tuberculosis for about four years, and Poe had tried, in both Philadelphia and New York, to find habitations on the urban outskirts, though that was not always possible or practical. The family lived in lower Manhattan near Washington Square, in a farmhouse on what is now the Upper West Side, and near Turtle Bay on the East River. Though Fordham proved to be Poe's last residence, after Virginia's death in 1847 he traveled for significant periods, pursuing backers for his still-unrealized magazine as well as a new wife. He spent much of the second half of 1848 away from Fordham, with five trips to Providence, RI, the home of Sarah Helen Whitman, and at least two to Lowell, MA, the home of Annie Richmond, as well as a trip to Richmond, where he visited a long-lost love interest, Elmira Royster Shelton. He spent the first half of 1849 back in Fordham, but left in June for Richmond, with excursions to Philadelphia and Norfolk. He spent his last three months living out of a suitcase—or trunk—before he died in Baltimore on October 7, 1849.

In short, Poe changed residences on average of about once a year throughout his life, and his itinerancy underscores the central experience of his life: rootlessness, precariousness, and instability. He created a family with Virginia and Maria, but for the most part they simply shared his vagabondage. Place mattered to Poe, and home mattered, but by the end of his life there was no place like home, which is to say no place he could call home.

THE QUESTION OF MOTIVE

During Poe's adolescence and early adult years especially, Richmond had been home, but it was a home Poe had to leave repeatedly. Poe's anguished letters to John Allan in March 1827 attest to the eighteen-year-old's struggle with this separation. He lists his grievances against Allan, makes clear his intention to leave, and yet continually begs for support and affection. Allan must have told Poe that he was incapable of surviving on his own (or something to that effect), for Poe adds, "[I]f you still have the least affection for me, As the last call I shall make on your bounty, To Prevent the fulfillment of the Prediction you this morning expressed, send me as much money as will defray my passage...[.]" He concludes the letter, "If you fail to comply with my request—I tremble for the consequence" (O 1:11). He writes again the next day, still in Richmond, conjuring images of himself without food, wandering the streets, and promising, "I sail on Saturday." The final line before his sig-nature is "Give my love to all at home—" and the postscript reads, "I have not one cent in the world to provide any food" (O 1:13).

Of course, Poe and Allan were not through with each other. Poe sought reconciliation over the next four years, repeatedly using the word "home" in reference to Richmond and Moldavia. In February 1829, writing from Fort Monroe and trying to account for what went wrong two years earlier, he explains to Allan, "I had never been from home before for any length of time" (O 1:20). In July 1829, writing from Baltimore upon receiving some money from Allan, he refers to "the length of time I have been from home," and, heartbreakingly, asks "for information as to what course I must pursue—I would have returned home immediately but for the words [in] your letter 'I am not particularly anxious to see you'—I know not how to interpret them" (O 1:37–38). Even after Frances Allan's death in 1829, and until John Allan's remarriage in 1831, Poe continued to refer to Richmond as home. He probably had hoped to regain Allan's affection—and a share of his fortune—when he entered West Point; the two men had recon-ciled somewhat as Poe sought the appointment.

Thus, his self-inflicted court-martial from the US Military Academy in 1831 might be regarded as another departure from Richmond as much as from West Point, precipitated as it was by John Allan's cutting off communication around the time of his remarriage. In his letter to Allan announcing his intention to be expelled for neglecting his duties, Poe writes, "As to your injunction not to trouble you with farther commu-nication rest assured, Sir, that I will most religiously observe it. When I parted from you—at the steam-boat, I knew that I should nev[er] see you again" (O 1:61). Poe probably did not see Allan again, though he did write him at least six more times, failing to observe Allan's injunc-tion. And yet, at the time, Poe was resolutely leaving "home" once again: in a note asking for a certificate of his class "standing," he informs the Superintendent of the Military Academy, "Having no longer any ties which can bind me to my native country—no prospects—nor any friends—I intend by the first opportunity to proceed to Paris with the view of obtaining...an appointment (if possible) in the Polish Army" (O 1:65). Having decided against that plan, two months later he asked a Baltimore newspaper editor for a job, explaining that "Mr. Allan has married again and I no longer look upon Richmond as my place of resi-dence" (O 1:66).

Poe repeated this drama, in somewhat muted form, almost exactly a decade after his departure for Boston, when he left Thomas White and the *Southern Literary Messenger* in 1837. Having found his first editorial success, a steady outlet for his fiction, and a regular paycheck, Poe nonetheless either quit his position or was fired, possibly both. While White was probably ready to be rid of Poe by early 1837, Poe had come to resent his employer, feeling unappreciated and underpaid.[14] Financial difficulties, which forced White to suspend publication for two months in late 1836, had something to do with the breakup—as did Poe's drinking and his acerbic reviews, both of which White repeatedly implored him to temper. But White's letters to Poe and to Beverly Tucker suggest a replay of the strained, ultimately broken foster-father-and-son relationship Poe had had with John Allan only a dozen or so blocks away from the *Messenger*'s office. White wrote to Tucker, not long before Poe moved to New York: "Poe pesters me no little—he is trying every manoeuver to foist himself on some one at the North...[.] He is continually after me for money. I am as sick of his writings as I am of him, —and am rather more than half inclined to send him up another dozen dollars in the morning, and along with it all his unpublished manuscripts."[15] For his part, Poe later referred to White as "illiterate and vulgar, although well-meaning" (O 1:236). In both cases, Poe left Richmond in reluctant rebellion against a father figure, heading north with no real prospects for employment. In the novel that is Poe's life, these episodes prefigure a third departure from Richmond in 1849, another journey to New York that leads to the weeklong period preceding his hospitalization and death.

I have suggested that Poe's departures from Richmond and West Point were largely acts of self-assertion and rejection of a father figure; of course, they were also motivated by Poe's literary ambitions and publishing opportunities, as were all of his inter-city removals. Not long after arriving in Boston in 1827, he arranged for the publication of *Tamerlane*; leaving the Army in 1829, he moved to Baltimore, where he quickly found a publisher for *Al Aaraaf, Tamerlane and Other Poems*; within weeks of leaving West Point in 1831, he published *Poems* in New York City. White's offer of an editorial job led Poe back to Richmond in 1835, and when he departed Richmond for New York in 1837, his primary aim seems to have been to find a publisher for *The Narrative of Arthur Gordon Pym*, which he did, with Harper & Brothers. There was no job waiting for him in Philadelphia when he moved there in 1838, but it was a periodical publishing mecca, *Godey's Lady's Book* enjoying the highest circulation figures in the nation. Poe quickly landed an editorial position with *Burton's Gentleman's Magazine* and began planning his own *Penn Magazine*. When he left Philadelphia for New York in 1844, he was once again likely motivated by publishing opportunities.

Poe's motives for his many intra-city moves are more obscure. Always a renter, he was subject to the uncertainties of local housing markets, which likely included unpredictable rent hikes, difficult neighbors, and disputes with landlords. Given Poe's constant poverty, he easily could have been evicted for failure to pay rent on more than one occasion. In New York, particularly, renters relocated frequently; a combination of law and custom made May 1 a notoriously chaotic annual moving day throughout the city. In fact, Poe commented on this phenomenon in his "Doings of Gotham" series, written not long after his move from Philadelphia to New York in 1844: "We are not yet over the bustle of the first of May. 'Keep moving' have been the watchwords for the last fortnight. The man who, in New-York, should be so bold as *not* to peregrinate on the first, would, beyond doubt, attain immortality as 'The Great Unmoved'—a title applied by Horne, the author of 'Orion,' to one of his heroes, Akineros, the type of the spirit of Apathy."[16] Poe's moves in New York—not confined to May 1—reflect the predicament in which he found himself in the mid-1840s. He moved to New York to be at the center of the publishing world, which was downtown in the area surrounding Fulton and Nassau Streets, but at the same time he wanted a healthy environment for Virginia, whose symptoms included coughing and difficulty breathing, surely aggravated by polluted air and crowded spaces. Poe's optimistic letter to Maria, written soon after his arrival in New York with Virginia, alludes to Virginia's health—"Sissy coughed none at all"—as well as other concerns, namely the cost of living and Poe's need to keep sober: "The house is old & looks buggy, [but] the landlady…gave us the back room…night & day & attendance, [for 7$ the cheapest board I] ever knew, taking into consideration the central situation and the living…[.] We have now got 4 $ and a half left. Tomorrow I am going to try & borrow 3 $—so that I may have a fortnight to go upon. I feel in excellent spirits & have'nt drank a drop—so that I hope so[on] to get out of trouble" (O 1:437–438).

Poe wrote that letter from 130 Greenwich Street, where he, Virginia, and eventually Maria would spend several weeks before moving to a farmhouse over five miles to the north: I would speculate that the "central situation" of the boarding house in lower Manhattan lost out to cleaner air, more space, and even cheaper lodging beyond the developed portion of the city.[17] But eventually, with the success of "The Raven" in early 1845, the advantages of living downtown again held sway, at least for a few months, until the family moved to the less crowded lower East Side, and then, in late 1845, back to a more central location, 85 Amity Street, near Washington Square. But once again, Poe sought a more remote habitation, moving briefly to a property near Turtle Bay, near the East River at what is now mid-town, and then, probably on May 1, to a cottage in rural Fordham.[18] This survey of Poe's moves in New York over a two-year period suggests either that he was forced to move frequently for financial reasons or that he believed each move—away from the city, back to the city, farther away from the city—offered some new advantage for his career or for his family.

No Direction Home, Sweet Home

Humanistic geographers identify "home" in various ways, but generally define it in terms such as a "socio-spatial entity" or "psycho-spacial entity."[19] Alison Blunt and Robyn Dowling describe home as "grounding of identity, an essential place…an anchoring point through which human beings are centered."[20] This notion of home as combining space and identity formation would have made sense to Poe and his contemporaries, though their notions of what kind of identity "the home" should form were narrowly conscribed by antebellum American ideals. The ideology of home as the locus of virtue and the determining influence in one's life gained unprecedented currency in mid-nineteenth-century America. As scholars such as Nancy F. Cott and Karen Halttunen have demonstrated, the home came to be imagined as a refuge or sanctuary, the counterpoint to "the world of strangers," or simply "the world."[21] Though we might imagine that dichotomy in terms of a single household—overseen by a wife and mother, in accordance with domestic ideology of the time—it also applies more broadly to a home community or "hometown," particularly at a time when many young people left rural or semi-rural homes for urban boarding houses. In her essay, "Reclaiming Sentimental Literature," which draws primarily from mid-nineteenth-century American sources, Joanne Dobson posits that "the principal theme of the sentimental text is the desire for bonding, and it is affiliation on the plane of emotion, sympathy, nurturance, or similar moral or spiritual inclination for which sentimental writers and readers yearn. Violation, actual or threatened, of the affectional bond generates the primary tension in the sentimental text and leads to bleak, dispirited, anguished, sometimes outraged representations of human loss."[22] The locus of that bonding and affiliation was the traditional home.

Thus, sentimental poems, plays, novels, and popular songs validated this psychic and emotional need, most often expressed as a loss, or home-sickness. John Howard Payne's "Home, Sweet Home," which debuted on stage in 1823, became one of the century's most popular songs:

> Mid pleasures and palaces, though we may roam,
> Be it ever so humble, there's no place like home,
> A charm from the sky seems to hallow us there,
> Which, seek through the world, is ne're met with elsewhere.
> Home, sweet home!
> There's no place like home.[23]

Bridget Bennett traces the song's popularity and influence throughout the nineteenth century (and into the twentieth), noting that it was a run-away bestseller in sheet music, was performed regularly by Jenny Lind on her mid-century American tour, and that Adeline Patti's rendition for Abraham and Mary Todd Lincoln famously moved the first couple and added to the song's reputation.[24] An archetypal Civil War legend features Union and Confederate army bands playing "Home, Sweet Home" together in the field on the eve of the Battle of Stones River in Murfreesboro, TN, in 1862.[25] Of course, by then the trope of longing for home had become a staple of minstrel songs, perhaps most famously Stephen Foster's "Old Folks at Home" and "My Old Kentucky Home." John Howard Payne's biographer cites a letter in which he describes his own homesickness: "My yearnings toward Home become stronger as the term of my exile lengthens ... I feel the want of you, parts of myself, in this strange world, for though I am naturalized to vagabondage, still it is *but* vagabondage ... I long for a Home about me."[26] Though Poe found and maintained a family with Virginia and Maria, the broader notion of home—not only as a permanent residence but also as an "anchoring point," a place where one is rooted, a community—remained elusive, so that "Home, Sweet Home" evoked not so much a loss as a lack, a state of belonging he knew about but had never known. From infancy, as I have suggested, Poe was naturalized to vagabondage.

And what of that family, and the domestic life shared by Edgar, Virginia, and Maria? Though then as now, families came in many configurations, theirs was certainly atypical, given Virginia's age at the time of marriage and subsequent delicate health, and (largely a result of these circumstances) their childlessness. Though husband, wife, and mother (-in-law) remained devoted to one another, poverty and Poe's alcoholism must have strained their domestic harmony. The hopefulness of Poe's letter to Maria upon moving to New York is undercut by his oblique references to those very problems ("have'nt drank a drop ... hope ... to get out of trouble"). With Virginia's death, Poe lost even that semblance of domestic tranquillity, and he never regained it. Poe's desperate pursuit, toward the end of his life, of a second Mrs. Poe attests not only to his need for companionship but also his desire for "Home, Sweet Home."

While Poe was probably not consciously mining his own domestic anxieties for gothic plots, his stories are fairly consistent in troubling the waters of conventional domesticity. The fictional home most associated with Poe—the House of Usher—implodes under the strain of the familial relationship it contained. Corpses are hidden underneath living spaces in "The Cask of Amontillado" and "The Tell-Tale Heart."[27] When the narrator's home in "The Black Cat" burns to the ground, the *bas relief* in the shape of his feline nemesis appears, conspicuously, on the wall above his and his wife's bed. In a recent essay focusing on that story, Heidi Hanrahan argues that Poe persistently challenges the efficacy of domestic virtues in their depiction of irrational violence: "Unwilling or unable to buy into the promises of domesticity, Poe's fiction instead frequently shows the system breaking down."[28]

But more often in Poe's fiction, there is no domesticity, no home, to deconstruct. Geographer Yi-Fu Tuan has usefully described "cosmos" and "hearth" as opposite "ends of the geographic scale," roughly synonymous with the open, unpredictable "world" and the "home" as locus of identity and security. While recognizing that much of the world's population has little choice but to remain at the hearth, Tuan explores the pull that individuals in modern, post-Enlightenment societies experience between the two: "Hearth, though nurturing, can be too confining; cosmos, though liberating, can be bewildering and threatening."[29] Poe certainly felt that pull, but we might say that the "cosmos" was thrust upon him by his itinerant life. Whether he wanted to be or not, Poe was a cosmopolitan, at least in Tuan's formulation, well before he wrote *Eureka*, his theory of the cosmos, in 1848. Broadly considered, Poe's writing reflects this cosmopolitan disposition in its refusal to give in to, or in many cases even acknowledge, the gravitational pull of the hearth.

In his landmark 1925 chapter on Poe, William Carlos Williams uses the terms "local" and "place" repeatedly, describing him as "a genius intimately shaped by his locality and time," who asserts "a *new locality* ... the first great burst through to expression of a re-awakened genius of *place.*"[30] But for Williams, Poe's locality is himself, and his place is an America that comes into being only when someone—an inventor, an explorer, an artist like Poe—makes it *new*: "What he wanted was connected with no particular place; therefore it *must* be where he *was.*"[31] Williams clarifies his point by comparing Poe to a writer with a more conventional relationship to the local: "what Hawthorne *loses* by his willing closeness to the life of his locality in its vague humors; his lifelike copying of the New England melancholy; his reposeful closeness to the town pump—Poe *gains* by abhorring; flying to the ends of the earth for 'original' material."[32] In light of Williams's insight, my reading of Poe's biography suggests that his predicament—no direction home—might well have been the basis for his achievement as a writer. If, in his longing for a home, Poe was quintessentially antebellum, he was preternaturally modern in being not *up*rooted but *un*rooted.

NOTES

1. Arthur Hobson Quinn, *Edgar Allan Poe: A Critical Biography* (1941; rpt. Baltimore and London: Johns Hopkins, 1997), 373.

2. W. H. Auden, "Introduction" [*Edgar Allan Poe: Selected Prose and Poetry*, 1950], rpt. In *The Recognition of Edgar Allan Poe*, ed. Eric W. Carlson (Ann Arbor, MI: University of Michigan Press, 1966), 221.

3. Wilbur, "The House of Poe," *Recognition*, 258. My italics.

4. *Voices and Visions: Walt Whitman.* New York Center for Visual History, 1988. Film.

5. Elise Lemire, "'The Murders in the Rue Morgue': Amalgamation Discourses and the Race Riots of 1838 in Poe's Philadelphia," In *Romancing the Shadow: Poe and Race*, ed. J. Gerald Kennedy and Liliane Weissberg (New York: Oxford University Press, 2001), 177–204; J. Gerald Kennedy, "'Trust No Man': Poe, Douglass, and the Culture of Slavery," *Romancing the Shadow*, 225–257; and David Leverenz, "Poe and Gentry Virginia," In *The American Face of Edgar Allan Poe*, ed. Shawn Rosenheim and Stephen Rachman (Baltimore and London: Johns Hopkins, 1995), 210–236.

6. Ian Urbina, "Baltimore Has Poe: Philadelphia Wants Him," *New York Times*, September 5, 2008, http://www.nytimes.com/2008/09/06/us/06poe.html (accessed October 15, 2016).
7. Ibid.
8. A second debate was held at Boston College on December 17, 2009. For more on Poe tourism and the bicentennial celebrations, see J. Bowers, "Chasing Edgar: The Tourist Rhetoric of the Poe Bicentennial," *Poe Studies* 43 (2010): 59–82.
9. Chris Kaltenbach, "Poe Kin to Have Say on City with Best Claim to Legacy," *Baltimore Sun*, January 10, 2010, http://articles.baltimoresun.com/2010-01-10/entertainment/bal-ae.poe10jan10_1_poe-descendant-poe-foundation-edgar-allan-poe (accessed October 15, 2016).
10. The biographical facts in this section are well established, but my primary sources are *The Poe Log*, Quinn, and Kenneth Silverman, *Edgar A. Poe: A Biography* (New York: HarperCollins, 1991).
11. Silverman, 23.
12. Ibid., 49.
13. Ibid., 63–67.
14. Quinn, 262; Silverman, 127–129.
15. Silverman, 129.
16. Edgar Allan Poe, "Doings of Gotham [Letter 1]," *Columbia Spy* (Columbia, PA), XV, no. 4 (May 18, 1844): 3, col. 2. "Akineros" is a misspelling of "Akinetos." For another description of Moving Day in the 1840s, see Lydia Maria Child, *Letters from New York*, ed. Bruce Mills (Athens, GA: University of Georgia Press, 1998), 175–178. See also Edwin G. Burrows and Mike Wallace, *Gotham: A History of New York City to 1898* (New York: Oxford University Press, 199), 476.
17. See Scott Peeples, "Poe, Brennan Farm, and the Literary Life," *Poe Studies* 49 (2016): 5–18.
18. Evidence for Poe's stay near Turtle Bay comes mainly from reminiscences by members of the John C. Miller family, who lived there in the 1840s. Quinn reports it as fact (506). Mary E. Phillips cites at length the accounts of John LeFevre Miller and Sarah F. Miller, both of whom were children at the time. Phillips believes that Poe, Virginia, and Maria might have stayed with the Brennan family again during this time, but the Brennans' property was too far from Turtle Bay for Poe to have been a neighbor of the Millers. See Mary E. Phillips, *Edgar Allan Poe: The Man* (Chicago: John C. Winston Co., 1926), vol. 2, 1109–1114.
19. Hazel Easthope, "A Place Called Home," *Housing, Theory and Society* 21 (2004): 134.
20. Alison Blunt and Robyn Dowling, *Home* (London and New York: Routledge, 2006), 11.

21. Nancy F. Cott, *The Bonds of Womanhood: "Women's Sphere" in New England, 1780–1835* (New Haven and London: Yale University Press, 1978); Karen Halttunen, *Confidence Men and Painted Women: A Study of Middle-Class Culture in America, 1830–1870* (New Haven and London: Yale University Press, 1986).

22. Joanne Dobson, "Reclaiming Sentimental Literature," *American Literature* 69 (1997): 267.

23. "Home Sweet Home" debuted in Payne's operetta *Clari; or, the Maid of Milan* (1823); quoted from Bridget Bennett, "Home Songs and the Melodramatic Imagination: From 'Home, Sweet Home' to The Birth of a Nation," *Journal of American Studies* 46 (2012): 171.

24. Bennett, 178.

25. James M. McPherson, *Battle Cry of Freedom: The Civil War Era* (New York: Oxford University Press, 1988), 580.

26. Grace Overmyer, *America's First Hamlet* (New York: New York University Press, 1957), 210; quoted in Bennett, 178.

27. The strongest bonds of romantic, marital love appear in stories and poems in which the beloved woman is dead (a partial list: "Ligeia," "Eleonora," "The Oblong Box," "The Raven," and "Annabel Lee"); just as often, Poe depicts loveless or troubled marriages ("Berenice," "Morella," "Ligeia" again, "The Oval Portrait," and comic tales such as "The Thousand and Second Tale of Scheherzade" and "Some Words with a Mummy").

28. Heidi Hanrahan, "'A Series of Mere Household Events': Poe's 'The Black Cat,' Pet-Keeping, and Domesticity in Nineteenth-Century America," *Poe Studies* 45 (2012): 49.

29. Yi-Fu Tuan, *Cosmos & Hearth: A Cosmopolite's Viewpoint* (Minneapolis: University of Minnesota Press, 1996), 2.

30. William Carlos Williams, *In the American Grain* (1925; rpt. New York: New Directions, 1956), 216. The italics are Williams's, here and elsewhere in this paragraph.

31. Ibid., 220.

32. Ibid., 228.

PART II

Geographical Places

CHAPTER 2

Poe and Boston

Katherine J. Kim

In his keynote address at the Edgar Allan Poe Bicentennial Celebration held at Boston College on January 15, 2009, Scott Peeples proposed that in addition to viewing Edgar A. Poe as connected to a number of locations in which he lived and worked, what needs to be emphasized is neither Poe's "placelessness" nor his "identification with a single place," but rather his "relationship to place," which he characterized as "strikingly modern and American: Rootless, down-at-the-heels, opportunistic, and cosmopolitan."[1] What Peeples suggests is a geo-critical approach to Poe that explores his life, writings, and ideas in connection not only with specific places, but also with multifaceted understandings of place and space.

Such a perspective can be helpful when examining connections between Poe and the specific location that is the city of his birth, Boston. While other cities such as Baltimore, Philadelphia, and New York have preserved residences and other landmarks associated with the author, many of the physical places related to Poe in and around Boston have been unceremoniously destroyed or transformed. *Poe-Land* author J. W. Ocker notes that the currently standing Poe houses in New York, Philadelphia, and Baltimore are not located in ideal tourism locations

K. J. Kim (✉)
Boston College, Newton, MA, USA

© The Author(s) 2018
P. E. Phillips (ed.), *Poe and Place*,
Geocriticism and Spatial Literary Studies,
https://doi.org/10.1007/978-3-319-96788-2_2

21

and that Boston "could have had a literary mecca just two blocks from the tourist sweet spot that is the Boston Common, making the area an even more desirable destination."[2] Indeed, there are a few humble markers with Poe's name in Lowell and Westford, Massachusetts, yet in Boston, which shows great pride in its literary history, there has been a significant lack of reference to the Boston-born author for years.[3] Most heartbreaking is the fact that the location of Poe's birth in a boarding house at 62 Carver Street (currently 62 Charles Street South) was razed to the ground in 1959 to make way for a parking lot. Because of the erasure of such locations, a discussion of Poe and Boston relies less on the modern-day experiential learning that occurs through visiting pre-served sites than those connecting Poe to other cities. Perhaps such erasure contributed to a lack of much critical discussion in the twentieth century regarding the significance of examining Poe and Boston except when mentioning Poe's mother (Elizabeth Arnold Poe) and the "Frogpondians" (adherents of New England transcendentalism) with whom Poe verbally combatted. Consequently, twentieth-century discussions about Poe and his birthplace have focused more on the antebellum literary scene in Boston than on how the city and the writer may have affected each other.

This approach has been shifting somewhat, however, due to a recent reclaiming of Poe in Boston that acknowledges the multifaceted relationship between the author and the city. On the morning of October 5, 2014, artist Stefanie Rocknak unveiled her statue, "Poe Returning to Boston," at Edgar Allan Poe Square on the corner of Boylston and Charles Street South in Boston (Fig. 2.1). The aptly-named, life-sized statue is strategically situated to portray Poe walking from the train station toward the location of his birth. Rocknak makes clear that having Poe confidently turn his back to the Boston Common with its Frog Pond contributes to the statue's reflection of Poe's "conflicted relationship with the city":

> This is a triumphant Poe, returning confidently after 165 years of literary success. Unlike the work of the "Frogpondians," including Longfellow and Emerson, that Poe mocked, this sculpture is neither pretentious nor didactic. The imagery is obvious and immediate. The raven represents his global fame and endurance, the trunk full of papers symbolizes the scope and power of his work, and the trailing pages are engraved with texts published in or written about Boston.[4]

Fig. 2.1 "Poe Returning to Boston," bronze, by Stefanie Rocknak (Photo used with permission)

The fact that this permanent work of public art addresses Poe's conflicted relationship with Boston is important because it emphasizes shifting sentiments about Poe over time, thus highlighting a dimension of spatiotemporality with which geo-criticism is concerned. In addition, the statue's position facing Poe's "home" and away from the Frog Pond (possibly inadvertently) contributes further to this complex relationship because Poe is also depicted as walking away from the locations of his first and last publications, both of which are situated close to where his mother and grandmother lived after immigrating to the USA.

As Poe himself acknowledged about writing, "[to] be appreciated you must be *read*," and so even though the statue's back is to the didactic Frogpondians, there is an acknowledgment that such a position does not negate or trivialize the impact that Poe had on the city's literary landscape and vice versa (O 85).

While Poe's published skirmishes with members of Boston's literary elite are significant to understanding his relationship with Boston both during the author's lifetime and after his death, this relationship is more complex than previously noted. As some critics have shown, the connection was not all pure animosity. Even when vitriolic words were exchanged, Poe's criticisms directed toward Bostonian writers can also apply to New England writers and the didacticism and puffery in their writings, many of which were published in the "Athens of America."[5] Furthermore, it can be argued that Boston represented an axis or epicenter for Poe, a place not for plodding through copious volumes of low-paying work, but of recalibrating that coalesced past experiences and present desires for future aspirations. In fact, many key locations significant to Poe's success, fame (or infamy), and legacy exist within an easy walking distance in Downtown Boston. Yet, to understand the dynamics that led to Poe's vilification by many of the Boston literary elite, it is necessary to consider Poe as intimately connected to Boston because of its intellectual and publication scenes as well as many aspects of Poe's life, including family, performance and the stage, romantic relationships, and financial needs.

Poe's relationship with Boston began long before he was born. On January 3, 1796, his mother Elizabeth ("Eliza") Arnold arrived in Boston Harbor with her mother Elizabeth after a perilous winter crossing of the Atlantic Ocean from Gravesend in England. Elizabeth first appeared at Covent Garden Theatre on February 28, 1791, and she continued to progress to more major roles, some which Eliza later would perform in America.[6] Elizabeth hazarded the journey for a better life with her nine-year-old daughter Eliza because she was hired by Charles Stuart Powell (who later built the Haymarket Theatre at 175 Tremont Street in Downtown Boston) as what was publicly deemed by the *Massachusetts Mercury* a "valuable [acquisition]" for the burgeoning American theater scene.[7] The Arnolds arrived soon after Boston's repeal of a 1750 Puritan law that illegalized performing and attending plays, and just two years after construction of the Federal Street Theatre at 1 Federal Street, designed by Charles Bulfinch, was completed.[8] Thus, as the Arnolds settled into their rooms at 14 State Street and prepared for Elizabeth's debut on February 12, the city's theater scene was in a nascent stage, still receiving some resistance from Puritan prejudices, and required many actors to supplement their incomes with grueling performance tours in different cities.

Philip Edward Phillips has argued that Poe was influenced by his mother's difficult but highly celebrated career on the American stage, one that began in Boston soon after she and her mother arrived from England.[9] By the time that Poe was born in Boston on January 9, 1809, Eliza had lost both her mother and her first husband to yellow fever, gotten remarried to David Poe, Jr. (a less talented actor who was the son of a Baltimore merchant and Revolutionary War veteran), and given birth to her first child, William Henry Leonard Poe, on January 30, 1807.[10] However, she remained a successful actress, performing three complete theatrical seasons (1806–1809) at the Federal Street Theatre, the location at which she and her mother frequently performed.[11] Although Poe spent his earliest days in Boston, he and his siblings were orphaned in Richmond on December 8, 1811, as Eliza's final performance in Boston occurred on May 16, 1809, at the Boston Exchange Coffee House[12] (Fig. 2.2). David Poe had previously abandoned his family, and Eliza had been engaging in multiple benefits and

BOSTON EXCHANGE COFFEE HOUSE, BUILT 1808...BURNT 1818.

Fig. 2.2 Boston Exchange Coffee House (Harry Lee Poe Collection)

tours to support her three very young children alone.[13] Biographer Kenneth Silverman notes that beyond a miniature of Eliza, some letters, and a watercolor sketch of Boston Harbor attributed to her with the note, "For my little son Edgar, who should ever love Boston, the place of his birth, and where his mother found her *best*, and *most sympathetic* friends," Poe was left with "a subtler inheritance as well: the fragmentary knowledge of Tekeli, the Ushers, Dan Dilly, January 3, 1796; the sense of someone who had stirred in a world of singers and dancers, scenery and demon traps; the dim remembrance of herself."[14] Phillips even asserts that Poe's witnessing of Eliza's death "surely formed deep-seated associations between beauty, the theater, and death."[15] Silverman and Phillips both suggest that the significance of Eliza and Boston resonated throughout Poe's life and writings despite Poe's young age by the time Eliza succumbed to illness, Silverman pointing out inspiring names and moments such as Eliza's first sight of Boston and Phillips explaining the "unmistakable" "influence of the American stage on him" and the author's pride in his parents' occupation.[16] It is thought-provoking to imagine how Poe's life and literary career would have differed had Eliza not died in Richmond but returned home with her children to Boston.

Eliza's death while on tour in Richmond meant that her children were orphaned far from the city that she urged Poe to love. However, her skills as an accomplished actress had brought her and her children charity from locals. Consequently, Poe was taken in by the local Scottish merchant John Allan and his wife, Frances Allan, despite the fact that Allan "disapproved of acting [...] and frowned upon stager performers."[17] Thus began Poe's difficult relationship with the man who never formally adopted him but had him baptized with the middle name "Allan" and provided him a "home" and a fine education.

Although Poe spent little of his childhood physically in Boston, he appears to have been drawn there multiple times during his abbreviated adult life for various personal reasons and professional opportunities in the eminent city filled with wealth, education, democracy, and a literate population. Once his relationship with Allan became sufficiently strained, Poe wrote to Allan on March 19, 1827, that he determined to leave and "find some place in this wide world, where I will be treated—not as you have treated me—" (O 10). That place turned out to be Boston.

Poe's decision to leave Richmond and return to the city of his birth in hopes of what he thought would be better treatment and future success proved significant to the author personally and to publishing history. There is some possibility that Poe attempted to be a clerk and a reporter after arriving from Virginia.[18] However, most likely due to a lack of gainful employment, Poe enlisted for a five-year term in the First Regiment of Artillery of the US Army on May 26 in Boston, several blocks east of his mother and grandmother's first residence after their arrival in America. Enlisting under the name "Edgar A. Perry" and claiming that he was 22 when he was actually 18, Poe was stationed initially at Fort Independence in Boston Harbor (which today has a plate with an etching of Poe along with various information about the location)[19] (Fig. 2.3). Silverman attributes Poe's decision to join the military in Boston to "his grandfather's association with the Revolutionary army; his own earlier service in the Morgan Junior Riflemen; [his] admiration for the martial ambitions of Byron and Tamerlane; [and] the prospect of familylike camaraderie."[20] Such a blending of family history, past personal experiences, and future ambitions as motivations appears plausible, and it also enhances a perspective of Boston as a point of past and future intersection as well as one of calibration for Poe throughout his

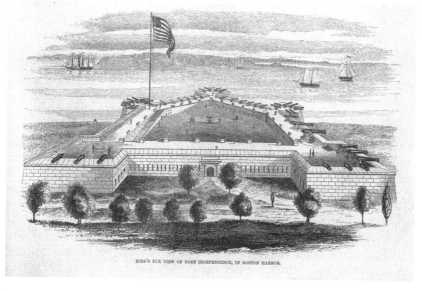

Fig. 2.3 Bird's eye view of Fort Independence, in Boston Harbor. 1852 (Harry Lee Poe Collection)

life. Here, rather than shirking his duties (or being viewed as a disappointment by Allan), Poe thrived in the army and soon distinguished himself as both capable and trustworthy. Soon promoted to "Assistant to the Assistant Commissary of Subsistence," Poe later became a company clerk and eventually took a pay increase through his role as an artificer. Military records indicate that Poe was noted as "exemplary in his deportment" and "highly worthy of confidence," and on New Year's Day in 1829, he was promoted to the highest rank for noncommissioned officers, sergeant major for artillery.[21] Poe's successful two years in the military attest to his self-discipline, reliability, and conscientiousness.

In addition to positioning himself in a more successful financial and professional state, Poe found support for his writing aspirations. It was while he was serving at Boston's Fort Independence that fifty copies of his first book, *Tamerlane and Other Poems*, a slim volume whose author was only identified as "a Bostonian," was quietly published in 1827 at One State Street (previously 70 Washington Street) by Calvin F. S. Thomas, a teenage printer whose family, according to Silverman, may have been acquainted with Poe's parents.[22] This print shop stood only steps away from his mother and grandmother's 1796 residence and was situated across the street from the location where Poe's most famous short story, "The Tell-Tale Heart," would later be published by James Russell Lowell in 1843 (67 Washington Street).[23] That Poe cited himself as "a Bostonian" rather than using some alteration of his name or a previously used pseudonym (such as Edgar A. Perry, Henri Le Rennet, or Edgar Allan) could be viewed as a strategic move to capitalize on his connections to the city, a genuine nod to a place dear to him, or (and probably likely) a combination of both. Furthermore, Philip Beidler underscores how significant Poe's time in the military (and later at the United States Military Academy at West Point) was to his future writings, explaining that it "[supplied] major elements of well-known stories ranging from 'The Gold Bug' to 'The Cask of Amontillado'" as well as "The Man that Was Used Up."[24] For instance, "The Cask of Amontillado" purportedly was influenced by what Poe heard about a famous duel between two lieutenants that occurred at Fort Independence in 1817.[25] Beidler adds that "in terms of an understanding of general antebellum cultural relations, such disparate postings as Charleston and Boston must have given the young adult Poe a notable survey of the regional politics of the era, with the former already by the late 1820s and early 1830s a hotbed of pro-slavery and states rights' agitation and the latter digging in as firmly as a bastion of Unionism and Abolitionism."[26] William F. Hecker even connects Poe's poetic theories, laid out in "The Poetic Principle," to the author's work as an artificer precisely calculating bomb construction, writing that "Poe's desire that his poems act as aesthetic 'bombs' figures him both as a poet-artillerist and artillerist-poet."[27]

By the time he published his second volume of poetry in 1829, Poe had moved to South Carolina with his regiment and found a replacement to complete his five-year enlistment. In Baltimore, Poe waited to attend West Point after Allan helped him procure recommendation letters (and included a cold one from himself in which he states, "Frankly sir, do I declare that He is of no relation to me whatever.")[28] Although raised as a young gentleman in Richmond, Poe never attained a sense of belonging with Allan. However, Boston still lingered in his mind. Poe dedicated this publication, *Al Aaraaf, Tamerlane and Minor Poems*, to John Neal, the Boston-based editor of *The Yankee and Boston Literary Gazette* located at 3 Center Plaza, a few streets west of Poe's mother and grandmother's former residence at 28 State Street. In the September issue of the publication, Neal had included excerpts from Poe's "Heaven" (later renamed "Fairyland"). He also wrote a highly complementary article which stated, "What more can we do for the lovers of genuine poetry? Nothing. They who are judges will not need more; and they who are not—Why waste words upon them? We shall not."[29] In a letter to Neal, Poe expresses his gratitude to the editor for being one of his earliest professional supporters, writing that Neal's praise of "Heaven" was "the very first words of encouragement I ever remember to have heard" (O 52). Neal's complimentary language, as well as several mixed reviews and notices in Boston and Baltimore publications, finally brought Poe some early validation and exposure.

Poe would end up never moving back to Boston, instead relocating to New York, Baltimore, Richmond, and Philadelphia at various points. However, some of his later writings may reflect distant memories of Boston. For instance, "The Fall of the House of Usher," which appeared in *Burton's Gentleman's Magazine* in 1839, is thought by some to have been inspired by the Usher House in Boston, which was built in 1684 and taken down in 1830.[30] The name "Usher" also could be a reference to Eliza Poe's friends Noble and Harriet Usher, two fellow actors who aided Eliza as her health declined.[31] Despite not residing there, Poe continued to publish works in Boston during the last decade of his life.

One of the most notable pieces, "The Tell-Tale Heart," was published by James Russell Lowell (whom he had not yet met in person) in the first issue of *The Pioneer*, a magazine housed at 1 Boston Place and located just one street away from where *Tamerlane* had been published in 1827. Although Poe already had begun to affirm his loathing of didacticism, transcendentalism, and puffery closely tied to the Boston-area literary scene, he found a supporter and admirer in Lowell, who claimed that Poe was "almost the only *fearless* American critic."[32] Lowell also accepted the poem "Lenore" and the essay "Notes Upon English Verse" from the author eager to provide pieces monthly for whatever Lowell could afford. Only after Poe sent "Eulalie—A Song" to Lowell did he discover that the journal ceased publication after just three months due to the saturated market of American magazines and Lowell's worsening eye problems. The struggling author wrote to Lowell that there was no need for apology or the sending of a "few dollars" that Lowell owed him, stating in a letter, "give yourself not one moment's concern about them. I am poor, but must be very much poorer, indeed, when I even think of demanding them" (O 393). The letter continues by asserting that the demise of *The Pioneer* constituted "a most severe blow to the good cause—the cause of a Pure Taste. I have looked upon your Magazine, from its outset, as the best in America, and have lost no opportunity of expressing the opinion" (O 393). In addition to sending a copy of some published praise that he had given, Poe mentioned his hopes for a periodical named *The Stylus* and his desire to publish works by Lowell as well as another Massachusetts-born writer, Nathaniel Hawthorne. Despite being in great need of money and resisting the "Bobby Buttons" of the world (Boston critics whom Poe also likened to porpoises because they talked about running in schools), Poe provided compassion, comradeship, and encouragement to the young editor from just outside of Boston, positive attributes that later would be obfuscated by Poe's literary executor Rufus Wilmot Griswold.[33]

Although Poe published in and travelled to Boston several times during the final years of his life, his 1845 trip to deliver a lecture at the Boston Lyceum would prove to be momentous. As several scholars have noted, the October 16, 1845 events began far before that fateful evening when publications such as the *Boston Daily Atlas* and Boston's *Evening Transcript* contradicted the *New York Daily Tribune*'s praise of Poe and his recent Society Library performance in New York. In addition to his accusations of plagiarism against beloved New England authors such as

Henry Wadsworth Longfellow, Poe responded to the editor Cornelia Wells Walter's demeaning *Evening Transcript* poem about him by further mocking and offending the Boston literary establishment.[34] The transcendentalism scene in Boston was a strong one that included the likes of Ralph Waldo Emerson, Margaret Fuller, and Henry David Thoreau. Scholars such as Richard Kopley have examined Poe's outspoken criticism of transcendentalism, including the "Dialism" issuing from 15 West Street's *The Dial* magazine.[35] Thus, the stage was set for Poe to return to Boston in hopes of obtaining sorely needed funds and desired praise, but also with the possibility that "a coalition of Longfellow supporters would likely hoot him from the stage, as both the *Boston Daily Atlas* and the *Evening Transcript* had warned."[36]

The stage on which Poe would deliver his poem was, in fact, one that he had been on in the past (Fig. 2.4). The Odeon, formerly known as the Federal Street Theatre and located just a few blocks from the *Evening Transcript* headquarters, was not only where Poe's lecture was to take place, but it was also the same venue where his mother had performed until about ten days before, and just weeks after, Poe's birth.[37] However, Poe, who was already anxious and unable to deliver the new poem that was expected of him by the Lyceum Planning

Fig. 2.4 The Boston Theatre, Federal Street. 1828 (Harry Lee Poe Collection)

Committee, was kept waiting for what seemed like an interminable two and a half hours by the opening lecture of the Hon. Caleb Cushing, late Ambassador to China. Eventually, Poe gave some opening remarks before commencing a reading of "Al Aaraaf" and concluding with a recitation of his acclaimed recent publication "The Raven." Although many of the Boston reviews of Poe's performance were negative, noting the lack of a new poem and the diminishing number of audience members as the event progressed, Thomas Wentworth Higginson provided another perspective several decades later of the event, which he and some schoolmates from Harvard College had attended. In *Short Studies of American Authors*, Higginson recalls that Poe began with "an apology for his poem, and a deprecation of the expected criticism of the Boston public; reiterating this in a sort of persistent, querulous way, which did not seem like satire, but impressed me at the time as nauseous flattery."[38] Poe's recitation of the lengthy "Al Aaraaf" "mystified" the audience, but eventually Poe's voice transformed into an entrancing melody, and by the end of the night, Higginson "[remembered] nothing more, except that in walking back to Cambridge my comrades and I felt that we had been under the spell of some wizard. Indeed, I feel much the same in the retrospect, to this day."[39] Apparently, not all the ticketholders for that evening's event were dissatisfied.

Yet immediately after the Lyceum event, publications such as the *Yankee Blade, The Sunday Times and Messenger*, and the *Daily Evening Traveller* were less than positive. Additionally, Walter, who had already instigated back-and-forth jabs with Poe in *The Boston Evening Transcript*, again goaded him to respond. Two weeks after the Boston Lyceum lecture, Poe wrote in his lengthy, and notorious, November 22 *Broadway Journal* response:

We like Boston. We were born there—and perhaps it is just as well not to mention that we are heartily ashamed of the fact. The Bostonians are very well in their way. Their hotels are bad. Their pumpkin pies are delicious. Their poetry is not so good. Their common is no common thing—and the duck-pond might answer—if its answer could be heard for the frogs. But with all these good qualities the Bostonians have no soul. They have always evinced towards us individually, the basest ingratitude for the services we rendered them in enlightening them about the originality of Longfellow … [.] Perhaps, however, we overrated our own importance, or the Bostonian want of common civility—which is not quite so manifest as one or two of their editors would wish the public to believe … [.] The Bostonians are well-bred—as *very* dull persons very generally are. (P 298)

Critics including Silverman have claimed that Poe's multiple explanations about his lecture as a hoax, his assertion that the Boston audience was not worthy of a new work, and his allegation that a "certain *clique* of the Frogpondians" [...] "clearly arose from the torment he felt over his inability to write a poem for the event and having a Boston audience walk out on him."[40]

Sandra M. Tomc provides a different perspective, arguing that the antebellum literary industry was one that "embraced and cultivated dysfunction as a condition of authorial productivity and repute."[41] Tomc argues that a number of contemporary writers, such as Nathaniel Parker Willis and Griswold, similarly compulsively enacted supposed deficiencies in ways that brought about attention but eventually backfired. Consequently, Poe can be viewed as "[coining] his own flaws and deficiencies—his envy, animosity, and alienation—in the production of a public self whose enormous currency lay precisely in its antisocial character."[42] He, in effect, tried to be scandalous because he knew that that was how he would gain viewership and recognition, but the effect of developing and portraying a "disturbed" public self was internalization. Tomc thus asserts that "[although] the tendency in Poe scholarship is to attribute his professional failure to psychic peculiarities that rendered him 'unfit' for the demands of the popular market, Poe's value to this market was, as ever, contingent upon his record of failure and defeat."[43] Indeed, even if what Tomc argues was not completely the case, Phillips accurately notes that "[what] was disastrous for Poe was his reaction to his critics in the first issue in his new capacity of editor and proprietor of *The Broadway Journal*…[.]"[44] Poe prolonged his arguments about the Lyceum event long after the night of the lecture.

Despite Poe's histrionic rants about Boston, some more recent scholarly views consider the author's vehement words as reflecting an unfulfilled desire to be accepted and praised as a son of the city seen as an American epicenter of cultural and political activity. Instead of simply favoring art for art's sake over didacticism and transcendentalism (which Poe vilified while also expressing some of its tenets in his own writings), and rejecting much of the puffery among popular New England writers of the day, Poe additionally desired to reinstate himself in the city that had highly praised his mother's talent on the stage and that Eliza instructed her young son to love.[45] In arguing that Poe's hatred of Boston has been somewhat exaggerated and regards the broader New England literary establishment rather than those just in the city, Phillips argues that the value of Boston to Poe must not be overlooked: "Poe takes such an extreme position toward the city of his birth in his journalistic writing because it does matter to him: it was his mother's city, the city that he should live, the city that was the 'Athens of America,' and in an ideal sense, the place that should recognize and promote real literary merit."[46] The October trip to the Boston stage of the Odeon was supposed to be a financial and professional success, a pivotal and triumphant homecoming performance. The notion that Poe's ideas were blasted could explain his compulsion to save face and brush off the lecture as a mocking of the Boston crowd after receiving multiple negative reviews. Perhaps his desire finally to be accepted and considered successful was one that he would not fully admit even to himself.

Attacks by the "Tomahawk Man" (a nickname Poe earned due to his sharp tongue as a critic) such as the ones after the Boston Lyceum performance harmed Poe's reputation and a number of his connections. For instance, after receiving negative reviews from Poe, Lowell famously wrote in his poetic satire, *A Fable for Critics*, "There comes Poe, with his raven, like Barnaby Rudge, / Three-fifths of him genius and two-fifths sheer fudge" (Poe, of course, counterattacked with a scathing review of Lowell's text, albeit anonymously).[47] However, members of the publishing world certainly profited from Poe's scandalous words and actions. Tomc notes that Louis Godey of the popular *Godey's Lady's Book* hired Poe to write a series of pieces on the New York literati that began appearing in mid-1846 for the small cost of $172: "The series, because of Poe's reputation for vitriol—because, that is, of the very conditions that rendered Poe unemployable—was so wildly popular that, in Godey's words, 'the May edition was exhausted before the first of May, and we have had requests for hundreds from Boston and New York, which we could not supply.'"[48] Apparently, even in the city that supposedly shared a mutual distaste for Poe, the author's words gained notoriety, popularity, or both.

In addition to Boston's reading public continuing to consume Poe's writings in the years following the Lyceum lecture (despite many of the city's literary elite deriding him), Poe continued to visit and pursue professional and romantic relationships in and near Boston. On November 5, 1848, he supposedly attempted suicide by laudanum in a Boston hotel in order to draw the married "Annie" Nancy Locke Heywood Richmond to his deathbed.[49] He had been on his way to Providence to see another woman, the poet Sarah Helen Whitman. Additionally, a little over a month before his death, Poe wrote to Mrs. Maria "Muddy" Clemm that he was considering moving to Lowell, Massachusetts (located approximately thirty miles from the heart of Boston) to be near Annie (O 831). In his final months, Poe was sustained professionally and financially by a Boston-based publisher and was pulled emotionally toward the area by Annie. While he never moved there, Mrs. Clemm did eventually reside in Massachusetts with the Richmonds for a time after Poe's mysterious death on October 7, 1849.

Boston eventually became the "birthplace" of Poe's last published works. During Poe's final year of life, the Boston newspaper *The Flag of Our Union*, located on Tremont Street, was the only publication to pay for and print his new works. His final completed four poems and five short stories to be published included "Landor's Cottage," "A Valentine," and the sonnet "To My Mother," which honored both "Muddy" Clemm and Eliza Poe, one mother whom he wished to bring to the Boston area and another mother who first stepped foot in the USA in Boston.[50] Both James M. Hutchisson and Silverman advance the notion of a fateful "return" to the beginning of things with Eliza Poe by noting that the story Poe was working on when he died, one about a lighthouse keeper and written in journal format, ends with a final entry on January 3, 1796.[51] Silverman views this untitled tale as blending text and author, commenting that "[with] the blank for January 4 … he vanished himself off the page. Remarkably, he timed his existence to end on January 3, 1796, the same day and the same year that the young actress Eliza Poe … arrived with her mother for the first time in America, in Boston."[52] The story that ends where Poe's mother's story in America begins, at the border of water and land, depicts the unnamed and solitary writer's increasing anxieties about his mental and physical stability as well as the lighthouse's foundation. Yet for Poe, ending at the beginning creates not separate beginning and end points, but a circle that obfuscates such distinctions and possesses not one single base point. There are returns, but those returns turn back on themselves. In a sense, Poe can be seen as not vanishing himself, but instead as securing his own immortality through an infinite loop to and from his mother and the city of his birth.

Despite such a circle closing through a merging of beginning and ending, the relationship between Poe and Boston continues to shift. Perhaps in part due to the bad blood between Poe and the Boston literati (which was exacerbated by Griswold's infamous obituary and scathing biography of Poe that included forged documents), a successful public celebration in Boston of the author's centenary failed to materialize. Still, a group of writers put together a small celebration at Boston University. Paul Lewis and Dan Currie have traced other Boston-based efforts at reclaiming the author during the twentieth century, noting that Boston's city council named the intersection of Broadway and Carver Street "Edgar Allan Poe Square" in 1913, but it was renamed after a World War I veteran in 1920. Similar attempts also proved only temporarily successful. On Poe's birthday in 1924, the Boston Authors Club installed a bronze tablet that eventually went missing, and in 1959, of course, the boarding house at 62 Carver Street in which Poe was born was torn down to create a parking lot. Later, in 1989, an Edgar Allan Poe Memorial Committee installed a plaque on Michael Moskow's building on the southeast corner of Boylston and Charles Street South and had the city name "Poe Way," but that sign disappeared and was never restored.[53]

Although Poe has been viewed worldwide as a critical shaper of and contributor to American literature, detective mysteries, the Gothic, Dark Romanticism, poetry, and more, and regardless of revelations that Griswold forged defamatory writings to and from Poe to further discredit and disgrace the author after his death, Boston's connections to Poe remained relatively undervalued and uncelebrated until as a graduate student at Boston College I approached Lewis about why Boston, a city still known for its intellectual vigor and its commemoration of many historical events and people, did not celebrate and explore its connections with the renowned author. The answer that I received regarding the city's ambivalence due to past quarrels did not satisfy me. Determined to enact change, I approached both Lewis and the city's mayor Thomas M. Menino's office in the first half of 2008 about joining forces to celebrate Poe's upcoming birthday bicentennial in 2009; from the former I received a bit of hesitation and doubt about the potential success of the venture, and from the latter there was silence.

However, the tides changed a few months later when Lewis reconsidered the idea and worked tirelessly with me to co-organize a birthday celebration at Boston College on January 15–16, 2009, consisting of readings and a celebration on the first night and a film screening of an independent film about Poe on the second night. Despite the bitter cold that first evening, the auditorium was packed with Poe enthusiasts who heard talks by Peeples and the popular author Matthew Pearl, recitations and comedy skits by Boston College students, and the reading of Mayor Menino's declaration (secured by Lewis) of January 2009 as Edgar Allan Poe Month by Boston poet laureate Sam Cornish. Lewis also spearheaded an effort that led to Mayor Menino naming the intersection of Charles and Boylston streets, a few steps from Poe's birthplace, Edgar Allan Poe Square that April. A group consisting of Paul Lewis, independent scholars Dan Currie and Rob Velella, collection owner Susan Jaffe Tane, me, and several Boston College students created the Boston Public Library exhibit, "The Raven in the Frog Pond: Edgar Allan Poe and the City of Boston," that December, which drew over 23,000 visitors.[54] This exhibit included a number of the Library's holdings along with many rare pieces on loan from Tane's extensive collection, including her copy of *Tamerlane*, one of only twelve known existing copies of Poe's first book (Fig. 2.5).

Finally, members of the museum group, along with Philip Edward Phillips and other Poe supporters, formed the Edgar Allan Poe Foundation of Boston, Inc., in 2010 with the aim of installing a permanent piece of public art near the author's birthplace.[55] The Foundation members organized events to celebrate Poe and raise funds for the artwork, including several lectures at the Boston Public Library. After releasing a call to artists in 2011, which drew 265 submissions from around the globe, the Foundation announced the selection of New York sculptor Stefanie Rocknak's design for the permanent public art sculpture, "Poe Returning to Boston." The life-sized bronze statue was unveiled by the Foundation, the Trustees of the Edward Ingersoll Browne Trust Fund, and the Boston Art Commission on October 5, 2014, at 2:00 p.m. one day before the 165th anniversary of Poe's mysterious death. It was preceded by a pre-unveiling event at the Boston Park Plaza Hotel which reviewed the process of Boston reclaiming its connections to Poe and the completion of Rocknak's statue. The day's momentous events were attended by the likes of former national poet laureate Robert Pinsky, Boston's Mayor Marty Walsh (Mayor Menino's successor, who passed away a few weeks after the statue's unveiling), Boston's NPR News Station WBUR's arts reporter Andrea Shea, and author Matthew Pearl, and hundreds of Poe admirers. While the author never truly could be disconnected from his city of birth due to their lingering mutual shaping of and effects on each other, Boston finally officially celebrated its multifaceted and sometimes problematic connections to Poe.

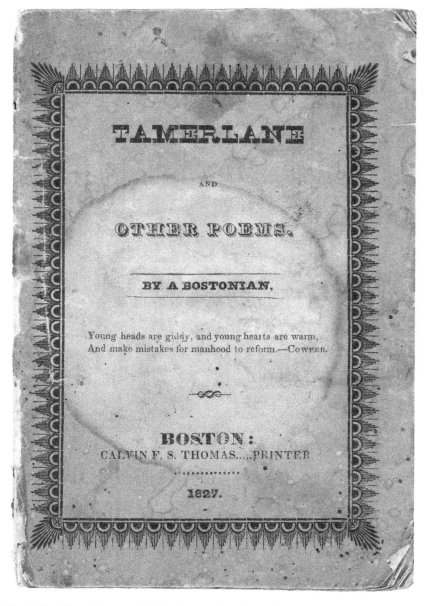

Fig. 2.5 *Tamerlane and Other Poems. By a Bostonian.* 1827 (Susan Jaffe Tane Collection)

No one can predict how the relationship between Poe and Boston will develop in the future, but at the very least, such a permanent fixture like a statue is harder to purloin in the dead of night than the previous street signs and plaques that have been installed in the city. Now, visitors can frequently be seen taking their pictures with the triumphant Poe statue. However, no matter what physical memorials may or may not exist, it is impossible to erase the impact that Boston had on Poe because of its cultural prominence in the early decades of the USA's history, as the place of Poe's birth to an immigrant who first set foot on American soil at Boston Harbor, and as a city where Poe continued to pursue personal and professional connections and aspirations up until his untimely death. It was a place where Poe sought aid, found inspiration, and looked toward the future in his youth and later on in life. Additionally, the author and the Bostonian proponents of didacticism and transcendentalism pushed each other to define and defend their craft (sometimes to less successful, more trifling degrees). The revolutionary author and the birthplace of the American Revolution cannot be divorced from each other, as their bonds have influenced, and continue to influence, the tastes and minds of the American public.

NOTES

1. Scott Peeples, "Nowhere Man: The Problem of Poe and Place." Keynote Address, Edgar Allan Poe Bicentennial Celebration, Devlin Hall, Boston College, Boston, MA, January 15, 2009.
2. J. W. Ocker, *Poe-Land: The Hallowed Haunts of Edgar Allan Poe* (Woodstock: The Countryman Press, 2015), 22–23.
3. See Chapter 1 of Ocker's text.
4. "The Designer & the Design," *The Edgar Allan Poe Foundation of Boston.* www.bostonpoe.org/design.
5. Philip Edward Phillips, "Poe's 1845 Boston Lyceum Appearance Reconsidered," in *Deciphering Poe: Subtexts, Contexts, Subversive Meaning,* ed. S. Alexandra (Bethlehem: Lehigh University Press, 2013), 41–52.
6. Arthur Hobson Quinn, *Edgar Allan Poe: A Critical Biography* (New York: D. Appleton-Century Company, 1941), 3.
7. Geddeth Smith, *The Brief Career of Eliza Poe* (London and Toronto: Associated University Presses, 1988), 15–16.
8. Ibid., 16.
9. See Philip Edward Phillips, "The American Stage," in *Edgar Allan Poe in Context,* ed. Kevin J. Hayes (Cambridge: Cambridge University Press, 2013), 118–128.

10. James M. Hutchisson, *Poe* (Jackson: University Press of Mississippi, 2005), 4–5.
11. Paul Lewis and Dan Currie, "The Raven in the Frog Pond: Edgar Allan Poe and the City of Boston," in *Born in the U.S.A.: Birth, Commemoration, and American Public Memory*, ed. Seth C. Bruggeman (Amherst: University of Massachusetts Press, 2012), 221.
12. Ibid., 221.
13. Kenneth Silverman, *Edgar A. Poe: Mournful and Never-Ending Remembrance* (New York: HarperCollins, 1991), 8.
14. Ibid., 9.
15. Phillips, "The American Stage," 121.
16. Ibid., 118.
17. Ibid., 121.
18. Theodore Pease Stearns, "A Prohibitionist Shakes Dice with Poe," *The Outlook* 126, no. 1 (September 1, 1920): 25–26.
19. Ocker, 38–39.
20. Silverman, 42.
21. Ibid., 42–43.
22. Ibid., 38.
23. Lewis and Currie, 223.
24. Philip Beidler, "Soldier Poe," *Midwest Quarterly* 53, no. 4 (2012): 330.
25. Ocker, 38.
26. Beidler, 330.
27. William F. Hecker, Introduction to *Private Perry and Mister Poe: The West Point Poems, 1831* (Baton Rouge: Louisiana State University Press, 2005), xxxviii.
28. Silverman, 48.
29. Susan Jaffe Tane, *Nevermore: The Edgar Allan Poe Collection of Susan Jaffe Tane* (Ithaca: Cornell University Press, 2006), 79.
30. For detailed information on the Usher House, see: William Sidney Rossiter, *Days and Ways in Old Boston* (Boston: H. R. Stearns and Company, 1915).
31. Silverman, 151–152.
32. Ibid., 201.
33. Lewis and Currie, 224.
34. Katherine Hemple Prown, "The Cavalier and the Syren: Edgar Allan Poe, Cornelia Wells Walter, and the Boston Lyceum Incident," *The New England Quarterly* 66, no. 1 (1993): 116–117.
35. Richard Kopley, "Naysayers: Poe, Hawthorne, and Melville," in *The Oxford Handbook of Transcendentalism*, ed. Joel Myerson, Sandra Harbert Petrulionis, and Laura Dassow Walls (Oxford: Oxford University Press, 2010), 598

36. Prown, 117.
37. Phillips, "Poe's 1845 Boston Lyceum Appearance Reconsidered," 46–47.
38. Thomas Wentworth Higginson, *Short Studies of American Authors* (Boston: Lee and Shepard, 1880), 13.
39. Higginson, 15.
40. Silverman, 268–270.
41. Sandra M. Tomc, "Poe and His Circle," in Hayes, 22.
42. Tomc, 27.
43. Ibid., 33.
44. Phillips, "Poe's 1845 Boston Lyceum Appearance Reconsidered," 42.
45. For example, see Heidi Silcox, "Transcendentalism," in Hayes, 269–278, and Kopley.
46. Phillips, "Poe's 1845 Boston Lyceum Appearance Reconsidered," 49–50.
47. Silverman, 405.
48. Tomc, 38.
49. Hutchisson, *Poe*, 228.
50. Tane, 67; Lewis and Currie, 225–226.
51. Hutchisson, 248. The date of the fourth is written, but there is no journal entry for it.
52. Silverman, 414.
53. Lewis and Currie, 235.
54. Ibid., 236–237.
55. Poe Foundation of Boston board members included Dan Currie, Paul Lewis, Patricia Bartavian, John LaFleur, Rob Velella, Katherine J. Kim, Richard Kopley, Philip Edward Phillips, Susan Jaffe Tane, and (after her statue design was chosen) Stefanie Rocknak.

CHAPTER 3

Poe's Richmond and Richmond's Poe

Christopher P. Semtner

While Poe made an indelible mark on Richmond's culture, business, and tourism, Richmond also left its imprint on Poe and his work. Antebellum Richmond served as the incubator for the ideas with which Poe would change the face of world literature. Poe grew up, received his earliest education, developed his storytelling skills, wrote his first poetry, and began his career in journalism in Richmond. The people and places Poe knew there helped inspire not only his aesthetic but also some of the settings and content for his fiction and poetry (Fig. 3.1).

The Richmond Poe entered in 1810, a year after his birth, was a city in transition. Having become the capital of Virginia just thirty years earlier, Richmond remained a rowdy frontier town of about six thousand residents (about a tenth of the nation's largest city, New York). Roughly half of the city's residents were African American, and nearly two-thirds of them were enslaved. Located at the falls of the James River, Richmond was a prosperous center for the export of tobacco and flour to Europe and the distribution of slaves to the Deep South.

The region was home to wealthy landowners whose families had ruled the area's plantations for nearly two centuries, and this planter class continued to occupy the highest level of society and government. By the

C. P. Semtner (✉)
Edgar Allan Poe Museum, Richmond, VA, USA

© The Author(s) 2018
P. E. Phillips (ed.), *Poe and Place*,
Geocriticism and Spatial Literary Studies,
https://doi.org/10.1007/978-3-319-96788-2_3

43

Fig. 3.1 Richmond, Virginia in 1810 (Courtesy of the Edgar Allan Poe Museum, Richmond, Virginia)

time of Poe's arrival, this Virginia aristocracy had produced three of the nation's four presidents, and, by the time of Poe's death, seven of the twelve presidents had been born in Virginia. This aristocracy was, however, on the decline. Centuries of tobacco crops had damaged the soil, making the plantations less profitable than in earlier days. The wealth was being transferred to the emerging merchant class, which oversaw the import and export of goods on the river and canal. Poe's foster father, John Allan (1779–1834), was one of these merchants. As if to usurp the planter class's power, Allan married a woman from a planter family and purchased Moldavia, the former home of Mary and David Randolph, cousins of Thomas Jefferson, John Marshall, Harry Lee, and Robert E. Lee.

Since it served as the site of the Virginia Convention of 1775 at which Patrick Henry stirred the Patriots to action with his "Liberty or Death" speech on the eve of the American Revolution, Richmond had been a focal point for political thinkers and politicians. It was also in Richmond that Jefferson, author of the Declaration of Independence, composed the Virginia Statute of Religious Freedom, a forerunner of the First Amendment of the US Constitution in its separation of Church and

State. In addition to declaring America's independence of both government and religion, Jefferson signaled the nation's architectural and aesthetic independence when he designed the Virginia Capitol, a building which broke from British models and defined the new nation's official style of Neoclassical architecture, which embodied its Republican ideals. The city was soon filled with imitations of Greek and Roman temples. Poe paid tribute to this blend of architectural styles in the lines, "To the glory that was Greece,/And the grandeur that was Rome," in his poem "To Helen" (1831) (Fig. 3.2).

This idealistic city also had a dark side. As the nation's crime rate reached record lows, Virginia's murder rate was significantly higher than that of the rest of the USA and double that of New York and Philadelphia, the northern cities with the highest murder rates.[1] The small city was home to boy gangs who practiced such violent tactics as throwing rocks at adults and plucking enemies' eyes out of their sockets.[2] In fact, Richmond's first mayor, William Foushee, boasted that, after a

Fig. 3.2 Thomas Jefferson's Virginia Capitol from an 1831 engraving by William Goodacre (Courtesy of the Edgar Allan Poe Museum, Richmond, Virginia)

political disagreement, he had an eye plucked out of his socket so that it hung over his cheek by its ocular nerve.[3]

As unprofitable Virginia plantations were rapidly selling their enslaved laborers to larger farms in the Deep South, Richmond became a center of the domestic slave trade. Enslaved people feared being separated from their families and sent south while the city's white citizens lived in constant danger of the next slave uprising. Only nine years before Poe's birth, an enslaved person named Gabriel conspired to eliminate the whites living along the James River. Gabriel's Insurrection, as it came to be known, only failed because a sudden storm made a creek impassible long enough for one of the conspirators to lose his nerve and divulge the plan to the authorities. Gabriel was publicly hanged about a block from what would become one of Poe's boyhood homes. In 1831, in nearby Southampton County, Nat Turner's Slave Rebellion resulted in the deaths of dozens of whites and inspired the Virginia General Assembly to pass laws restricting the activities and education of African Americans in the state. Even with the constant threat of more insurrections, slave auctions were a common sight in downtown Richmond throughout the time Poe lived and worked there. Many such sales were held in the hotel directly across Main Street from the buildings in which Poe worked while editing the *Southern Literary Messenger*, and the Exchange Hotel, in which he performed his last public reading, also hosted slave auctions.

Despite the unavoidable presence of the slave trade in Poe's Richmond, Poe does not share his views on the contentious matter of slavery in his essays or reviews. The fear of slave rebellion may, however, be reflected in his novel, *The Narrative of Arthur Gordon Pym* (1838), in which black-skinned natives massacre a group of white explorers. In his late tale "Hop-Frog" (1849), an enslaved jester exacts a brutal vengeance on his king/master for cruel treatment. While "Hop-Frog" is primarily a horror story, Poe narrates it in a slightly comic tone and treats the jester/slave in a sympathetic light.

For its white citizens, at least, Richmond was a place of lax morals and scarce religious institutions. Richmond historian Samuel Mordecai observed in his 1856 account, *Richmond in By-Gone Days*, "It is a remarkable fact that Richmond was without a church of any denomination in the early part of the present century, and previously, except the venerable old parish church of St. John's on Church Hill, where religious service was performed before the Revolution."[4] With one church serving six thousand residents in 1810, only a few Richmonders could have attended weekly services.

In his *History of Richmond*, John P. Little observes that the city was "more famous for its amusements in racing, drinking and frolicking... than for those of a higher intellectual character."[5] It should be mentioned that the northern press still condemned the theater as "the very exchange for harlots."[6] While theater had only been legal in Boston for sixteen years, Richmonders of all classes had long enjoyed the raucous entertainment the stage provided. It was the lively, decadent world of the Richmond Theater that brought Poe to Richmond with his mother, the celebrated actress Eliza Poe (1787–1811).

There is an unverifiable tradition that the infant Poe appeared on the Richmond stage as a cherub in the play *Cinderella, or The Little Glass Slipper*, in which his mother played the role of one of the three Graces (PL 9). Even if he did not appear onstage himself, Poe bore the stigma of having been the son of an actress throughout his early years in class-conscious Richmond society. His classmate John T.L. Preston recalled that his peers knew "that his parents were players" and "this had the effect of making the boys decline his leadership" (PL 53). Even his foster father, John Allan, repeated a rumor that Poe's mother had conceived his sister out of wedlock.[7]

Poe was only two when Eliza Poe died from tuberculosis at the age of twenty-four. Her husband having recently abandoned her and disappeared from history, Eliza Poe depended upon the support of charitable society ladies, including Frances Valentine Allan (1785–1829) and her friend Jane Scott Mackenzie (1783–1865). Mrs. Mackenzie, who already had nine children, fostered Poe's sister Rosalie (1810–1874), and his brother Henry (1807–1831) went to Baltimore to live with their paternal grandparents, David and Elizabeth Poe. The childless Mrs. Allan took in Poe. Her Scottish-born husband, John Allan, was the co-owner of the Ellis and Allan Firm, which exported tobacco and imported British goods.

Just over two weeks after Eliza Poe's death, Richmond's carefree climate was shattered when the Richmond Theater burned on the night after Christmas, 1811, taking the lives of seventy-two of the city's most prominent citizens. The city and the nation plunged into public mourning with the US Congress wearing black armbands for a month and Richmond banning acting.

Because the victims, who included Governor George W. Smith, were indistinguishable from one another, the city entombed the "mangled, burnt and undistinguishable remains of many of the victims"[8] in two large boxes buried on the site of the theater and constructed an Episcopalian Church over them as their monument. This unusual building, appropriately named Monumental Church, was decorated with emblems of mourning and death. The architect Robert Mills went so far as to model the structure itself after a tomb.

Parishioners paid for the construction by purchasing pews. US Supreme Court Chief Justice John Marshall owned Pew Twenty-Three, and the Allans bought Pew Eighty. It was there that the young Poe attended Sunday services with Frances Allan.

Within a few decades, Richmond evolved from a fairly secular city to a fervently religious one in which the Second Great Awakening (1780–1840) brought a flood of Baptists and Methodists. The city's religious tolerance meant that Quakers, Jews, and Catholics worshipped alongside the established Episcopalians.

Thanks to Poe's traditional Protestant upbringing, his works are replete with Biblical references, but his extensive reading on other world religions is also reflected in his writing. Unlike his Baltimore-raised Presbyterian brother William Henry Leonard Poe, whose first two poems "Psalm 139th" (1827) and "Jacob's Dream" (1827) addressed Biblical subjects, Edgar Poe's early poems *Al Aaraaf* (1829) and "Israfel" (1831) borrowed themes from George Sale's (1697–1736) English translation of the Koran published in 1734.[9]

A year after Poe moved into the Allan home, the USA entered the War of 1812. Since the trade with Britain upon which the Ellis and Allan Firm relied was cut off during the conflict, the business greatly suffered. When Poe was six, Allan attempted to save the firm by starting a London branch. Having traveled there with the Allans, Poe spent the next five years in London. The journey across the Atlantic might have served as inspiration for his seafaring tales *The Narrative of Arthur Gordon Pym* (1837) and "MS Found in a Bottle" (1833), and London provided the settings for "William Wilson" (1839) and "The Man of the Crowd" (1840) (Fig. 3.3).

Failing to establish his business in London, Allan brought his family back to Richmond, where Poe received his education in Clarke's and Burke's academies. Allan intended to prepare the young Poe for a business career by placing him in the Ellis and Allan Firm's counting room, but Poe seems to have spent some of his time as Allan's unpaid employee writing poetry on the backs of ledgers and on various scraps of paper.[10]

Fig. 3.3 Moldavia, one of Poe's boyhood homes in Richmond, from a photograph taken in 1890 (Courtesy of the Edgar Allan Poe Museum, Richmond, Virginia)

Disparaging of Poe's dreams of becoming a poet, Allan wrote that Poe's "talents are of an order that can never prove a comfort to their possessor."[11] After Allan's death, Poe ridiculed businessmen like Allan in the short story "Peter Pendulum, Businessman."

This is not to say, however, that Poe did not benefit from his exposure to Allan's business. The ships departing from and arriving at Rockett's Landing from exotic lands brought the latest British magazines, such as *Blackwood's*, and books, including those of Poe's boyhood hero, George Gordon, Lord Byron (1793–1824).

If Richmond's high crime rate inspired a taste for violent stories in the young Poe, the city also fostered a love of beauty and refinement. The wealthy gentry with whom the Allans associated lived in large mansions in the city and often owned plantations in the surrounding counties.

Poe also developed a love of nature and of landscape gardens. On the western edge of town, Charles Ellis purchased an entire city block and devoted himself to building a walled garden on the site. Richmonders flocked to private and public gardens like French Garden and Haymarket Garden as relaxing escapes from the filth and noise of the city, and Ellis's garden became a favorite spot for young lovers, including Poe, who reputedly courted his first fiancée Elmira Royster (1810–1888) there.

The Ellis garden became a lasting source of inspiration for the poet. Years later, he identified such gardens with Paradise in poems like "To One in Paradise," which may contain a description of the Ellis garden in the lines, "a green isle in the sea, love, a fountain and a shrine, all wreathed in fairy fruits and flowers...[.]"[12] (Mabbott).

In Poe's tale, "The Domain of Arnheim" (1842), Ellis becomes the character Ellison, a fabulously wealthy poet who decides that the fullest expression of the poetic ideal is to be found in the creation of a landscape garden. The unnamed narrator espouses on the poetry of gardens:

> No definition had spoken of the landscape-gardener as of the poet; yet it seemed to my friend [Ellison] that the creation of the landscape-garden offered to the proper Muse the most magnificent of opportunities. Here, indeed, was the fairest field for the display of imagination in the endless combining of forms of novel beauty; the elements to enter into combination being, by a vast superiority, the most glorious which the earth could afford... And in the direction or concentration of this effort...he perceived that he should be employing the best means...in the fulfilment, not only of his own destiny as poet, but of the august purposes for which the Deity had implanted the poetic sentiment in man.[13]

The small city that Poe knew occupied a valley and two steep hills stretched along the Falls of the James River. A short walk from his boyhood homes was Harvey's Woods, a favorite haunt of his occupying a high bluff overlooking the city and river. Thanks to scenery that surrounded him during his childhood, Poe's early poetry abounds with a love of nature in works like "Tamerlane" (1827), "To the River__" and "The Lake" (1827). With a little imagination, the rocky shore in the latter poem, which Poe wrote by the age of eighteen, could describe the James River at Richmond, where he whiled away countless hours in his youth. In "The Premature Burial" (1844), Poe specifically names the James River, near Richmond, as the setting.

In 1826, at the age of seventeen, Poe enrolled in Thomas Jefferson's new University of Virginia in Charlottesville. The first non-sectarian university in America, Jefferson's "Academical Village" embodied the secular Enlightenment ideal. While the typical American university was a religious institution with a chapel at its core, Jefferson took the bold step of removing the chapel and replacing it with a library, housed in the Rotunda, a half-size replica of the Pantheon. Two long rows of buildings extended southward from the Rotunda to house the students, the professors, and the classrooms while neighboring taverns supplied meals. In addition to designing the campus, Jefferson recruited the professors and planned the curriculum. He envisioned the institution as an experiment in which he could put his educational theories into practice. When most universities prepared their students for a life in the church or classroom, he sought to equip students with practical skills for public service (Fig. 3.4).

By the time Poe entered the University on Valentine's Day 1826, Mr. Jefferson's University was in a state of chaos. The sons of wealth and privilege found the isolated campus a perfect environment for drinking, gambling, and fighting. Poe's letters from the University to John Allan describe an unruly environment in which "a common fight is so trifling an occurrence that no notice is taken of it."[14]

Recalling his University days thirteen years later in the 1839 tale, "William Wilson," Poe places his title character at "the most dissolute

Fig. 3.4 The University of Virginia from an 1831 engraving by William Goodacre (Courtesy of the Edgar Allan Poe Museum, Richmond, Virginia)

university of Europe." Having lost heavily at cards himself, Poe makes Wilson, the story's villain, a gambler who, in his words, sought "acquaintance with the vilest arts of the gambler by profession, and, having become an adept in his despicable science, to practice [sic] it habitually as a means of increasing [his] already enormous income at the expense of the weak-minded among [his] fellow collegians."[15]

Writing in 1841 to Rufus Griswold, Poe admitted that, while in Charlottesville, he had "led a very dissipated life, the manners of the college being at that time extremely dissolute."[16] This account Griswold quotes in his profile of Poe in *The Poets and Poetry of America*, and Griswold expands on it for his "Memoir" of the author in *The Works of Edgar A. Poe* (1850–1856) by falsely claiming "gambling, intemperance, and other vices, induced [Poe's] expulsion from the university."[17] Although Poe helped create this legend of his "dissipated life" at the University, the truth might be less exciting. According to William Wertenbaker, who served as the University's Librarian during Poe's time,

[Poe] certainly was not habitually intemperate, but he may occasionally have entered into a frolic. I often saw him in the Lecture room and in the library, but never in the slightest degree under the influence of intoxicating liquors. Among the Professors he had the reputation of being a sober, quiet, and orderly young man and to them and the officers his deportment was uniformly that of an intelligent and polished gentleman.[18]

Despite the dissolute atmosphere and the fact that Allan had provided him less than a third of the funds necessary to pay his expenses, Poe excelled in his classes. Unable to afford a French textbook, Poe wrote Allan for assistance and received an Arithmetic book in reply—even though Poe was not enrolled in that class. Without a textbook, Poe was unable to study French outside of class. His classmates were astonished that he would arrive at "the lecture-room utterly unprepared to recite if called upon. But his brain was so active and his memory so excellent, that only a few moments' study was necessary, and then he was ready to make the best recitation, in the class."[19] At the conclusion of his first term, the student without a French book was among the top eight students in that subject.

In spite of his high grades, Poe's gambling debts—combined with the money he owed the University—prevented him from returning for a second term. Had Allan either provided sufficient funds when Poe first entered the University or paid them at the end of the term, Poe would have been allowed to continue his studies.

In addition to the University itself, the landscape around Charlottesville also left its mark on Poe's writing. He sets "A Tale of the Ragged Mountains (1844)" in "the chain of wild and dreary hills that lie westward and southward of Charlottesville and are there dignified by the title of the Ragged Mountains."[20] Just as Poe may have enjoyed hiking through these wooded hills, the story's narrator, Bedloe, explores this landscape, providing a description that still holds true for those who visit the present day Ragged Mountains Nature Preserve:

> The scenery which presented itself on all sides, although scarcely entitled to be called grand, had about it an indescribable and to me a delicious aspect of dreary desolation. The solitude seemed absolutely virgin. I could not help believing that the green sods and the gray rocks upon which I trod, had been trodden never before by the foot of a human being.[21]

Among the professors who influenced Poe was George Tucker (1775–1861). Two years before Poe entered the University, Tucker published one of the first pieces of Plantation Literature, *The Valley of Shenandoah* (1824). The year after Poe left Charlottesville, Tucker published the early science fiction novel *A Voyage to the Moon: With Some Account of the Manners and Customs, Science and Philosophy, of the People of Morosofia, and Other Lunarians* (1827) which could have inspired Poe's own "The Unparalleled Adventure of One Hans Pfaall" (1835) in which the title character takes a trip to the moon.

Tucker may also be a source for Poe's aesthetic theory. Poe's theory of "unity of effect," could have originated in Tucker's call for each composition to "have a certain degree of singleness."[22] Just as Poe's essay "The Philosophy of Composition" describes beginning a composition with the final effect and working backwards from there, Tucker theorized that a writer should "begin in the tone with which he means to proceed," arranging his composition "so that one part may seem to rise naturally out of the other...by easy gradations to the conclusion."[23] While Poe's distaste for didacticism in poetry is thought to have been influenced by Coleridge's *Biographia Literaria*, Tucker's theory that the goal of a poem is pleasure may also be a source. Even Poe's definition of poetry as "the rhythmical creation of beauty" may originate in Tucker's belief that music is the foundation of poetry.[24]

After leaving the University, Poe returned to Richmond to find that his engagement to his childhood sweetheart, Elmira Royster, had been broken by her father and that she was engaged to the wealthy shipper Alexander Shelton. About four months later, after an especially violent quarrel with John Allan, Poe stormed out of the Allan home and stowed away aboard a coal ship for Boston, where he would publish his first book of poetry, *Tamerlane and Minor Poems* (1827). Both the title poem and the minor poem, "Song," could reflect Poe's broken engagement. *Tamerlane* tells of two young lovers roaming the countryside together until the boy's pride and thirst for glory and conquest draw him away from her in the same way that Poe's ambition took him to the University. Upon his return, the boy, having become the conqueror Tamerlane, finds that she has died during his absence. Similarly, Poe returned to Richmond to find that he had lost Elmira. In "Song," a bride is filled with shame on her wedding day because she realizes she is about to marry the wrong man.

Over the course of the next four years, Poe served as an enlisted soldier under the pseudonym of "Edgar A. Perry" in the US Army, later attended the US Military Academy at West Point, and still found time to publish two more books of poetry. While Allan aided Poe's application to West Point, he refused to pay the substitute Poe secured to serve the remainder of his enlistment. Allan's reluctance to pay Poe's expenses, coupled with Allan's remarriage after Frances Allan's 1829 death, brought about a rift between Poe and his foster father. The two were estranged by the time of Allan's death in 1834. The following year, Poe finally returned to Richmond in order to accept a position on the staff of the new *Southern Literary Messenger*.

Just as Jefferson had declared America's independence in government, religion, and architecture, the *Southern Literary Messenger* called for America's—and specifically the South's—literary independence. The editor, James Heath, introduced the first issue with a message meant to inspire Southern patriotism:

> Are we doomed forever to a kind of vassalage to our northern neighbors—a dependence for our literary food to our brethren, whose superiority in all the great points of character,—in valor—in eloquence, and patriotism, we are no wise disposed to admit? We ought forthwith, to buckle up our armor and assert our mental independence.[25]

In the same issue, J. K. Paulding writes that Virginia is an ideal environment to cultivate literary production, but he regrets its publications until that time have mainly been devoted to politics:

Hitherto your writings have been principally political; and in that class, you have had few rivals. The same talent, directed to other pursuits in literature, will, undoubtedly, produce similar results, and Virginia, in addition to her other high claims to the consideration of the world, may then easily aspire to the same distinction in the other branches that she has attained in politics.[26]

At the time of the *Messenger*'s inception, Richmond's periodicals were devoted to partisan politics. The leading newspaper editor in the city was Thomas Ritchie of the Richmond *Enquirer*, the "Bible of the Democrats."[27] Ritchie's rival was John Hampden Pleasants, editor of the *Richmond Whig*, a paper supporting the opposition party.

In the early years of the Republic, politicians had reason to doubt the young country would last, and politicians believed the decisions they made would either save or doom their nation. With such high stakes, it is little surprise Richmond's political journalism became a matter of life and death. Richmond journalists who died in duels in the early nineteenth century include Meriwether Jones, John Daly Burk, Skelton Jones, and John Hampden Pleasants. Poe himself challenged Richmond *Semi-Weekly Examiner* editor John Moncure Daniel to a duel in 1848. Although that confrontation never took place, Daniel did take part in eight other duels before his death from tuberculosis in 1865.

The state of Richmond's literary and artistic community in Poe's time is best illustrated by an incident that took place during Charles Dickens's 1842 visit to the city. A group of merchants led by Thomas Ritchie entertained the author. The hosts admitted they had not found the time to read any of their guest's books but that their wives enjoyed them very much. As Agnes Bondurant Marcuson observed, "It was not the planters but the professional and business men of Richmond who were responsible for the promotion of literary culture in the city."[28] It is only fitting that the *Messenger*'s founder, Thomas Willis White (1788–1843), a printer of humble origins and meagre education, was the one who started the city's first important literary magazine.

With few creative writers of note in Richmond, the *Messenger* sought contributions from authors throughout Virginia and the South. In Poe's time, Virginia writers associated with the *Messenger* included

George Tucker, its first editor James Ewell Heath (1792–1862), and Nathaniel Beverley Tucker (1784–1851). As mentioned earlier, George Tucker was a professor at the University of Virginia. James Ewell Heath, who was not compensated for his editorial work at the *Messenger*, served as state auditor for Virginia from 1819 until he was fired in 1849 following the release of his political satire *Whigs and Democrats; or, Love of No Politics.*

Although they never met in person, Poe corresponded with the College of William and Mary professor Nathaniel Beverly Tucker, who served as his advisor and contributor. Poe deemed Tucker's book *George Balcombe* (1836) "the *best* American novel."[29] Among Tucker's contributions to the *Messenger* was a favorable review of two staunchly pro-slavery books, James Kirk Paulding's *Slavery in the United States* (1836) and William Drayton's *The South Vindicated from the Treason and Fanaticism of the Northern Abolitionists* (1836) in the April 1836 issue.

The March 1835 issue of the *Southern Literary Messenger* introduced Poe to its readers with his short story "Berenice," a tale of premature burial and horrific mutilation for which White reprimanded the author. In stark contrast to the plantation literature of Nathaniel Beverley Tucker and James E. Heath, Poe's tale ignores the popular issues of southern politics and slavery to focus on violence, horror, and abnormal psychology. Rather than set his story in the South, Poe places his narrative in an unnamed country in an unspecified time. Upon its publication, "Berenice" shocked and offended the public such that Poe felt the need to defend it in an April 30, 1835, letter to his frustrated employer. In this note, Poe does not justify his submission of "too horrible" a story by placing it in the context of Southern literature. Instead, he compares it with successful European fiction and even advises White to emulate the practices of Edinburgh's *Blackwood's Magazine.* Poe assures him that "[t]he history of all Magazines shows plainly that those which have attained celebrity were indebted for it to articles similar in nature — to Berenice...[.]"[30] Poe continues by explaining that originality and style are the necessary elements of an effective short story and concludes by stating that the success of the work is better determined by the magazine's circulation than by a few readers' angry letters.

Other periodicals soon took note of Poe's contributions. The *Augusta Chronicle* praised "Morella" as "one of the best of those wild and gloomy exhibitions of passion" while regretting that Poe's choice of subject matter is "injurious to correct taste."[31] The Charleston, Virginia

Kanawha Banner condemned "Morella" as "the creation of a fancy unrestrained by judgment and undirected by design" but had reason to believe its author "truly imaginative and [possessing] great powers of language...[.]"[32]

If Poe's tales of terror were receiving mixed reviews, his humorous stories prompted more favorable responses. The *Baltimore Republican* deemed Poe's comic story "Lion-izing" "an admirable piece of burlesque, which displays much reading, a lively humor, and an ability to afford amusement or instruction...[.]"[33] The Charleston, South Carolina *Daily Courier* deemed "Hans Phaal" "one of the most exquisite specimens of blended humor and science that we have ever perused."[34]

Not everyone, however, was impressed with Poe's humor. James M. Garnett wrote Thomas White on June 22, 1835, that Poe's tale "Lion-izing" "has neither wit nor humor; or, that if it has any, it lies too deep for common understandings to fathom it" (Fig. 3.5).[35] In the midst of this flurry of creative work, Poe kept up with his editorial responsibilities, which included news articles, filler, and criticism of new books. During his second month with the magazine, Poe wrote the first of his "slashing" reviews, a brief notice of Laughton Osborne's *Confessions of a Poet* that Poe begins by observing "the most remarkable aspect of this production is the bad paper on which it is printed" and concludes by advising the author to shoot himself.[36]

As a devoutly southern literary critic, Poe took aim at the established northern literati. In his review of the anonymously written 1835 novel *Norman Leslie*, which had been puffed by the *New York Mirror*, Poe begins by revealing that the author is Theodore S. Fay, an employee of the very same *New York Mirror* that had "bepuffed, beplastered, and be-Mirrored" it. "For the sake of every thing puffed, puffing, and puffable," Poe continues by declaring the novel "the most inestimable piece of balderdash with which the common sense of the good people of America was ever so openly or so villainously insulted."[37]

Writing for the *Messenger* allowed Poe to experiment with a variety of literary forms and literary genres, from his first horror story, "Berenice," to his pioneering science-fiction tale, "The Unparalleled Adventure of One Hans Pfaall." He also wrote—and abandoned—what would be his only attempt at a play, *Politian* (1835), as well as the first two chapters of *The Narrative of Arthur Gordon Pym* (1837), the only novel he would complete. With "Autography" (1836), Poe merged fiction with criticism as he pretended to analyze the handwriting of authors and celebrities in

Fig. 3.5 The office of *The Southern Literary Messenger* (center, on the corner) and John Allan's counting house (right of center building) from a 1914 photograph (Courtesy of the Edgar Allan Poe Museum, Richmond, Virginia)

order to ridicule them. In the article "Maelzel's Chess Player" (1836), Poe exposed a hoax by employing the same combination of acute observation and reasoning his fictional detective C. Auguste Dupin would use five years later in "The Murders in the Rue Morgue."

By the time Poe returned to Richmond to assume a position at the *Messenger*, both of his foster parents had died, and he was no longer welcome in his former home where John Allan's second wife and her three sons then lived. Although Allan had provided for his illegitimate children, his will failed to mention Poe. As an actress's son who had never been legally adopted, Poe's place in the Virginia aristocracy had always been a precarious one, but, as an adult, he was entirely excluded. He did however maintain friendships with some of his boyhood friends, including Robert Craig Stanard, who was then a judge. Poe also received invitations to the city's balls, where he demonstrated ample dancing skills.

Poe lodged at a boarding house on Bank Street, facing Capitol Square. It stood within two blocks of two of his boyhood homes and about six blocks from the current Allan mansion. A few months after his arrival, Poe suffered a bout of depression and turned to alcohol for comfort. Ultimately, he sought solace in the company of his aunt Maria Poe Clemm (1790–1871) and her daughter Virginia (1822–1847). Making a sudden trip to Baltimore, he retrieved them and took them back to Richmond, where they moved into the boarding house of Mrs. James Yarrington on Bank Street. It was in this house that he married Virginia in a small ceremony on May 16, 1836. Poe's friend Thomas Cleland signed Poe's marriage bond, verifying that the bride was "of the full age of twenty-one years." She was actually thirteen, and Poe was twenty-seven.

For the next eleven years, Poe devoted himself to providing for his wife's happiness. Despite his poverty, he supplied her with tutors, music instructors, and a piano. His letters reveal the intensity of his dedication to her while he mentions her by name in his poem "To My Mother." Meanwhile, Virginia's only surviving poem reflects her own devotion to her husband.

If Poe's home life brought the poet peace and emotional stability, his relationship with White was becoming increasingly turbulent. After seventeen months of complaining about Poe's drinking, erratic behavior, and offensive book reviews, White dismissed him. While this would be the first of a series of editorial jobs held by Poe over the next decade, it also proved to be Poe's longest period of employment at any magazine.

In February 1837, Poe relocated to New York, where he completed and published *The Narrative of Arthur Gordon Pym* (1838). The novel features Richmond as the setting in which the narrator meets a young man named Edgar A. Poe, the *Southern Literary Messenger* editor who convinces him to write the account of his Antarctic voyage that comprises the narrative referred to in the title. Although Poe would not return to Richmond for over a decade, he remained in contact with his Richmond friends and business associates. After the death of Thomas White in 1843, Poe wrote his son to inquire about purchasing the *Southern Literary Messenger*. Poe was unsuccessful, but he did make contact with the new editor Benjamin Blake Minor (1818–1905) who invited Poe to contribute some articles.

His search for magazine work brought Poe to Philadelphia in 1838 and back to New York in 1844. Eleven years passed before he finally returned to his hometown. In September 1848, Poe visited Richmond to meet the *Messenger's* new editor John Ruben Thompson (1823–1873), who purchased several of Poe's articles over the following year. In this same period, Poe also sold revised versions of his poems "The Raven" (1845) and "Dream-Land" (1844) to the Richmond *Semi-Weekly Examiner* in spite of having challenged the paper's editor to a duel.

During a lecture tour in which Poe intended to sell subscriptions to a proposed literary magazine to be called *The Stylus*, he returned to Richmond in July 1849. The reasons for his visit were not entirely professional. Having heard that his former fiancée Elmira Royster Shelton had been widowed, Poe sought to renew her acquaintance. Shelton was by then a wealthy widow and mother living in a fashionable new Greek Revival house on Church Hill. Poe paid her regular visits over the course of the summer and made plans to settle permanently with her in Richmond. Despite accusations that he was courting her for her money, their engagement was well-known throughout the city. With his meagre funds, he was able to procure a suit for their wedding, an engagement ring, a locket bearing their initials on the verso, and a decanter and drinking glass set. In anticipation of starting a new life in Richmond, Poe joined the local division of the Sons of Temperance, pledging to abstain from the use of alcohol.

In August, Shelton wrote to Maria Clemm, inviting her to live with them in Richmond. For the first time since he left the Allan home, Poe would finally live in luxury, without the necessity of earning his living from his writing. How this would have changed his writing will never be known because, only ten days before they would have married, Poe died suddenly in Baltimore on his way to an editing job in Philadelphia. The exact cause of his early demise remains a mystery.

Shelton never remarried after the loss of her first and last fiancé. In the years to come, she seldom spoke of Poe, whose posthumous reputation suffered after Rufus Griswold published his vindictive memoir of the author. After the Civil War, Shelton's fortune declined, and she moved into her daughter's Ashland, Virginia home for a few years. While there, her daughter forbade her to mention Poe's name. Elmira Shelton's granddaughter later admitted she had been completely ignorant of her grandmother's relationship with Poe before reading about it in Elmira's obituary in 1888.

Poe's sister Rosalie Mackenzie Poe lived in Richmond until the Civil War when she relocated to Powhatan County and Mathews County, Virginia. Never having married, she supported herself in her later years by selling photographs of her famous brother on the streets of Richmond and Baltimore. She died in poverty in Epiphany Church Home, a

Washington, D.C., charity home, in 1874. Dependent on the support of her brother's admirers, she was found clutching one of their donations.

In the years after Poe's death, Richmonders helped disseminate a combination of information and misinformation about Poe's life. By the early 1860s, John Rueben Thompson began delivering the lecture *The Genius and Character of Edgar Allan Poe*. As one of a number of talks about Poe being delivered at the time, Thompson's lecture provides little new information about Poe, but, in its final version, it proposes the theory that Poe's death resulted from cooping, a form of voter fraud in which the victim is drugged and forced to vote multiple times.

Another Richmonder, the poet Susan Archer Talley Weiss (1822–1917), was Poe's sister Rosalie Poe's neighbor during the 1840s and entertained the poet at her house in 1849. Her acquaintance with Poe and her access to Poe's sister qualified her to be an expert on the author. In 1866, Weiss published the first of a number of articles about Poe, and, in 1907, she published the wildly inaccurate but entertaining biography *The Home Life of Poe*.

William G. Stanard (1888–1928), a relative of Poe's "first, purely ideal love"[38] Jane Stith Craig Stanard, served as both the secretary of the Virginia Historical Society and the editor of the *Virginia Magazine of History and Biography*. His wife, Mary Newton Stanard (1865–1929), took advantage of her access to local legends when writing her own Poe biography, *The Dreamer: A Romantic Rendering of the Life-Story of Edgar Allan Poe* (1909).

The great number of people in Richmond with first-hand experiences of Poe proved a treasure trove of information for biographers in the second half of the nineteenth century. Elmira Shelton occasionally granted interviews, most notably with Edward Valentine in 1875 and with John Moran around 1885 for the book *Edgar Allan Poe: A Defense*. Poe's former classmates and friends provided romanticized descriptions of Poe's early years. Offering a different perspective on Poe, Thomas Ellis, son of John Allan's business partner Charles Ellis, wrote that Poe was a scoundrel whose "ingratitude, falsehood and deceptions contributed to [Mrs. Allan's] death."[39] John Allan's widow Louisa Gabriella Allan told a biographer that "all I heard of [Poe] from those who had lived with him was a tissue of ingratitude, fraud and deceit"[40] (Fig. 3.6).

Before moving to Richmond around 1880, James Howard Whitty (1859–1937) had devoted himself to collecting Poe memorabilia and to researching the author's life. In this pursuit, he wrote Poe, Allan, and

Mackenzie relatives to request information about artifacts. The jewel of his collection, purchased from the estate of former *Southern Literary Messenger* editor Benjamin Blake Minor, was the desk Poe used while editing the magazine.

In 1906, Whitty joined former Virginia Lieutenant Governor Joseph E. Willard, attorney James E. Cannon, journalist Charles Marshall Graves, and Rabbi Edward N. Calisch as a founding member of the Poe Memorial Association, a group whose mission was to erect a statue of Poe in Richmond.

Richmond, however, was not interested in memorializing its greatest author. While the City Council approved the allocation of the land on which to place the statue, the Poe Memorial Association struggled to raise the money for the statue itself. The public's opinion of the project may be reflected in a 1906 editorial in the *Richmond News Leader* that states, "We found it impossible to develop any internal enthusiasm on the subject [of the Poe monument]."[41]

In 1921, Whitty and preservationists Archer and Annie Jones reorganized the Poe Memorial Association under the name Poe Foundation, Inc. and devoted themselves to establishing a Poe Shrine (Fig. 3.7).

Mrs. Jones used the bricks and granite salvaged from the *Southern Literary Messenger* office, from John Allan's counting house, and from the boarding house in which Poe lived while working at the *Messenger* to construct a walled garden and pergola on the site of an old junkyard behind the city's oldest house. Over the course of the next ninety-six years, the Poe Shrine, which soon changed its name to the Poe Museum, amassed a collection of thousands of Poe artifacts, first editions, letters, and manuscripts.

In 1956—fifty years after the Poe Memorial Association tried and failed to erect a statue of Poe in Richmond—the retired physician Dr. George Barksdale commissioned from the Pennsylvania artist Charles Rudy a full-length bronze sculpture of the poet seated holding a pen and paper. When Barksdale donated his statue to the Commonwealth of Virginia, the General Assembly sent it to a warehouse for two years while deciding what to do with it. When it was finally installed on the Capitol Square in 1958, the General Assembly apparently deemed it unworthy of a location near Jefferson's Capitol, where it would have stood alongside bronze versions of George Washington, Patrick Henry, Thomas Jefferson, and other celebrated figures.[42] The General Assembly's ambivalence about Poe's worth, as evidenced by the placement of his statue,

Fig. 3.6 Poe's desk and chair from the office of *The Southern Literary Messenger* (Courtesy of the Edgar Allan Poe Museum, Richmond, Virginia)

Fig. 3.7 The Poe Shrine in the Enchanted Garden of Richmond's Edgar Allan Poe Museum in a photograph taken around 1927 (Courtesy of the Edgar Allan Poe Museum, Richmond, Virginia)

continued to reflect the long-held view that Poe might just be unworthy of being remembered. While the Civil War homes of Robert E. Lee and Jefferson Davis have been preserved as historic landmarks, the nine Richmond homes in which Poe lived have all been demolished.

Even if Poe was officially dismissed by both his hometown and state, he still managed to find support in Richmond's creative community. Sculptor and historian Edward Virginius Valentine not only contributed to Poe studies by interviewing Elmira Shelton and one of John Allan's slaves but also collected Poe's letters to John Allan for his family's museum.

During the early twentieth century, the city's most prominent authors acknowledged Poe's influence on their own work, and several contributed to the formation of the Poe Museum. Born four years after Poe's death, Thomas Nelson Page (1853–1922) was only eleven years old at the close of the Civil War. His novels, like *Red Rock* (1898) and *The Negro* (1905), praise the Antebellum South and glorify slavery. Writing of Poe as the South's most important writer, Page opines, "The first evidence of culture which was accepted abroad after the long night of silence which covered the South after the departure of the great fathers of the Republic, was the work of Edgar A. Poe."[43]

Fantasy novelist James Branch Cabell (1879–1958), whose grandfather once lost to a fifteen-year-old Poe in a six-mile swimming contest in the James River, was a founding member of the Poe Foundation. Having grown up reading Poe's works, Cabell declared him the first American literary genius and modeled his own early poetry after Poe's.[44]

Cabell's friend Ellen Glasgow (1873–1945), who won the Pulitzer Prize for her 1941 novel *In This Our Life*, also financially supported the newly founded Poe Museum. As a Southern writer, Glasgow wrote that she "felt a curious (because an improbable) kinship with Poe."[45] When enumerating the qualities that made his work Southern, she identified the "formalism of his tone, the classical element in his poetry and in many of his stories, the drift toward rhetoric, the aloof and elusive intensity…[.]"[46]

Two-time Pulitzer Prize-winning Civil War historian and *Richmond News Leader* editor Douglas Southall Freeman (1886–1953) was the president of the Poe Foundation from 1924 until 1947. His leadership navigated the struggling Poe Museum through both the Great Depression and World War II while overseeing the acquisition of important artifacts.

While Richmond has since produced a diverse array of writers, visual artists, and filmmakers, the most prominent are known for work, which much like Poe's examines crime, violence, and death. Patricia Cornwell (born 1956) lived and set twelve of her crime procedural novels in Richmond, where she worked at the Office of the Chief Medical Examiner of Virginia, which, by coincidence, stood on the site of the Exchange Hotel where Poe gave his last public reading. Cornwell's character Kay Scarpetta is one of many fictional detectives derived from Poe's character C. Auguste Dupin. In fact, she won the 1991 Edgar Allan Poe Award from the Mystery Writers of America for her 1990 novel, *Postmortem* (Fig. 3.8).

Richmond's internationally famous rock band GWAR wears extravagant monster costumes while performing such violent and explicit live shows that the group was banned from performing in the city for several years. Members of the Grammy-nominated[47] band have claimed Poe's dark persona, as inaccurate as it might be, as an inspiration. When asked about Poe's influence on their work, the band's late lead singer Dave Brockie (1963–2014), who portrayed the character Oderus Urungus during the band's live shows, explained, "We're from Virginia. Poe used to hang around Virginia."[48]

Author Tom Wolfe (1931–2018) grew up in Richmond and attended St. Christopher's School before establishing himself as a journalist in New York. In his book, *The Bonfire of the Vanities*, Wolfe entitles a chapter "The Masque of the Red Death" and makes several references to Poe's fiction and poetry.[49] Wolfe has stated that Poe's mastery of

Fig. 3.8 Lead singer of the band GWAR posing with an Edgar Allan Poe cut-out in 2014 (Courtesy of the Edgar Allan Poe Museum, Richmond, Virginia)

language and the musical quality of his poetry were his great contributions to literature, but, Wolfe quipped, "The literary world turned against rhyme, and today Poe would probably be writing jingles for some television show."[50]

On the bicentennial of his birth, in 2009, Virginia's General Assembly finally passed a resolution honoring Poe for his significant contributions to literature. While Poe's influence on genre fiction, poetry, and aesthetic theory are well known, lesser known is the important role that Poe played in making Richmond the cultural and artistic center that it is today. Against all odds, Poe began his literary career in an artistic backwater whose most prominent writers told Dickens they had no time to read his novels. In such an unpromising environment, Poe's reviews and short stories in the *Southern Literary Messenger* elevated not only the city's but also the nation's literature and set Poe on a course toward the literary fame he would soon find in New York and Philadelphia. Poe has since inspired many other Richmond creative thinkers, like James Branch Cabell, Ellen Glasgow, and GWAR, who also launched their careers in the city. In some small way, Richmond's hard-won reputation as an artistic center with one of the nation's largest comprehensive art museums and one of the highest-ranked art schools in the US[51] can be attributed to Poe for blazing the trail for others to follow.

NOTES

1. Randolph Roth, *American Homicide* (Cambridge: Harvard University Press, 2009), 180–182, 200.
2. Virginius Dabney, *Richmond: The Story of a City* (Garden City: Doubleday & Company, 1976), 146, 205–206.
3. Dabney, 35.
4. Samuel Mordecai, *Richmond in By-Gone Days: Being Reminiscences of a Very Old Citizen* (Richmond, VA: George M. West. 1856), 117.
5. Quoted in Dabney, 39.
6. J. Kingston, *Particular Account of the Dreadful Fire at Richmond, Virginia* (Baltimore: J. Kingston, 1812), 33.
7. In a November 1, 1824, letter to Poe's brother Henry, John Allan writes, "At least She [Rosalie Poe, Edgar Poe's sister] is half your Sister & God forbid my dear Henry that We should visit upon the living the Errors & frailties of the dead" (Thomas, 62).
8. Mordecai, 141.

9. T. Mabbott, *Collected Works of Edgar Allan Poe* (Urbana: University of Illinois Press, 2000), 1:95–96 (hereafter cited in text as M).
10. Thomas, 63.
11. John Allan wrote this comment on the back of a February 21, 1831 letter from Poe. See John Ostram, Burton Pollin, and Jeffrey Savoye, eds., *The Collected Letters of Edgar Allan Poe* (New York: The Gordian Press, 2008), 1:65 (hereafter cited in text as O).
12. M 1:211–215.
13. M 3:1272.
14. Poe to Allan, May 25, 1826 (O 1:5–6.)
15. M 2:440.
16. The original manuscript for Poe's autobiography is in the collection of the Edgar Allan Poe Museum of Richmond, Virginia. It is written on the lower half of a letter to Griswold dated May 29, 1841. The upper half is owned by the Boston Public Library.
17. Rufus Griswold, ed., *The Works of the Late Edgar A. Poe* (New York: Redfield, 1850), 3:ix.
18. Thomas, 75.
19. Sherley, 247.
20. M 3:942.
21. M 3:942–943.
22. Robert Colin McClean, *George Tucker: Moral Philosopher and Man of Letters* (Chapel Hill: The University of North Carolina Press), 139.
23. Ibid., 139.
24. Ibid., 139–140.
25. James E. Heath, "Southern Literature," *Southern Literary Messenger* (August, 1835): 1.
26. J. K. Paulding, "From J. K. Paulding," *Southern Literary Messenger* (August 1, 1835): 1.
27. Dabney, 129.
28. James Branch Cabell, "The Arts in Gaza: The State of Culture in Virginia," *The Saturday Review of Literature* (New York) (August 1, 1942): 7.
29. Pollin, Burton R., Collected Writings of Edgar Allan Poe, ed. Burton R. Pollin and Joseph V. Ridgely (New York: Gordian Press, 1985–1997), 344 (hereafter cited in text as P).
30. O 1:84–88.
31. Thomas, 156.
32. Ibid., 156.
33. Ibid., 158.
34. Ibid., 161–162.
35. Ibid., 159.

36. P 7–8.
37. P 60–62.
38. Poe uses these words to describe Jane Stanard in an October 1, 1848 letter to Sarah Helen Whitman recorded in O 2:692–700, ibid., 60.
39. Thomas H. Ellis, "Edgar Allan Poe," *Richmond Standard* (May 7, 1881): 2.
40. Ibid., 2.
41. Anonymous, "Not a Poe Enthusiast," *Richmond News Leader* (December 6, 1906): 4.
42. In November 2017, the statue suffered the indignity of being moved to a distant corner of Capitol Square to make way for new monuments.
43. The Thomas Nelson Page quote is preserved in the files of the Poe Museum, Richmond, Virginia.
44. M. Thomas Inge, ed., *James Branch Cabell Centennial* Essays (Baton Rouge: Louisiana State University Press, 1982), 28.
45. Blair Rouse, ed., *Letters of Ellen Glasgow* (New York: Harcourt, Brace, 1958), 27.
46. Ellen Glasgow, *A Certain Measure: An Interpretation of Prose Fiction* (New York: Harcourt, Brace, 1938), 132–133.
47. GWAR's 1992 video "Phallus in Wonderland" was nominated for the Grammy Award for Best Long Form Music Video.
48. Mark MacQueen, "Exclusive Interview with GWAR," *Música* (October 18, 2010).
49. Jeffrey Meyers, *Edgar Allan Poe: Life and Legacy* (New York: Cooper Square Press, 1992), 302–304.
50. Louis Llovo, "Letters Show Evidence of Poe's Imagination," *Richmond Times-Dispatch* (May 26, 2014).
51. *US News & World Report* ranks Virginia Commonwealth University's School of the Arts as the second-best art school in the US in 2016.

CHAPTER 4

The Realm of Dream and Memory: Poe's England

J. Gerald Kennedy

In 1842, Edgar Poe voiced disdain for US literary nationalism and American themes, asserting his preference for the "foreign subject" (ER 1027). But even though he later wrote tales set in Virginia, South Carolina, and New York, he rarely delineated real places. Situating "A Tale of the Ragged Mountains" around Charlottesville, for example, Poe turned an Appalachian forest into an oriental panorama. Apart from his "Doings of Gotham" journalistic pieces, he mostly avoided depicting the cities where he lived—Baltimore, Boston, Philadelphia, or New York. "The Gold-Bug" stands virtually alone as a Poe narrative that hinges on local geography, sketching the sandy terrain of Sullivan's Island near Charleston, where Poe served in the US Army in 1828. As a critic, he hailed the narrative power of verisimilitude but in fiction rarely aimed for topographical accuracy. Rather, he invented surreal scenes of dread, thus anticipating the psychospatial "landscapes of fear" identified by geographical theorist Yi-Fu Tuan.[1] Many of Poe's most compelling stories conjure an invented, continental Europe, which he had never seen, or

J. G. Kennedy (✉)
Louisiana State University, Baton Rouge, LA, USA

© The Author(s) 2018
P. E. Phillips (ed.), *Poe and Place*,
Geocriticism and Spatial Literary Studies,
https://doi.org/10.1007/978-3-319-96788-2_4

71

else portray unspecified sites of violence. But a few intriguing exceptions to Poe's usual practices suggest that his childhood years abroad
left enduring images of England and Scotland. Traces of that experience
color "Ligeia" and "The Fall of the House of Usher," and two subsequent tales, "William Wilson" and "The Man of the Crowd," represent
complicated explorations of the England Poe remembered.

AN AMERICAN BOY IN THE OLD WORLD

In 1815, six months after the end of the second war between Great
Britain and America, young Edgar accompanied his foster parents, John
and Frances Allan, as well as Ann "Nancy" Valentine (Frances's sister),
on a voyage to England. Allan planned to establish a London branch of
the tobacco and dry goods business he ran with Charles Ellis. Setting off
from Richmond, the travelers boarded the *Lothair* in Norfolk on June 22,
and after several wretched weeks at sea, they arrived in Liverpool on July
28. For the next five years, until the summer of 1820, young Edgar lived
mainly in London or at nearby boarding schools. But his sojourn began
and ended with visits to John Allan's home county, Ayrshire, Scotland,
where relatives lived in Irvine and Kilmarnock; Poe also enjoyed a three-
month summer holiday there when he was ten. On their arrival in Britain,
the family journeyed to London by way of Greenock, Glasgow, and
Edinburgh, with stops in Newcastle, Sheffield, and Leeds. In the capital
they lodged briefly in Blake's Hotel, 57 Jermyn Street, before finding a
flat in Bloomsbury at 47 Southampton Row. There, the merchant portrayed himself, in a letter of October 30, enjoying "a snug fire and seated
in a nice little parlour" while his foster son was "reading a little Story
Book" (PL 26). The Americans kept that address for two years but moved
in 1817 to a nearby house at 39 Southampton Row, where they resided
until returning to the USA.[2] Allan hoped to reap profits from direct
sale of Virginia tobacco—and for a while he did. Opposite the Guildhall
in King Street, with its vast, medieval banquet hall that featured giant
wooden statues of Gog and Magog, Allan opened a shop at 18 Basinghall
Street. Tucked within the ancient London Wall in a commercial district
near the old guild halls of the Masons and Weavers, the firm known as
Ellis and Allan in Richmond did business in England as Allan and Ellis.

The record of that sojourn in the *Poe Log* provides hints of young
Edgar's movements but reveals little about their effect on his emerging
psyche or his consciousness of the larger world. On the Atlantic crossing,

whatever anxieties the ocean aroused, the boy was "highly pleased with being at sea" (PL 26) and declared that he had not been afraid. Yet when the Allans arrived on October 7, London presented an overwhelming spectacle. Unlike Richmond, which counted perhaps 10,000 inhabitants in 1815, the English capital boasted a population of more than one million, extended roughly 25 square miles, and ranked as the greatest metropolis in the Western world.[3] A young friend from Richmond aptly remarked: "I expect Edgar does not know what to make of such a large City as London" (PL 30). The visitors from America saw palaces, cathedrals, and grand public buildings, but they also discovered vile quarters and noisy streets, filled with carts, carriages, pedestrians, and animals.

Poverty abounded in Regency England: The Napoleonic Wars left crippling debts, and the new Corn Law of 1815 had inflated food prices, stirring social unrest. Several popular uprisings, including the Peterloo Massacre of 1818, occurred during the Allans' residence abroad. The Prince Regent, who ruled in place of the insane King George III, personified the extravagance and excess that provoked working-class resentment of the nobility. He responded to protests and rallies with military force. The shocking contrast in London between luxury and misery gave the native-born Americans, Frances, "Nancy," and Edgar, a first glimpse of the rigid class system that expatriates James Fenimore Cooper and Catharine M. Sedgwick later deplored. In the six months between the Allans' arrival in the city and Edgar's enrollment in a boarding school, the family apparently enjoyed urban sightseeing—likely visiting the Inns of Temple, St. Paul's Cathedral, and the Tower of London; crossing London Bridge; strolling down the Strand, Piccadilly, and The Mall; and perhaps seeing St. James's Palace or the Queen's Palace as well as Westminster Abbey and Westminster Hall, where the British Parliament then met.

Like any child newly relocated, Poe felt curious to explore his neighborhood, which included fashionable Russell Square and Bloomsbury Square. The nearest green space, Queen's Square, lay opposite the Allan flat, down Little Ormond Street. On Southampton Row, Poe lived literally around the corner from the mansion that housed the British Museum. Founded in 1753, the museum had by 1815 nearly outgrown Montague House; its collection of archeological artifacts had expanded dramatically of late, thanks partly to cultural treasures obtained through conquest and plunder. These holdings included the Rosetta Stone, acquired in 1802, as well as the statues and friezes removed by

Lord Elgin from the Parthenon and placed on exhibit in 1817. At the British Museum, Poe surely formed an inchoate idea of the glory that was Greece by gazing on gods, goddesses, martial scenes, and mythic forms (like centaurs). He gauged the grandeur of Rome by heroic sculptures and busts. There, he saw Egyptian treasures, including mummies and sarcophagi, and marveled at the immense bust of Rameses II, which inspired Shelley's "Ozymandias."[4] Free and open to the public three afternoons weekly, the museum (a mere eight-minute walk from the Allans' address) presented an irresistible attraction to expatriate Americans, citizens of a country barely forty years old.

What Poe saw of London must remain necessarily conjectural, but historical maps convey an idea of the possibilities. In April 1816, when Edgar Allan (as he was known there) set off for the school of the Misses Dubourg in Chelsea, the hackney carriage that transported him probably followed main thoroughfares from Great Russell Street and Tottenham Court Road to Oxford Street, turning south on Park Lane and right at Hyde Park Corner as it entered Knightsbridge before reaching Sloane Street on the left. Such a route passed through neighborhoods quite different from genteel Russell Square. Another route, following High Holborne to Broad and High Streets, would have skirted the notorious Seven Dials district, then a rookery of poverty, crime, and prostitution southwest of Bloomsbury, less than a mile from Southampton Row.[5] The school managed by the Dubourg sisters at 146 Sloane Street stood on the edge of London, close to the Royal Military Asylum, the Ranelagh Gardens, and the Wellington Tea Gardens. There, Poe studied geography, spelling, penmanship, church history, and probably Latin.[6]

The trip to the Manor House School in Stoke Newington, which the boy probably first made in early August of 1818, would have followed the northern periphery of built-up London, through Islington, and into the Middlesex countryside. Quaint, tree-lined Stoke Newington had a tradition as a Dissenting community, and its former residents included Daniel Defoe and Mary Wollstonecraft. Defoe was an enduring presence, and Poe's attachment to *Robinson Crusoe* probably dates from his time at Rev. Bransby's boarding school. His residence there began inauspiciously—Poe gashed his hand at the end of August and required ointment and bandages for several weeks (PL 37). The school he attended looked nothing like the rambling Gothic mansion portrayed in "William Wilson"; it was a rectangular stone building of two floors at the corner of Edward's Lane and Church Street. A large house across the street, which according to William Bittner, "dated from Queen Elizabeth's time," became Poe's focus for "imagining mysterious stories."[7] In this bucolic setting, Poe lived mostly inside the school walls, although each Sunday, students marched to nearby St. Mary's Church for two services. At Bransby's school, young Edgar continued to learn Latin and began to study French (Chapter 13, Phillips and Poe, on young Edgar's French studies). Stoke Newington felt distant from London and yet Poe resided barely four miles from Bloomsbury; in November 1818, he returned to Southampton Row for a single day, perhaps to see an aunt visiting from Scotland. Probably the most memorable event of Poe's residence abroad came in late January 1820 when mad King George III, the tyrant vilified in the American Declaration of Independence, finally died at Windsor Castle. Church bells tolled endlessly and unforgettably, even in Stoke Newington. Some of Rev. Bransby's pupils may have obtained leave to attend the London funeral procession; Edgar did not or would have mentioned it later.

Poe's visits to Scotland formed a key facet of his foreign experience. In addition to the six weeks the family spent in Irvine and Kilmarnock in 1815, Edgar passed nearly three months in the summer of 1819 in Irvine with his aunts Mary Allan and Jane Johnston. The journey from London by stagecoach likely passed the Lake District and the haunts of Wordsworth and Coleridge.[8] In Ayrshire, as family relatives would have reminded him, the boy was in Robert Burns country and probably saw a few sites associated with the poet. It seems likely that Allan's sisters would have taken the boy to see picturesque Kilwinning Abbey and nearby Eglinton Castle (Fig. 4.1). Built in the twelfth century, the abbey had been pillaged during the Reformation, and by 1815, the former monastery lay mostly in ruins, though Poe perhaps saw the surviving tower under reconstruction.[9] Eglinton Castle, a superb Gothic mansion completed in 1802, lay close by, and its crenellated towers, reminiscent of the feudal era, would have presented an unforgettable sight (Fig. 4.2). In Kilmarnock, Poe may also have seen Dean Castle, where (like the fictional House of Usher) a zigzag crack ran down the façade of the keep. Just south of Irvine lay Dundonald, a village overlooked by the imposing ruins of a castle built for Robert II, king of the Scots, in the fourteenth century. Visits to Scotland surely provided Poe vivid mental images of the great houses and ancient strongholds that recalled a legendary past.

Family letters from Britain reveal few facts about where Poe went or what he saw during those years, but his stories contain clues that confirm

Fig. 4.1 Kilwinning Abbey Ruins in Kilwinning, North Ayrshire, Scotland, 1901 (Wiki Commons)

Fig. 4.2 Eglinton Castle, north side. A small wooden bridge over the Lugton Water is visible. Irvine, North Ayrshire, Scotland, 1811 (Wiki Commons)

the deep imprint of the Old World. That is particularly true for the tales of terror composed between 1838 and 1840, but Poe also slipped references to London, Edinburgh, and British culture into several satirical pieces. His 1838 satire, "How to Write a Blackwood Article," as well as the accompanying parody, "A Predicament," loosely tracks the literary activities of a Philadelphia bluestocking in Edinburgh. For reasons easy to surmise, Poe gave the lecherous Irishman Sir Pathrick O'Grandison of "Why the Little Frenchman Wears his Arm in a Sling" John Allan's London address of 39 Southampton Row. A vapid tale of 1841, "Three Sundays in a Week," likewise takes place in London, where the Greenwich Prime Meridian tacitly figures in a dispute between two captains who have sailed the world in opposite directions. Their quarrel about which day is Sunday comically resolves a lovers' dilemma: Bobby's miserly uncle, Rumgudgeon, will let him marry cousin Kate only when three Sundays fall in one week. Trivial as these last two pieces may be, they reflect persisting resentment of the foster father who had disinherited Poe.

The literary impact of Poe's years in England seems easier to discern than the geographical impression. If he had not been aware of contemporary literature when he was reading little story books, by 1818, when he reached Rev. Bransby's academy, he had become a precocious reader with an emerging literary bent. Among other commodities, John Allan apparently sold books and periodicals, enabling Poe to browse titles and scan magazines like *Blackwood's*. Fiction exerted a magical influence, and that was especially true for *Robinson Crusoe*, which Poe later associated with "those enchanted days of our boyhood" (H 8:169). But he was probably also aware of current excitements in the English novel. Jane Austen had delighted Regency-era readers with *Sense and Sensibility* (1811), *Pride and Prejudice* (1813), and *Emma* (1815), but Poe would have been more likely drawn to her posthumous mock-Gothic novel, *Northanger Abbey* (1818). When the Allan family arrived in Britain, however, the immediate sensation was the "Great Unknown," the anonymous Scots author who had burst on the scene in 1814 with *Waverley*, a success followed by *Guy Mannering* (1815), *Rob Roy* (1817), *The Heart of Midlothian* (1818), and *Ivanhoe* (1820). The reclusive Sir Walter Scott, not widely identified as the novelist until the 1820s, had introduced the historical romance, weaving documented events into a fictional plot. Poe would later proclaim *The Bride of Lammermoor* (1819) "the master novel of Scott," and he surely identified with the haughty, scornful hero, Edgar Ravenswood, whose beloved is forced to marry another man. Poe possibly first read this "magic tale" (H 8:234) before returning to America. At Stoke Newington, schoolboy banter may also have enticed Poe to read Mary Shelley's strange new novel, *Frankenstein* (1818).

English poetry exerted an equally powerful attraction to boarding school students forced to memorize, translate, and "construe" Latin verse. They would have talked eagerly about the most recent works by leading British poets. Poe lived abroad during the heyday of Romanticism when Coleridge and Wordsworth were cultural celebrities, when Byron and Shelley enjoyed a glamorous notoriety, and when Keats was the emerging young star of English poetry. While classical verse shaped school pedagogy, Rev. Bransby's neighbor, Dr. John Aiken, was preparing an anthology, *Selected Works of the British Poets* (1820), for younger readers. Whether Poe used this textbook, it seems quite likely that Aiken's influence would have been felt by Bransby's pupils. A physician, editor, and freethinker, Aiken was compiling his volume for the revolutionary purpose of educating young people in the beauties of early modern poetry. Although Aiken avoided verse "unsuited to the perusal of youths" and ignored the controversial Romantics, the boys of Manor House School would have welcomed his elevation of such poets of melancholy as Thomas Gray and William Collins to schoolroom respectability.

But young Poe was more attracted, as his later writings attest, to Coleridge, Byron, Shelley, and Keats. Like other boys enamored of dark fantasy, Poe probably developed a fondness for poems such as "The Rime of the Ancient Mariner" and "Christabel" during his years in Stoke Newington. Soon after its publication, he may likewise have read Shelley's indignant sonnet, "England in 1819," which captured popular resentment of the monarch and regent as well as bitterness about the Peterloo Massacre. He perhaps caught Byron's sardonic questioning, in *Childe Harold's Pilgrimage*, of Britain's theft of Greek artifacts as well as their relocation of "shrinking Gods" to "Northern climes abhorred."[10] Publishing the last two cantos of his famous poem of exile in 1818, Byron projected a defiance that would have been attractive to Regency-era schoolboys, who aped the Romantics the way contemporary youth idolize rock stars. But Poe may also have shared the more complicated anguish expressed in Keats's sonnet, "On Seeing the Elgin Marbles." First published in Leigh Hunt's *Examiner* for March 9, 1817, the poem reflects on mortality but closes by acknowledging a heart-wrenching "feud"—the conflict evoked by a vision of "Grecian grandeur" that at once discloses "the rude/Wasting of old Time"—a ruin effected both by passing millennia and archeological piracy over "a billowy main."[11] If Poe did not, in 1817, grasp the controversy surrounding British Museum's purchase of the Elgin Marbles, the boy's visits to Montague House would nevertheless have made the interventions of Byron and Keats compelling lessons in the public work of poetry.

Important evidence suggests that in Stoke Newington, young Edgar became infatuated with the idea of becoming a poet himself. A credible report holds that soon after returning to the USA in 1820, John Allan showed Richmond schoolmaster Joseph H. Clarke a "manuscript volume of verses" (PL 47) mostly composed abroad—or so the timing suggests—by his precocious foster son. Allan pondered the wisdom of allowing their publication, and his decision to deny Edgar's dream no doubt intensified Poe's belief that his boyhood years in England had revealed his true vocation and uniquely prepared him to pursue it. He had absorbed the culture of Romanticism at its source, stood where famous poets had stood, and saw the landscape and ruins that inspired so much renowned poetry. The orphan had followed his foster parents to a foreign land, only to be shuttled off to boarding schools far enough from Southampton Row that he felt displaced even from his London "home." For a future author who epitomized his childhood in a poem called "Alone," his own Romantic agony had begun.

REMEMBERING BRITANNIA

During Poe's adolescence, he read British poetry and fiction to keep alive thoughts of England. In Richmond, we must assume, the Old World also persisted in memories and dreams. Poe's verse from 1827 to 1831, however, reflects the influence of England only obliquely: He questioned the authority of the Lake School, venerating Coleridge but mocking Wordsworth in his introductory "Letter to B—"; he emulated Byron's orientalism in "Tamerlane" and "Al Aaraaf"; and he evoked Keats's meditation on the Elgin Marbles and "old Time" in his "Sonnet—To Science," musing on the way empirical knowledge—that "true daughter of Old Time"—displaces fancies with "dull realities" (M 1:91). After his break with John Allan in 1827, Poe cultivated the Byronic pose of the scorned outcast and threatened to avenge Allan's rejection by winning the world's approval (L 1:17). But nothing in his early poetry explicitly evokes remembered English places, and his one topographical poem about Europe, "The Coliseum," portrays a Roman site glimpsed only in paintings and engravings. As critics have noted, his poetry more often conjures places defying geospatial location, "wild weird clime(s)" situated "out of Space—out of Time" (M 1:344).

Realizing that he would never inherit John Allan's fortune, Poe in 1831 confronted the attendant reality that he could not sustain himself publishing poetry. He decided instead to become a "magazinist," writing tales for the periodicals then proliferating in the USA. This change of course motivated a review of leading British and American magazines, and evidence of Poe's homework lies in the "Folio Club" pieces he composed in Baltimore. These tales, five of which appeared in the *Philadelphia Saturday Courier* in early 1832, represent an exercise in adaptation: Poe reinvented himself as a writer by repurposing popular sub-genres of magazine fiction. These exaggerated, mostly parodic versions of recognizable story types included a Gothic tale of horror, a *Blackwood's* tale of sensation, a Captain Marryat-inspired sea narrative, a grotesque faux-classical farce, a florid Venetian romance (with Byronic hero), and two separate burlesque accounts of bargaining with the devil.

Michael Allen has argued that Poe's long immersion in the "British magazine tradition" inspired hyperbolic stories pitched simultaneously to two different audiences—one vulgar and easily duped, the other elitist, shrewd, and appreciative of self-referential ironies.[12] Allen further suggests that Poe absorbed from Byron the defensive, self-parodic tendencies that distanced him from the unwashed masses. The clearest evidence of Poe's reliance on the British magazine tradition surfaces in his 1832 tale, "A Decided Loss," and an 1835 farce, "Lion-izing." The former bills itself as "a tale neither in nor out of 'Blackwoods'" and reconstructs the horrific misadventures of Mr. Lackobreath, a cuckold who literally loses his breath and gets buried alive. The latter satirizes the elegant literary salons of Fum-Fudge (London) by staging an outrageous gathering of "lions." Poe mocks the celebrity culture excited by periodical puffery as well as the attentions of the nobility. The tale alludes to fashionable Jermyn Street, with social venues such as Almack's Assembly Rooms, where noble "Lady Patronesses" enforced exclusivity but also created celebrities by admitting penniless poets like Thomas Moore.

More than a dozen years after returning from England, Poe began devising tales of that land, and "King Pest" (*Southern Literary Messenger*, September 1835) marked his first tale set explicitly in London. The narrative lacks geographical interest, however, and contains only a slight clue to the author's boyhood perambulations—a passing reference to "St. Andrew's Stair." This name surely alludes (*pace* Mabbott) to the steps leading up to St. Andrew-by-the-Wardrobe, a church dating back to the twelfth century, located near the Thames, and identified by its proximity to the building for garment storage commissioned by Edward III in the fourteenth century. Poe locates his story in the "chivalrous" reign of that same monarch, during a time of plague, and sets principal scenes in taverns near the river, as well as in the "filthy lanes and alleys" that spawned the contagion. Young Edgar may have observed ancient pubs near St. Andrew's, one of which, "The Cockpit" still stands opposite a side entrance to the church.[13] Poe's humor throughout "King Pest" remains forced, but one paragraph bears closer inspection. It describes a particularly squalid quarter filled with "fallen houses" and "poisonous smells" (M 2:243–244), and thus hints at an impetus for Poe's subsequent tales of England.

In a broad sense, that inspiration came from the reading entailed by Poe's appointment in August 1835 as editorial assistant and reviewer for the *Southern Literary Messenger*. Always a voracious reader, Poe's access to new titles had been limited in recent years.[14] At the *Messenger* office, however, he found scores of books fresh from US publishers and current periodicals as well. Perusing this material to compose eight or ten reviews per month formed an exhausting challenge, but the task also summoned memories of his childhood abroad.

His monthly reviews typically included several British titles, and these pirated volumes ranged from novels and memoirs to histories and travel writings. They also aroused in Poe a sense of critical authority. As he realized, his years in London had shaped his upbringing in a way unique among the American literati, and they conferred special insight into many works he was reviewing. Evaluating *The Literary Remains of the Late William Hazlitt*, for example, Poe remarks that when Hazlitt returned from Paris, he lived with his brother "in Great Russell Street, Bloomsbury" (H 9:141), a neighborhood the reviewer recalled. In a critique of Frederick Von Raumer's *England in 1835*, Poe mentions "the attic bas-reliefs, and the works from the Parthenon and Phigalia, to be found in the British Museum" (H 9:63). His recapitulation of J. F. Dalton's "piquant" *Peter Snook* traces the hero's movements from Bishopsgate Street to various genteel establishments in London and thence to stops along the Thames. Reviewing compatriot Alexander Slidell's *An American in England*, Poe displayed his familiarity with London in a shorthand summary of "fine passages" that offered glimpses "of some groups in a London coffee-room—of a stand of hackney-coaches—of St. James Park—of a midnight scene in the streets—of the Strand—of Temple-Bar—of St. Paul's and the view from the summit" (H 8:217). For those who know London, Poe implies, such minimal notation suffices.

Poe's reviews of 1835–1836 also identify the British authors he admired—Dalton, Henry Chorley, Benjamin Disraeli, and Lady Dacre among them. But he most revered Sir Walter Scott, whose name recurs often, especially in notices of American novels, as a standard of critical comparison. James French's *Elkswatawa* clumsily emulates "mannerisms" that in Scott add "great force and precision" to plot development, while Robert Montgomery Bird's *The Hawks of Hawk-Hollow* delivers "a bad imitation of Sir Walter Scott" (H 9:123; H 8:73). In the Bird review, as well as two others published in 1836, Poe extolled the aforementioned *Bride of Lammermoor*, remarking that the novel surpassed anything written by Bulwer (H 8:223) and more nearly approached the power of Greek tragedy (H 8:234) than any other modern work. Poe often criticized Bulwer but ranked him high among English novelists, as seen in a review of *Rienzi, the Last of the Tribunes* that lauds the author's imaginative gifts (H 8:223). Poe likewise admired William Godwin, whose *Caleb Williams* he perhaps discovered in Stoke Newington; Poe's review of *Lives of the Necromancers* pays tribute to the "premeditation" and restraint in Godwin's "artificial" but "inestimable" style. That review asserts that only Coleridge exceeded Godwin in his "appreciation of the value of *words*" (H 8:92–93), and in a later review of the great poet's *Letters, Conversations, and Recollections* he expatiated on "the majesty of Coleridge" and his "gigantic mind" (H 9:51).

But no author influenced Poe's mid-career swerve to British materials more obviously than Charles Dickens, who commanded Poe's attention in two reviews of 1836. To be sure, the anonymous pieces later ascribed to "Boz" had begun to appear in the London *Monthly Magazine* in December, 1833. About *Watkins Tottle*, the first collection under that famous *nom de plume*, Poe noted in a June 1836 review that many of the sketches were "old and highly esteemed acquaintances" (H 9:45), implying his familiarity with their earlier periodical incarnations. Poe's memories of Southampton Row would have drawn his attention to such 1834 *Monthly Magazine* pieces as "The Bloomsbury Christening" or "The Boarding-House." But it was Dickens's sketch of London "Gin-shops," first published on February 19, 1835, in the *Evening Chronicle*, that most discernibly stirred Poe's creative imagination, for Dickens's description of the "miserable" quarter near Drury-Lane inspired passages in both "King Pest" and "The Man of the Crowd."[15] Poe's June review also manifests his admiration for Dickens's genius, his ability to achieve "unity of effect" in a "brief article," and his deft management of both comic and tragic materials (H 9:46). For Poe, the sketches of Boz delivered vivid images of quintessential London scenes—such as "The Pawnbroker's Shop"—and he closed his review by citing the entire "Gin-shop" piece. His shorter notice in November of *Pickwick Papers* hailed Dickens's "delineation of Cockney life" (H 9:205) and quoted approvingly the conclusion of "A Madman's MS," implicitly justifying the strategy Poe used in "Berenice" (1835)—revealing insanity in the disjunction between rational affect and mad conduct. The sketches and tales of Dickens reawakened memories of Poe's own London childhood and propelled him toward "William Wilson" and "The Man of the Crowd"

(Chapter 6, Amy Branam Armiento, on Poe's meeting with Dickens in Philadelphia).

If writing reviews stirred latent nostalgia for Poe's English boyhood, it also produced a critical epiphany. As early as mid-1835, Poe began to express both sympathy for British authors unfairly castigated by American reviewers and irritation with nationalistic overrating of native works. A resentment of such chauvinism already informs his May 1835 review of the *Journal* of Frances Anne Butler (the British actress Fanny Kemble), in which Poe notes that Mrs. Butler's letters on American society, however just or cogent, provoked US critics to ignore the "merits" of her work. Indeed, Poe adds, unfavorable foreign opinions of America tend to create among national pundits "a superfluous frenzy of indignation" (H 8:25). A similar "national soreness of feeling," Poe observes elsewhere, tainted judgments of Frances Trollope's work on America (H 9:17). In a review of his compatriot John Armstrong's *Notices of the War of 1812*, Poe lamented the "unhappy sources of animosity between America and the parent country" and warned that loose talk of the sort promulgated by Armstrong might yet produce "a future mountain of mischief" (H 9:22). At the same time, he perceived, a corollary nationalist arrogance inflated critical judgments of homegrown compositions, producing a glut of worthless novels such as Theodore Fay's *Norman Leslie* or Morris Mattson's *Paul Ulric*. Poe wanted to believe, as he said in one of his first reviews for the *Messenger*, that "no sensible American will like a bad book the better for being American" (H 8:49). But a few months on the job at the *Messenger* forced him to conclude otherwise. In the famous "Drake-Halleck" review of April 1836, he wrote:

> So far from being ashamed of the many disgraceful literary failures to which our own inordinate vanities and misapplied patriotism have lately give birth, and so far from deeply lamenting that these daily puerilities are of home manufacture, we adhere pertinaciously to our own original blindly conceived idea, and thus often find ourselves involved in the gross paradox of liking a stupid book the better, because, sure enough, its stupidity is American. (H 9:277)

On the cusp of his own turn to English stories and settings, Poe pushed back against the literary nationalism that was souring US opinions of British authors while vaunting American vulgarity.

Memory Speaks

Poe's first tentative effort to meld recollections of England into a significant Gothic tale came in 1838 when he began writing "Ligeia." The geography of the tale shifts from an old German city on the Rhine, where the narrator lives with Ligeia, to an abbey in "one of the wildest and least frequented portions of fair England" (M 2:320) where he marries his detested second wife, Rowena. But this English location remains altogether indefinite. Instead, Poe draws on cultural associations to signify "England": The ruined abbey evokes Henry VIII's dismantling of Catholic religious houses in the sixteenth century; the Joseph Glanvill references summon up English metaphysical debates of the seventeenth century; recurrent references to opium recall Thomas De Quincey's *Confessions of an English Opium Eater*; the narrator's hallucination (as Benjamin F. Fisher IV has noted) replicates the effect of Dickens's "A Madman's MS"[16]; and Poe conjured Rowena Trevanion straight from Scott's *Ivanhoe*. Her family name and the village (Tremaine) associated with her origins both signify Cornwall.[17] One other association with England was purely personal: Poe first glimpsed sarcophagi "from the tombs of the kings over against Luxor" (M 2: 322) in the British Museum (Chapter 12, Emily James Hansen, for a fuller account of Poe, Egypt, and Egyptomania).

The following year, the locale of "The Fall of the House of Usher" proved similarly obscure, though allusions again insinuate an English setting. Mabbott linked the Usher name to American friends of Poe's parents (M 2:393), but Poe probably recalled the name from childhood memory: The Usher distillery was prominent in Edinburgh in 1815. That family name was also common in the Scots Lowlands and had been established in Britain since the eleventh century. Poe thus depicts a Gothic mansion of "excessive antiquity" associated with a "very ancient family," for its dungeon saw use "in remote feudal times" (M 2: 398, 400, 410). Another hint of English culture attaches (as in "Ligeia") to the narrator's implied familiarity with opium. But Poe inserted the most telling signs of an English setting in the romance the narrator reads to Usher. The knight Ethelred recalls the Anglo-Saxon King Ethelred the Unready, who ruled England for four decades. His slaying of the dragon, however, mirrors the heroism of St. George, patron saint of England. In naming the romancer Sir Launcelot Canning, Poe fused the forename of the legendary Arthurian knight with the surname of George Canning, foreign secretary and head of Parliament in England from 1822 to 1827. On the rise politically during Poe's years in England, Canning faced fierce questioning of his worthiness, as the son of an actress, to hold lofty government positions.[18] These oblique associations with England or Scotland signal the pull of a place Poe had not seen in twenty years, and in his very next tale, he made explicit use of childhood memories.

One month after "Usher," *Burton's Gentleman's Magazine* published "William Wilson." Poe got the idea for the story from Washington Irving, but Irving credited Lord Byron, who once projected a poem about a Spanish nobleman maddened by the imagined pursuit of a shadowy double (M 2:422–424). Poe's eagerness to credit Irving for the inspiration hides an equally salient fact: The tale hinged on his memory of Manor House School. It opens there and culminates in a puzzling scene of nocturnal surveillance before moving on to briefer episodes at Eton and Oxford and thence to the great cities of Europe before finally ending in Rome. But the narrator's struggle with a nemesis emerges from memories of a specific place and evokes a crisis of identity that becomes more suggestive when understood in relation to Poe's marginal status as an American boy at an English boarding school.

Nowhere else in his fiction does Poe recall a real locale with such palpable affection. The fourth paragraph of "William Wilson" betrays a significant attachment:

> My earliest recollections of a school-life are connected with a large, rambling, Elizabethan house, in a misty-looking village of England, where were a vast number of gigantic and gnarled trees, and where all the houses were excessively ancient. In truth, it was a dream-like and spirit-soothing place, that venerable old town. At this moment, in fancy, I feel the refreshing chilliness of its deeply-shadowed avenues, inhale the fragrance of its thousand shrubberies, and thrill anew with undefinable delight, at the deep hollow note of the church-bell, breaking, each hour, with sullen and sudden roar, upon the stillness of the dusky atmosphere in which the fretted Gothic steeple lay imbedded and asleep. (M 2:427–428)

But memories of Stoke Newington (located by the reference to Rev. Bransby's school) form the crux of a curious problem: The school marks a site of both happiness and self-ruin. The narrator says that "minute recollections" of the place form his chief pleasure in the aftermath of the tale's conclusion. Remembrance of the "misty-looking village" produces a dream-like contentment, even spiritual bliss; the narrator re-experiences those cool, shaded streets and hears the familiar bell from the town's church (St. Mary's old church), where Rev. Bransby preached on Sundays.

Memories of that school elicit from the narrator, and perhaps from Poe himself, something like nostalgia. Wilson likens the "rambling" house to a "palace of enchantment" (429) almost infinite in its windings; even the low, Gothic "school-room," associated with tedium and discipline, figures in his musings. He speaks of the "intense excitement" even in the "dismal monotony" of daily activities and concedes the profound influence of his "very early existence" there (430). About the school routine, he says: "The morning's awakening, the nightly summons to bed; the connings, the recitations; the periodical half-holidays, and perambulations; the play-ground, with its broils, its pastimes, its intrigues; — these, by a mental sorcery long forgotten, were made to involve a wilderness of sensation, a world of rich incident, an universe of varied emotion, of excitement the most passionate and spirit-stirring" (431). Those schooldays form a magical epoch despite Rev. Bransby's "Draconian Laws" and the deadly enmity that arose there—his revulsion toward a classmate of similar appearance bearing an identical name and the same birthday (Poe's own).

One suspects that Poe experienced similar anxieties at Manor House School. Surrounded by sons of the gentry, he learned how prep schools prepared wealthy young Britons for lives of privilege. Poe would have stood out, as an American and the ward of a dry goods merchant. If he was not the poorest boy in the school, he must have been among lowest in social standing, immersed in a culture preoccupied with rank and status. The market prosperity of 1818 that probably allowed Allan to send Poe to Stoke Newington ended abruptly in 1819, when the tobacco market collapsed. Perhaps Poe interiorized the chagrin of social inferiority as a hatred of his mercantile, American origins; perhaps he fantasized an alternate existence as a well-bred young gentleman of ample means, leading the life he might have led under other circumstances. Such reflection invites a more nuanced understanding of what Manor House School presumably meant to Poe and suggests a productive way to reimagine the antagonism between Wilson and his counterpart.

To different purposes, Russ Castronovo, David Peyser, and Paul Giles have all briefly critiqued "William Wilson" in ways that identify the despised (possibly imaginary) second Wilson as democratic. Castronovo positions the tale as "a proleptic commentary on democracy and reproduction," even a projection of "the future condition of mass culture within democracy."[19] He observes that the duplication performed by the second Wilson, an act of "democratic leveling," outrages the narrator: "In Poe's tale, the copying of Wilson punctures ... the narrator's obnoxious sense of aristocratic entitlement."[20] The tale's great paradox is that the craving for originality and distinctiveness excited by democratic society inevitably produces public mimicry. Peyser's explication delivers a more conventional close reading but also emphasizes the maddening "equality" represented by the second Wilson's imitative genius. The tale thus illustrates "the truly Gothic quality of the democratic predicament" insofar as democracy "turns every citizen into a potential competitor" and generates contempt for one's equals, the look-alikes and peers who mirror one's lack of originality.[21] Noting Poe's ambivalence toward British culture, Giles says Poe "positions himself on an eerie dividing line between British convention and American independence" and in "William Wilson" situates this "fissure" within a "specifically transatlantic context" as the narrator tells the story of "his youth and upbringing in England, where he was always haunted by a shadow self."[22] While Castronovo, Peyser, and Giles all regard the confrontation between Wilson and his doppelganger as a clash of political values, however, none ascribe American nationality to the nemesis.

Yet Poe's association of the second detested Wilson with "equality" surely authorizes a reading of this figure as the American self from which the narrator wishes to distance himself. The association of the democratic Wilson with rebellion against the narrator's "despotism" (431) strengthens such an interpretation. The narrator's vexation comes partly from the ordinary name he shares with his adversary, for despite his own "noble descent," this "uncourtly patronymic" and "very common, if not plebian praenomen" has long seemed the "common property of the mob" (431, 434), a denial of the rank the narrator obsessively asserts. That his counterpart bears the same name and loves to repeat it intensifies the latter's indignation at the other Wilson's assumed equality. Poe here comes close to replicating the idea that "all men are created equal" as a denial of aristocratic entitlement. The narrator insists that he and his adversary are not related, yet they are also, perversely enough, inseparable "companions" (431). The second Wilson embodies all that the haughty narrator hates about himself—his resemblance to an outright commoner, an American at that. In this sense, "William Wilson" prefigures Henry James's "The Jolly Corner" as a frightening encounter between a narrator and the vulgar person he might otherwise have been, but in Poe's tale the truly terrifying figure proves to be not the American but the debased European self.

The latter portions of "William Wilson" indeed suggest that if the double is a lowborn American, associated (in the English boarding school context) with Poe's internalized self-contempt, the narrator personifies the hedonism of the English aristocracy. As Wilson practices his villainy, his successive moves to Eton and Oxford represent a path to social dominance very much like the ones Poe's more affluent classmates at Manor House School must have projected for themselves. He writes tellingly about Wilson's admission to Oxford: "Thither I soon went, the uncalculating vanity of my parents furnishing me with an outfit and annual establishment, which would enable me to indulge at will in the luxury already so dear to my heart — to vie in profuseness of expenditure with the haughtiest heirs of the wealthiest earldoms in Great Britain" (440). This munificence, so unlike the meager allowance John Allan gave his college-bound foster son, perhaps represented for Poe a dark social fantasy, the unlived life of a pampered, Europeanized self who might have emerged from Stoke Newington.

But here, despite his aversion to the Jacksonian "mob," Poe reveals his own democratic sympathies. The amoral Wilson craves only superiority and dominance. Once the narrator leaves the venerable town where his transformation has begun, the tale follows a wild course across Europe; after his shameful departure from Oxford, Wilson moves to Paris, Rome, Vienna, Berlin, and Moscow. Even Naples and Egypt figure in his fugitive course before the narrative returns to Rome. But by that point, Wilson has become confused about his identity: He cannot distinguish his odious counterpart—the ethical, American Wilson—from his own mirror image. Poe thanked Irving for the literary idea of the pursuing double but privately invested "William Wilson" with conflicted schoolboy memories of loving and hating Manor House School and of alternately deploring his American lack of status and despising the arrogant boys who taunted him.

The idea of an imagined European double apparently haunted Poe. His critical encounter with Charles Dickens (years before their 1842 meeting in Philadelphia) pushed him in 1840 to write "The Man of the Crowd," a tale that simultaneously recycled *Sketches of Boz* and distilled subjective impressions of London from two decades earlier.

Steven Rachman has provided an illuminating account of Poe's borrow-ings from Dickens in "The Man of the Crowd," probing the psychology of plagiarism as a key to the tale's complex intertextuality. He suggests that "Poe's text shadows Dickens, as the narrator shadows the man of the crowd, and Dickens haunts Poe's text the way the old man occupies the psyche of Poe's narrator."[23] Yet, as in the case of "William Wilson," there is more than literary borrowing going on. If, as Rachman suggests, Poe derives details from Dickens "to pretend to the same kind of inti-mate knowledge of the city," we must be mindful that Poe too remem-bered London.[24]

The mishandled German quotation that opens and closes "The Man of the Crowd" uses the metaphor of an unreadable book to under-score the difficulty of "reading" both individual lives and urban aggre-gations.[25] As Robert Byer, Dana Brand, Bran Nicol, and others have observed, recent criticism has been influenced by Baudelaire's reflections on the story and by Walter Benjamin's longer critique, "The Paris of the Second Empire in Baudelaire."[26] While Baudelaire popularized the *flaneur*, a figure derived from Poe, as a model of the artist's relation to modernity, Benjamin regarded Poe's rendering of the city as a study of alienation. The stranger's unreadability indeed seemed to mark the ori-gin of the detective story. For several decades, discussion of "The Man of the Crowd" has thus hinged on the puzzling stranger, the urban multi-tude, and the paradoxical loneliness of the throng. But this commentary has nevertheless neglected several problems that evoke the buried history of Poe's English boyhood.

One lies in the oddly generic city represented in "The Man of the Crowd." The narrator portrays himself as keenly observant, and from the window of the "D____ Coffee-House" (M 2:507) he scrutinizes the metropolitan horde.[27] But when he descends into the street, his attention narrows to the stranger's appearance and movements, and he makes no effort, oddly, to particularize the geography of London. The tale opens and closes on "one of the principal thoroughfares of the city" (507), but the street remains unnamed. The suppressed name of the "D____ Hotel" (513) creates the illusion of precision without risking identification.[28] The narrator later mentions a nameless square, follows his prey through an anonymous bazaar, and turns toward "the river," where "one of the principal theatres" (514) is closing its doors. At last, on the "verge of the city," he enters a squalid ghetto, but through which one he cannot say. In the 1830s, when Dickens began writing about rookeries and slums, St. Giles would have best fit the description of a "noisome quarter" (514), but this area lay near the heart of London, not on its periphery.

Though this absence of geographical particularity may reflect mere forgetfulness in the lapse of two decades since Poe lived in the city, it seems puzzling in light of the reading he had lately done as a book reviewer. The narrator's indifference to place names may, however, represent a more authentic rendering of Poe's childhood experience of London.[29] Until children achieve spatial independence, they rarely remember street names, even though they may fear becoming lost or abducted by a stranger. Tuan says children often wish to become policemen or firefighters to make cities less threatening and to "overcome their sense of impotence and anxiety before both the physical environment and strange adults."[30] The London scene in "The Man of the Crowd" becomes more ominous as a result of darkness, fog, and rain, but also because the vile crowd now includes beggars, invalids, lepers, prostitutes, and drunkards (509–510). Rather illogically, a decrepit old man models the idea of deep crime, and the narrator's surveillance supposedly confirms his amorality. This observation seems calculated to remove some mystery from the city.

The truly fascinating part of "The Man of the Crowd" thus remains hidden: the *terror* produced by the narrator himself. Nicol calls "The Man of the Crowd" "Poe's strange stalking story" without once considering how stalkers frighten their prey.[31] Poe so efficiently rivets the reader's attention on the old man that he makes the narrator invisible. Indeed, the narrator himself believes he can't be seen. Three times he reassures us on this point: "he did not observe me" (512); "at no moment did he see that I watched him" (513); "he noticed me not" (515). Yet he also describes following the old man closely enough to see the texture of his linen; seeing him cross and re-cross the same street before spinning around, "nearly detecting" the narrator; and pursuing the man down empty, "people-less lanes" (513). And why might the narrator-stalker excite anxiety? This gumshoe (wearing "caoutchouc overshoes") has also, earlier in the evening, donned a mask against the damp air: "Tying a handkerchief about my mouth, I kept on" (512, 513). Although he insists that he has never been seen, he describes the eyes of the old man several times, indicating that he has been in the stranger's line of sight. Incredibly, the narrator stands in front of the old man at the end of the tale and still insists that he is not seen. All of the old man's evasive actions have been to no avail. The narrator does not stop stalking his victim until he himself is "wearied unto death" (515) and then unconvincingly explains the reactions *he himself has provoked* as evidence of criminality.[32]

But there is another wrinkle. Many readers, including Nicol, have noticed that "The Man of the Crowd," like "William Wilson," involves the doppelganger motif. But unlike the narrator of "William Wilson," who becomes obsessed by doubling, the narrator of "The Man of the Crowd" never perceives a connection. He portrays himself as the sagacious, discreet observer of a tormented psychopath. Yet in fact, as many readers perceive, both figures are "men of the crowd," and the narrator truly describes himself in remarking of the stranger, "He refuses to be alone" (515). The narrator's loneliness triggers his pursuit, which causes the stranger to seek crowds and avoid isolated places—all to elude the madman following him. But what then is the deep relationship binding this odd couple?

Poe provides geographical particularity only once in "The Man of the Crowd," when his narrator remarks that the number of pedestrians in an unnamed London street has decreased to "about that number which is ordinarily seen at noon in Broadway near the Park" (512). Is this reference to New York merely an aside to Poe's original American audience in *Graham's Magazine* or a broad hint that this narrator, who does not bother to identify a single London street, is in fact an American? If so, he is an ugly American, eager to stereotype everyone and to sniff out criminality, which he discerns in a frail old fellow, presumably English. This man wanders the streets of London with "a diamond and a dagger" (512) under his cloak, or so the narrator imagines. Has Poe produced a sequel to "William Wilson?" The opening paragraph of "The Man of the Crowd" almost invites this analogy with its meditation on "conscience" (507) and the plight of a man so burdened by horrible misdeeds that death alone can relieve his anguish. But unlike the conflict with conscience that produces a crisis for the profligate Wilson, "The Man of the Crowd" casts the Englishman as a "decrepid" (511) figure, stalked remorselessly by a moralizing, voyeuristic American who won't leave him alone.

But there is no reason to insist on a doubling of doubling. "The Man of the Crowd" contains no palpable allusions to "William Wilson" and indeed, once we understand the ratiocinative project as unconsciously sadistic, the tale transforms the figure of "conscience," the narrator, into an unwitting monster, a would-be sleuth who hounds a pedestrian almost to death because he cannot read the man's appearance. Poe hides this perverse cruelty behind the illusion of rational cleverness, a ploy not unlike the one the narrator adopts in "The Tell-Tale Heart." "The Man of the Crowd" effectively concluded the sequence of tales variously inspired by Poe's English boyhood, and it did so ironically, recasting Dickens to produce a grotesque American misreading of a London pedestrian.[33]

Drawn into the controversy over literary nationalism in the 1840s, Poe lamented US deference to "the Golden Calf of the British opinion" (ER 1083) and decried American writers who pandered to the English audience. In 1845, he insisted that "in Letters as in Government we require a Declaration of Independence" (ER 1078). His own tales from the mid-1840s indeed show increased attention to American subjects and settings, and except for the opening pages of "The Balloon Hoax," with a launch in North Wales, Poe never again portrayed in fiction the Britain of his boyhood. He did insert two Britons into the New York debate staged in "Some Words with a Mummy" and pointedly identified Dickens as a correspondent in "The Philosophy of Composition." But Poe's homage to Dickens in "The Man in the Crowd" also seems to have exorcised his nostalgia for England, even as it served as a prototype for the new literary genre that emerged a few months later in "The Murders in the Rue Morgue." In that hallmark narrative, Poe left behind memories of London and began imagining the Paris of Monsieur Dupin.

Notes

1. Thanks to Caleb Doan for valued editorial assistance. Tuan explains that certain kinds of places—wild and "civilized"—become associated with frightening ideas in *Landscapes of Fear* (Minneapolis: University of Minnesota Press, 1979).

2. The address was subsequently renumbered and today corresponds to 83 Southampton Row. Oppressed by London smoke and noise, Frances Allen several times sought relief from illness by rusticating in the west of England.

3. London in 1820 extended about seven miles east to west and two to four miles north to south; the metropolitan population had surpassed one million residents by 1811. See *The Picture of London for 1820*, 21st ed. (London: Longman, Hurst, Rees, Orme, and Brown, 1820), 50, 69.

4. The bust was first displayed in 1818, according to Marjorie L. Caygill, *The Story of the British Museum*, 3rd ed. (London: British Museum Press, 2002), 24.

5. This milieu figures in Andrew Taylor's historically meticulous mystery, *The American Boy* (New York: Harper, 2004), in which young Edgar Allan plays a role—as does his father, David Poe, long presumed dead in America.

6. On June 22, 1818, at the end of Edgar's second year at the school in Chelsea, Allan remarked in a letter: "Edgar is a fine Boy and reads Latin pretty sharply." *The Poe Log: A Documentary Life of Edgar Allan Poe, 1809–1849*, eds. Dwight Thomas and David K. Jackson (New York: G.K. Hall & Co., 1987), 36.

7. See William Robert Bittner, *Poe: A Biography* (Boston: Little, Brown, 1962), 26–27. For corrective information on the house, including its name, see A. P. Baggs, Diane K. Bolton, and Patricia E. C. Croot, "Stoke Newington: Growth, Church Street," *British History Online*, accessed on May 3, 2018. http://www.british-history.ac.uk/vch/middx/vol8/pp163-168. The salient reference reads: "The Laurels, square built and standing back from the road ..., one of the so-called Manor Houses, an 18th-century five-bayed building behind fine iron gates, was demolished in 1875."

8. In a plate article on Stonehenge, published in *Burton's Gentleman's Magazine* for June 1840, Poe gives the impression of having seen the site, comparing its appearance from a distance with a closer view. But unless the Allans detoured to Salisbury, it seems unlikely that Poe saw Stonehenge en route to Scotland in 1819.

9. This is where Poe must have witnessed the traditional shooting of the "popingo" or popinjay, mounted on the church tower, as referenced by Mabbott glossing the "painted paroquet" in "Romance." See M 1:128–129.

10. The lines in question appear in *Childe Harold's Pilgrimage*, Canto II, stanzas xiii–xv. Thanks to Jerome McGann for the benefit of his expertise.

11. The salient phrases from "On Seeing the Elgin Marbles" occur in lines 10–14 of the 1817 sonnet.

12. See *Poe and the British Magazine Tradition* (New York: Oxford University Press, 1969).

13. At 7 St. Andrew's Hill (called in the Regency Era Puddle Dock Hill), the Cockpit, built in the sixteenth century, was long associated with illegal cockfights. Lying between St. Paul's Cathedral and Blackfriars Bridge, St. Andrew's was reconstructed by Sir Christopher Wren after the great fire of 1666, then suffered massive damage in WW2 but was again rebuilt.

14. Poe may also have borrowed books in Baltimore from his mentor, John Pendleton Kennedy.

15. Mabbott's estimated date of 1834 for the composition of "King Pest" (M 2:239) should be revised to spring or summer 1835, based on this connection.

16. See "Dickens and Poe: *Pickwick* and 'Ligeia,'" *Poe Studies* 6 (June 1973): 14–16.

17. See John Burke, Esq., *A Genealogical and Heraldic History of the Landed Gentry*, vol. I (London: Henry Colburn, 1837), 253.

18. See R. K. Webb, *Modern England: From the 18th Century to the Present* (New York: Dodd, Mead, 1968), 168–169. Webb provides background on Canning's career and identifies him as the prototype for Bulwer's *Vivien Grey* (a novel admired by Poe). Webb thus challenges the view of literary critics who regard the novel as Disraeli's sardonic self-portrait.

19. See "Death to the American Renaissance: History, Heidegger, Poe," *ESQ: A Journal of the American Renaissance* 49, no. 1–3 (2003): 187, 189.

20. Ibid., 188.

21. See "Poe's William Wilson and the Nightmare of Equality," *The Explicator* 68, no. 2 (2010): 101–103.

22. See *Transatlantic Insurrections: British Culture and the Formation of American Literature, 1730–1860* (Philadelphia: University of Pennsylvania Press, 2001), 188.

23. See Stephen Rachman, "'Es lässt sich nicht schreiben': Plagiarism and 'The Man of the Crowd,'" in *The American Face of Edgar Allan Poe*, edited by Shawn Rosenheim and Stephen Rachman (Baltimore: Johns Hopkins, 1995), 72.

24. Ibid., 75.

25. As Rachman and others note, the German phrase "er lässt sich nicht lessen" should have begun with a neuter pronoun ("es") if alluding to a book (das Buch). But the faulty masculine "er" hints at the task of reading a man.

26. See Robert H. Byer, "Mysteries of the City: A Reading of Poe's 'The Man of the Crowd,'" in *Ideology and Classic American Literature*, edited by Sacvan Bercovitch and Myra Jehlin (New York: Cambridge University Press, 1986); Dana Brand, "From the Flaneur to the Detective: Interpreting the City of Poe," in *The Spectator and the City in Nineteenth-Century American Literature* (New York: Cambridge University Press, 1991); Bran Nicol, "Reading and Not Reading 'The Man of the Crowd': Poe, the City, and the Gothic Text," *Philological Quarterly* 91, no. 3 (2012): 465–493.

27. Monika Elbert notes that Poe's tales vacillate between social and solitary perspectives and that he shows greater interest in the masses in this tale

than elsewhere in his fiction. See "'The Man of the Crowd' and the Man Outside the Crowd: Poe's Narrator and the Democratic Reader," *Modern Language Studies* 21 (Autumn 1991): 16–30.

28. Perhaps Poe had in mind the Dubourg Hotel at 61–63 Haymarket Street, nearly the only London hotel of the late 1830s (according to city directories) beginning with a D, but Poe seems unlikely to have known of its existence.

29. In the *Broadway Journal* for November 1, 1845, Poe commented on an article on the Reading Room at the British Museum, recalling it as a place in which to get "some work respectably done" before "sally[ing] out among the multitudes of London." He closed by remarking: "Let no man undervalue this who has not felt the solitude of London, the monotony of the streets, and the want of those out-of-door sympathies so freely shared in Paris" (ER 1090). The allusion to Paris signals a fictionalizing of past experience, but Poe seems to express personal appreciation of the Reading Room and evokes the tone of "The Man of the Crowd."

30. Tuan, *Landscapes of Fear*, 156.

31. Nicol, "Reading and Not Reading 'The Man of the Crowd,'" 473.

32. This paragraph amplifies an argument I made in "The Limits of Reason: Poe's Deluded Detectives," *American Literature* 47 (May 1975): 184–196.

33. "Three Sundays in a Week," the farce set on Southampton Row, actually appeared a year later, in November 1841.

CHAPTER 5

Poe and Baltimore:
Crossroads and Redemption

Jeffrey A. Savoye

Any exploration of Edgar A. Poe's connections to a specific geographical location needs to address biographical, personal, and literary associations, but there is generally a greater expectation that such a study must go beyond a list of mere facts. A scholar should attempt also to deal with more difficult questions of subtle influences of time and place, and what those connections mean, even when such questions are inherently problematic and necessarily limited by what we can plausibly determine from a distance of more than a century. Poe's first collection of poetry, *Tamerlane and Other Poems*, was published in Boston in 1827 (with the author given only as "By a Bostonian") (Katherine Kim, Chapter 2, Fig. 2.5. *Tamerlane and Other Poems*). The flimsy pamphlet, crudely printed but with pages teeming with the author's pent-up artistic aspirations and early ambitions, is surely important, and the details of its printing are necessary building blocks of bibliographies and biographies. Should one assume, however, that this volume's publication in Boston is inherently significant to the poems themselves simply because they first became indelibly embodied there in paper and printer's ink?

J. A. Savoye (✉)
Baltimore, MD, USA

© The Author(s) 2018
P. E. Phillips (ed.), *Poe and Place*,
Geocriticism and Spatial Literary Studies,
https://doi.org/10.1007/978-3-319-96788-2_5

Poe almost certainly did not write any of the poems during his brief visit to the city, his clear intent for traveling there being to find a publisher for poems already written. Poe composed his most famous poem, "The Raven," in New York, but did Poe write it *because* he happened to be living in New York at the time? There is nothing expressly New-York-ish about the poem, in whatever way we might define such a characteristic, and it embodies discernable traces of earlier poems written long before he moved to New York. Would the poem have been substantially different if it had been written elsewhere? Poe's great treasure-hunting tale, "The Gold-Bug," takes place on Sullivan's Island, South Carolina, a detail of considerable significance to the plot, but Poe wrote it while living in Philadelphia. "The Murders in the Rue Morgue," also written in Philadelphia, expressly takes place in Paris. While many readers may want to assign tangible roots to Poe's works, Poe himself ardently resists such efforts in works like "The Fall of the House of Usher" that are set in no particular geographical location and take place in an indistinct time.

Based on his surviving letters, literary manuscripts, and chronology of publications, we know that Poe first began to write short stories while living in Baltimore in the early 1830s. That simple and verifiable fact allows us to date to that period at least fourteen of the early tales and a handful of poems, but does it necessarily mean that they recognizably reflect the environment in which they were written? Morella's poetic plea to the Virgin Mary would be fully at home in the Maryland of Poe's time, a rare place in the English colonies where Catholics had been permitted to practice freely and openly from the mid-eighteenth century, but the castles of the Metzengerstein and Berlifitzing families are not to be found even among the grand estates that once surrounded the city of Baltimore. For "Berenice," we are fortunate to have a letter of April 30, 1835, written by Poe to Thomas Willis White (1788–1843), the owner and publisher of the *Southern Literary Messenger*, in which Poe conveniently states that "The Tale originated in a bet that I could produce nothing effective on a subject so singular, provided I treated it seriously."[1] As Lucille King documented, this bet almost certainly emerged from the report of an actual incident of grave robbing "for the sake of obtaining human teeth" in Baltimore, a brief account being published in the *Baltimore Saturday Visiter* for February 23, 1833. Even such precise information, however, does not help us to determine where lay the "gloomy, grey, hereditary walls" of the family mansion of the tale's protagonist, with its suggestively European buttresses, frescos, and tapestries. When we do find specific details, there seems to be an overt attempt at name-dropping of exotic locales. The ship in "MS. found in a Bottle" sails not from Baltimore, in spite of the city's strong nautical connection, but from the harbor of Java, and it ends by plunging into the mythical depths of the earth at the South Pole. Poe's early tales are conspicuously sprinkled with references to Venice, Padua, Gottingen, Jerusalem, and ancient Antioch. Poe presumably wrote all of these works while living in Baltimore, and yet not one of them makes any direct mention of the city or its environs.

It should not be surprising, therefore, that Baltimore does not enjoy an obvious place of prominence in Poe's writings. The only direct mention of the city appears in "The Premature Burial" (1844), which opens with a particularly unpleasant report of what is claimed as an actual example of such a dreadful fate. Although it is introduced as being one of "very remarkable character, and of which the circumstances may be fresh in the memory of some of my readers," no case clearly fitting Poe's description has been identified.[2] If we are willing to extend our search to the broader realms of influence, however, there are some who suggest that Baltimore is often lurking in the shadows, just out of sight. Among the most frequently noted connections are those in the story "Eleonora," first published in 1841. While there is some coincidence of a few significant details in the story and in Poe's life in Baltimore nearly a decade earlier, we should perhaps feel more reservation in asserting, as May G. Evans did exactly a century later, that "the first part" of "Eleonora" necessarily "depicts the happy life together of the two cousins [Edgar and Virginia], the gradual unfolding of their love, the vow of constancy," or that "the humble little Amity Street is transformed, by the enchantment of the poet's pen, into the resplendent Valley of the Many-Coloured Grass."[3] Similarly, we should perhaps feel at least a little less confident than did John C. French in 1955 in suggesting even more specifically as the inspiration for the setting of this same story "the valley of Gwynn's Falls at a point not more than a mile and a half west of Amity Street."[4] W. F. Melton went so far as to assert that Baltimore was the "kingdom by the sea" of "Annabel Lee," the last poem Poe appears to have written.[5] While we may not be able to provide a list of precise cause and effect between people and locales of Baltimore and characters and settings of stories and poems, it is true that Poe's roughly five-year residence in Baltimore marked a pivotal moment in his literary career. As John C. French says, "In those years he had for the first time in his life since babyhood a home in which there was unmixed affection, and in that humble home he had that richest of graces the consciousness of genius growing into the maturity of its powers."[6]

In a strange way, one can state that Baltimore defines the beginning and ending of Poe's life—indeed, several beginnings, serving as a crossroads for a formative period and as a launching pad for a new career as a literary critic, editor, and magazinist. Although Poe had been born in Boston, his personal disappointments and a long-fed professional resentment seem to have led him consciously to suppress that fact.[7] For whatever reason, Poe allowed biographical material published during his lifetime to print as fact the erroneous assertion that he was born in Baltimore. In his brief autobiographical note, sent to Rufus Wilmot Griswold as part of a letter dated May 29, 1841, Poe states only: "Born January, 1811 [sic]. Family one of the oldest and most respectable in Baltimore." Griswold essentially copied this vague reference, including Poe's own erroneously asserted birth year, in the short note on Poe in his anthology of *The Poets and Poetry of America* (first published in 1842), but in the similar note for *The Prose Writers of America* (first published in 1847), Griswold more overtly reveals his assumption that "Mr. Poe was born in Baltimore, in January, 1811."[8] Poe almost certainly saw both of these notes, but he appears to have made no effort at correction as Griswold would give the same information again in his infamous "Ludwig" obituary of Poe and in the subsequent memoir for the Redfield collection of Poe's works, which would largely shape Poe's biography for the next 25 years.[9]

Poe's family was indeed rooted in Baltimore. Poe's father, David Poe, Jr., had been born in the city on July 18, 1784, and Edgar's grandfather, David Poe, Sr., having himself been born in Ireland about 1742, came to the city as a young man and adopted it as his home until his death on October 18, 1816. The grandfather was a tradesman, a wheelwright, and a prominent member of the First Presbyterian Church of Baltimore, which boasted among its congregation many of Baltimore's first citizens. Bearing the honorary title of "General," David Poe had participated in the Revolutionary War and the War of 1812 (Battle of North Point) and served as the Assistant Deputy-Quartermaster General for the city of Baltimore beginning in 1779. Edgar Poe himself, not yet carrying the middle name of Allan, was brought by his parents to be presented to his grandparents within a few weeks of his birth. His older brother, William Henry Leonard Poe (1807–1831) (usually called Henry), was left with his grandparents while Edgar and the infant Rosalie (1810–1874) accompanied their mother as she continued her tour of the South with her theatrical company. If not for the odd circumstances of her death in Richmond in 1812, and the philanthropic stepping forward of citizens of that town to assume responsibility for the orphaned children, they most likely would have ended up in Baltimore as well.[10]

It would be virtually impossible to surmise the Baltimore of the 1820s from the sprawling modern city of today. Only isolated fragments of the old town have survived the generations of expansion, changes in taste and preferences for style, the great fire of 1904, and the waves of development following the Civil War and both of the great world wars. Only one house that Poe lived in still stands, along with the site of his death in 1849. Even his burial place has been altered radically, chiefly by the building of a large church on the property a few years after Poe's first burial. As Poe no doubt would have quickly realized, Baltimore was larger and more diverse than Richmond, but smaller and less cosmopolitan than New York, and with a publishing industry that was active but not nearly as established as in New York, Boston, or Philadelphia. One constant has been the importance of the port, certainly the original reason for Baltimore being established in 1729 at the deepest estuaries of the Potomac River as it runs toward the upper waters of the Chesapeake Bay. The inner harbor always has been the heart of the city, and it was even more important during Poe's day, before the advent of a national railway system and other alternatives to shipping by water. In the 1830s, a mixture of mostly single- and two-story buildings of wood and brick tightly lined dirt streets, mostly laid out in neat blocks and leading away from the great wharves and warehouses of the harbor area through the shops and small houses of workers, who chiefly found the rewards of their labors in the concentration of supporting businesses, and out past the large farms and estates that surrounded the city.

Being south of the Mason-Dixon line, Maryland, and especially the city of Baltimore, had strong southern sympathies, but blended with a more northern inclination for business and manufacturing. Beneath the veneer of southern gentility, however, were strong elements of less civil behavior and even outbursts of brutish violence. Elections were frequently characterized by drinking and general rowdiness, with many taverns serving as voting places. A protracted series of riots broke out in 1835, when frustration erupted over the failure of the Bank of Maryland. The homes of the bank directors, and even the mayor, were raided.

Bonfires were built in the streets, fed by books, furniture, and other possessions taken from these houses. Wine stolen from well-stocked cellars helped to fuel the uprising. By 1838, a letter to the editor of one of the local newspapers would lament that the city had earned the unsavory nickname of "mob town," a designation that may have helped to crystalize Poe's deep distrust of the baser instincts of democracy (as noted in "Some Words with a Mummy" and "Mellonta Tauta").[11] It might also be noted that not all of the merchants of Baltimore were engaged in entirely honorable pursuits. The city was the northernmost center of the slave trade, with at least a dozen prominent businesses involved in the transportation and selling of slaves. Slave ships, bound for Charlestown, New Orleans, and other southern ports, were frequently moored in the area of Fell's Point, and slave pens were scattered around the city, mostly clustered on or near the east–west corridor of Pratt Street, for easy access to the harbor. One of the most notorious slave dealers, Austin Woolfolk (fl. 1818–1841), kept a pen at Pratt and Cove streets, only a few blocks from where Poe was living in 1833.[12]

Given the strongly mercantile nature of the bustling city (featuring precisely the men of business and method that Poe mercilessly parodied in 1840 in "Peter Pendulum, the Business Man"), it is only reasonable that the most visible and enduring aspects of the artistic scene tended to serve civic or utilitarian purposes.[13] Generally, the city was a follower and imitator rather than a driver of style, but it did enjoy an array of lectures, public readings, and other refined entertainments. Singing schools began in Baltimore about 1789, increasing substantially in number in the 1830s, and there were numerous choral associations, often, but not exclusively, associated with churches. In addition to gatherings in private homes, small concerts for various combinations of voice and musical instruments were regularly advertised and held in venues throughout the city. Theatrical events relied primarily on traveling performers. Indeed, Poe's mother, Elizabeth Arnold, had appeared on the Baltimore stage, seasonally, in 1799–1802, playing various parts and singing.[14]

One of the more pervasive aspects of cultural life in Baltimore was literature, with both the consuming and creation of written matter in all its forms: news, educational and moral essays, tales, poems, and novels. John C. French, citing an unpublished dissertation by Dr. John E. Uhler, notes "that in the years from 1815 to 1833, inclusive, no less than 72 new periodicals were announced for publication in Baltimore. A few of these never got beyond the prospectus stage, and forty-seven of them did not survive more than twelve months."[15] It was, however, a world of two extremes. At one end, literature was the plaything of wealthy dilettantes, an opportunity to show off one's erudition and the cultural interests of the leisure class. At the other end were penniless scribblers who, if they were lucky, obtained positions as editors slaving away on the thankless labors of preparing magazines or newspapers as they discovered how difficult it was to scratch out a living merely by the efforts of their own pens. Many of these would-be literary figures moved regularly and came and left the city in their search for more comfortable opportunities. While the poet Edward Coote Pinkney (1802–1828) was praised by John Greenleaf Whitter and has achieved a minor reputation, mostly in academic circles, the names of Baltimore's literary community in the 1820s and 1830s would hardly draw much attention today. A number of more significant literary figures had Baltimore connections of varying degrees, including John Neal (1793–1876), William Wirt (1772–1834), Jared Sparks (1789–1866), and Francis Scott Key (1779–1843), but who now remembers Rufus Dawes (1803–1859), John Hill Hewitt (1801–1890), John N. McJilton (1806–1875), or Susan Rigby Morgan (1810–1887)? Perhaps Baltimore's most prominent writer was John Pendleton Kennedy (1795–1870), who, somewhat unexpectedly, would play an important role in Poe's life.

Baltimore would not have a truly free public library until the Enoch Pratt main library opened in 1886, but Poe would not have been entirely deprived of access to books. There were numerous bookstores and book auctions in the city, and buying, reading, and reselling books was a common practice.[16] He might also have exchanged books within his circle of friends, but there was also a more prominent source of which he presumably availed himself. The Library Company of Baltimore was founded in 1795 and incorporated in 1797. Access to books and journals was intended primarily for paying members, on a subscription basis, although surviving documents clearly show the considerable difficulty in collecting the payments due. Non-members could borrow materials for a deposit that was twice the value of the books. The library was open daily, except for Sundays and designated holidays. An impressive catalog of 3616 books, divided into various categories, was printed in 1809, with supplements in 1816, 1823, 1831, and 1841. There is no direct evidence that Poe ever visited the Library Company, but it seems hard to imagine that he would not have done so, particularly when he was living in the Fells Point area, which was within easy walking distance.[17]

Perhaps the most important of Baltimore's literary institutions, in regard to Poe's writings, was the Delphian Club, a private gathering of mostly elite citizens, engaging in literary pursuits chiefly for their own artistic and social pleasure. It was established by seven members in 1816 and, after a two-year interruption, continued with the active participation of roughly sixteen members until 1825. These members met regularly to exchange epigrams, squibs, barbs and puns, sing songs and present their own more extended creations, generally of a humorous nature, in terms of stories, poems, and essays. During 1816–1818, many of these works appeared in the *Portico*, edited by Tobias Watkins (1780–1855) and the *Journal of the Times*, edited by Paul Allen (1775–1826), both published in Baltimore. The members adopted pseudonyms that were simultaneously pompous and silly: Jehu O'Cataract (John Neal), Solomon Fitz-Quizz (Paul Allen), Blearix von Crambograph (John Didier Readel), and Pertinax Particular (Tobias Watkins). They also adopted equivalent titles. Paul Allen, for example, was the self-assigned Professor of Chrononhotonthology, who specialized in describing small things in many words. In one lecture, he expended over 300 words to say merely that the Sun had risen.[18]

The Delphians met on Saturday nights in the homes of the various members. At their gatherings, in addition to their literary pursuits, they feasted on cheese, oysters, and duck, smoked cigars, and drank whiskey. Their proceedings were dutifully recorded by J. D. Readel (1790–1854), in a beautiful print-like hand that strongly reminds one of Poe's own early manuscripts. Although the club had disbanded by the time Poe came to Baltimore, many of its members were well known, even after Poe's death, and stories about the club were almost certainly still in circulation, especially among some of its former members of Poe's acquaintance, including John Hazelhurst Boneval Latrobe (1803–1891), William Gwynn, and John P. Kennedy. There were also tangible remains, in the periodicals that had been associated with the club, chiefly the *Portico* (for which a set could be found in the shelves of the Library Company of Baltimore), *Journal of the Times*, and the small book written by Tobias Watkins, *Tales of the Tripod, or a Delphian Evening* (Baltimore: F. Lucas, Jr. 1821). The club's fame lasted long enough that it was considered worthy of mention in the obituary of Readel, printed in the *Baltimore County Advocate* in 1854, and obituaries of John Pierpont (1785–1866) more than a decade later. Some speculation is required, but the probability that Poe was familiar with the lore of the Delphians seems self-evident in his own proposed collection, *Tales of the Folio Club* (1833).[19]

It was into this lively and complicated milieu that Poe made many of his first staggering steps in the literary world. Toward the end of March in 1827, Poe, having feuded bitterly with his foster-father, John Allan (1779–1834), left Richmond and stopped by Baltimore, presumably to visit with his brother, Henry. The only tangible evidence of this visit are the poems "To Margaret," written in the album of Miss Margaret Bassett, and "To Octavia," written in the album of Octavia Walton (dated by Miss Walton as May 1, 1827).[20] The dating seems reasonable, as *Tamerlane and Other Poems* was printed in Boston by August of 1827 (when it was listed in the *United States Review and Literary Gazette*). Furthermore, Lambert A. Wilmer (ca. 1805–1863) wrote a play called "Merlin," based on Poe's thwarted romance with Elmira Royster (1810–1888) and published in August–September 1827.[21] Soon afterward, Poe enlisted in the army under the false name of Edgar A. Perry, still eluding debtors or John Allan. By the end of 1828, Poe had grown weary of the drudgery of a soldier's life and wrote to Allan, hoping to be relieved of his service and to be granted admission to West Point. It would yet be several months before Poe was officially discharged. After a brief visit to Richmond, and to Washington, D. C., about May 1829, Poe once again found himself at a crossroads, and with nowhere else to turn, sought refuge in Baltimore. Poetry was still his great passion, and this period in Baltimore boasts several poetic relics. Among these, Poe wrote two minor trinkets in the form of acrostics in the album of his cousin, Elizabeth Herring (1815–1889), the poems now known as "To Elizabeth" and "An Acrostic." More significantly, he wrote a new poem in the album of Lucy Holmes, a poem to which he gave only the legend "Original," but has long been assigned the title of "Alone." This poem (beginning "From childhood's hour I have not been…") is a rare example of a heartfelt work that was never printed during his lifetime or even offered for publication, perhaps because it was so personally revealing.[22]

At this time, while awaiting his appointment to West Point, Poe was actively seeking to publish the second and last of his long poems, the recently completed "Al Aaraaf." The lack of encouragement appears not to have dimmed his enthusiasm. Poe almost certainly showed the manuscript of the poem to William Gwynn, who printed excerpts in his *Federal Gazette and Baltimore Daily Advertiser*, of May 18, 1829. He also loaned the manuscript to William Wirt, who wrote him a letter, presumably returning the manuscript, on May 11, 1829, admitting that he did not understand the poem and suggesting that it was perhaps too "modern" for his tastes.[23] Poe continued his epistolary dance with John Allan, hoping to extract financial support without actually offering anything in return other than emotional appeals. On May 18, 1829, John Allan deposited $100 in the Union Bank of Maryland for Poe's benefit. Poe wrote to Issac Lea (of the publishing firm of Carey, Lea and Carey), with the hope that they could be persuaded to fulfill the dream that had faltered in Boston. On July 28, 1829, he wrote them again, requesting the return of his manuscript and claiming that he had "made a better disposition of my poems than I had any right to expect." That disposition was presumably mostly false bravado, but in a few months, he was able at last to hold in his hands the little book that he, at least at this time, considered to be the true first edition of his poetical works, *Al Aaraaf, Tamerlane and Minor Poems* (Baltimore: Hatch and Dunning, 1829) (Fig. 5.1). Using the money chiefly obtained from John Allan, Poe apparently managed to convince a fledgling Baltimore publisher to issue the slightly expanded collection of his poems.[24] The thin volume was only a slightly more refined production than had been *Tamerlane and Other Poems* two years earlier, but the new collection had the added dignity of a hard cloth binding. The claim in his November 18, 1829 letter to John Allan that the publisher would give him 250 copies of the book probably accounts for the full number printed. The book materialized in December of 1829. The much-hoped-for swell of public embrace of the poems did not emerge, and Poe resumed his efforts to settle for a career of a soldier, but without entirely abandoning his ambitions to acquire a reputation as a poet.[25]

By late May, 1830, Poe was a cadet at West Point. He found its demanding schedule of learning and rigid military code of conduct to be unsatisfactory, and he conspired to achieve a court-martial on February 8, which took effect on March 6, 1831. By about the beginning of May of 1831, after a brief period in New York City, and again with nowhere else to go, he was back in Baltimore. This time, he moved in with his aunt, Maria Clemm (1790–1871), and her little family, which included her two children, Henry and Virginia Clemm, her mother, Elizabeth Cairnes Poe (1756–1835) (who was also Poe's grandmother), and Edgar's older brother, also named Henry. They were all living in rooms in a house in Mechanic's Row on Wilks Street. Henry Poe, who had been ill for some time, died on August 1, 1831, and was buried in his grandfather's lot in the Western Burial Ground of the First Presbyterian Church, at the corner of Fayette and Greene

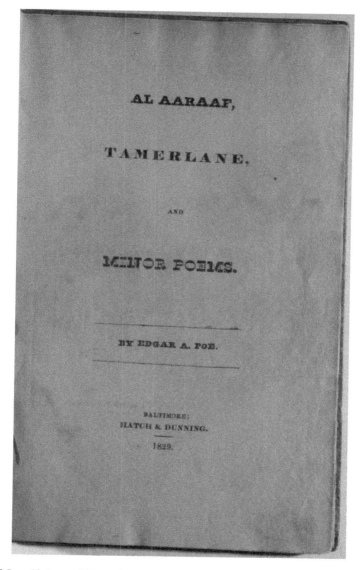

Fig. 5.1 *Al Aaraaf, Tamerlane and Minor Poems* (Susan Jaffe Tane Collection)

streets. Presumably out of a combination of unhappy associations and a concern for the health of the grandmother, who was frail, paralytic, and bedridden, and on whose annuity they were financially dependent, as well as for the children, they moved from the Fell Point area to the western outskirts of the city. (At this time, medical theory held that illness could be caused by poor air, precisely like that of the marshy areas that surrounded the harbor, particularly on the eastern side of the city.) Sometime in 1832, or certainly by very early in 1833, they had moved to the southern half of a narrow brick duplex that was long known as no. 2, now 203, Amity Street. During this period, Poe and Henry Clemm may have been working as general laborers in a local brickyard, or stone mason's yard.[26]

While perhaps resigning himself to the daily struggle of existence, Poe never abandoned his literary ambitions. Although many of the later recollections are of dubious validity, it seems that Poe was busy pursuing the attention of various young ladies, an activity in which he took full advantage of his ability to compose poems. Among the few surviving examples, he wrote "To Elizabeth" ("Wouldst' thou be loved...") in the album of his cousin Elizabeth Herring in 1833.[27] More importantly, something truly remarkable happened somewhere around this time—Poe began to broaden his production from poetry to writing short stories. He may have been inspired, in part, by his brother, Henry, who had written and published a number of minor items in the short-lived Baltimore publication the *North American*.[28] Poe, clearly inspired by the kind of prose works he had read in British magazines, such as *Blackwood's Magazine*, wrote tales in a variety of styles that were a mixture of homage and parody. Whether or not they were originally composed as such, they began to form a collection, which Poe would eventually call *The Tales of the Folio Club*. (The context for these tales, a literary club of gentlemen with such absurd names as Convolvulus Gondola, Horribile Dictu, and Chronologos Chronology, bears unmistakable echoes of the Delphian Club.) Unable to find a publisher for the full collection, Poe was compelled by opportunity or need to seek an audience for the individual pieces. Responding to a contest announcement in the *Saturday Courier*, a Philadelphia newspaper, Poe failed to win an award but did achieve the pleasure of seeing his first five tales in print.[29]

His fortunes would improve very shortly, and the event of his winning the contest of the *Baltimore Saturday Visiter* was clearly important to Poe, both professionally and personally, becoming one of his most repeated biographical trinkets. The literary contest was announced in the *Visiter* for June 15, 1833. The judges were named as John Pendleton Kennedy, John H. B. Latrobe, and Dr. James Henry Miller (1788–1853). All three made their money in various professions, but were at least dabblers in literary matters, perhaps coincidentally having been members of the Delphian Club. Being the last of these gentlemen still alive in 1877, Latrobe left a detailed account of the event, which has appeared in many biographies.[30] Two prizes were offered, one for the best tale and one for the best poem. Poe submitted a number of poems, including "The Coliseum," and several stories, probably including "Lionizing," "The Visionary," "Shadow," "Epimanes," "Siope," and "MS. Found in a Bottle," all almost certainly composed during his time in Baltimore. Of these, we still have a fragment of "Siope" and a full manuscript for "Epimanes", (Fig. 5.2) the later having been sent by Poe to the father and son editors of the *New-England Magazine* on May 4, 1833, but not published, acknowledged, or returned. Both manuscripts show the "imitation of printing" noted by Latrobe in his recollections. This striking visual characteristic distinguished Poe's manuscripts from those of his competitors, although it was ultimately the "unquestionable genius and great originality of the writer" that won over the judges, who already having decided on the winning author had to reread all of his entries for the difficult process of selecting just one winning tale (30). As Poe would repeatedly tell the story, he had won both prizes and, in effect, had been cheated out of the one for poetry. The fact that the now winning poem was written by John Hill Hewitt, an editor for the newspaper, seemed to make the nature of the conspiracy clear to him, and it was something for which he never quite forgave Hewitt. The claim that Hewitt had submitted his poem, "The Song of the Wind," under a pseudonym persuaded Poe of nothing. Although the poetry prize was the lesser of the two awards, to Poe it might have been considered the greater. According to Hewitt, he met Poe on the street one day and Poe's famously fiery anger boiled over into an actual exchange of fists.[31]

The decision was publicized in the *Saturday Visiter* for October 15, 1833, giving the names of the winners as Edgar A. Poe and Henry Wilton (Hewitt). The sting of not having won the poetry prize must have been somewhat eased by the words of high public praise about his submitted tales. It also may have helped to validate his choice to begin writing short stories. Perhaps, more importantly, these events introduced Poe to John P. Kennedy, who, as Poe later admitted, "has been at all

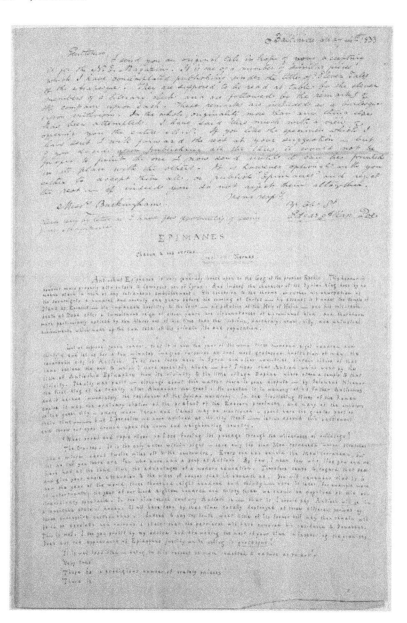

Fig. 5.2   Manuscript of "Epimanes," 1833 (Susan Jaffe Tane Collection)

times a true friend to me—he was the first true friend I ever had—I am indebted to him *for life itself.*"[32] Kennedy did indeed intervene at this crucial moment. Decades later, Kennedy himself noted in his journal, "It is many years ago, I think perhaps as early as 1833 or 1834, that I found him in Baltimore in a state of starvation. I gave him clothing, free access to my table, and the use of a horse for exercise."[33] Kennedy took an active interest in advocating for Poe, soliciting publishers with the material that Poe had prepared for *Tales of the Folio Club.* Eventually, Kennedy recommended that Poe write to Thomas Willis White, who had recently started the *Southern Literary Messenger* in Richmond, VA, and who was in need of editorial assistance. Checking Poe's references, White wrote to Kennedy, and Kennedy replied that Poe "is very clever with his pen—classical and scholarlike." He also described Poe as being "highly imaginative, and a little given to the terrific," further noting that "He is at work upon a tragedy, but I have turned him to drudging upon whatever may make money."[34] Partly based on this recommendation, Poe accepted a position with White, and he moved to Richmond about mid-August 1835. After a brief falling out with White, Poe returned to Baltimore only a month later. Apologizing, and receiving White's forgiveness, Poe moved back to Richmond by about October 3, 1835, taking Mrs. Clemm and Virginia with him. He would never live in Baltimore again.[35]

Over the next few years, Poe contributed tales to *The Baltimore Book for 1838,* and three items to the short-lived Baltimore periodical the *American Museum,* co-edited by his friend, Joseph Evans Snodgrass (1813-1880).[36] In addition, Poe appears to have visited Baltimore at least once each year thereafter (often on his way to other places, usually Richmond or Washington, D. C.), although it is difficult to account precisely the number and timing of these visits. In a letter to Neilson Poe, Poe states, "we all speak very frequently of yourself and family, and regret that, hitherto, we have seen and known so little of each other," specifically mentioning that he "had no opportunity of seeing you during my last visit to Baltimore."[37] On January 31, 1844, Poe repeated his lecture on "The Poets and Poetry of America" in the Egyptian Saloon at the Odd-Fellows Hall, on Gay Street (the building was demolished about 1892 and the site now serves as the War Memorial Plaza, in front of City Hall). According to Robert D'Unger (ca. 1825–1908), he first met Poe in Baltimore in 1846, in a chance encounter at Guy's Coffee House, at Monument Square and Fayette Street.[38]

The lack of more substantial activity in Baltimore may be attributed to two potentially related matters. The first matter was what Poe perceived as active antagonism from his Baltimore cousin, Neilson Poe (1809–1884). Overtly, Poe seems to have maintained more or less cordial relations with Neilson, but privately he was harshly critical, calling Neilson "the little dog" and stating that he was "the bitterest enemy I have in the world."[39] In later years, this troubled relationship may have softened somewhat, with Poe using Neilson's services to sell a lot to John B. Morris for $22.[40] Some of this earlier antagonism was perhaps wound up in the second matter. On August 8, 1839, Poe wrote to John Beauchamp Jones (1810–1866), replying to a letter in which Jones apparently informed Poe of an unfavorable notice in the *Baltimore Sun* for August 6, 1839, in which the current issue of *Burton's Gentleman's Magazine* was criticized for "a palpable want of tact in the manner in which it has been gotten up." A similar attitude toward Poe appears to have still be present at the newspaper in 1840, when a brief notice of Poe's proposed magazine plans was dismissed with: "NEW MAGAZINE. — Edgar A. Poe, Esq. assistant editor of Burton's Magazine, has issued proposals for a monthly literary journal to be published in Philadelphia to be called the 'Penn Magazine.' A good many pens, and much paper will be wasted upon it" (*Baltimore Sun*, June 5, 1840). Several months later, another notice stated: "GIVEN UP. — Edgar A. Poe, Esq., has given up the idea of publishing the Penn Magazine, and has connected himself with Graham's Magazine. He superintends the review department. He wields a slashing pen" (*Baltimore Sun*, February 22, 1841). It was more complimentary when noticing the current issue of *Graham's Magazine*, singling out Poe's tale "A Descent into the Maelstrom" as "the best paper in the book" and describing it as "a highly original and masterly production" (*Baltimore Sun*, May 10, 1841). Whatever may have been the original difficulties, the tone of the *Sun* was decidedly more favorable over the coming years. It reprinted several of Poe's tales, including "A Descent into the Maelström" (May 11–12, 1841), "The Gold-Bug" (July 24–27, 1843), "The Black Cat" (August 25, 1843), "Raising the Wind; or, Diddling Considered as One of the Exact Sciences" (October 16–18, 1843), and "A Tale of the Ragged Mountains" (March 23, 1844).[41]

Despite its relatively minor role during the last decade of his life, Baltimore would unexpectedly become central once again, as the site of his tragic death in 1849. The facts of this event remain shrouded in mystery and obfuscation. Several long articles and at least three short books have been written on the topic, but nothing has done much to lift the veil from this dark episode.[42] A summary necessarily omits much detail of interest. Poe, at the time, was living in the little cottage in Fordham, but had been away for several months on a trip through the south to publicize, once again, his long-desired magazine project. In Richmond, he had apparently managed to become engaged to his childhood sweetheart (Elmira Royster, now the widowed Mrs. Shelton). Depending on the account one accepts, Poe left Richmond on September 28 or October 1, 1849. His plan was to pass through Baltimore on his way to Philadelphia, where he was to be paid $100 to edit the poems of Mrs. Marguerite St. Leon Loud, and then to go on to New York, where he would collect Mrs. Clemm and return to Richmond. In Baltimore, he appears to have checked his trunk at the train station. No one has left any recollections of seeing Poe until October 3, an election day for local offices, when he was found at or near a tavern known as Gunner's Hall or Ryan's Fourth Ward Polls. After some discussion between his old friend, Dr. Snodgrass, and his uncle, Henry Herring (1792–1868), both of whom lived nearby, he was sent to the building variously known as the Washington University Hospital or the Baltimore City Marine Hospital. There, after a few days in which he seemed to have improved slightly but then taken a sudden turn for the worse, he died early in the morning of October 7, 1849. Having died in Baltimore, away from home but near close family, he was buried in the Westminster Burial Grounds, in the Poe family lot owned by his grandfather, David Poe, where the remains of both of his grandparents rested, and where his brother Henry had been buried nearly two decades earlier. It was a short ceremony, presided over by Rev. W. T. D. Clemm, a relative on his wife's side, attended only by five or six people, and without pomp or even a tombstone. Over the course of the next several months, a flurry of obituary notices for Poe was printed, reprinted, and extracted in newspapers across the country, often including "The Raven," "The Bells," or "Annabel Lee." If anyone thought that Poe would be forgotten, however, and quickly fade into the mists of obscurity, that person would be very surprised to find out what actually happened.

In one of many curious twists in Poe's life and legacy, all of the cities where he lived and worked, which paid him so little attention during his lifetime, now eagerly clamor for a piece of his enduring fame. Baltimore may have been the first to sluff off its former indifference to Poe. In the years following Poe's burial, the literary world initially seemed to have brought out the knives and carved away at his reputation, aided substantially by the "Ludwig" obituary and the longer "Memoir" included with the posthumous collected edition of Poe's works edited by Rufus Wilmot Griswold.[43] Newspapers across the country repeated or reprinted Griswold's distorted version of Poe's life and personality, and old enemies, who had been licking their wounds (real and perceived) from Poe's critiques, took the opportunity to kick Poe's literary corpse. Perhaps unexpectedly, Poe also enjoyed some very public defenses, from N. P. Willis, C. Chauncey Burr, John Neal, George Rex Graham, and others. During this first decade, articles seem to have alternated between puritanical finger-pointing, typified by "A Great Man Self Wrecked" (an anonymous article first published in the USA in the *National Magazine* in October 1852 and still widely appearing in newspapers as late as 1862) and such elegiac poetry as "Caelicola" by T. H. Chivers (*Petersen's Magazine* (Philadelphia, PA), vol. XVII, no. 2, February 1850, 102) and "A Lament for Edgar A. Poe," by Julia Granby Stickney (*Independent* (NY), January 5, 1860).

The moralistic attacks on Poe were somewhat muted by the sad details of his life, the tragic nature of his death, and the continuing and very public mourning of Mrs. Clemm, characterized as Poe's motherly angel, left alone and penniless. From the strange brew of charges and countercharges, there emerged a growing public opinion that Poe had been his own worst enemy, that one should not speak ill of the dead, and that whatever might have been his personal failings, his memory was redeemed by his love and loss of Virginia and the beauty of his best-known poems. Almost from the beginning, his place of burial became a focus of interest. People actively sought it out and wrote about the cemetery and the fact that his eternal resting spot was unmarked. By 1854, isolated comments began to consolidate into a movement to erect some type of memorial over Poe's grave. The momentum of the movement grew but was interrupted by the outbreak of the Civil War, quickly resuming once the Confederacy was defeated and life began to return to normal. On October 7, 1865, the Teachers' Association of Baltimore City gathered for their regular meeting. In addition to whatever business made up the usual agenda, they also discussed the formation of a committee to propose and fund a monument to Poe. They met, appropriately enough, on the 16th anniversary of Poe's death, at the Western Female Public School, which sat directly adjacent to the property of the Westminster Presbyterian Church. A young school teacher and elocutionist, Sara Sigourney Rice (1831–1909), was quickly selected to coordinate the efforts, and an initial fund-raiser was held. Many more events would be organized, but money was accumulated only very slowly, and the movement was in danger of failing when George William Childs (1829–1894), then living in Philadelphia but who as a publisher had known Poe and was himself born in Baltimore, was prevailed upon to contribute a sum sufficient to fulfill the proposed project. The monument was dedicated with great fanfare and national attention on November 17, 1875 (Fig. 5.3).[44]

Suddenly, Poe's reputation was enjoying something of a renaissance. As the years progressed, the graffiti painted by Griswold in such brash colors and broad brush strokes over Poe's personal character began to be scraped away and in some cases to be covered by white-wash. Redemption was at hand. William James Widdleton (1829–1882) was the publisher who had in 1860 inherited from J. S. Redfield responsibility for the four-volume edition of Poe's works first printed in 1850–1856 and who kept it in print at least annually until the death of Mrs. Clemm in 1871. Capitalizing on the spurt of publicity surrounding the dedication of the monument, Widdleton resumed publication of the set, replacing Griswold's memoir of Poe with the far more sympathetic essay by John H. Ingram.[45] The increase of attention reached a crescendo as the centennial of Poe's birth approached in 1909. Baltimore commissioned an elegant statue to be erected in a public setting, enlisting the talents of the celebrated artist Moses Jacob Ezekiel, the native son of Richmond, Virginia, who, from his studios in Italy, populated cemeteries and public squares with monuments, often dedicated to heroes of the Confederacy. Various difficulties, including World War I, delayed the delivery of the completed statue until 1921, several years after the death of the artist in 1917. It was dedicated on October 20, 1921. Having accomplished its goal, the Poe Memorial Association disbanded, but quickly re-formed as the Edgar Allan Poe Society of Baltimore, which held its first annual commemorative program in January 1923 and is currently approaching its centenary. Evidence of the surprising reach of Poe's continued popularity in the city is perhaps most clearly demonstrated by the naming of the new football team, the Baltimore Ravens, in 1996 (with a raven mascot named Poe).

In his "Fifty Suggestions," Poe noted: "In lauding Beauty, Genius merely evinces a filial affection. To Genius Beauty gives life—reaping often a reward in Immortality."[46] The elegant slab of marble sitting in

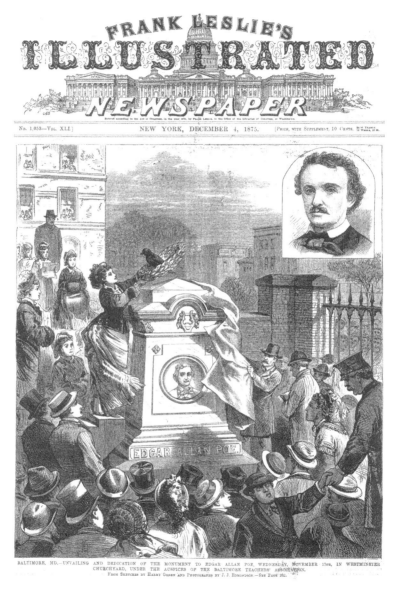

Fig. 5.3 Unveiling of the Poe Monument, Baltimore (Photo by Jeffrey A. Savoye)

a little plot of soil in an obscure cemetery at the corner of Fayette and Greene streets in Baltimore may seem an odd tourist destination, and yet this humble spot has served as a shrine for more than a century, annually drawing thousands of visitors from around the world. For Poe, his genius gave him little solace in life, but it shines in all that he wrote, and through it, he has achieved his own immortality.

Notes

1. The tales noted are, respectively, "Morella" (1835), "Metzengerstein" (1832), "Berenice" (1835), and "MS. Found in a Bottle" (1833). For texts and publication details, see Thomas Ollive Mabbott, ed., *The Collected Works of Edgar Allan*, vol. 2, *Tales and Sketches, 1831–1842* (Cambridge: Belknap Press of Harvard University Press, 1978) (hereafter cited in text as M). The prayer recited by Morella was later published as a separate poem with the title of "Catholic Hymn," in Poe's own *Broadway Journal* for August 16, 1845. For Poe's letter to White, see John W. Ostrom, Burton R. Pollin, and Jeffrey A. Savoye, *The Collected Letters of Edgar Allan Poe* (New York: Gordian Press, 2008), 1: 84–86 (hereafter cited in text as O). The letter also shows that Poe's ideas for what made a marketable story were already fully formed by 1835. For the source of "Berenice," see Lucille King, "Notes on Poe's Sources," *University of Texas Studies in English*, no. 10 (1930): 130.

2. It is worth noting that the *Baltimore Sun* of November 30, 1834 does contain an account of resuscitation after interment. An advertisement from about January 14, 1844 promotes a life-preserving coffin, patented on November 15, 1843 by Christian Henry Eisenbrandt and manufactured in Baltimore by Bobeth and Schulenberg.

3. May Garrettson Evans, "Poe in Amity Street," *Maryland Historical Magazine* 36, no. 4 (December 1941): 379–380.

4. John C. French, "The Maryland Scene and Poe's 'Eleonora'," *Maryland Historical Magazine* 50, no. 1 (March 1955): 65.

5. Wightman F. Melton, "Some Autobiographical References in Poe's Poetry," *South Atlantic Quarterly* 11, no. 2 (April 1912): 175–179.

6. John C. French, "Poe's Literary Baltimore," *Maryland Historical Magazine* 32, no. 2 (June 1937): 112.

7. Poe's self-identification as a southerner is clear in his frequent advocacy for writers outside of the northern clique, and perhaps even more clearly from his statement in a letter of June 26, 1841 to F. W. Thomas: "I am a Virginian—At Least I Call Myself One ..." (O 1:287). In an editorial in the *Broadway Journal* for November 1, 1845, Poe states, "We

like Boston. We were born there—and perhaps it is just as well not to mention that we are heartily ashamed of the fact" (see Pollin, *The Collected Writings of Edgar Allan Poe* [New York: Gordian Press, 1986], 3, 297 [hereafter cited in text as P].)

8. Rufus W. Griswold, *The Poets and Poetry of America* (New York: Carey & Hart, 1842), 387 and *The Prose Writers of America* (New York: Carey & Hart, 1847), 523. Poe provided the information, including the 1811 date, in a letter to Griswold of May 29, 1841 (O 1:273).

9. The "Ludwig" obituary of Poe is so-called because that was the pseudonym Griswold used when it was published in the *New York Daily Tribune* for October 9, 1849. The posthumous collection of Poe's works was edited by Griswold and published initially by J. S. Redfield, supposedly for the benefit of Poe's indigent aunt, Maria Clemm, with the first two volumes appearing early in 1850, a third being added later in 1850, followed in 1856 by a fourth and final volume. The set was regularly printed for nearly 25 years.

10. According to Mrs. Clemm, Poe was brought to Baltimore by his parents about the time he was 5 weeks old and left with his grandparents for 6 months (Mrs. Clemm to Neilson Poe, August 19, 1860, see Miller, 1977, 46–47). David Poe, Sr., is listed in *The Citizen Soldier at North Point and Fort McHenry, September 12 & 13, 1814* (Baltimore: Nathaniel Hickman, 1858), 37, the first edition apparently having been published in 1822.

11. *Baltimore Sun* (February 13, 1838), 4.

12. Ralph Clayton, *Cash for Blood: The Baltimore to New Orleans Domestic Slave Trade* (Bowie, MD: Heritage Books, 2002).

13. Baltimore was named the Monumental City by President John Quincy Adams in a toast at a dinner on October 15, 1827. Poe himself would refer to Baltimore as "the City of Monuments" in a September 19, 1841 letter to J. E. Snodgrass (O 1:309).

14. See Quinn, *Edgar Allan Poe: A Critical Biography* (New York: D. Appleton, 1941), 700–705. The information for Baltimore performances was obtained from manual examination in the 1930s of surviving newspapers of the period, for which comprehensive files are often lacking. It is also possible that performances were chiefly advertised through separate flyers, for which we have a few examples in other cities, but most of which, being such an ephemeral form, have not generally endured the passing of time. The entries in Quinn give two names for locations of performances in Baltimore: the New Theater and the Baltimore Theater. Both of these names appear to have been used as different incarnations of the same building, later known as the Holliday Street Theatre, which formerly stood on Holliday Street near Fayette, but burned to the ground in 1873. (The site is now occupied by the current city hall and the War Memorial Plaza.)

15. French, "Poe's Literary Baltimore," 104.
16. One of the more famous bookstores of the era was that of Edward Johnson Coale (1776–1832), at 4 Calvert Street (see Allen and Mabbott, *Poe's Brother* [New York: George H. Doran Company, 1926], 26). Like many purveyors of books, Coale was also a publisher.
17. Stuart C. Sherman, "The Library Company of Baltimore, 1795–1855," *Maryland Historical Magazine* (March 1944): 6–24. We know, from a letter of September 3, 1841 by F. W. Thomas to Poe, that Thomas, who shared Poe's difficult financial circumstances, did frequent the Library: "I often stole out to the Baltimore Library and devoured the works upon Poetry, Oratory and Biography" (see J. A. Harrison, *The Complete Works of Edgar Allan Poe*, vol. 17: Letters [New York: T. Y. Crowell, 1902], 17, 96 [hereafter cited in text as H]. Although Harrison, following Thomas's own error, gives the date as August, Harrison condenses the text of the letter.)
18. For a history of the Delphians, see John Earle Uhler, "The Delphian Club: A Contribution to the Literary History of Baltimore in the Early Nineteenth Century," *Maryland Historical Magazine* 20, no. 4 (December 1925): 305–346.
19. See Alexander Hammond, "Edgar Allan Poe's Tales of the Folio Club: The Evolution of a Lost Book," *Poe at Work: Seven Textual Studies* (Baltimore: Edgar Allan Poe Society, 1978), 13–43. The design of the fictional Folio Club is strongly reminiscent of the actual Delphian Club. Although Poe was never able to find a publisher for his proposed collection, the individual tales were printed separately over the course of several years. In that form, they lacked the apparatus that would have given context to the stories as part homage, part parody, and designated by Poe as having been written by the various imaginary authors named and described in his manuscript introduction.
20. For these poems, see M 1969, 1:14–16 and 1:16–17.
21. *Merlin* appeared in three installments in the Baltimore periodical the *North American* (August 18, 25 and September 1, 1827). It was reprinted by T. O. Mabbott in *Merlin, Together with Recollections of Edgar A. Poe* (New York: Scholar's Facsimiles and Reprints, 1941). Elmira married Alexander B. Shelton in 1828. Both widowed, Poe reputedly became engaged again to Elmira in 1849, a planned marriage being interrupted by his death. Questions about the engagement have been raised primarily due to Mrs. Shelton's denials repeated to various inquiries in the years after Poe's death, but probably prompted by her family's disapproval. The recently resurfaced beginning half of Poe's letter of August 29, 1849 to Mrs. Clemm states: "We are solemnly engaged to be married within the coming month (Septr)—but I make no doubt that in a week or 10 days, all will be over. I enclose you her last note—that

you may see how we stand. I got angry with her for wishing to defer it till January & wrote her a cross letter—to which the one enclosed is her reply. We made it up & she now sanctions my writing to you, announcing the marriage in a month. She went nearly frantic when I told her I would nt [sic] have her—went out to Mackenzie's after me & all about town—so that every body [sic] knows of our engagement. It was reported, indeed, that we *were* married last Thursday. Her relations—her married daughter especially—are opposed to it—because their pecuniary interests will be injured—but she defies them & seems resolved." Previously unprinted, and long hidden as an unsigned Poe relic among the treasures of an autograph collector in Italy, this portion of the letter was sold at auction on June 4, 2015 and is now in the collection of Susan Jaffe Tane. The full text of the letter may be read at URL: http://www.eapoe.org/works/letters/p4908280.htm.

22. The title was first assigned by E. L. Didier in *Scribner's Magazine* (September 1875): 10, 608. To the facsimile of the poem, Didier added the title "Alone" and a date, "Baltimore, March 17, 1829," which raised unnecessary suspicions about the authenticity of the poem for several years (M 1969, 1:145n1).

23. For a history of the poem, see M 1:97–98. For Wirt's letter, see Stanard, 131–132. About November 1829, Poe also sent extracts of several of the poems to John Neal, who, having moved from Baltimore, was then living in Boston, where he edited the *Yankee and Boston Literary Gazette* (which printed the extracts in the issue of December 1829). In his introductory notes, Neal states that Poe was "entirely a stranger to us," and his comments are not entirely favorable, admitting some "faults," but also noting that parts were "extraordinary" and that the author might "deserve to stand high—very high—in the estimation of the shining brotherhood." Poe was eager to embrace any encouragement, and he included a dedication to Neal for "Tamerlane" in the 1829 book. He also personally inscribed a copy of his 1831 *Poems* to Neal, now in the collection of Susan Jaffe Tane. Writing to the older author in 1840, Poe acknowledged Neal as having given him "the first jog in my literary career" (see Poe to Neal, June 3, 1840).

24. It is also possible that part of the money came from the December 10, 1829 sale of Edwin, a 21-year-old slave owned by Poe's aunt, Maria Clemm, for which Poe acted as agent. The term was for a period of nine years, for the price of $40. The buyer, Henry Ridgway, was a free black, and the sale presumably resulted in Edwin's freedom. See May Garrettson Evans, "When Edgar Allan Poe Sold a Slave," *Baltimore Sun* (April 6, 1940).

25. Much of the general history given here in the form of an overview is well-trodden ground and has been more thoroughly detailed in various biographies of Poe, for which particularly, see A. H. Quinn, 1941 and Thomas and Jackson, *The Poe Log* (1987).

26. See Robert Thomas Pichett Allen (Letter to the Editor), *Scribner's Monthly* 11 (November 1875): 142–143.

27. Among these accounts are questionable recollections by Mary Starr, also known as Mary Deveraux (Augustus Van Cleef, "Poe's Mary," *Harper's New Monthly Magazine* 78, no. 3 [March 1889]: 634–640) and Kate Bleakley (see Mary E. Phillips, *Edgar Allan Poe, the Man*, 2 vols. (Chicago: John C. Winston, 1926), 1, 421–423).

28. See Allen and Mabbott, *Poe's Brother*, 1926.

29. The five tales, with their dates of publication, were "Metzengerstein" (January 14, 1832), "The Duke de L'Omelette" (March 3, 1832), "A Tale of Jerusalem" (June 9, 1832), "A Decided Loss" (November 10, 1832), and "The Bargain Lost" (December 1, 1832).

30. A detailed account of the contest and judging, written by J. H. B. Latrobe, may be found in S. S. Rice, *Edgar Allan Poe: A Memorial Volume* (Baltimore: Lucus, 1877). Mabbott considered the recollections to be "highly inaccurate" (M 1:544). Although some details concerning "Hans Pfaall" do suggest that Latrobe is conflating multiple meetings into one, there seems no reason to mark Latrobe for special censure.

31. See J. H. Hewitt, *Shadows on the Wall* (Baltimore: Turnbull Bros., 1877), 41.

32. Poe to F. W. Thomas, July 4, 1841 (O 1:292–293).

33. Quinn, 1941, 208.

34. The letter from Kennedy to T. W. White, April 1835, is quoted in Griswold, "Memoir of the Author," *The Works of the Late Edgar Allan Poe* (New York: Redfield, 1850), XIII.

35. There is a tradition that Poe married Virginia in a ceremony in Baltimore (M 1:546 n7). Why there would have been a second ceremony in Richmond is unclear and has cast a shadow of doubt over claims for the earlier wedding.

36. To *The Baltimore Book*, Poe contributed "Siope, A Fable," an interesting choice since it was one of the *Tales of the Folio Club*, written in Baltimore about 1832 and the only tale known to have been part of the original collection and not already published by 1837. To the *American Museum*, Poe contributed the tale "Ligeia" (September 1838), the poem "The Haunted Palace" (April 1839), and the miscellany "Literary Small Talk" (January and February 1839).

37. Poe to Neilson Poe, August 8, 1845 (O 1:515–516).

38. See John E. Reilly, "Robert D'Unger and His Reminiscences of Poe in Baltimore," *Maryland Historical Magazine* 88 (1993): 60–72.

39. Poe to Snodgrass, October 7, 1839 (O 1:197).

40. A newly discovered letter, Poe to Neilson Poe, Heritage Auction, Beverly Hills, CA, October 8–9, 2014, item 49209. http://www.eapoe.org/works/letters/p4601020.htm.

41. The publishers of the *Baltimore Sun* also owned the *Philadelphia Public Ledger* and the *Philadelphia Dollar Newspaper*.

42. A few of the many attempts to delve into these depths include John E. Walsh, *Midnight Dreary: The Mysterious Death of Edgar Allan Poe* (New Brunswick, NJ: Rutgers University Press, 1998); Matthew Pearl, "A Poe Death Dossier: Discoveries and Queries in the Death of Edgar Allan Poe" (Parts 1 and 2), *Edgar Allan Poe Review* 7, no. 2. (Fall 2006) and 8, no. 1 (Spring 2007): 4–29, 8–31; and Michael A. Powell, *Too Much Moran: Respecting the Death of Edgar Poe* (Eugene, OR: Pacific Rim University Press, 2009).

43. The obituary signed "Ludwig" appeared in the *New York Tribune* for October 9, 1849. *The Works of the Late Edgar Allan Poe*, edited by R. W. Griswold, was issued initially in two volumes in January 1850, with a third, now including the memoir by Griswold, in September 1850. (A fourth and final volume was added to the set in 1856.)

44. For a general account of the history of the monument, see Sara Sigourney Rice, *Edgar Allan Poe, A Memorial Volume* (Baltimore: Turnbull Brothers, 1877), 43–47.

45. Widdleton had continued to print a separate volume of Poe's poems, in various formats. Late in 1875, although bearing the imprint and copyright date of 1876, Widdleton essentially reissued the four-volume set with Ingram's memoir in place of Griswold's, removing the "To the Reader" letter from Mrs. Clemm, who had died in 1871, and inserting the poem "Alone" as it had appeared in facsimile in *Scribner's Magazine* (September 1875). Ingram had been in contact with Widdleton sometime before September 11, 1875, when he wrote to Sarah Helen Whitman and mentioned what appears to have been a very complicated sequence of correspondence between the editor and publisher (see Miller, *Poe's Helen Remembers*, 1979, 325). By early in 1876, Widdleton had reprinted the edition again, adding to the introductory material in the first volume information about the Baltimore memorial and the dedication ceremonies as well as Dr. Moran's dubious account of Poe's final days, these additional items apparently being reprinted from the *New York Herald*. The newer edition also rearranged volumes and included some of the miscellaneous Poe items Ingram had added to his 1874–1875 Edinburgh collection.

46. See item 39, *Graham's Magazine* (June 1849): 364.

CHAPTER 6

Poe in Philadelphia

Amy Branam Armiento

Nathaniel Hawthorne's Puritan New England, Washington Irving's New York, Henry David Thoreau's Walden Pond, and James Fenimore Cooper's American frontier represent clear examples of writers' connections to place. In most cases, however, Poe's works eschew this link—at least overtly. In 1838, when Edgar A. Poe moved to Philadelphia with his wife, Virginia, and mother-in-law, Maria Clemm, the city was flourishing. A network of railroads operated throughout the city. Jefferson Medical College had improved its prestige by breaking off from its parent institution, Jefferson College, and becoming its own university. Traders and financiers flocked to the Philadelphia Exchange each workday. The innovative correctional facility, Eastern State Penitentiary, had been operating for nearly ten years, along with a separate facility, the House of Refuge, which housed underage criminals. The residents supported thirteen daily newspapers, seventeen weeklies, and thirteen periodicals. The Arch Street, Chestnut Street, and Walnut Street Theatres produced numerous shows for high- and low-brow audiences.

With a population of over **90,000**, Philadelphia offered a big-city atmosphere without the crowd press, noise, or pollution that characterized New York, which had a population of more than three times that of

A. B. Armiento (✉)
Frostburg State University, Frostburg, MD, USA

© The Author(s) 2018
P. E. Phillips (ed.), *Poe and Place*,
Geocriticism and Spatial Literary Studies,
https://doi.org/10.1007/978-3-319-96788-2_6

123

this city. J. Gerald Kennedy writes, "the country's first public high school opened in Philadelphia, and the new Museum Building provided an elegant setting for the display of natural specimens and cultural artifacts."[1] Kenneth Silverman notes, "Neat, clean, quiet, so most visitors described Philadelphia."[2] He also comments that the city's "long parallel streets, crossing each other at right angles, the gridiron design that its founder William Penn had been the first to impose on an American city" struck those who came to the city for the first time.[3] Inspiration abounded to pique an imaginative mind such as Poe's.

This chapter will discuss Poe's literary relationship with Philadelphia using broad geocritical assumptions. Bertrand Westphall identifies "three fundamental concepts" of this method: spatiotemporality, transgressivity, and referentiality.[4] The first and third concepts are the foci of this chapter. Poe's link to Philadelphia is inextricable from the specific time in which he lived there (spatiotemporality), and the imagery and descriptions employed in his literary worlds, I argue, are drawn from real objects, people, and events in the city space of Philadelphia (referentiality). The concept of transgressivity applies to the discussions of Poe's displacements, setting works that he writes in Philadelphia in other locales. Like it did on Charles Brockden Brown's novels, Philadelphia made an indelible mark on Poe's works. Although he may not have set most of the pieces in Philadelphia, most of the works that he composed here reflect Philadelphia and its happenings.

The expansion west from the banks of the Delaware River to the Schuylkill moved at a rapid pace. *A. McElroy's Philadelphia Directory for 1839* specifies fourteen wards bound on the west by the Schuylkill River, on the east by the Delaware River, on the north by Vine Street, and on the south by Cedar Street. Mrs. C. Jones is also listed in the directory. The abbreviation "b.h." designates that she was the proprietor of a boardinghouse. The newly arrived Poe family rented rooms at her establishment, 202 Mulberry Street.[5] The home shared the block with the Arch Street Theatre and was near the City, Golden Swan, and Philadelphia Hotels.[6]

After a few months, Poe was in debt, and the family moved from these lodgings on the border between the Lower Delaware and High Street Wards to a home in the Locust Ward, an area much more removed from the hustle and bustle of the city center. Only a couple of blocks away from Rittenhouse Square, the apartment was nestled in a beautiful area. Its relatively remote location would have provided an ideal spot for a peaceful, domestic setting.[7] At this time, *The Narrative of Arthur Gordon Pym* created a small sensation, which may have inspired Poe later to write such adventure works as *The Journal of Julius Rodman* and "Descent into the Maelstrom." By year's end, Poe remitted the amount of money that he owed to Mrs. C. Jones.

In April 1839, Poe netted additional money with the publication of a ghost-written textbook, *The Conchologist's First Book*. The popularity of the work resulted in a second edition that appeared later that year. In June, he began working at *Burton's Gentleman's Magazine* as assistant editor. Located at the corner of Dock Street and Bank Alley, the magazine's office required Poe to take a twelve-block walk down either Walnut or Spruce Streets. In either case, he crossed over the Philadelphia Railroad tracks. If he chose the path down Spruce Street, he saw the stately Pennsylvania Hospital, with its two spires, two large wings, manicured front lawn, large trees, and stone fence. It occupied the block between Eighth and Ninth Streets. The four-story brick building of St. Joseph's Orphan Asylum on Seventh abutted the sidewalk. It featured a statue of the Virgin Mary perched atop the building. Most of Poe's walk along Spruce passed by homes and churches of various Christian denominations, including Catholic, Episcopalian, Presbyterian, and Quaker.

The walk down Walnut Street brought Poe closer to businesses and schools, including the Jefferson Medical College, the University of Pennsylvania, the Walnut Street Theatre (featuring second-story arched windows), Washington Square, Independence Square, the pointed roof and eight columns of the US Bank, Carpenters Hall with its latticed windows and cupola, and the Friends' Almshouse. Similar to the route along Spruce, Poe passed by churches as well.

On occasion, Poe may have selected a third route by walking along Locust about eight blocks through residences before coming to Washington Square and then selecting either Walnut or Spruce to finish his journey. In those blocks, he saw the Medical Institute and the First Unitarian Church of Philadelphia, replete with its four, impressive columns. The *Gentleman's Magazine* office was nestled among the Custom House, the City Tobacco Warehouse, a variety of insurance companies, *The American Sentinel* and *The Evening News* newspaper buildings, and the impressive rotunda of the Philadelphia Exchange (Fig. 6.1).

During these perambulations, it is not difficult to imagine how some of the material for the stories composed at this time relates to these sights.[8] For instance, "Peter Pendulum, The Business Man" mocks

Fig. 6.1 Philadelphia Exchange (Harry Lee Poe Collection)

the popinjays who pursue this line of work. The eponymous character, devoted to a certain type of ill-conceived method, catalogs his various experiences from his counting house debacle to his modeling
career to his incarceration to his de-evolution into a thug and scammer
(or "diddler" as Poe designates the confidence man in "Raising the
Wind"). Although many critics read the story as a veiled profile of his
foster father, Poe witnessed firsthand the risky trade at the Philadelphia
Exchange, the eager clients depositing and withdrawing funds at the US
Bank, and the indigent at the Almshouse.[9] To conceive of a character
who tries and fails at this enterprise—who moves from the legitimate
business realm to an illicit one—is Poe's way of lampooning the types of
men employed at the Philadelphia Exchange.

Poe's contempt for investors also extends to clerks. "The Man of the Crowd" is displaced from Philadelphia to London. When observing the clerks, he describes them with the same scorn directed at the business-men. The young ones are "gentlemen with tight coats, bright boots, well-oiled hair, and supercilious lips [...]. They wore the cast-off graces of the gentry," and the older clerks display an "affectation of respect-ability" (M 508). The distinction between appearances and personality is clearly demarcated, and the story implies that the two do not corre-spond. Poe's daily exposure to a variety of clerks for the bank and insur-ance companies near Burton's office allows him to describe their kind with confidence.

In addition to the influence of the financial world on Poe's imagina-tion, the Jefferson Medical College, the Pennsylvania Hospital, and the Medical Institute may have encouraged Poe's inclusion of medical dis-course and imagery in some of the tales that he composed at this time.[10] For instance, the following lines in "The Fall of the House of Usher" indict the medical community:

The brother had been led to his resolution (so he told me) by consider-ations of the unusual character of the malady of the deceased, of certain obtrusive and eager inquiries on the part of her medical men, and of the remote and exposed situation of the burial ground of the family. I will not deny that when I called to mind the sinister countenance of the person whom I met upon the staircase, on the day of my arrival at the house, I had no desire to oppose what I regarded as at best but a harmless, and not by any means an unnatural precaution. (M 409)

Poe's unfavorable description of the doctor probably formed while he mingled with them on his walks. The doctor's "sinister countenance" is a direct result of the rumors that the medical colleges raided cemeter-ies to supply cadavers to the students. Around the time that Poe com-posed the story, an article in the *Philadelphia Public Ledger* reported on an attempted grave robbery in which a passerby frightened the robbers: "Just at the moment the coffin was to be lifted, one of the [robbers] remarked in a serious voice, 'Arise, and come to judgment!' Much to their surprise, there arose a white-clad figure from behind a neighbor-ing tombstone who responded with equal seriousness, 'Yea, Lord, I'm coming.'"[11] The same piece highlights that the deceased had died "of a rare disease." This humorous yet morbid anecdote contributed to the impression that the doctors stalked the dead, especially the freshly dead, to advance their educations.[12]

Body snatching was related to the need for specimens at the University of Pennsylvania's Anatomical Museum. In an 1832 catalog of the collection, hundreds of body parts, human and non-human, are listed, including "Lung, tubercular consumption of" and "Small polypus from lining membrane of trachea, producing suffocation and death, after symptoms of consumption."[13] Poe's focus on disease incarnate in "The Mask of the Red Death. A Fantasy" is most assuredly influenced by Virginia's diagnosis of tuberculosis.[14] However, the Great White Plague, as it was dubbed, threatened all residents of large cities. The study of this disease and others, especially in surgical theaters and dissections, was commonplace. For example, the University of Pennsylvania charged its students a $10 fee to observe surgeries or dissections during its 1838–1839 Session.[15]

The most common types of surgery were amputations, tumor and cataract removals, and other surgeries considered minor today.[16] According to the Penn Medicine's "History of Pennsylvania Hospital" page, advertisements were routinely posted to inform the public of the upcoming procedures.[17] It is likely that Poe would have perused these flyers, for his attention to popular entertainments is a hallmark of his success as an author.[18] "The Tell-Tale Heart" and "The Man that Was Used Up" feature the man afflicted with a cataract and the amputee, respectively, within their plots. In the former, the narrator describes "a pale blue eye, with a film over it" (M 792). His nightly visitations to the old man's bedroom loosely resemble the surgeon preparing to operate in the surgical theater. He insists that he is the star and invites the reader to imagine a reenactment, "But you should have seen *me*. You should have seen how wisely I proceeded — with what caution—with what foresight— with what dissimulation I went to work!" (M 729, italics in original). The bed is the stage, and the shaft of lamplight corresponds to the candlelight used to illuminate the patient, or more accurately, to pinpoint "precisely [...] the damned spot" (M 795). Rather than remove the offending eye, the narrator takes drastic measures to rid himself of the eye.[19] He suffocates the old man. This over-reaction to the man's affliction mimics the large amount of blood loss during surgeries and the great numbers of patient fatalities. His means of collecting the blood also followed the operating room procedures. He says, "There was nothing to wash out—no stain of any kind—no blood-spot whatever. I had been too wary for that. A tub had caught all" (M 796). According to Lindsey Fitzharris, medical historian, "In hospital operating theatres, a wooden box was placed under the patient to catch blood and pus during the surgery. Additionally, sawdust was placed under the floorboards to catch the overflow."[20] The vulnerability of the floorboards as a potential indicator of the grisly business is echoed in the tale. The narrator assures the reader, "I then replaced the boards so cleverly, so cunningly, that no human eye—not even his—could have detected anything wrong" (M 796). He even plays the part of resurrectionist when he disinters the body from "the very spot beneath which [it] reposed" (M 796).[21] Following the suffocation, the narrator "dismembered," or amputated, the old man's head and limbs.

Similarly, Brevet Brigadier General A.B.C. Smith undergoes numerous losses of limbs. However, the story's ludicrous ending begs the question of whether he should have been given the opportunity to survive, for he, as the ending overtly states, "was the man that was used up" (M 389). The "exceedingly odd-looking bundle of something," with its barely perceptible voice, could hardly be considered human (M 386). This story is rare in that it is set specifically in Philadelphia. Many of Philadelphia's amputees were well served by John F. Thomas, who had cornered the market in cork leg making.[22] Smith refers to Thomas at "Race street, No. 79"; *McElroy's Philadelphia City Directory for 1843* lists him at 99 Crown Street, although he may have moved between the composition of the story and the publication of the directory (M 388).[23]

"The Psyche Zenobia" and "Life in Death" concern dissection as well. In "The Psyche Zenobia," Poe exposes the layers of how to compose a sensationalist work for *Blackwood's* while the companion piece, "The Scythe of Time," represents the finished product.[24] "The Scythe of Time" uncovers the physical reactions the female protagonist experiences while slowly being decapitated. Unlike "The Tell-Tale Heart" and "The Man that Was Used Up," this story's tone is much more humorous. The comedy derives from the incongruity of the decapitated person relaying her own "predicament." Like the proverbial chicken with its head cut off, she maintains an ability to amble about for a short period after her beheading before she utters her dying words, "I have done" (M 356). A severed head is the sort of item one could view in the anatomical museum. In fact, the University of Pennsylvania possessed at least three human heads (or significant parts thereof) in addition to animal skulls.

Besides storing actual body parts, the Anatomical Museum exhibited models and other artistic renderings of the body. Poe's "Life in Death" (later, "The Oval Portrait") emulates the concept of a death mask. The Anatomical Museum held seven replicas of death masks and several paintings and models of anatomical features. In essence, these materials serve to understand the beings they represent. The lives have ceased, yet the lifelikeness persists. In Poe's story, the reader learns that the painter's wife "sat meekly for many weeks in the dark high turret-chamber where the light dripped upon the pale canvas only from overhead" (M 665). This description mirrors the amphitheater of the Pennsylvania Hospital: The top floor is the home of the nation's oldest surgical amphitheater, the "dreaded circular room," which served as the operating room from 1804 through 1868. Surgeries were scheduled for sunny days between 11:00 a.m. and 2:00 p.m. because there was no electricity during Poe's time.[25] Similar to many patients in the hospital, in the round turret of the story, the painter drains his subject of her life. The line, "And he *would* not see that the tints which he spread upon the canvas were drawn from the cheeks of her who sat beside him," refers to the blush caused by the blood rushing to the face (M 665, italics in original). Poe likens the artist's process to the surgeon, who persists in his art to the detriment of his patient. Although the artist captures his subject's beauty or the surgeon removes the cancer, the question of the wisdom of the endeavor is brought to bear on those who become absorbed in their work, "which went on from hour to hour and from day to day," only to result in death (M 665).

Pseudo-medical discourse is present in "Ligeia" as well. Her unnatural eyes arrest the narrator's attention. While Ligeia pours through tomes, the narrator studies her. He says,

> The "strangeness," however, which I found in the eyes of my Ligeia was of a nature distinct from the formation, or the colour, or the brilliancy of the features, and must, after all, be referred to the *expression*. Ah, word of no meaning! behind whose vast latitude of mere sound we intrench [sic] our ignorance of so much of the spiritual. The expression of the eyes of Ligeia! How, for long hours have I pondered upon it! How have I, through the whole of a mid-summer night, struggled to fathom it! What was it — that something more profound than the well of Democritus — which lay far within the pupils of my beloved? What was it? I was possessed with a passion to discover. Those eyes! those large, those shining, those divine orbs!

They became to me twin stars of Leda, and I to them devoutest of astrologers. Not for a moment was the unfathomable meaning of their glance, by day or by night, absent from my soul. (M 313, italics in original)

Like a medical student, he spends "long hours" speculating upon the "strangeness" of her eyes. Unlike the student, however, he relinquishes his examination. Because he cannot provide an explanation, he elects to designate their meaning to a divine understanding. Following Ligeia's death, the narrator takes a new wife. The bridal chamber, like the attic in "Life in Death," is placed in a remote and high place reminiscent of the surgical amphitheater:

The room lay in a high turret of the castellated abbey, was pentagonal in shape, and of capacious size. Occupying the whole southern face of the pentagon was the sole window—an immense sheet of unbroken glass from Venice—a single pane, and tinted of a leaden hue, so that the rays of either the sun or moon, passing through it, fell with a ghastly lustre upon the objects within. Over the upper portion of this huge window extended the open trellice-work [sic] of an aged vine which clambered up the massy walls of the turret. The ceiling, of gloomy-looking oak, was excessively lofty, vaulted, and elaborately fretted with the wildest and most grotesque specimens of a semi-Gothic, semi-druidical device. From out the most central recess of this melancholy vaulting, depended, by a single chain of gold, with long links, a huge censer of the same metal, Arabesque in pattern, and with many perforations so contrived that there writhed in and out of them, as if endued with a serpent vitality, a continual succession of particoloured fires. (M 321)

Unlike the Pennsylvania Hospital's operating theater, this is a perverted space in which the opium-addled narrator can observe his patient's demise rather than her recovery. Although he refused to persist in his study of the woman he loved, he does not feel the same regard for the Lady Rowena. The pendant's light corresponds to the candlelight used in the operating space. However, the lighting is contorted to underscore the narrator's motives and to obscure his operations. When Lady Rowena falls ill, doctors are called to her aid, prescribing "light wine" (M 325). If read that the narrator is the one to administer the "three or four large drops of a brilliant and ruby-colored fluid" to Rowena's tonic, then he is the one to conduct the experiment that resurrects Ligeia at the cost of Lady Rowena's life (M 325).

These stories are not the only ones to explore the deterioration of the body. "The Conversation of Eiros and Charmion" and "The Colloquy of Monos and Una" consider the diminishing consciousness after corporeal death. In the former, Eiros describes how a comet enters the Earth's atmosphere, resulting in its spontaneous combustion. In the latter, Una directs a postmortem of sorts when she requests that Monos relay what happened to him "when, the fever having abandoned you, you sank into a breathless and motionless torpor, and I pressed down your pallid eyelids with the passionate fingers of love" (M 609). Most of the story consists of Monos's monologue, in which he describes what he does and does not perceive and senses and does not sense. Along with "Shadow—A Parable," "Morella," "A Decided Loss," "The Facts in the Case of M. Valdemar," "Mesmeric Revelation" (a work similar in content and form to "The Colloquy of Monos and Una"), "The Island of the Fay," and "Ligeia," these two works may be categorized as Poe's eschatological works. He had begun writing these types of stories early in his career and persisted to do so in Philadelphia. He fluctuated among the depictions of the body, the mind, and the soul in his pieces. Although the focus on the body that was taking place in the nascent medical fields regarding surgery and dissection arrested the attention of the Philadelphia medical community, Poe never lost interest in the soul's ultimate fate.

Although he had turned to the afterlife in other stories and poems before his time in Philadelphia, the number of churches near his home and on his way to work probably induced more speculation upon the subject. "The Devil in the Belfry," "The Masque of the Red Death," and "Never Bet the Devil Your Head" feature the antics of the fiend. He considers the power of curses in "Eleonora" and concludes, at least in this story, that loved ones who have died desire the survivor's happiness notwithstanding promises made when they were still living. Moreover, living within the city that housed so many churches and the Liberty Bell, Poe highlighted chiming and bell tolls in two of his stories: "The Devil in the Belfry" and "The Masque of the Red Death." In the case of the latter, Paul Haspel asserts that Poe was tapping into the public interest in the recent name change of the Independence Bell to the Liberty Bell.[26]

Other sights bombarded him on Philadelphia's streets. Seeing the children outside of St. Joseph's Orphan Asylum on his meanderings could have unleashed memories of the loss of his parents and of his boarding school days abroad. The description of the school in "William

Wilson" does not match the austere, four-story building on Seventh and Spruce Streets nor does the asylum feature a "high and solid brick wall, topped with a bed of mortar and broken glass" (M 428). However, as an orphan himself, Poe might have reflected on his alternative fate as contrasted with the children placed in this institution. Similar to "The Man of the Crowd," Poe the Philadelphian displaces the story to a setting in London. The description by a local historian of the "long processions of demur and decorous orphans through [Philadelphia's] streets" echoes Poe's own portrayal of the students being "paraded in the same formal manner to the morning and evening service in the one church of the village" (M 428).[27] In addition to this connection, Thomas Peyser asserts that the tale reenacts America's break from Britain. He discusses Poe's rhetorical choices to describe William Wilson's independence from his parents as reminiscent of the words in the Declaration. It is an easy leap for readers to connect this discussion to the fact that Poe pens this work in the very city where the colonies voted to secede from Britain.[28] Brit Theron has linked the story to Poe's historical moment, and Philadelphia specifically, believing that Poe's involvement in Harrison's campaign brought to the forefront of his imagination the reality that "a new class of voters [...], for the first time, entered significantly into national politics. Property and religious qualifications for voting had been recently abolished in most states; and new states joining the Union in general had made their constitutions receptive to the popular will."[29] Theron concludes that Wilson's demise stems from his insistence on his individuality at a time when equality of all is the way of the land.

By September 1842, the Poe family moved closer to the Schuylkill River to a home on Coates Street near Eastern State Penitentiary. On his way to the office of *Graham's Magazine* on W. Third Street and Chestnut, which was within a couple of blocks of Burton's old location, Poe could select a myriad of routes. When he walked directly east on Coates Street to Third, he passed the formidable walls of the prison and, six blocks later, the House of Refuge, a juvenile detention center with window slits and corner towers (Fig. 6.2).

Slightly over a year before this relocation, Poe had published "The Murders in the Rue Morgue" in *Graham's Magazine*. Dwight Thomas speculates that "[w]hen Poe wrote 'The Murders in the Rue Morgue,' he would have been mindful of the popular sensation caused by the exhibition of the ourang outang at the Masonic Hall, Chestnut Street, during August and September 1839" (PL 265). Elise Lemire ties the story

PENITENTIARY, PHILADELPHIA.

Fig. 6.2   Eastern Penitentiary, Philadelphia (Harry Lee Poe Collection)

to other contemporary events, namely the riots between the free blacks, abolitionists, and whites that took place. She provides ample evidence to show the conflation of blacks with orangutans during Poe's time.[30] Living in close proximity to these houses of detention could not fail to inspire stories of gruesome murders. At this address, he wrote "The Tell-Tale Heart," "The Black Cat," "Pit and the Pendulum," and "The Mystery of Marie Rôget." In all of these cases, the perpetrators are human. He could delve into the criminal mind and society's inventions of disciplinary machinations.

"The Tell-Tale Heart" and "The Black Cat" end in scenes depicting justice for the victims. In each case, the criminal confesses his crime, and the police are present to apprehend the offender. Both stories are told in the past tense as the narrator recalls his crime while incarcerated. Poe's use of the second person implies that the narrator of "The Tell-Tale Heart" may be presenting his defense in court or expostulating with a psychologist. Similarly, "The Black Cat" opens with a narrator facing execution the next day. He begins, "For the most wild, yet most homely narrative which I am about to pen, I neither expect nor solicit belief. Mad indeed would I be to expect it, in a case where my very senses reject their own evidence. Yet, mad am I not—and very surely do I not dream. But to-morrow I die, and to-day I would unburthen my soul" (M 849). Either one of these stories could provide the backstory for an inmate at the Eastern State Penitentiary. John E. Reilly argues that an article that ran in the July 16, 1842 issue of the *Public Ledger* provided the content for the final discovery scene in "The Black Cat."[31]

"The Pit and the Pendulum" engages the theory of the panopticon for guarding prisoners. Eastern State was partially designed using this model. The facility has a central hub from which the guards monitor the prisoners. However, Eastern State's fluctuation in Bentham's theory was to incorporate solitary confinement. This combination of surveillance and seclusion is the crux of "The Pit and the Pendulum," which is set in the prison of Toledo, Spain. Both Joan Dayan and Jason Haslam connect Poe's story to Eastern State and the discourse on the penal system.[32] Haslam writes, "Poe's tale helps to highlight telling fractures in the shift in the discourse of punishment from bodily torture and public suffering to narratives of mental and ideological control."[33] His analysis provides a history of this transition in thinking about the purpose of the penal system and how Poe engages it.

Based upon the success of "The Murders in the Rue Morgue," Poe felt emboldened and tried his hand at solving a real-life crime in "The Mystery of Marie Rôget." If he had solved this New York City case, he might have had a future in private detection. In his defense, he argued that he did not have all of the pertinent facts on which to base his conjectures, and consequently, he misidentified the killer. Enticed by a contest with a cash prize, Poe returned to the detective story at the end of the year. He submitted "The Gold-Bug" to Philadelphia's *Dollar Newspaper's* contest, and it won first place. He sets the story in a place well known to him, Sullivan's Island, South Carolina, a place where he had been stationed during his brief military career. Soon after its appearance, the story was adapted for the stage and included as part of a benefit performance at the Walnut Street Theatre (PL 434). Thus, in a manner of speaking, Poe became the third member of his family to "take the stage" in Philadelphia.[34]

From his home on Coates Street, Poe could take alternating routes into the city that avoided the penal institutions. Depending on his path, he could pass by the Blind Institution, Logan Square, the Botanical Garden, or Wills Hospital for the Lame and Blind.[35] The many beautiful lawns and squares in the city likely influenced "The Landscape-Garden." Ellison, the protagonist, observes, "A poet, having very unusual pecuniary resources, might, while retaining the necessary idea of art, or culture, or, as our author expresses it, of interest, so imbue his designs at once with extent and novelty of Beauty, as to convey the sentiment of spiritual interference" (M 1276). One cannot help but notice that Poe is a poet. This statement seems self-referential. If Poe had the financial means, he could conceive of a much more beautiful landscape garden—one that perfectly melds the natural with the artificial. Jeffrey Hess traces elements of the story and its later revision to the Hudson River School painter Thomas Cole and the landscape artist Andrew Jackson Downing.[36] He could have added the five squares of Philadelphia. While living near Rittenhouse Square, Poe would have noticed that the city had started to introduce landscaping to the park. Nancy Heinzen writes, "Carts of soil were brought in to level out the ponds and pits, saplings were planted, and graveled walks in a formal crisscross pattern showed up as early as 1838 on a survey map."[37] Similarly, Logan and Washington Squares received humble improvements. Logan Square, as described by John Thomas Scharf, featured "an open paling fence, walks had been laid out, trees planted, and the ground had been leveled."[38] According to Bill Double, Washington Square had "circular gravel walks [...] set amid an arboretum of trees," and the park was surrounded by an "iron palisade fence."[39] These nascent attempts to beautify the public spaces were daily present to Poe. Ellison insists that the best place for a landscape garden is "a spot *not far* from a populous city" (M 1277, italics in original). Rittenhouse and Logan Squares were near but not within the concentrated urban population of Philadelphia at this time.

In April 1843, the Poes moved to their final Philadelphia address, 234 North Seventh Street. This location brought the family much closer to the Delaware River. Perhaps, on days when Virginia felt up to it, they strolled to Franklin Square, five blocks south. If she was feeling particularly strong, they could have walked or ridden to the city center, which was about ten blocks south of their new home.

Poe's works about the body persisted. In "The Premature Burial," the narrator believes that he has regained consciousness in a coffin after being misdiagnosed as deceased. Silverman posits, "Poe addressed a widespread anxiety in the period, in part owing to uncertainty over the physiology of dying."[40] Of course, the ending reveals that this is a ruse used as a radical treatment for the narrator's phobia of being buried alive. Silverman interprets the message, saying it "warns against too much concern with the grave."[41] On the other hand, Virginia's wavering health probably brought thoughts of the grave to Poe's mind. In his analysis of "The Oblong Box," a story written soon after this one, Silverman observes, "it so starkly enacts Poe's feelings about Virginia."[42] Therefore, imagining the body in the coffin, which he does in both of these stories, seems likely under the circumstances.

"The Spectacles" seems to return Poe to the days of witnessing the patients milling about the Blind Institution or Wills Hospital for the Lame and Blind. Here, he mocks the narrator who refuses to wear the apparatus that can cure his inability to see, his eyeglasses. Napoleon Bonaparte Simpson confesses,

> My eyes are large and gray; and although, in fact, they are weak to a very inconvenient degree, still no defect in this regard would be suspected from their appearance. The weakness, itself, however, has always much annoyed me, and I have resorted to every remedy — short of wearing glasses. Being youthful and good-looking, I naturally dislike these, and have resolutely refused to employ them. I know nothing, indeed, which so disfigures the countenance of a young person, or so impresses every feature with an air of demureness, if not altogether of sanctimoniousness and of age. An eye-glass, on the other hand, has a savor of downright foppery and affectation. (M 889)

A victim of vanity, the narrator foolishly rejects the remedy to his affliction. Unlike the patients who could never see again, no matter how strong the magnification of the glass, Simpson had the means to live a sighted person's life. Ernest Freeberg notes how the students at Philadelphia's Blind Institution "put on hundreds of exhibitions."[43] Poe, like most Philadelphians, probably marveled over the wonders performed by the educated blind children at the school under the direction of Julius Friedlander. Whereas most of them could never see again, Simpson merely had to visit a shop like the one listed at the back of *McElroy's Directory for 1839*. An advertisement features a pair of eyeglasses and reads, "William Patten, S.E. corner of Arch and Sixth sts [sic], has constantly for sale an assortment of spectacles."[44] Although no conclusive evidence has surfaced to make this connection, Poe's awareness of contemporary news and entertainment makes it likely that he knew about these students and probably saw them ambling on the lawn outside of the school.

Poe's strolls also brought him into contact with a creek running near his homes on Locust and Coates Streets. Although he did not write "Morning on the Wissahiccon" until he returned to the east side of Philadelphia, he was probably one of those "few adventurous pedestrians" who went to admire its beauty in the wake of Fanny Kemble's book (M 864). In fact, Poe directs would-be hikers on how to access the stream and which route to follow. The ending features a humorous twist on Poe's imaginings, which ties into the accompanying illustration. Nevertheless, this fantasy piece is rooted in the reality of the natural beauty of Philadelphia's outskirts.

In addition to his prolific writing in Philadelphia, Poe managed to meet Charles Dickens during the celebrated writer's visit to the city from January 4–7, 1842. Many scholars have identified similarities between Poe's works and those of Dickens.[45] Poe admired the works of the Englishman, and it is thought that Poe's "The Raven" evolved from the one mentioned in Dickens's *Barnaby Rudge*, a tribute to Dickens's own raven, Grip. Although Poe did not publish his famous poem until after leaving Philadelphia, some maintain that he had drafted it in this city (PL 435, 437).[46] If true, this poem is the only major one in his oeuvre composed during his six-year residence[47] [Chapter 4, Kennedy, England].

During Poe's residence there, Philadelphia offered much to engage his imagination and to include in his literary worlds. Geocriticism allows for speculation on the phenomenon of how place impacts its inhabitants and, for literature specifically, how real places influence imagined worlds. Many of the examples posed in this chapter are ideas and images repeated in Poe's early works from Richmond and continued into works that he would write in New York. However, Philadelphia itself provided additional substance for Poe to expand his use of monomaniacal narrators and, arguably, encouraged him to persist in writing sensationalist, homicidal tales. The flexibility of writing similar types of works in different cities and locating them in different places connects to the geocritical idea of transgressivity. Nevertheless, references to Philadelphia, overt and covert, are interpolated into his texts.

While in Philadelphia, Poe experienced a number of setbacks that are all the more poignant considering the promise the city seemed to offer when he had settled there. Initially, it appeared that Poe would find stable employment at *Burton's*. His regular paycheck covered household expenses and afforded him some ability to clear previous debts. However, Mr. Burton's interest in the stage resulted in his sale of the periodical to Graham. Poe attempted to capitalize on this situation by seeking to found and edit his own magazine, *The Penn*. When Poe finally gained the momentum necessary to secure funding for the project, the economy plummeted, and, to make matters worse, Poe succumbed to illness. Although he tried to resurrect the enterprise, even renaming it *The Stylus*, Poe had to postpone the project, which never materialized. Although he published *The Tales of the Grotesque and Arabesque*, Poe never found a publisher willing to issue a second collection of works titled *Phantasy-Pieces*. His inability to secure a government position at the Custom House exacerbated his financial situation, pushing him to take the position of book editor at *Graham's*. Charles Cantalupo succinctly sums up Poe's writing career in lines 11–12 of his poem, "Poe in Philadelphia": "He left as a failure – his most famous/ Tales for sixteen cents a day"[48] [Poem, "Poe in Richmond," by Charles Cantalupo, at the beginning of this volume].

Under these employment and financial strains, Poe's efforts to create a tranquil domestic life seemed futile. However, he persevered. Even when he found himself without steady work, he contributed stories, previously printed poems, critical essays, and miscellany to periodicals in and outside of Philadelphia.[49] He supplemented his meager income with lectures, and he continued to build networks with the literati, including Lydia Sigourney and Charles Dickens. In the end, the elements over which he had control were not those that would destroy his home life. The tuberculosis that manifested itself in Virginia in January 1842 ravaged her body for the next five years. After achieving limited successes and facing bitter disappointments in Philadelphia, Poe uprooted his family and returned to New York.

NOTES

1. J. Gerald Kennedy, "A Brief Biography," in *A Historical Guide to Edgar Allan Poe*, ed. J. Gerald Kennedy (Oxford: Oxford University Press, 2001), 40.
2. Kenneth Silverman, *Edgar A. Poe: Mournful and Never-Ending Remembrance* (New York: Harper Perennial, 1992), 140.

3. Ibid., 140.
4. Bertrand Westphall, "Foreword," in *Geocritical Explorations: Space, Place, and Mapping in Literary and Cultural Studies*, ed. Robert T. Tally, Jr. (London: Palgrave Macmillan, 2011), xv.
5. Ellis Paxson Oberholtzer, *The Literary History of Philadelphia* (Philadelphia: George W. Jacobs, 1906), 286.
6. *McElroy's Philadelphia City Directory* (Philadelphia: A. McElroy and Co, 1839), 302.
7. For places nearby Poe's homes, see Thomas G. Bradford, *Philadelphia* (Map) (Boston: Weeks, Jordan, 1838), David Rumsey Map Collection.
8. J. A. Leo Lemay, "Poe's 'The Business Man': Its Contexts and Satire of Franklin's Autobiography," *Poe Studies/Dark Romanticism: History, Theory, Interpretation* 15, no. 2 (1982): 29–37. Lemay connects the story again to Philadelphia by pointing out its ironic relationship to the Philadelphian statesman and writer Benjamin Franklin.
9. For more discussion of this story as a reaction against John Allan, see Dawn B. Sova, *Edgar Allan Poe: A to Z* (New York: Checkmark Books, 2001), 40. For an analysis of this story's commentary on manhood, see Leland S. Person, "Poe and Nineteenth Century Gender Constructions," in *A Historical Guide to Edgar Allan Poe*, ed. J. Gerald Kennedy (Oxford: Oxford University Press, 2001), 158–159.
10. Michael Sappol draws many connections between Poe and medical discourse of the nineteenth century in his book. See Michael Sappol, *A Traffic of Dead Bodies* (Princeton: Princeton University Press, 2002), 26, 215, 357.
11. Suzanne M. Shultz, *Body Snatching: The Robbing of Graves for the Education of Physicians in Early Nineteenth-Century American* (Jefferson, NC: McFarland, 1992), 52.
12. For more on the role of medicine in this story, see David E. E. Sloane, "Usher's Nervous Fever: The Meaning of Medicine in Poe's 'The Fall of the House of Usher,'" in *Poe and His Times: The Artist and His Milieu*, ed. Benjamin Franklin Fisher, IV (Baltimore: Edgar Allan Poe Society, 1990), 146–153.
13. Wistar Institute of Anatomy and Biology, *Catalogue of the Anatomical Museum of the University of Pennsylvania: With a Report to the Museum Committee of the Trustees* (Philadelphia: Lydia R. Bailey, 1832), 18, 17.
14. See Silverman, 180–181 and William Bittner, *Poe: A Biography* (Boston: Little, Brown, 1962), 177; James Hutchisson, Poe (Jackson, MS: University Press of Mississippi, 2005), 137.
15. "Ticket to the Healing Arts: Medical Lecture Tickets of the 18th and 19th Centuries," *Penn University Archives and Records Center*, accessed

May 3, 2018, http://www.archives.upenn.edu/histy/features/medical_lecture_tickets/anatomy.html.

16. "Surgical Amphitheatre," *Penn Medicine*, accessed May 3, 2018, http://www.uphs.upenn.edu/paharc/tour/tour5.html.

17. Ibid.

18. For instance, John Cleman connects two Philadelphia court cases that invoked the insanity defense to Poe's "The Tell-Tale Heart" and "The Black Cat" (624). See John Cleman, "Irresistible Impulses: Edgar Allan Poe and the Insanity Defense," *American Literature* 63, no. 4 (1991): 623–640.

19. For more on other medical discourses evoked by the tale, see Edward Pitcher, "The Physiognomical Meaning of Poe's 'The Tell-Tale Heart,'" *Studies in Short Fiction* 16 (1979): 231–233.

20. Lindsey Fitzharris, "The Horrors of Pre-Anesthetic Surgery," The Chirurgeon's Apprentice (blog), July 16, 2014, https://thechirurgeonsapprentice.com/2014/07/16/the-horrors-of-pre-anaesthetic-surgery/.

21. For readings on how the story depicts the narrator's mental state, see Clemans andPaige Matthey Bynum, "'Observe How Healthily-How Calmly I Can Tell You the Whole Story': Moral Insanity and Edgar Allan Poe's 'The Tell-Tale Heart,'" in *Literature and Science as Modes of Expression*, ed. Frederick Amrine (Dordrecht: Kluwer Academic, 1989), 141–152.

22. Mabbott's text includes a note that identifies contemporary vendors who may correspond to Bishop. See 389, n. 24. Thomas Ollive Mabbott, *The Collected Works of Edgar Allan Poe* (Urbana: University of Illinois Press, 2000), 389.

23. *McElroy's Philadelphia City Directory* (Philadelphia: Orrin Rogers, 1843), 278.

24. Reynolds points out that the story "is an exemplum of how *not* to write a peril story" (239, italics in original). David Reynolds, *Beneath the American Renaissance* (Cambridge: Harvard University Press, 1989).

25. "Surgical Amphitheatre."

26. Paul Haspel, "Bells of Freedom and Foreboding: Liberty Bell Ideology and the Clock Motif in Edgar Allan Poe's 'The Masque of the Red Death,'" *Edgar Allan Poe Review* 13, no. 1 (2012): 46. Also, Hutchisson draws a parallel between the Philadelphia New Year's Parade featuring the Mummers and Poe's figure of the Red Death (138).

27. Eleanor C. Donnelly, *Life of Sister Marie Gonzaga Grace* (Philadelphia: Author, 1900), 85.

28. Thomas Peyser, "Poe's 'William Wilson' and the Nightmare of Equality," *Explicator* 68, no. 2 (2010): 101–103.

29. Theron Britt, "The Common Property of the Mob: Democracy and Identity in Poe's 'William Wilson,'" *Mississippi Quarterly* 48, no. 2 (1995): 197.

30. Elise Lemire, "'The Murders in the Rue Morgue': Amalgamation Discourses and the Race Riots of 1838 in Poe's Philadelphia," *Romancing the Shadow*, ed. J. Gerald Kennedy (Oxford: Oxford University Press, 2001), 185–187.

31. John E. Reilly, "A Source for the Immuration in 'The Black Cat,'" *Nineteenth-Century Literature* 48, no. 1 (1993): 93.

32. See Joan Dayan, "Poe, Persons, and Property," *American Literary History* 11, no. 3 (1999): 405–425.

33. Jason Haslam, "Pits, Pendulums, and Penitentiaries," *Texas Studies in Language and Literature* 50, no. 3 (2008): 270.

34. Silverman, 3.

35. In her recent book, Barbara Cantalupo describes the impact that the sight of the Institution for the Deaf and Dumb had on "To Helen." She also discusses the influence of Chinese décor in "The Devil in the Belfry." See Barbara Cantalupo, *Poe and the Visual Arts* (University Park, PA: The Pennsylvania State University Press, 2014), 7, 88–90.

36. Jeffrey A. Hess, "Sources and Aesthetics of Poe's Landscape Fiction," *American Quarterly* 22 (1970): 177–189.

37. Nancy M. Heinzen, *The Perfect Square: A History of Rittenhouse Square* (Philadelphia: Temple University Press, 2009), 25.

38. John Thomas Scharf, *History of Philadelphia, 1609–1884* (Philadelphia: L. H. Everts, 1884), 1849.

39. Bill Double, *Philadelphia's Washington Square* (Mt. Pleasant, SC: Arcadia Publishing Library Editions, 2009), 37–38.

40. Silverman, 227.

41. Ibid., 228.

42. Ibid.

43. Ernest Freeberg, "The Meanings of Blindness in Nineteenth-Century America," *Proceedings of the American Antiquarian Society* 110, no. 1 (2000): 122.

44. *McElroy's* (1839), n.p.

45. See Burton R. Pollin, "Dickens' Chimes and Its Pathway into Poe's 'Bells,'" *Mississippi Quarterly* 51, no. 2 (1998): 217–231; Laurence Senelick, "Charles Dickens and 'The Tell-Tale Heart,'" *Poe Studies* 6, no. 1 (1973): 12–14; Adeline R. Tintner, "A Possible Source in Dickens for Poe's 'Imp of the Perverse,'" *Poe Studies* 18, no. 2 (1985): 25; Burton R. Pollin, "Nicholas Nickleby in 'The Devil in the Belfry,'" *Poe Studies* 8 (1975): 23; Rodney Stenning Edgecombe, "'The Fall of the House of Usher' and Little Dorrit," *Victorian Newsletter* 101 (2002): 32–34;

Edward Strickland, "Dickens' 'A Madman's Manuscript' and 'The Tell-Tale Heart,'" *Poe Studies* 9 (1976): 22–23; Edith S. Krappe, "A Possible Source for Poe's 'The Tell-Tale Heart' and 'The Black Cat,'" *American Literature* 12 (1940): 84–88.

46. For an amusing read on the idea that Poe wrote "The Raven" in Philadelphia, see "Poe and Philadelphia," *New York Times*, April 27, 1919, http://query.nytimes.com/mem/archive-free/pdf?res=9A0DE2DB1F3BE03ABC4F51DFB2668382609EDE.

47. Excepting "The Haunted Palace" and "The Conqueror Worm," which appeared in "The Fall of House of Usher" and "Ligeia," respectively, and will not be treated separately here, Poe wrote "Lenore" and "Eulalie."

48. Charles Cantalupo, "Poe in Philadelphia," in *Poe's Pervasive Influence*, ed. Barbara Cantalupo (Bethlehem, PA: Lehigh University Press, 2012), 112.

49. It is unclear whether Poe wrote "Thou Art the Man" and "The Purloined Letter" before leaving Philadelphia or shortly after arriving in New York.

CHAPTER 7

Outside Looking In:
Edgar Allan Poe and New York City

John Gruesser

How should a person broach the topic of Edgar Allan Poe and New York City, a subject with as much intrigue, complexity, and diversity as the author and the metropolis themselves? Should the focus be temporal (Poe's stints in New York in 1831, 1837–1838, and 1844–1849), spatial (his residences and places of employment in what are now the Financial District, Greenwich Village, the Lower East Side, Turtle Bay, the Upper West Side, and the Bronx), social (his dealings with figures such as Anne C. Lynch), commercial (his professional relationships with everyone from Charles Anthon to Walt Whitman), literary (his texts written in and about the city), or metaphorical (what might be characterized as his "New York state of mind")? Because Poe often made sense of things—particularly those he grappled with that related to New York—by means of oppositions, the approach in what follows will be to discuss Poe as an outsider and an insider vis-à-vis the nation's largest city.

I am grateful to J. Gerald Kennedy, Scott Peeples, Carole Shaffer-Koros, and Philip Phillips for their suggestions for improving this essay.

J. Gruesser (✉)
Sam Houston State University, Huntsville, TX, USA

P. E. Phillips (ed.), *Poe and Place*,
Geocriticism and Spatial Literary Studies,
https://doi.org/10.1007/978-3-319-96788-2_7

Born in Boston but raised in Virginia, Poe lived in New York City for two extended periods, from early 1837 to early 1838 and from April 1844 until his death in October 1849. After establishing himself as an editor, critic, and literary artist at—and being fired from—the *Southern Literary Messenger* in Richmond, he moved to the nation's most important publishing hub because it appeared to offer him opportunities to advance his literary career. His toast at the 30 March 1837 Booksellers Banquet—"The Monthlies of Gotham—Their distinguished Editors, and their vigorous Collaborateurs"[1]—indicated his desire to play a role in the city's publishing industry, but the severe economic depression that began shortly thereafter frustrated his ambitions, and by the following spring he had moved to Philadelphia.[2] During the first sixteen months that followed his return to New York a half dozen years later, he experienced high points, such as the sensations created by the "The Balloon Hoax" in April 1844 and "The Raven" in late January 1845, invitations to literary *soirées*, and the realization of his dream of sole editorial control (and shortly thereafter sole ownership) of a magazine. However, in the fall of 1845 and throughout 1846, his fortunes plummeted. The Boston Lyceum debacle in October 1845 was followed by the demise of the *Broadway Journal*, which ceased publication with the January 3, 1846, issue, and, soon afterward, a scandal involving the poets Frances Osgood and Elizabeth Ellet led to fallacious reports that Poe had been institutionalized for mental illness. This combination of misfortunes resulted in his being effectively exiled from the New York publishing world. That spring both he and his wife were ill, making it difficult for Poe to work, and he produced far fewer texts, especially fictional ones, in 1846 than he had during the previous two years. The nadir came in December 1846 when there were appeals for donations to support Poe, his dying wife, and his mother-in-law, who were described as living in dire poverty in the Bronx (PL 577–585, 614–315, 622–624, 672–678) (Fig. 7.1).

During his second extended New York sojourn, Poe published two nonfiction series about the city that were loosely structured around an opposition between inside and outside, as well as a short story about a deadly rivalry between an insider and an outsider: *Doings in Gotham* (seven installments, May 18 to July 6, 1844 in the *Columbia* [Pennsylvania] *Spy* newspaper), a kind of travelogue by a non-native who shares what he has learned about the city with provincial readers; *The Literati of New York City* (six installments, May through October 1846 in the Philadelphia-based *Godey's Lady's Book*), a mix of gossipy portraits

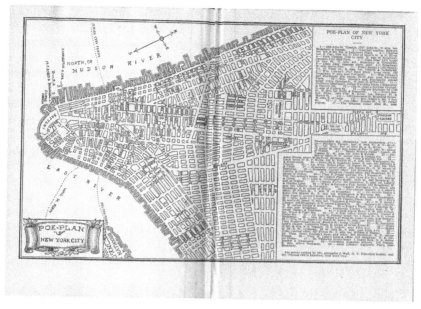

Fig. 7.1   Poe Plan of New York City (Harry Lee Poe Collection)

and glib assessments of New York writers from the perspective of a purported insider; and "The Cask of Amontillado" (*Godey's* November 1846), a tale in which an out-of-favor nobleman walls up his popular foe in a crypt.[3]

Poe relies on several oppositions in *Doings* and the *Literati*, notably quacks versus geniuses, public/printed opinion versus private/spoken opinion, fancy versus imagination, nonsense versus sense, and the provinces/Philadelphia/Pennsylvania versus New York City. Similarly, "Cask" pits the well-liked, happy-go-lucky Fortunato, who belongs to the Masons, against the disliked and disgruntled Montresor, who is not a member of the secret fraternity. All of these binaries might be subsumed under the opposition between in and out. In *Doings*, Poe presents himself as an outsider looking in on New York, identifying himself as someone familiar with Philadelphia and its environs, which he often uses as points of comparison in describing the larger metropolis. Located inside New York and providing specific (inside) information about it to an audience of outsiders, he nevertheless writes as an outsider in *Doings*. In the

Literati, he again writes about New York City for an outside, specifically Philadelphia/Pennsylvania audience—although the highly successful *Godey's* was distributed nationally. This time, however, he does so as a self-proclaimed insider, someone not only based in New York but also as an author himself, someone privy to inside opinion and thereby uniquely qualified to share gossip with his audience of outsiders. Although Poe was still living in Manhattan when the *Literati* began to appear, he had by that time, as noted above, once again become an outsider *vis-à-vis* the New York literary scene, a status reinforced when he and his family moved thirteen miles <u>outside</u> of the city to a cottage in Fordham in May 1846, in part because of his consumptive wife's precarious health (PL 638–639) (Fig. 7.2).

   In his letters and several published works, most notably "Some Secrets of the Magazine Prison-House," which appeared in the *Broadway Journal* in February 1845, Poe decries the cruel dynamics of the ante-bellum literary scene. The lack of an international copyright law makes

Fig. 7.2 Edgar Allan Poe's Cottage, Kingsbridge Road, Fordham, NY (Harry Lee Poe Collection)

the publication of books by American writers rare because publishers can print volumes by established foreign authors without having to pay royalties. As a result, magazines have become the only practical means of finding an audience; however, the "poor devil authors" receive little or nothing for periodical publication.[4] He explains the harmful effects this situation has had on "our national literature" in a September 1845 *Marginalia* entry. It keeps out of print "the efforts of our men of genius, for genius, as a general rule, is poor in worldly goods and cannot write for nothing." Meanwhile, "editors and proprietors" put into their magazines, typically without compensation, the writings of "gentleman of elegant leisure," who "have been noted, time out of mind, for the insipidity of their productions," their "obstinately conservative" nature, and their "imitation of foreign, more especially of British models."[5] Because the wages (and, as the cliché goes, the stakes) were so low, the antebellum publishing world not only bred enmity between writers of "genius" and "quacks" but also spawned bitter personal animosities. After two years in the crucible of the New York literary scene, having seen his fortunes rise and precipitously fall and having written extensively about the factors responsible for the mediocre quality of American letters, Poe wrote a story devoted to the rivalry between an insider and an outsider, "The Cask of Amontillado," his only new work of fiction to be written and published in 1846. In the light of Poe's experiences in New York in 1844, 1845, and 1846, we can fruitfully see him and, I contend, he must to a certain extent have seen himself as both Montresor and Fortunato.

Looking [In] on Gotham

As Scott Peeples has discussed, the writing of a series of letters from and about New York had become a popular practice by the early 1840s, one in which Nathaniel Parker Willis, Lydia Maria Child, and George G. Foster participated. Whereas Child and Foster wrote for specific outside audiences—Bostonians, abolitionists, Fourierists—Willis, portraying himself as the consummate insider, wrote for people residing inside the city and for those outside of it. As Peeples notes, Poe clearly had Willis in mind while penning *Doings*, mentioning him several times, quoting his poems in full, and even, at least initially, affecting the style of the man who would employ him at the *New York Mirror* from the fall of 1844 until the spring of the 1845, publish "The Raven" in late January 1845, and staunchly defend him against his many detractors after his mysterious demise in 1849. As Peeples aptly remarks, "reading 'Doings in Gotham' against other New York Letters series deepens our appreciation for how enmeshed Poe was in the network of New York journalism."[6] Yet, despite its links to other such New York series and the writings of Willis in particular, Poe unmistakably left his own fingerprints all over *Doings*.

The first paragraph of the initial installment alerts readers that Poe's approach to his task will be deliberately random because, as he explains, "I must deal chiefly in *gossip*," an "unlimited" subject "engrossing at least seven-eighths of the whole waking existence of Mankind" that has "neither beginning, middle, nor end" and recognizes no "law."[7] Therefore, he reserves the right to swerve from his "avowed purpose" of depicting New York, indulging in "a frequent hop-skip-and-jump, over the hedges, into the tempting pastures of digression" and "touching [...] upon everything and something besides."[8] Although I agree with Peeples's observation that Poe abandons a Willisesque style after the opening paragraph, I must take exception to his contention that "throughout most of 'Doings in Gotham,' Poe presents himself not as the new arrival that he was but as a curmudgeonly Knickerbocker."[9] Poe decidedly does not adopt the pose of a New York insider in the series. Described by the *Spy* as a correspondent "from the City of New-York, where he has taken up residence for the present" (rather than a native New Yorker or a permanent transplant),[10] Poe frequently aligns himself with his provincial readers, evoking the gingerbread "in some of the Dutch boroughs of Pennsylvania," referring to an article in "a Philadelphian paper," and contrasting New York's most famous thoroughfare with those in the "City of Brotherly Love": "Foreigners are apt to speak of the great *length* of Broadway. It is no doubt a long street; but we have many much longer in Philadelphia"[11] (Fig. 7.3). In this passage, he clearly dissociates his readers and himself from New Yorkers (whom he consistently refers to as "the"—rather than "we"—"Gothamites" in the series) through the use of the first-person plural. At times, Poe assumes the role of the literary traveler—walking the streets, riding in boats, describing merchants' wares, remarking landmarks, deploring the noise and filth of the streets, critiquing architecture and city planning. He memorably offers the following advice to his readers, should they ever journey to the city: "When you visit Gotham, you should ride out the Fifth Avenue, as far as the distributing reservoir, near forty-third street, I believe. The prospect from the walk around the reservoir, is particularly beautiful. You can see, from this elevation, the north reservoir

Fig. 7.3 Broadway from the Bowling Green, 1848 (Harry Lee Poe Collection)

at Yorkville; the whole city to the battery; with a large portion of the harbor, and long reaches of the Hudson and East rivers."[12]

At other times, Poe delivers his opinions on the visual arts, local and national politics, corruption, "mob-disorder," celebrated trials, and, of course, writers and the publishing world. Rufus Griswold, in particular, suffers at the hands of Poe the critic, who as early as the mid-1830s was given the nickname the "tomahawk man" for the scathing reviews he published in the *Southern Literary Messenger*. In the sixth installment of *Doings in Gotham*, after mentioning that Griswold served for a time as the editor of *The Opal*, a holiday annual, Poe states, "By the way, if you have *not* seen Mr. Griswold's 'American Series of the Curiosities of Literature,' then look at it, for God's sake—or for mine. I wish you to say, upon your word of honor, whether it is, or is not, per se, the greatest of *all* the Curiosities of Literature, or whether it is as great a curiosity as the compiler himself."[13] Poe does not specify exactly what makes Griswold's American appendix to Isaac Disraeli's *Curiosities of Literature* so odd. On the one hand, some of its contents make fascinating reading even today, including a ballad entitled "Bold Hawthorne," which Griswold recovered and first reprinted in 1842, about the commander of the *Fair American*, "wounded in the head by a musket ball" while battling the British during the Revolutionary War, who was "an ancestor of the inimitable author, Nathaniel Hawthorne, of Salem."[14] On the other hand, "The Curiosities of American Literature" contains notable errors, such as the assertion that Anne Bradstreet's verse was first printed in the colonies in 1640.[15] Perhaps what may have irked Poe in particular was Griswold's decision, as he explains in "To the Reader," a Preface dated November 1843, "to exclude everything relating to contemporaries" from the "Curiosities."[16] As for Griswold's own eccentricities, Poe may have already divined these from his own dealings with the man, whom he first met in 1841, and the accounts of others.[17] In the seventh and final letter of *Doings*, Poe returns to the subject, dispelling any possible ambiguity his previous comments may have generated: "It is preposterous, also, to hear anything like commendation of that last and greatest of all absurdities, Griswold's Appendix to D'Israeli's 'Curiosities of Literature.'"[18]

Miscellaneous items in *Doings* often let readers in on subjects that relate in fascinating ways to Poe's own life and writings. In the first installment, he talks about the ongoing "bustle of the first of May," the date on which so many New Yorkers, particularly boarders like Poe and his family, move out of one place of residence and into another.[19] The third letter contrasts Edward Bulwer-Lytton's visit to the USA with that of Charles Dickens, whom Poe met in Philadelphia in 1842. In the fourth installment, he describes the sensation created by a "foot-race" watched by 11,000 people, yet is not impressed by the winner's time—"Touching the actual feat in question—ten miles within the hour—I have not only accomplished it myself, but firmly believe that there are at least one thousand men, in our western districts, who could perform, with proper training, *twelve*, with all ease."[20] The use of the esoteric word *porphyrogenitus*, which Poe translates as "born in the purple,"[21] in the opening paragraph of the series recalls his 1839 poem "The Haunted Palace," later incorporated into "The Fall of the House of Usher." References to detection, stereotomy (a type of pavement), Mary Rogers, and "gift-books" evoke the Dupin trilogy—"The Murders in the Rue Morgue," "The Mystery of Marie Rôget," and "The Purloined Letter." (The latter story was published in the *The Gift* for 1845, a volume that Poe predicts "will bear away the palm" among the Christmas annuals for that year.)[22] A long paragraph in the fourth installment about Antarctic exploration, which includes two mentions of "Reynolds," relates to his 1838 novel *The Narrative of Arthur Gordon Pym* (as well as to accounts of the supposed ravings of a delirious Poe while on his deathbed).[23] Moreover, Poe makes explicit reference to his own "Balloon Hoax," recently perpetrated in New York, which he compares and contrasts to Richard Adams Locke's earlier "Moon-Story," thereby anticipating his long discussion of Locke's hoax two years later in the final installment of the *Literati*.[24]

LETTING SOME SECRETS OF THE NEW YORK LITERATI OUT

Portraying himself as an insider lifting the veil to reveal what is really true about the New York literary scene by sharing what writers and editors actually say about their peers behind closed doors, Poe makes the outside–inside opposition that is implicit in *Doings* overt in the *Literati*. He asserts, "With one or two exceptions I am well acquainted with every author to be introduced, and shall avail myself of the acquaintance to convey, generally, some idea of the personal appearance of all who, in this regard, would be likely to interest the readers of the magazine."[25] In doing so, he further extends the binary, often criticizing the inaccuracy of official (public, outside) portraits, which he remedies by offering his own (private, inside) descriptions of people's physical characteristics. He explains that he limits himself to "New York literature" not because it is unique but rather because it "may be taken as a fair representation of that of the country at large. The city itself is the focus of American letters. Its authors include, perhaps, one-fourth of all in America," and their influence is "extensive and decisive."[26] Over a year previous to this, an anonymous New York *Evening Mirror* item entitled "Why Have the New Yorkers No Review?" that biographers have attributed to Poe, asserted, "We are the chief city in the Union in all respects, and in no respect more especially than in the number and eminence of our literary men—in the number and merit of the books they write."[27]

As J. Gerald Kennedy explains, Poe "was among the first to regard the republic of letters then emerging in the United States as a community imaginable across boundaries of region, party, and clique, and beyond differences of gender. His involvement in the magazine world and print culture [...] make him singularly representative of the practical realities of antebellum literary production."[28] In particular, as Kennedy goes on to state, "his various efforts to construct an idea of the literary nation and to install himself as critical kingpin, comprise an illuminating yet largely unappreciated dimension of Poe's achievement."[29] Just as Poe intended to incorporate the *Literati* into his subsequent unrealized projects, *The Living Writers of America* and *Literary America*, the origins of the 1846 *Godey's* series, as Kennedy convincingly argues, can be traced back to his series on "Autography" in the *Southern Literary Messenger* in 1836, a project he would resurrect and significantly expand in *Graham's Magazine* in 1841 and which, along with the *Literati* and other similar projects, complemented his long-term effort to found his own journal devoted to the productions of prominent writers from across the USA.

Given Kennedy's exhaustive efforts to enumerate Poe's multiple endeavors to map American literature and publishing in the antebellum USA, it is surprising that he makes no mention of Poe's extensive review of *The Complete Poetical Works of William Cullen Bryant*, published in *Godey's* the month before the start of the *Literati*. Poe refers to this critique in the opening sentence of the series: "In a criticism on Bryant published in the last number of this magazine, I was at some pains in pointing out the distinction between popular 'opinion' of the merits of contemporary authors and that held and expressed of them in private literary society."[30] Even though it was not officially part of the series that began in *Godey's* in May, Poe saw his April review as a key precursor to the *Literati* and an integral part of his larger project to chart the Republic of Letters because of Bryant's well-established position in the New York publishing world as both one of the nation's most lauded poets and the editor of the *New York Evening Post*.

In the Bryant review, Poe adopts the pose of a literary (and New York) insider. Speaking of members of "private literary circles," he states,

> The fact is, that when brought face to face with each other we are constrained to a certain amount of honesty by the sheer trouble it causes us to mould [*sic*] the countenance to a lie. We put on paper with a grave air what we could not for our lives assert personally to a friend without either blushing or laughing outright. That the opinion of the press is not an honest opinion, that necessarily it is impossible that it should be an honest opinion, is never denied by the members of the press themselves.[31]

The next month in the initial installment of the *Literati*, he returns to this subject:

But the very editors who hesitate at saying in print an ill word of an author personally known, are usually the most frank in speaking about him privately. In literary society, they seem bent upon avenging the wrongs self-inflicted upon their own consciences. Here, accordingly, the quack is treated as he deserves—even a little more harshly than he deserves—by way of striking a balance. True merit, on the same principle, is apt to be slightly overrated; but, upon the whole, there is a close approximation to absolute honesty of opinion.[32]

As a result of this private veracity and public dishonesty, "The most 'popular,' the most 'successful' writers among us, (for a brief period, at least,) are, ninety-nine times out of a hundred, persons of mere address, perseverance, effrontery—in a word, busy-bodies, toadies, quacks"; meanwhile, "men of genius," who refuse to "resort to these manoeuvers," struggle "because genius involves in its very essence a scorn of chicanery."[33] After repeating almost verbatim what he says about lying, blushing, and laughing outright in the Bryant review, he proceeds to contrast the reputations of Nathaniel Hawthorne and Henry Wadsworth Longfellow in order to illustrate the "very remarkable discrepancy between the apparent public opinion of any given author's merits and the opinion which is expressed of him orally by those who are best qualified to judge." The former, a "poor man," who is not a "ubiquitous quack," "is scarcely recognized by the press or by the public, and when noticed at all, is noticed merely to be damned by faint praise," even though his "extraordinary genius" has "no rival either in America or elsewhere."[34] In contrast, popular opinion regards the latter, "a man of property and a professor at Harvard" as "a poetical phenomenon, as entirely without fault as is the luxurious paper upon which his poems" are printed, yet in "private society he is regarded [...] as a determined imitator and dexterous adapter of the ideas of other people."[35] Poe implicitly associates himself with Hawthorne, a "poor devil author" at the mercy of the "fat," "pursy 'editor[s]'" and "bottle-nosed 'proprietor[s]'" he describes in "Some Secrets of the Magazine Prison-House."[36] In the *Godey's* series, Poe delivers on his promise to provide two types of often conflicting inside information—his "own unbiased opinion of the *literati* (male and female) of New York" and that of "conversational society in literary circles."[37] In the six installments, he profiles thirty-seven authors and editors, including Willis, Evert Duyckinck,

Margaret Fuller, Lydia Maria Child, and Catherine Sedgwick. Some of these figures he flatters, some he ridicules, and others he analyzes extensively and meticulously. Along the way, he often lashes out at Bostonians, particularly the Transcendentalists, and, once again, raises questions about the editorial choices and critical assessments of Rufus Griswold, who would exact a notorious revenge on Poe for this and other actual and perceived slights. Poe refers to Griswold by name seven times in the *Literati*, sometimes noting his errors, sometimes indirectly criticizing him, and sometimes openly questioning his judgment. In the section on James Aldrich in the third installment, after mentioning that "three, (or four,)" of Aldrich's poems appeared in Griswold's *The Poets and Poetry of America*, Poe accuses the poet of plagiarizing Thomas Hood, implicitly chiding Griswold for including the poems in his collection.[38] In the Henry Cary section in the same installment, Poe skewers Griswold, Charles F. Briggs (his one-time co-editor and co-proprietor at the *Broadway Journal*), and Cary himself. The article begins by noting Griswold's inaccuracies: "Doctor Griswold introduces *Mr. Cary* to the appendix of 'The Poet [sic] and Poetry,' as Mr. Henry Carey, and gives him credit for an Anacreontic song of much merit entitled, or commencing, 'Old Wine to Drink.' This was *not* written by Mr. C. He has composed little verse, if any, but, under the *nom de plume* of 'John Waters,' has acquired some note by a series of essays in 'The New York American' and 'The Knickerbocker.'"[39] Poe upbraids Briggs at considerable length for overpraising Cary, whom Poe judges to be a "fifth or sixth rate" essayist. Echoing his September 1845 *Marginalia* item, Poe faults Briggs and Griswold for promoting businessmen who dabble in literature: "Mr. Cary is what Doctor Griswold calls a 'gentleman of elegant leisure.' He is wealthy and much addicted to letters and *virtû*. For a long time, he was President of the Phoenix Bank of New York, and the principal part of his life has been devoted to business."[40]

In the initial section of Part V of the *Literati* devoted to Charles Fenno Hoffman, Poe once more deplores the tendency of critics to overpraise authors, and he accuses Griswold of indulging in crude favoritism: "Whatever may be the merits of Mr. Hoffman as a poet, it may be easily seen that these merits have been put in the worst possible light by the indiscriminate and lavish approbation bestowed on them by Doctor Griswold in his 'Poets and Poetry of America.' The compiler can find *no* blemish in Mr. H., agrees with everything and copies everything said in his praise—worse than all, gives him more space in the book than any two, or perhaps three, of our poets combined. All this is as much an insult to Mr. Hoffman as to the public, and has done the former irreparable injury—how or why, it is of course unnecessary to say."[41] In the opening section of the fourth installment, on Sarah Margaret Fuller, Poe again evokes Griswold's "Curiosities": "'Woman in the Nineteenth Century' is a book which few women in the country could have written, and no woman in the country would have published, with the exception of Miss Fuller. In the way of independence, or unmitigated radicalism, it is one of the 'Curiosities of American Literature,' and Doctor Griswold should include it in his book." Poe acclaims Fuller, whom he regards as the antithesis of dilettantes such as Cary, because of her "genius (for high genius she unquestionably possesses)."[42] Poe implies that just as Griswold missed Aldrich's plagiarisms, puffs amateurs like Cary, and allows bias to dictate his editorial decisions, he lacks the ability to recognize true genius such as Fuller's.[43]

Similar to *Doings*, Poe does not hesitate to make several explicit and covert references to himself in the *Literati*, ranging from the increase in circulation he effected at the *Southern Literary Messenger* to items he published in the *Broadway Journal* and *Godey's* to a facetious offer to forgive to Lewis Gaylord Clark for reviewing *The Raven and Other Poems*. Although the controversial nature of the *Literati* made it quite popular, the series did nothing to change Poe's marginal position in the New York publishing world; rather, it led to counterattacks and even a protracted libel suit Poe brought against the New York *Evening Mirror*.

INSIDE AND OUT: RIVALRIES AND REVENGE IN "THE CASK OF AMONTILLADO"

Just as the Bryant review, published in the April 1846 issue of *Godey's*, serves as a kind of preface to the six installments of the *Literati*, "The Cask of Amontillado," which appeared in the November issue of the magazine, might be regarded as a fictional epilogue to the series. In the tale, a man of French descent living in Italy recounts how fifty years earlier he exacted revenge on Fortunato, an Italian. A "quack" in his knowledge of "painting and gemmary," Fortunato takes pride in "his connoisseurship in wine," as does Montresor himself (M I:346). As he lures his foe to the fatal crypt, their conversation indicates Montresor's status as an outsider. Referring to the possible ill effects of the damp, nitre-encrusted catacombs on their physical well-beings, he contrasts himself with the popular, contented Fortunato: "You are rich, respected, admired, beloved; you are happy, as once I was. You are a man to be missed. For me it is no matter" (M I:348). Moreover, when Fortunato makes a gesture that Montresor does not comprehend, the former declares, "Then you are not of the brotherhood," referring to the Masons, a secret society to which he does and Montresor does not belong. Choosing carnival season so that both he and Fortunato are in disguise and ensuring that his servants are out of the house, Montresor uses a pipe of Amontillado as the MacGuffin to lead his enemy first into his family's catacombs, then inside "a deep crypt" in which there is an "interior crypt," which itself has "a still interior recess" that "seemed to have been constructed for no especial use within itself." When his victim enters this innermost crypt following his declaration, "herein is the Amontillado," Montresor chains Fortunato to the back of this "niche" and walls up the "figure within" (M I:349, 350, 351). Thus, in achieving his vengeance, Montresor transforms his enemy from a social insider into a literal one.

Since 1934 when *American Literature* published Joseph Schick's article on the subject, scholars have acknowledged the striking similarities between "Cask" and "A Man Built in a Wall," an account of an upright skeleton J. T. Headley saw in a church south of Florence in 1843.[44] Prompted by the claim of a physician accompanying him that the cause of death was suffocation, Headley tells a tale of vengeance in which the man was sealed alive behind the wall as his bitter enemy looked on. Although other sources have been proposed as the inspiration for Poe's story, none resembles it as closely as "A Man Built in a Wall." Like Poe, Headley asserts that the victim and the man responsible for his live burial were "men of rank," claims that the latter "stood leaning on his sword—a smile of scorn and revenge on his features—and watched the face of the man he hated," details the walling up of the immobilized victim tier by tier by a mason using a trowel, emphasizes the placing of the final stone to complete the entombment, and alludes to the death of the killer many years after he committed the murder. Additionally, to underscore the excruciating nature of the means by which the man died, Headley twice uses the phrase "At length,"[45] the same words Poe italicizes at the start of the third sentence of his story when Montresor states, "*At length*, I would be avenged" (M I:346).

Surprisingly, no Poe scholar has ever, apparently, attempted to establish the veracity of Headley's story. Had such a person done so, he or she would have discovered not the "skeleton" Headley writes about but a mummy known locally as *l'uomo murato* (the walled man). Wally, as I'll refer to him, was found when some repairs were undertaken in the Church of San Lorenzo in San Giovanni Valdarno in 1780 and was put on semi-public display there in 1820. He has been the subject of articles in history books, scholarly journals, and local magazines, is mentioned on several travel websites, and can even be seen in a three-minute YouTube video.[46] The 1843 edition of the *Handbook for Travellers in Central Italy*, which Headley almost certainly read, contains a brief description of Wally. Likely because of the stature Headley had achieved as a writer in the interim, the 1850 edition of the same guidebook quotes "A Man Built in a Wall" extensively, presenting it as if it were historical fact.[47]

A travel and nature writer, popular historian, and politician, Joel Tyler Headley (1813–1897) earned a divinity degree and briefly served as a minister in Stockbridge, Massachusetts, before suffering a breakdown in 1842, which led to his embarking on a long European tour. In 1843 and 1844, the *New York Tribune* published twenty-seven of his "Letters from Italy." In 1844, twenty-two of Headley's letters were published in the 64-page *Italy and the Italians*. Neither the *Tribune* series nor *Italy and the Italians* included "A Man Built in a Wall," which first appeared in the August 1844 issue of the *Columbian Magazine*, the same issue in which Poe's "Mesmeric Revelations" was published. From that point on, Headley became increasingly visible in the New York publishing world. Late June 1845 saw the appearance of Headley's 224-page *Letters from Italy*, containing forty-nine letters, the thirty-ninth of which was "A Man Built in a Wall." The book sold well and garnered considerable and mostly favorable critical attention, with some of the reviewers commenting specifically on "A Man Built in a Wall." In connection with the publication of *Letters from Italy*, the weekly *New York Mirror* printed "A Man in Built in a Wall" in its July 12, 1845 issue. In spring 1846, Baker and Scribner brought out Headley's initial foray into popular history and the firm's first best seller, *Napoleon and His Marshalls*, which was so successful that by 1861 it was in its fiftieth printing. The book received long, mostly positive reviews in the leading newspapers and journals of the day. Indicating the reputation that he had achieved by that time, in September 1846 Baker and Scribner published notices in the *Tribune* stating that Headley's *The Sacred Mountains* would be published in early October as an elaborately engraved gift book. It was the period from mid-1844, when "A Man Built in a Wall" was first published, through fall 1846, when *The Sacred Mountains* appeared, that transformed

Headley from a fledgling writer into a literary star (and by 1853, he had sold an astounding number of books—over 200,000 copies).[48] As noted earlier, these two and a half years would be pivotal and remarkably productive for Poe as well, although 1846, Headley's banner year, was Poe's *annus horribilis*.

Between 1844 and 1846, there were numerous connections between Poe and Headley. In 1845, Evert Duyckinck, who corresponded with both men, edited and actively promoted two books by each writer in the Library of America series. Moreover, that same year Poe reviewed Headley's books positively in the *Broadway Journal*. His assessment of *Letters from Italy*, in fact, explicitly mentions the "Man in the Wall" but does not comment further on it.[49] Anne C. Lynch attested that Poe and Headley attended a party she hosted in January 1846, and three and a half months later, Poe asked Duyckinck to supply him with the autographs of several authors, including Headley, indicating the intention to write something about him (PL 619–620; O I:570). Another key link between the men, hitherto unnoticed by scholars, concerns the commencement exercises held at the University of Vermont in August 1846. In April, Poe was invited to serve as commencement poet, an offer he declined, citing "engagements" and "ill health." When Duyckinck loyally complied with Poe's request that he publicize this honor, getting a brief notice about the university's invitation printed on the second page of the 1 May issue of the *Tribune* (O I:569–570; PL 637–638), it was overshadowed by Margaret Fuller's lengthy page one review of the initial volume of *Napoleon and His Marshalls*. Three months later, on 8 August, the front page of the *Tribune* featured a glowing account of the address Headley had delivered at the University of Vermont four days earlier.[50] Perhaps not coincidentally, in a letter to Philip Pendleton Cooke dated the very next day, Poe discusses his renewed plans for establishing the *Stylus*, "a journal in which the men of genius may fight their battles; upon some terms of equality, with those dunces the men of talent" (O I:597).

The clearest link between Poe and Headley has always been the former's savagely funny, posthumously published review of the *Sacred Mountains*, which appeared under the title "Joel T. Headley" at roughly the same time in the *Southern Literary Messenger* and the third volume of *The Works of the Late Edgar Allan Poe*. It describes Headley as the "Autocrat of all the Quacks" and asserts that "the thing he 'does' especially well is the public."[51] Many scholars have accepted Griswold's contention that "Joel T. Headley" was directly connected with the larger Literati project on which Poe was at work during his final years, even though the piece in question is clearly a review as opposed to a wide-ranging evaluation of a writer's life and career, which is the way Poe conceived of the installments of the Literati series. Because much of *The Sacred Mountains* was published in the *New York Observer* in the spring of 1846 while Poe was at work on the New York Literati series and the book itself appeared in print in early October of that year, I suspect that Poe wrote the review of Headley's book sometime in the fall of 1846, perhaps trying and failing to place it in a periodical or deciding for some reason not to publish it. If this is correct, then it is likely that Poe wrote the *Sacred Mountains* review within a few months or even weeks of composing "Cask," which was available to the public when the November issue of *Godey's* went on sale on October 20. Poe's statements about the "Living Writers of America," one of the names for the larger Literati project, bolster this argument. In his December 16, 1846 letter to George Eveleth, Poe says that in the "Living Writers" he will address "Historical Writing," very likely a reference to Headley (O I:602). Moreover, in his manuscript for the "Living Writers," which contains nothing to indicate that it was written after 1846, Poe devotes a paragraph to Headley, signaling his plan to include an article about him in the series.[52]

In asserting that Poe's story was to some extent a response not simply to "A Man Built in a Wall" but also to the meteoric trajectory of Headley's career, I do not mean to suggest that he regarded this incredibly prolific author as an enemy who had done him an evil turn in the way that critics such as Francis Dedmond see Poe using "Cask" to settle scores with the writer Thomas Dunn English and the editor Hiram Fuller, key figures in the aforementioned libel suit.[53] Rather, because wherever he looked in 1846 Headley was in (and Poe was out)—in New York dailies, in the pages of leading journals, and even in the ceremonies at the University of Vermont—he may have regarded Headley as epitomizing "those dunces the men of talent" (i.e. the "quacks"), who, in stark contrast to Poe, a writer "of genius," undeservedly enjoyed financial success and public acclaim. Thus, Headley, for Poe, may have represented fortune's favorite—that is, Fortunato—someone "respected, admired, beloved, [...] happy [...] a man to be missed," as Poe once was. What better way to get vengeance not on Headley per se but instead on fate itself than to use the semi-fictional sketch about Italy, "A Man Built in a Wall," by this exceedingly verbose writer (whom undiscriminating critics and the fickle public had anointed that year's literary celebrity) as the basis for a true work of art, a remarkably concise tale of incredible power with an Italian setting?

"The Cask of Amontillado" reflects Poe's experiences in New York in a variety of ways. On one level, he likely identified with the outsider Montresor's desire to obtain revenge on one of fortune's favorites, the "quacks" and "dunces the men of talent" who thrived in the antebellum publishing world. A key critical question about "Cask" concerns who gets the last laugh—Montresor or Fortunato. Poe may have enjoyed the first chuckle in writing the story—and in penning his hilarious assessment of *The Sacred Mountains* shortly thereafter. However, by the time the review appeared in print in 1850, the popular, successful, respected insider Headley, who would hike in the Berkshires with Hawthorne and Herman Melville in August of that year, could easily laugh off this attack from an outsider who had self-destructed so infamously and was the ongoing subject of one of the most vicious character assassinations in literary history, perpetrated by Rufus Griswold. Yet 170 years later it is Poe—or, if not Poe, then Literature itself—that has come out on top. The only reason anyone remembers Headley at all today is that his "A Man Built in a Wall" served as a key source for one of the most memorable and most carefully constructed tales by an undisputed master of the short story form. On a different level, as someone thoroughly familiar with the cutthroat world of literary publishing, someone with a love for a good joke, and someone willing to share the inside dope no matter what the cost to himself, Poe quite plausibly identified with the insensitive, carefree, (and inebriated) insider Fortunato in opposition to humorless, deceitful, distrusted, and vindictive Montresor-like men such as Griswold. However, on yet another level, Poe had to know that he himself, an insider and an outsider—and not English, Fuller, Griswold, Headley or anyone else— was often his own worst enemy. Throughout his career, but especially in 1845 and 1846, Poe's inability to refrain from attacking people kept hurrying him to his destruction. And how can we imagine that the author of "The Imp of the Perverse," published in the summer of 1845 and addressing this very subject, was not acutely aware of this?

Conclusion

Only an insider and an outsider could have produced both *Doings in Gotham* and *The Literati of New York City*. In the former, having recently returned to the city after a six-year absence, Poe the non-native noted how drastically things had changed and was able to predict accurately how rapidly they would continue to do so in New York. Moreover, with considerable experience as not only an editor for several magazines (and even, briefly, the proprietor of a doomed one) but also a "poor devil" author, Poe uniquely had the inside knowledge—as well as the temerity—to publish the "honest opinions" of the latter series. Similarly, what makes several of Poe's stories, foremost among them "The Cask of Amontillado" (which followed immediately on the *Literati*'s heels), so fascinating is that they can be convincingly interpreted in at least two (often diametrically opposed) ways. One group of critics has read this tale as a story about a man who plans and successfully executes the perfect act of revenge, and thus they regard Montresor as a reliable narrator. Meanwhile, an opposing critical camp views Montresor, like other narrators in the writer's most famous tales, as unreliable and unsuccessful in punishing his foe "with impunity." Relating "The Cask of Amontillado" to Poe's experiences as a New York outsider and insider, we can profitably read him as Montresor, as Fortunato, and as both Montresor *and* Fortunato.

NOTES

1. Kevin J. Hayes, *Poe and the Printed Word* (New York: Cambridge University Press, 2004), 56.
2. Poe states in the first letter of *Doings in Gotham* (May 18, 1844): 3, "Business has experienced a thorough revival, and 'all goes merry as a marriage bell,'" indicating that, after seven years, New York had finally emerged from the doldrums caused by the Panic of 1837.
3. Between *Doings* and the *Literati*, Poe began another nonfiction series, *Marginalia*, in which he emphasizes that these "scribblings," as he calls them, appear inside of a book but outside of its margins, the book itself providing both the text and the context for each musing although Poe often does not identify into which books he supposedly inscribed these jottings, thereby taking them out of their text and context. "*Marginalia*," *United States Magazine and Democratic Review* (November 1844), 485.
4. "Some Secrets of the Magazine Prison-House," *Broadway Journal* (February 15, 1845): 103.
5. "Marginal Notes.—No. II," *Godey's Lady's Book* (September 1845): 121.
6. Scott Peeples, "'To Reproduce a City': New York Letters and the Urban American Renaissance," in *Poe and the Remapping of Antebellum Print*

Culture, eds. J. Gerald Kennedy and Jerome McGann (Baton Rouge: Louisiana State University Press, 2012), 118.

7. *Doings in Gotham, Columbia Spy* (May 18, 1844): 3.

8. Ibid.

9. Peeples, 111.

10. *Doings in Gotham, Columbia Spy* (May 18, 1844): 3.

11. *Doings in Gotham, Columbia Spy* (June 15, 1844): 3; *Columbia Spy* (June 29, 1844): 3; *Columbia Spy* (June 1, 1844): 3; *Columbia Spy* (June 29, 1844): 3.

12. *Doings in Gotham, Columbia Spy* (June 1, 1844): 3.

13. *Doings in Gotham, Columbia Spy* (June 29, 1844): 3.

14. Rufus W. Griswold, "Curiosities of American Literature," in *Curiosities of Literature, and the Literary Character Illustrated, with Curiosities of American Literature*, ed. I. C. D'Israeli (New York: D. Appleton & Co., 1846), 37–38. Hathorne (1731–1796) engaged the British off the coast of Portugal in 1777.

15. Bradstreet's first book of poems appeared in London in 1650. An expanded collection of her poems was published posthumously in Boston in 1678.

16. Griswold, 2.

17. For an overview of the relationship between the two men, see the "Edgar Allan Poe and Rufus Wilmot Griswold" page of the E. A. Poe Society of Baltimore's website, http://www.eapoe.org/geninfo/poegrisw.htm.

18. *Doings in Gotham, Columbia Spy* (July 6, 1844): 3.

19. *Doings in Gotham, Columbia Spy* (May 18, 1844): 3.

20. *Doings in Gotham, Columbia Spy* (June 8, 1844): 3.

21. *Doings in Gotham, Columbia Spy* (May 18, 1844): 3.

22. *Doings in Gotham, Columbia Spy* (June 29, 1844): 3.

23. *Doings in Gotham, Columbia Spy* (June 8, 1844): 3.

24. Ibid.

25. *The Literati of New York City* [Part 1], *Godey's Lady's Book* (May 1846): 195.

26. Ibid.

27. "Why Have the New Yorkers No Review?" *Evening Mirror* (New York) (January 8, 1845): 2.

28. J. Gerald Kennedy, Introduction in *Poe and the Remapping of Antebellum Print Culture*, 9.

29. J. Gerald Kennedy, "Inventing the Literati: Poe's Remapping of Antebellum Print Culture," in *Poe and the Remapping of Antebellum Print Culture*, 13.

30. *The Literati of New York City* [Part 1], 194.

31. Edgar A. Poe, "Literary Criticism," *Godey's Lady's Book* (April 1845): 182.

32. *The Literati of New York City* [Part 1], 194.
33. Ibid.
34. Ibid.
35. Ibid., 194–195.
36. "Some Secrets of the Magazine Prison-House," 104. In the *Literati* and elsewhere, as Maurice S. Lee remarks, Poe "presents himself as both a maven and a victim of print culture. On the one hand, he displays an insider's knowledge of the personal habits of writers and editors and the secret practices of the literary establishment. On the other hand, he presents himself as an outsider--objective, independent, and persecuted." See Lee's "Poe by the Numbers: Odd Man Out?" *Poe and the Remapping of Antebellum Print Culture*, 233.
37. *The Literati of New York City* [Part 1], 195. In a 15 December 1846 letter to George Eveleth, Poe asserts that in the *Literati* he "had no other design than critical *gossip*" in *The Collected Letters of Edgar Allan Poe*, 2 vols. ed. John Ward Ostrom, 3rd rev. ed. (New York: Gordian Press, 2008).
38. *The Literati of New York City* [Part 3], *Godey's Lady's Book* (July 1846): 16.
39. Ibid., 18.
40. Ibid.
41. *The Literati of New York City* [Part 6], *Godey's Lady's Book* (October 1846): 157–158.
42. *The Literati of New York City* [Part 4], *Godey's Lady's Book* (August 1846): 72.
43. Poe also mentions Griswold in the Elizabeth Bogart section of Part 5 of the *Literati* (*Godey's Lady's Book*, September 1846, 130).
44. Joseph Schick, "The Origin of the Cask of Amontillado," *American Literature* 6 (March 1934): 18–21.
45. J. T. Headley, *Letters from Italy* (London: Wiley and Putnam, 1845), 193–195.
46. Simonetta Berbeglia, "L'uomo murato' in San Lorenzo nei racconti dei viaggiatori stranieri," *Memorie Valdarnesi* 172 (2007): 147–156; *L'enigma della "mummia*,"" Valdarnotizie.com, http://www.valdarnotizie.com/attualita/lenigma-della-mummia, July 6, 2011; *La leggenda dell'uomo murato a San Giovanni*, YouTube video, https://www.youtube.com/watch?v=BA_B3W9HI7s, March 30, 2010. I am not the first person to connect *l'uomo murato* to "The Cask Amontillado." Simonetta Berbeglia does so in passing in a 2010 article concerning a lost poem that Robert Browning wrote about Wally in the 1840s or 1850s, "A Skeleton in the Wall: Robert Browning's Italian Story," *Journal of Browning Studies* 1 (February 2010): 70–79, 104.
47. *Handbook for Travellers in Central Italy* (London: John Murray, 1843), 206; Octavian Blewitt, *Handbook for Travellers in Central Italy*, 2nd ed. (London: John Murray, 1850), 236–237.

48. Writers' Program of the Works Projects Administration in the State of New York, *New York: A Guide to the Empire State* (New York: Oxford University Press, 1940), 147. For several months during 1847, Headley engaged in a public battle with Rufus Griswold arising from competing books about George Washington and his generals prepared by the two men, a feud Headley effectively won when the *New York Daily Tribune* printed a letter in which he declared, "I should not have taken the trouble to contradict the ridiculous accusations he made, if your paper had been confined to the city where he is understood. A man to whom even his friends have been accustomed to say, 'is that a Griswold or a fact,' I can well let pass where he is known, but in other parts of the country where *The Tribune* circulates, people are not well acquainted with matters." See Headley's Letter to the Editor, *New York Daily Tribune* (November 11, 1847): 2, and Joy Bayless, *Rufus Wilmot Griswold* (Nashville: Vanderbilt University Press, 1949), 132–136.

49. Edgar Allan Poe, review of *Letters from Italy*, by Joel T. Headley, *Broadway Journal* (August 9, 1845): 75.

50. "City Items," *New York Daily Tribune* (May 1, 1846): 2; [Margaret Fuller], "Headley's Napoleon," *New York Daily Tribune* (May 1, 1846): 1; "Vermont University Commencement—Rev. J. T. Headley's Address," *New York Daily Tribune* (August 8, 1846): 1.

51. "Poe on Headley and Channing," *Southern Literary Messenger* (October 1850): 610.

52. "Text: Edgar Allan Poe, 'The Living Writers of America,' (A), Manuscript, 1846–47," E. A. Poe Society of Baltimore, http://www.eapoe.org/works/misc/livingw.htm, May 16, 2014.

53. Francis B. Dedmond, "'The Cask of Amontillado' and the War of the Literati," *Modern Language Notes* 15 (1954): 137–146.

PART III

Imaginative Spaces

CHAPTER 8

Fantastic Places, Angelic Spaces

William E. Engel

Picturing Angels

Ah, distinctly I remember it was in the bleak December,
And each separate dying ember wrought its ghost upon the floor.
Eagerly I wished the morrow; — vainly I had tried to borrow
From my books surcease of sorrow — sorrow for the lost Lenore —
For the rare and radiant maiden whom the angels name Lenore —
Nameless here for evermore. (ll.7–12)[1]

The second stanza of "The Raven" identifies the grieving speaker's beloved by what amounts to her angel name. Only angels can invoke her now, posthumously, as she is no longer here—but there, among angels: "Nameless here for evermore." What is the nature of these angels?

A preliminary draft of this essay was presented at the "SymPOEsium on Place" at Middle Tennessee State University on April 8, 2015. Taking into account the variants in Poe's published works quotations follow whichever version or edition was judged to be the most apt relative to the point being made and will be duly cited.

W. E. Engel (✉)
The University of the South, Sewanee, TN, USA

© The Author(s) 2018   169
P. E. Phillips (ed.), *Poe and Place*,
Geocriticism and Spatial Literary Studies,
https://doi.org/10.1007/978-3-319-96788-2_8

Where do they abide when not "here," naming this "rare and radiant maiden"? Will the speaker eventually rejoin her; and, if so, then where? This latter consideration is reiterated in his last-ditch, desperate appeal to the bird to confirm whether "within this distant Aidenn" he might at last "clasp a sainted maiden whom the angels name Lenore" (l.94). Edgar A. Poe's choice of this unusual spelling of *Aiden*, the Arabic word for Eden,[2] seems to have had a special meaning for him as he uses it elsewhere, most tellingly in his angelic dialogues, "The Conversation of Eiros and Charmion" and "The Power of Words." A chilling poetic effect is created by the ambiguity regarding the status of these angels whose presence is palpable throughout "The Raven." It is augmented further by the intimated Arabesque features of Lenore's destination, as well as by the chiastic resonance activated by Poe's deliberate verbal echoing of the opening and closing stanzas. The underlying intent of Poe's careful arrangement of setting, tone, and sonic effects, however, is undermined wholly by the commercial interests of later illustrators, most notably Gustave Doré (1832–1883)[3] (Fig. 8.1).

Despite Doré's fertile imagination and dogged insistence on tackling this text notwithstanding his failing health,[4] the angels represented in his deluxe version of *The Raven* (first published 1884, posthumously) are indistinguishable from those that previously had populated his versions of Milton's *Paradise Lost* (1866) and Dante's *Purgatorio* and *Paradiso* (1887).[5] His conception of the angelic was consonant with that of the Pre-Raphaelites, seen, for example, in the work of Edward Burne-Jones[6] (Fig. 8.2). Such imagery can be traced back to Attic-Greek vase paintings of Eos, goddess of dawn, depicted as a beautiful woman with dove wings. This classical way of representing and alluding to a host of deities was adopted in early Christian art to denote the angelic,[7] a visual shorthand that persists to this day in the Western visual imagination.[8]

Accordingly, Doré's angels are associated with things at once aethereal and divine (hence their wings), executing God's will—whether battling Lucifer's rebel angels (who are differentiated from the heavenly host by their leathery, pointed bat wings) or encircling the Mystic Rose—and wear diaphanous robes of a generic, indeterminate classical style. Such imagery has come to be associated with the Romantic era's depiction of angels on tombs,[9] holiday greeting cards, and in Bible illustrations. In fact, among Doré's greatest accomplishments was his 1866 Bible, which included his much-copied image of "Jacob Wrestling with the Angel" (1855) depicting a masculine version of the typical nineteenth-century angel[10] (Fig. 8.3). The angels in Doré's *Raven*, though, are distinctively

Fig. 8.1 Gustave Doré, "Nameless here Forevermore," *The Raven* (New York: Harper Brothers, 1884), 41; engraved by Fredrick Juengling (Newberry Library, Chicago)

Fig. 8.2 Edward Burne-Jones, "Angel Playing a Flageolet" (1878), Sudley House, Liverpool; Accession No: WAG 192

feminine throughout, making them something of a welcoming sister-hood enfolding Lenore into their ranks (see again Fig. 8.1). This gives a hint of consolation and a prospective happy ending to the story that by no means is self-evident in the poem. For it is precisely this space

Fig. 8.3 Gustave Doré, "Jacob Wrestling with the Angel" (1855), engraved by C. Laplante, reissued in *The Bible* (London: Cassell & Co, 1866), Gen. 32B (Newberry Library, Chicago)

between an expression of hope for an afterlife and an acknowledgment of the finality of death that characterizes the tension upon which Poe relied to consolidate and convey the poem's unsettling melancholy resonance.[11]

Having a triumphant choir of angels is consistent with Doré's approach, but it is not in keeping with the affective tenor and narrative arc of Poe's "The Raven." Doré's capacity to produce the kinds of images his audience wanted to see (such as benign, unthreateningly familiar angels) contributed to his being one of the most successful, prolific, and frequently imitated book-illustrators of the late nineteenth century.[12] He took the unknown and brought it comfortably within the scope of the known. Again, this is antithetical to Poe's craft that so often, especially through his use of the figure of the doppelgänger (in works ranging from "William Wilson" to "Liegia"), enabled him to create a sense of productive frisson between what we think we know and the uncanny.[13]

Angels in Poe are not the smiling cherubim of the Romantic popular imagination, strumming harps and singing hosannas. There is a salient difference in kind, not simply in degree, between Poe's references to angels as a comparative rhetorical trope (e.g., in "Annabel Lee"[14]) and when they are figured as mouthpieces to play out his ideas concerning cosmology and metaphysics (most especially in "The Power of Words," "Eiros and Charmion," and *Eureka*). As Charles A. Huttar has suggestively observed: "On the surface Poe's angels are fairly traditional, though with some teasing heterodox twists."[15] What then was at stake in Poe's choice to break with or twist free from orthodox tradition and give his readers some other version of the angelic, something hailing from "Aidenn," something that is not registered in the period's engravings? By way of answering this, let us consider first the characteristic features and essential nature of Poe's angels so as to examine his rationale for setting them up as he does. The underlying metaphysics of Poe's fantastic places inhabited by angels thereby will come into focus and reveal a fundamental element in the larger scheme of his literary lifework.

PLACING POE'S ANGELS

John Milton, to whom Poe was indebted at least for some turns of phrase in works such as "Al Aaraaf,"[16] was at pains to describe angelic intelligence insofar as it served the Reformed Christian framework of *Paradise Lost*.[17] Poe, although not at all bound to the religious sense of purpose driving Milton's expository dialogues between Raphael and

Adam (*Paradise Lost*, Books V and VIII), still was drawn to this pattern of Socratic discourse between one who knows and one seeking to know more. And yet when Poe's angels speak, they speak to one another—not to mortals. A fairly consistent perspective emerges concerning Poe's angels (what they are, where the dwell, and the range and limitations of their powers) when we look at how they operate in several key texts. As Poe's sophisticated if syncretic view of the cosmos comes into focus, so does his intellectual affinity for speculative description, especially as regards thresholds of human experience and the limits and liberties of mortal thought.

In the colloquy between the fledgling Oinos and more seasoned Agathos in "The Power of Words" (as in his two other Socratic dialogues involving celestial spirits), it is clear that angels, in fact, age and are capable of acquiring further knowledge while filling in gaps about the past. Poe's angels exist in a temporal continuum similar to that experienced by ordinary mortals; they have recollections of having once lived—and died. For example, Charmion instructs the bewildered Eiros saying: "It is now ten earthly years since I underwent what you undergo—yet the remembrance of it hangs by me still. You have suffered all of pain, however, which you will suffer in Aidenn."[18] So too Una, "born again," responds to Monos's explanation: "In Death we have both learned the propensity of man to define the indefinable."[19] The existence and place of Poe's angelic spirits are conditioned by a principle of extension,[20] especially as regards the notion of a timeline that approaches timelessness and which thus confounds our usual points of reference. They are figured as aethereal, disembodied entities, but who are still able to speak—the reverse of the problem of M. Valdemar, who can utter words once dead but does so from a body that otherwise has ceased to function.[21] The entities that we find *in medias res* in "The Power of Words" seemingly are more evolved versions of humans insofar as they retain their recollections of the world if only to comment on how facile and incomplete their apprehension of such things once was.

> *Oinos*: Pardon, Agathos, the weakness of a spirit new-fledged with immortality!
>
> *Agathos*: You have spoken nothing, my Oinos, for which pardon is to be demanded. Not even here is knowledge a thing of intuition. For wisdom, ask of the angels freely, that it may be given!
>
> *Oinos*: But in this existence, I dreamed that I should be at once cognizant of all things, and thus at once happy in being cognizant of all.

Agathos: Ah, not in knowledge is happiness, but in the acquisition of knowledge! In for ever knowing, we are for ever blessed; but to know all, were the curse of a fiend.

Oinos: But does not The Most High know all?

Agathos: *That* (since he is The Most Happy) must be still the *one* thing unknown even to HIM.

Oinos: But, since we grow hourly in knowledge, must not *at last* all things be known?

Agathos: Look down into the abysmal distances! — attempt to force the gaze down the multitudinous vistas of the stars, as we sweep slowly through them thus — and thus — and thus! Even the spiritual vision, is it not at all points arrested by the continuous golden walls of the universe? — the walls of the myriads of the shining bodies that mere number has appeared to blend into unity?

Oinos: I clearly perceive that the infinity of matter is no dream.

Agathos: There are *no* dreams in Aidenn — but it is here whispered that, of this infinity of matter, the *sole* purpose is to afford infinite springs, at which the soul may allay the thirst *to know* which is for ever unquenchable within it — since to quench it, would be to extinguish the soul's self. Question me then, my Oinos, freely and without fear. Come! we will leave to the left the loud harmony of the Pleiades, and swoop outward from the throne into the starry meadows beyond Orion, where, for pansies and violets, and heart's-ease, are the beds of the triplicate and triple-tinted suns.

Oinos: And now, Agathos, as we proceed, instruct me! — speak to me in the earth's familiar tones! I understood not what you hinted to me, just now, of the modes or of the methods of what, during mortality, we were accustomed to call Creation. Do you mean to say that the Creator is not God?

Agathos: I mean to say that the Deity does not create.

Oinos: Explain!

Agathos: In the beginning *only*, he created. The seeming creatures which are now, throughout the universe, so perpetually springing into being, can only be considered as the mediate or indirect, not as the direct or immediate results of the Divine creative power.

Oinos: Among men, my Agathos, this idea would be considered heretical in the extreme.

Agathos: Among angels, my Oinos, it is seen to be simply true.[22]

According to this colloquy about the nature of angels and the sorts of ideas they are capable of formulating and comprehending, it is given that their coming into being is only an indirect cause of the "Divine creative power," and that creation is ongoing by virtue of the physical power of words among celestial beings. Poe will develop these notions steadily throughout his career, from "Al Aaraaf" (1829) to *Eureka* (1848).[23] Specifically, a "maiden-angel," Ianthe, and her "seraph-lover," Angelo, are central to the narrative arc of "Al Aaraaf."[24] As Poe explained in a letter to the publisher: "Al Aaraaf of the Arabians [is] a medium between Heaven & Hell where men suffer no punishment, but yet do not attain that tranquil & even happiness which they suppose to be the characteristics of heavenly enjoyment."[25] What Poe took as the thinking and theology of "the Arabians,"[26] he gleaned less from the Qur'an and more from Thomas Moore's *Lalla Rookh* and *Loves of the Angels*.[27] As often was the case with Poe's building upon a fragment of philosophy or turn of phrase he encountered in his reading that fit his purpose (e.g., and closely aligned to the matter at hand, Pythagorean metempsychosis, the transmigration of souls, used explicitly in, among other works, "Metzengerstein" and "Liegia"), he constructed a consistent pseudo-Arabian cosmology that animates much of his angel-related writing. Moreover, the place of angels, when compared work-to-work, traces the contours of a self-consistent narrative frame, consistent within the terms of its own construction and also with respect to the universal constants as presented.

The place of Poe's angels as specified in "Al Aaraaf" is one such point of consistency. They abide in connection with a supernova in Cassiopeia discovered by Tycho Brahe. In a prefatory footnote, readers are told of the sudden appearance in 1572 and eventual winking out of the blazing star,[28] and this stellar nursery is the location of the spirit realm in "Al Aaraaf." (The "announcement by astronomers of a *new comet*" likewise figures significantly in "The Conversation of Eiros and Charmion."[29]) These angelic entities exist "somewhere between Heaven & Hell," such that Beauty in our world emanates from the tutelary spirit of this "anchored realm," Nesace, a Greek-derived name linking the words for "lady of the island" and "shadowy."[30] The poem opens with this personification of Beauty, who otherwise receives scant physical description, washing herself in the cosmic light of four stars, reminiscent of classical and early modern accounts of chaste Diana bathing in her Arcadian pool.

> O! nothing earthly save the ray
> (Thrown back from flowers) of Beauty's eye,
> As in those gardens where the day
> Springs from the gems of Circassy—
> O! nothing earthly save the thrill

Of melody in woodland rill —
Or (music of the passion-hearted)
Joy's voice so peacefully departed
That like the murmur in the shell,
Its echo dwelleth and will dwell —
Oh, nothing of the dross of ours —
Yet all the beauty — all the flowers
That list our Love, and deck our bowers —
Adorn yon world afar, afar —
The wandering star.

'Twas a sweet time for Nesace — for there
Her world lay lolling on the golden air,
Near four bright suns — a temporary rest —
An oasis in desert of the blest.
Away — away — 'mid seas of rays that roll
Empyrean splendor o'er th' unchained soul —
The soul that scarce (the billows are so dense)
Can struggle to its destin'd eminence —
To distant spheres, from time to time, she rode,
And late to ours, the favour'd one of God —
But, now, the ruler of an anchor'd realm,
She throws aside the sceptre — leaves the helm,
And, amid incense and high spiritual hymns,
Laves in quadruple light her angel limbs.

Now happiest, loveliest in yon lovely Earth,
Whence sprang the "Idea of Beauty" into birth,
(Falling in wreaths thro' many a startled star,
Like woman's hair 'mid pearls, until, afar,
It lit on hills Achaian, and there dwelt)
She look'd into Infinity — and knelt.
Rich clouds, for canopies, about her curled —
Fit emblems of the model of her world —
Seen but in beauty — not impeding sight
Of other beauty glittering thro' the light —
A wreath that twined each starry form around,
And all the opal'd air in color bound. (ll.1–41)[31]

Poe builds here on the doctrine of stellification, a Neoplatonic revival of the older view of an afterlife in the stars through a transformation into stellar or angelic substance after death.[32] Likewise, he selectively

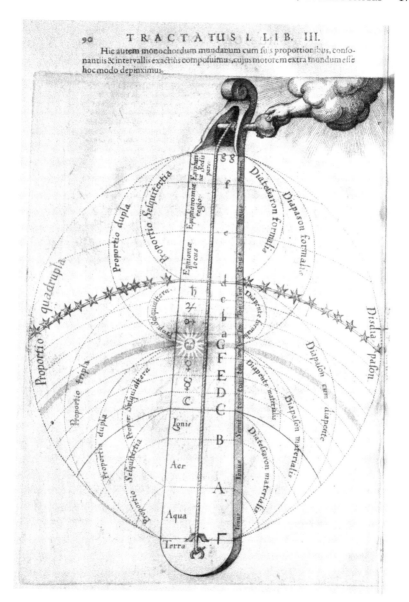

Fig. 8.4 Robert Fludd, "Universal Monochord," *Utriusque cosmi majoris scilicet et minoris metaphysica* (1617–1621) (Folger Shakespeare Library)

used notions promulgated by Renaissance polymaths such as those mentioned by name in the catalogue of Roderick Usher's Library,[33] including
Tommaso Campanella's *City of the Sun* and Robert Fludd's *Chiromancy*,[34]
which Poe either knew directly or, more probably, gleaned from Isaac
Disraeli's *Curiosities of Literature* and Jakob Bielfeld's *Elements of General
Erudition* (M 1973, 19:3–7). Fludd famously charted the intervals and
frequencies of the "cosmic monochord" connecting the microcosm and
macrocosm.[35] "Al Aaraaf" implicitly takes as a guiding premise that the
celestial spheres harmonize one with the other and open onto a world
of seemingly multiple worlds animated by Beauty of an aethereal order
which emanates from thence into our realm, where we too can catch a
glimpse and attend to its harmonious strains. This is a matter for poetry
(as *"The Rhythmical Creation of Beauty"*[36]) in accord with Poe's view of
the ennobling aspects of art: "We are often made to feel, with a shiver-
ing delight, that from an earthly harp are stricken notes which *cannot*
have been unfamiliar to the angels."[37] Fludd published a diagram of the
"Monochord" (spanning the divine, celestial, and mundane) that linked
the Ptolemaic universe to musical intervals[38] (Fig. 8.4). Along the same
lines, Poe maintained it was in Music that "the soul most nearly attains the
great end for which, when inspired by Poetic Sentiment, it struggles—the
creation of supernal Beauty."[39] Poe is in sympathy with Fludd here, for it
is the Music of Nature, sung by Ligeia in "Al Aaraaf," that is instrumental
to the poem's evocation of the figure of universal and cosmic harmony.
Regarding just such a musical paradigm of all creation, S. K. Heninger, Jr.,
explained that, according to this cosmological pattern, "the monochord
stretches from absolute materiality to absolute conceptuality, and the ulte-
rior intention of Pythagorean doctrine was to accomplish this ascent."[40]

Poe makes music and song of an aethereal order the province of the
poet—and indeed the principal subject of poetry itself—and of his own
poetry in particular. For example, in his Arabian-inflected view of the
celestial lyricist, Israfel, we have a description of a space that is appos-
itively not here, such that the poet imagines changing places with the
angel who sings "wildly well."

> IN Heaven a spirit doth dwell
> "Whose heart-strings are a lute;"
> None sing so wildly well
> As the angel Israfel,
> And the giddy stars (so legends tell)

Ceasing their hymns, attend the spell
Of his voice, all mute.

Tottering above
In her highest noon,
The enamoured moon
Blushes with love,
While, to listen, the red levin
(With the rapid Pleiades, even,
Which were seven,)
Pauses in Heaven.

And they say (the starry choir
And the other listening things)
That Israfeli's fire
Is owing to that lyre
By which he sits and sings —
The trembling living wire
Of those unusual strings.

But the skies that angel trod,
Where deep thoughts are a duty —
Where Love's a grown-up God —
Where the Houri glances are
Imbued with all the beauty
Which we worship in a star.

Therefore, thou art not wrong,
Israfeli, who despisest
An unimpassioned song;
To thee the laurels belong,
Best bard, because the wisest!
Merrily live, and long!

The ecstacies above
With thy burning measures suit —
Thy grief, thy joy, thy hate, thy love,
With the fervour of thy lute —
Well may the stars be mute!

Yes, Heaven is thine; but this
Is a world of sweets and sours;

Our flowers are merely — flowers,
And the shadow of thy perfect bliss
Is the sunshine of ours.

If I could dwell
Where Israfel
Hath dwelt, and he where I,
He might not sing so wildly well
A mortal melody,
While a bolder note than this might swell
From my lyre within the sky.[41]

Readers are told (in a footnote in some versions and a prefatory epigraph in later reprintings) that the Qur'an records: "And the angel Israfel, whose heart-strings are a lute, and who has the sweetest voice of all God's creatures."[42] This angel treads the skies and dwells somewhere within earshot of Heaven, but it clearly is an Islamically nuanced one ever so slightly different from and yet emphatically not the Judeo-Christian frame of reference.[43] For Poe, the celestial figure who, Orpheus-like, brings an awed hush in Heaven that all might attend to his song is Israfel, "The Burning One," an archangel in Islamic lore who sounds the trumpet at the end of days.[44] Israfel's counterpart in this regard in early Christian angelology is Raphael.[45] That Poe chose Israfel and not Raphael is precisely the point. This alien angel causes us to think outside the limits of how we, in the West (in the Anglo-American tradition), have come to imagine angels. Poe exploited the idea of "Arabianness," not to offer any serious examination of Muslim cultural thought or Islamic theology, but, as Betsy Erkkila adduces, "as figures of romantic *apartness* and otherworldliness."[46] Moreover, Travis Montgomery has argued persuasively that Poe's exotic vision of the Orient ultimately is subversive, used "to expose the limitations of poetic principles and verse forms in Britain and America."[47]

Poe would have his angels be thus tenuously conceived, just out of reach of our conceptualization—hence the merging of cosmologies as we have seen variously in the cosmic nursery of stars, Neoplatonic emanations, spirits "new-fledged with immortality," Ptolemaic correspondent harmonies, and an Arabian-inflected Heaven among the stars and above the Earth. The poem, "Israfel," is set near the Pleiades, recalling Agathos's description of the place where Poe's Socratically minded angels meet and discourse. Israfel, however, is a different kind of angel—solitary and bound to perform. His bearing and mien indicate there is something more still to be understood about the range of activities of the inhabitants of Poe's angelic precincts. Poe the poet would play out and outplay the angelic archetype of poetry itself, Israfel. He does so in a poetically conceived universe of his own creation and, in this gesture, is just following his own projection of angelic influence as continuing the pattern set in motion, according to Agathos, by "The Most Happy." Somewhere between Earth and the highest sphere, the *premium mobile* (the outermost sphere in the Ptolemaic model of the universe), Poe's angels create—and destroy—worlds through words. The analogy here to the poet's craft is clear, and it reveals the contours of a larger ontological framework in Poe's thought. An amalgam of Miltonic, Islamic, and Gnostic elements, angels in Poe's works collectively bespeak the essential place of cosmic wonder at the threshold of the human imagination. As will be disclosed in the final section, closer scrutiny of Poe's angelic spaces affords a glimpse into the fiery, starry crucible of his own poetic temperament.

Angelic Dwelling, Haunting, and Tenanting

A final piece of the puzzle concerning Poe's angels comes into focus through "The Domain of Arnheim," a work that, as he says in the closing paragraph of a letter to Mrs. Sarah H. Whitman, "expresses *much of my soul.*"[48] He reiterates the same sentiment on the copy of the *Columbian Magazine* he sent to her: "This story contains more of myself and of inherent tastes and habits of thought than anything I have written."[49] With such an endorsement about his habits of thought, this fantasy piece yields valuable insight into the end to which angels can be said to figure in Poe's work—contradistinct from his carefully considered and calculatingly chilling use of tone-setting demons.

> I repeat that in landscape arrangements alone is the physical nature susceptible of exaltation, and that, therefore, her susceptibility of improvement at this one point, was a mystery I had been unable to solve. My own thoughts on the subject had rested in the idea that the primitive intention of nature would have so arranged the earth's surface as to have fulfilled at all points man's sense of perfection in the beautiful, the sublime, or the picturesque; but that this primitive intention had been frustrated by the known geological disturbances — disturbances of form and color-grouping, in the correction or allaying of which lies the soul of art.

[...] It was Ellison who suggested that they were prognostic of *death*. He thus explained: — Admit the earthly immortality of man to have been the first intention. We have then the primitive arrangement of the earth's surface adapted to his blissful estate, as not existent but designed. The disturbances were the preparations for his subsequently conceived deathful condition.

"Now," said my friend, "what we regard as exaltation of the landscape may be really such, as respects only the [mortal] or human *point of view*. Each alteration of the natural scenery may possibly effect a blemish in the picture, if we can suppose this picture viewed at large — in mass — from some point distant from the earth's surface, although not beyond the limits of its atmosphere. It is easily understood that what might improve a closely scrutinized detail, may at the same time injure a general or more distantly observed effect. There *may* be a class of beings, human once, but now invisible to humanity, to whom, from afar, our disorder may seem order — our unpicturesqueness picturesque; in a word, the earth-angels, for whose scrutiny more especially than our own, and for whose death-refined appreciation of the beautiful, may have been set in array by God the wide landscape-gardens of the hemispheres."[50]

Ellison's pronouncement about a special class of angles, "human once" with a "death-refined appreciation of the beautiful," speaks volumes about Poe's drive to present a concept of angelic intelligence to advance his exposition of the role of Beauty in the ennobling of human experience through expressions of the Poetic Sentiment. Elsewhere Poe includes the composition of landscape gardens among the modes of expression where the "Poetic Sentiment" may develop itself, along with painting, sculpture, architecture, and "very especially in Music."[51] As we have seen with "Israfel," there is much more to music than what even angels are capable of producing—even fiery ones, to which Poe would compare himself and emerge the victor.

Historically, most readers focus on the demonic rather than the angelic in Poe, even though the bulk of writings tends toward the humorous and satirical rather than the abjectly moody and dire. Such a popular view is understandable though given Poe's telltale touch of the macabre and appreciation of the grotesque, for example, in works such as "The Imp of the Perverse" and "Silence—A Fable," the latter which begins: "'Listen to *me*,' said the Demon...."[52] Poe also gives an absurd characterization of angels as self-satisfied, perverse imps in his darkly humorous "Angel of the Odd" (July 1884), published shortly after—and in many ways a sly gloss on—"The Balloon Hoax" (April 1844). Taking into account the whole range of Poe's angels, as Charles Huttar concluded: "The symbolism of Poe's angels, then, is full of tensions."[53] To be sure, it is this sense of productive tension that Poe relied on to create some of his most affective images and jarring oppositions that goad readers to look beyond mere poetic allegory and commonplace themes. Although Poe uses features of allegory and elements of fable and parable selectively and often wryly, he remains ever alert that he is not at all in the business of allegory as was, say, Hawthorne, with whom Poe's work sometimes is linked by way of the sub-genre known as "Dark Romanticism." Northrop Frye quipped about "patterns of the 'Romantic agony'" that they seem "to provide all the disadvantages of superstition with none of the advantages of religion."[54] As for the putative advantages of religion, Poe will have none of it where his demons, like his angels, are concerned.

His much-anthologized poem "Dream-land" is an instructive case in point, presenting the reader with a place that is "[h]aunted by ill angels only."[55] This fantastic place is characterized as being "Out of Space—out of Time" (l.8); it is the exact opposite of the celestial clime where Oinos and Agathos indoctrinate their newly arrived friends from former lives on earth, for theirs is a place where space is identifiable by stellar regions and time is operative. "Dream-land," as Mabbott observed, is exactly that a place where "all of us meet phantoms of the real and unreal, of the dead and the living."[56] And we do well to remember that Poe's discoursing angel, Agathos, is emphatic that "There are *no* dreams in Aidenn." Angelic space is not dream-land space.

As such, "Dream-land" is of an entirely different order from the locale of Poe's high-minded discoursing angels. "Dream-land" is a place "[w]here dwell the Ghouls,-- / By each spot the most unholy—In each nook most melancholy" (ll.30–32), and so too "Ulalume," with its choric refrain of the "ghoul-haunted woodland of Weir."[57] Wailing ghouls essentially are tone-setting affective adornments constitutive of Poe's broader aesthetic scheme concerning what resides at the threshold of the human imagination, and their version of discordance is strikingly (and self-consciously) opposed to the well-plotted landscape garden explored in "Arnheim." This dichotomy is showcased and contained in "The Haunted Palace,"[58] which, because of its content no less than Poe's putting it in a variety of literary contexts during his career, allows us to see his reckoning of the angelic and the demonic as affective mirrors of one another.

"The Haunted Palace" traces a genealogy of the creation and destruction of what so majestically has been constructed; as such, it provides a suitable way to conclude this investigation of the place of Poe's angels and demons because, finally, the one requires the other for its rightful place in his cosmic ontology. This overriding vision of the human condition, like that of the universe itself (as *Eureka* makes abundantly clear), is one of entropy, of progressive collapse.[59] Where Poe's angels and demons are concerned, the one is not so much the opposite of the other as its doppelgänger—and it is not quite clear which is the original and which the shadow. This is consistent with the importance of vague indeterminacy at the heart of Poe's rationale for developing angelic space as he does; for example, his positioning of "Al Aaraaf" as "somewhere between Heaven & Hell," and his idiosyncratic spelling of "Aidenn" referred to among other places in "The Raven" (l.93). The raven itself moves from being considered a "prophet," with possible knowledge about where Lenore has been transported, to a "thing of evil! — prophet still, if bird or devil!" (l.91). This tantalizingly extensive ideological space of speculation, like the "somewhere between" of "Al Aaraaf," is for Poe the fulcrum upon which everything is held in balance; it is the Archimedean point upon which he creates (and destroys) worlds, extending his initial conception to reach the very limits of the human imagination: "wondering, fearing, / Doubting, dreaming dreams no mortal ever dared to dream before" ("The Raven," ll.25–26).

Poe's designation of the spirit realm of "Al Aaraaf" as somewhere between Heaven and Hell marks a significant departure from his putative Islamic source material, Sale's "Preliminary Discourse,"[60] which states there is a wall between Heaven and Hell.[61] Poe will have no such barriers. The indeterminate space imagined by Poe better suits his larger plan, and his decision to diverge from his source material reflects his concerted aim to keep the eschatology of Abrahamic religions at bay. It is this space of indeterminacy—without the armature of Christian teleology—upon which Poe relied to pursue a wider gamut of imaginative and affective possibilities in his writing. This is especially the case as regards the threshold between life and death, contextualized for example in "The Colloquy of Monos and Una" by one who formerly was human. As already has been observed (and it bears repeating in this present context): "In Death we have both learned the propensity of man to define the indefinable."[62] And yet, as Monos will qualify: "this was termed *Death* by those who stood around me. Words are vague things."[63] The same critique of language's implicit limitations is expressed in "The Premature Burial" in very similar terms: "The boundaries that divide Life from Death are at best shadowy and vague. Who shall say where the one ends and the other begins."[64] Words are vague things even as boundaries are, at best, vague, which helps to explain or at least provides a rationale as to why Poe eliminated the cosmic wall in Heaven when he was imagining and constructing his abode for the angels.

"The Haunted Palace," another of Poe's inspirited and vaguely determined spaces, receives an extended and refined life, much like Poe's pairs of angelic interlocutors who are characterized along the lines of the earth angels of "Arnheim" as having been "human once, but now invisible to humanity." The poem itself, "The Haunted Palace," like Poe's angels, represents an extension of a previous mode of being. It was first printed in *American Museum* (April 1839) and then almost immediately was given a renewed and extended life in "The Fall of the House of Usher" (September 1839). In whatever form it appeared though, the poem retained its title—one which evokes a classical-turned Gothic Memory Palace where, instead of finding signifying objects situated in an orderly fashion typical of place-system mnemonic schemes, we discover indistinct and unsettling traces of the departed whose intimated presence is a reminder of what once was but which now decisively no longer is there.[65] The affective tension of the poem turns upon the metaphysics of absence. The opening of "The Haunted Palace," appositive to "Dreamland" ("[h]aunted by ill angels only"), is situated "[i]n the greenest of our valleys / By good angels tenanted" (ll.1–2). By the final stanza though, everything is reversed:

> And travelers now within that valley
> Through the red-litten windows, see
> Vast forms that move fantastically
> To a discordant melody;
> While, like a rapid ghastly river,
> Through the pale door,
> A hideous throng rush out forever,
> And laugh—but smile no more. (ll.41–48)

The change that assailed the monarch Thought's high estate, we are told simply if vaguely, involves "evil things, in robes of sorrow" (l.33) starkly in contrast to the "good angels" who once were tenanted there. During the hay-day of the "stately palace," there could be found "a

troop of Echoes whose sole duty / Was but to sing, / In voices of sur-
passing beauty / The wit and wisdom of their king" (ll.29–32). Their
sole task, which defines their reason for being, bears comparison to
the cosmic role played by Israfel. Thought, the sovereign of the realm,
has been overthrown; "the glory" gone "that blushed and bloomed,"
now "but a dim-remembered story" (ll.37–39). Something though
clearly still resides there, in what might be more properly thought of as
a Haunted Memory Palace. Like a doppelgänger of what once was "by
good angels tenanted," we now find its dark double—the voices of sur-
passing beauty now a "hideous throng" cackling with hollow laughter
"but smile no more" (ll.47–48).

"The Haunted Palace," of course, is a mirror in miniature of "The
Fall of the House of Usher," the story in which it appears, emblemati-
cally echoing the world of the tale from within while at the same time
projecting a self-contained and irremediable melancholy (because
doomed) world of fragile beauty, one initially tenanted by good angels.
As with "Arnheim," which likewise exists in several incarnations,[66] we
find in the poem a "death-refined appreciation of the beautiful." And
this brings us back to Lenore, ever present through her absence, so
named by the angels and who remains otherwise "[n]ameless here forevermore." Everything hinges on the space between and encompassing
here and there. The affective tension brought out by Poe's evocation of
the angelic, whether modified as "good" or "ill," is central to and indicative of his own ongoing performance—executed "wildly well"—of an
aesthetic practice predicated on a metaphysics of absence.

NOTES

1. "The Raven," *American Review* (February 1845), following the text provided online by the Baltimore Poe Society (www.eapoe.org/works), with
   special thanks to Jeffrey A. Savoye. See also *Edgar Allan Poe, Complete
   Poems,* ed. Thomas Ollive Mabbott (Urbana and Chicago: Illinois University
   Press, 2000), 367.
2. *Complete Poems,* 374, n. 93.
3. *Gustave Doré, The Raven* (New York: Harper & Brothers, 1884), 41; this
   particular engraving was executed by Frederick Juengling (at the height
   of his career, Doré had in his employ as many as forty engravers to meet
   production demands).
4. Blanche Roosevelt, *Life and Reminiscences of Gustave Doré* (New York:
   Cassell & Company, 1885), 488.

5. For a representative sampling of Doré's stylized Romantic angels, see Carole Belanger Grafton, *Dore's Angels* (Mineola, NY: Dover Publications, 2004).

6. Edward Burne-Jones, "Angel playing a Flageolet" (1878), Sudley House, Liverpool, Accession No: WAG 192.

7. Therese Martin, "The Development of Winged Angels in Early Christian Art," *Espacio, Tiempo y Forma, Serie VII, Historia del Arte* 14 (2001): 11–30.

8. Charles Dempsey, *Inventing the Renaissance Putto* (Chapel Hill, NC: University of North Carolina Press, 2001), 44, *et passim*.

9. Philippe Ariès, *The Hour of Our Death: The Classic History of Western Attitudes Toward Death*, trans. Helen Weaver, 2nd ed. (New York: Vintage, 1982), Ch. 10: "The Age of the Beautiful Death."

10. Gustave Doré, "Jacob Wrestling with the Angel" (1855), reissued in Doré's *The Bible* (London: Cassell & Co, 1866), Gen. 32B; engraved by Charles Laplante.

11. See, for example, "The Philosophy of Composition," in *Edgar Allan Poe, Critical Theory: The Major Documents*, eds. Stuart Levine and Susan F. Levine (Urbana and Chicago: University of Illinois Press, 2009), 64: "Melancholy is thus the most legitimate of all the poetic tones."

12. Penny Brown, "Gustave Doré's Magical Realism: The *Nouveaux contes de fées* of the Comtesse de Ségur," *Modern Language Review* 95 (2001): 964–977.

13. Nicholas Royle, *The Uncanny* (Manchester: Manchester University Press, 2003), esp. 158–159; Betsy Erkkila, "Perverting the American Renaissance," in *Poe and the Remapping of Antebellum Print Culture*, eds. J. Gerald Kennedy and Jerome McGann (Baton Rouge: Louisiana State University Press, 2012), 65–100; Robert T. Tally, Jr., *Poe and the Subversion of American Literature: Satire, Fantasy, Critique* (New York and London: Bloomsbury, 2014), 45, 64, 109ff.

14. "Annabel Lee," *Complete Poems*, 478: "The angels, not so happy in Heaven, / Went envying her and me-- / Yes! That was the reason (as all men know, / In this kingdom by the sea) / That the wind came out of the cloud by the night, / Chilling and killing my Annabel Lee" (ll.21–26).

15. Charles A. Huttar, "Poe's Angels," in *Essays for Richard Ellmann*, eds. Susan Dick, et al. (Montréal: McGill-Queens University Press, 1989), 82–84, 82.

16. On Poe's debt to Milton, see Richard C. Frushell, "Poe's name 'Ligeia' and Milton," *American Notes and Queries* 11, no. 1 (Winter 1998): 18–20; Daniel Hoffman, "Poe," in *Encyclopedia of American Poetry: The Nineteenth Century*, ed. Eric L. Haralson (New York: Routledge, 1998), 341–345, 342; and William E. Engel, *Early Modern Poetics in Melville and Poe: Memory, Melancholy, and the Emblematic Tradition* (Farnham: Ashgate, 2013), 87, n. 45.

17. Joad Raymond, *Milton's Angels* (Oxford: Oxford University Press, 2010), esp. Ch. 10.

18. "Eiros and Charmion," *Edgar Allan Poe, Tales and Sketches*, 2 vols., ed. Thomas Ollive Mabbott (Urbana and Chicago: University of Illinois Press, 2000), I.456.

19. "The Colloquy of Monos and Una," *Tales and Sketches*, II.609.

20. From Aristotle on, extension is a principal determinate of space making possible the identification of "place," which in the Cartesian world-picture is a subordinate feature of matter and space. See Edward S. Casey, *The Fate of Place: A Philosophical History* (Berkeley: University of California Press, 1997), 156.

21. "The Facts in the Case of M. Valdemar," *Tales and Sketches*, II.1242: "the jaws and lips remained rigid as before…and at length the same hideous voice which I have already described, broke forth…."

22. "The Power of Words," *The Works of the Late Edgar Allan Poe* (1850), 2:271–275, 271–272 (http://www.eapoe.org/WORKS/tales/pwrwdsc. htm); cf. *Tales and Sketches*, II.1212–1213.

23. Barbara Cantalupo, "Preludes to Eureka: Poe's 'Absolute Reciprocity of Adaptation' in 'Shadow' and 'The Power of Words,'" *Poe Studies/Dark Romanticism* 29:1 (June 1996): 17–21; Harry Lee Poe, *Evermore: Edgar Allan Poe and the Mystery of the Universe* (Waco, TX: Baylor University Press, 2012), 56.

24. "Al Aaraaf," *The Raven and Other Poems* (1845), 56 (www.eapoe.org/works/poems/aaraafk.htm).

25. *Complete Poems*, 92; see also, Harry Lee Poe, *Edgar Allan Poe: An Illustrated Companion to His Tell-Tale Stories* (New York: Metro, 2008), 39.

26. See Jacob Rama Berman, *American Arabesque: Arabs and Islam in the Nineteenth Century Imaginary* (New York: New York University Press, 2012), esp. ch. 3, "Poe's Taste for the Arabesque," 109–137.

27. On Poe's allusions to ideas loosely derived from the Qur'an, see Betsy Erkkila, "The Poetics of Whiteness: Poe and the Racial Imaginary," *Romancing the Shadow: Poe and Race*, eds. J. Gerald Kennedy and Liliane Weissberg (Oxford: Oxford University Press, 2001), 41–74, 48; and Travis Montgomery, "Turning East: Poe's 1831 *Poems* and the Renewal of American Verse," Baltimore: The Edgar Allan Poe Society of Baltimore, 2011 (http://www.eapoe.org/papers/psblctrs/pl20061. htm#pn0026). On Poe's indebtedness to Thomas Moore, see Arthur Hobson Quinn, *Edgar Allan Poe: A Critical Biography* (1941; repr. Baltimore: The Johns Hopkins University Press, 1998), vii; and Travis Montgomery, "The Near East," *Edgar Allan Poe in Context*, ed. Kevin J. Hayes (Cambridge: Cambridge University Press), 53–62, 56.

28. "Al Aaraaf,"—*The Raven and Other Poems*—(1845), 56–73; *Complete Poems*, 96 and 99.

29. *Tales and Sketches*, I.457 [Poe's emphasis]; see also I.452 for Mabbott's discussion of the popular interest in comets during Poe's day.

30. *Complete Poems*, 115, n. 16.

31. *Complete Poems*, 99–101.

32. Alastair Fowler, *Time's Purpled Masquers: Stars and the Afterlife in Renaissance English Literature* (Oxford: Oxford University Press, 1996), argues the new astronomy of Copernicus and Brahe encouraged hopes of access to the uncorrupted spheres. Poe may also have seen the note in Thomas Moore's *Loves of the Angels* regarding a belief "common to all the religions and heresies of the East" that "the stars are either spirits, or the vehicles of spirits" (Mabbott, *Collected Poems*, 115, n. 16).

33. "The Fall of the House of Usher," *Tales and Sketches*, I.409.

34. On the place of Campanella and Fludd in Usher's library, especially as regards esoteric learning of the Renaissance, see Engel, *Poetics*, 110.

35. Francis A. Yates, *Art of Memory* (Harmondsworth: Penguin, 1966), 310–329.

36. Edgar Allan Poe, "The Poetic Principle," in *Critical Theory: The Major Documents*, eds. Stuart Levine and Susan F. Levine (Urbana: University of Illinois Press, 2009), 185 [Poe's emphasis].

37. Poe, "Poetic Principle," 184 [Poe's emphasis].

38. On this cosmological model and its larger cultural implications in the West, see Joscelyn Godwin, *Robert Fludd: Hermetic Philosopher and Surveyor of Two Worlds* (London: Thames & Hudson, 1979).

39. Poe, "Poetic Principle," 184.

40. S. K. Heninger, Jr., *Touches of Sweet Harmony: Pythagorean Cosmology and Renaissance Poetics* (San Marino: The Huntington Library, 1974), 185.

41. E. A. Poe, "Israfel" (1845–1848), the text reflecting minor manuscript revision of punctuation in the J. L. Graham copy of *The Raven and Other Poems* (Mabbott's copy-text for the final version), 16–17

42. See, for example, the note at the bottom of the page in *Poems by Edgar A. Poe* (1831), 43 (http://www.eapoe.org/works/poems/israfela.htm).

43. On Poe's angels, with special reference to Israfel, "as figures of 'other' ranges of thinking," see Jerome McGann," *The Poet Edgar Allan Poe: Alien Angel* (Cambridge, MA: Harvard University Press, 2014), 63.

44. While this information would have been available to Poe from his Orientalist sources, it is not mentioned directly in the Qur'an. Still Poe had access to the Qur'an, most likely George Sale's English translation (Quinn, 156; and Mabbott, *Complete Poems*, 95–96). Given his range of interests and the ease with which he procured books relating to his professional endeavors as a book reviewer, it is likely he had read at least the "Preliminary Discourse" introducing Sale's Qur'an (published in 1734 and then frequently thereafter). Even so Thomas Moore clearly used Sale's material in *Lalla Rookh*, with which Poe was quite familiar (see Killis Campbell, "Poe's Reading," *University of Texas Studies in English* (October 1925), 166–196, 196; Mabbott, *Complete Poems*,

96; and Travis Montgomery, "Poe's Oriental Gothic: 'Metzengerstein' (1832), 'The Visionary' (1834), 'Berenice' (1835), the Imagination, and Authorship's Perils," *Gothic Studies* 12, no. 2 (2010), 4–28, 25.

45. Gabriel, figured as the eschatological horn-blower, is the product of late medieval Byzantine Christian texts and Armenian liturgy and icons. See, for example, Jane Baun, *Tales from Another Byzantium: Celestial Journey and Local Community in the Medieval Greek Apocrypha* (Cambridge: Cambridge University Press, 2007), 391; and Thomas F. Matthews and Avedis K. Sinjian, *Armenian Gospel Iconography* (Washington, DC: Dumbarton Oaks, 1991), 162.

46. Erkkila, "The Poetics of Whiteness," 48.

47. Travis Montgomery, "Turning East" (cited above n. 28), which goes on to explain: "In their cultural conspicuousness, the Oriental images of 'Israfel' reflect the uniqueness of the new American verse that Poe wants to create, a verse liberated from the fetters of Western convention."

48. Letter to Sarah H. Whitman, October 18, 1848 (LTR-280) [Poe's emphasis] (http://www.eapoe.org/works/letters/p4810181.htm).

49. *Tales and Sketches*, II.1266.

50. "The Domain of Arnheim," *The Works of the Late Edgar Allan Poe* (1850), I.393–394 [Poe's emphasis] (http://www.eapoe.org/WORKS/tales/arnhmc.htm).

51. Poe, "Poetic Principle," 184.

52. *Tales and Sketches*, I:195 [Poe's emphasis].

53. Huttar, "Poe's Angels," 83.

54. Northrop Frye, *Anatomy of Criticism* (Princeton: Princeton University Press, 1973), 157.

55. *Complete Poems*, 343.

56. *Complete Poems*, 342.

57. *Complete Poems*, 415–419.

58. *Complete Poems*, 315–317.

59. Joel Porte, *In Respect to Egotism: Studies in American Romantic Writing* (Cambridge: Cambridge University Press, 1991), 100.

60. See above, n. 46.

61. *Collected Poems*, 96.

62. *Tales and Sketches*, I.609.

63. *Tales and Sketches*, I.612.

64. *Tales and Sketches*, II.955.

65. See William E. Engel, "Echoic Effects in Poe's Poetic Double Economy—of Memory," *Connotations* 23, no. 1 (2013/2014): 26–48.

66. "Arnheim" began its literary life as "The Landscape Garden" (1842); see Mabbott, *Tales and Sketches*, II.1266.

CHAPTER 9

Re-ordering Place in Poe's
Arthur Gordon Pym

Richard Kopley

The usual order of place in Edgar Allan Poe's 1838 novel *The Narrative of Arthur Gordon Pym* is, of course, that of the text, from beginning to end. We begin with Richmond and New York City and end past the 84th parallel, headed toward the South Pole. However, the significance of place in Pym's narrative is particularly critical because of Poe's subtle rendering of two other narratives—first, the narrative of his life and that of his family and, second, the narrative of the Fall of Jerusalem. I propose, therefore, to re-order place in *Pym* to reflect the order of place in these two narratives. We may thereby recover anew the undercurrents of Poe's novel.[1]

The Narrative of Poe and His Family

Poe's embedding his life in his work is familiar—we may think, for example, of Manor House School in Stoke-Newington for the short story "William Wilson," Jane Stith Stanard for the poem "To Helen," Elmira Royster for the poem "Tamerlane," and his wife Virginia for the short

R. Kopley (✉)
Penn State University, DuBois, PA, USA

© The Author(s) 2018
P. E. Phillips (ed.), *Poe and Place*,
Geocriticism and Spatial Literary Studies,
https://doi.org/10.1007/978-3-319-96788-2_9

story "Eleonora" and the poem "Annabel Lee." And I have shown how he embedded his life in the Dupin tales, as well—particularly his concern for his mother.[2] We may infer that Poe was egotistical—as he certainly was—but also that he was, in a sense, generous, in that he shared his life and that of his family covertly with his reader. *Pym* takes us from his older brother's birth in Boston to Poe's first stay in New York City, when *Pym* was about to be published by the Harpers. At the center of the book is his older brother's death in Baltimore; at the climax is his mother's performance in a play in Charleston. We should recall, in this regard, Poe's confiding to John Neal in an 1829 letter, "There can be no tie more strong than that of brother for brother—it is not so much that they love one another, as that they both love the same parent" (O 1:47).

Boston, 1807–1809

Edgar Poe was born to David and Eliza Poe in Boston on January 19, 1809. The family probably lived at 62 Carver Street. Edgar was the couple's second son: his brother William Henry Leonard was born on January 30, 1807.[3] Poe suggests the births of his brother and himself in the early chapters of *Pym*.

Arthur Gordon Pym is, as the rhythm of the name suggests, Edgar Allan Poe. Augustus Barnard—two years older than Arthur, a drinker, a teller of tales of his travels, who dies on August 1—is Henry Poe, two years older than Edgar, a drinker, a teller of tales of his travels, who also died on August 1. Their mother, Eliza Poe, whose maiden name was Arnold, is suggested early on anagrammatically, through mention of "Mr. E. Ronald's academy on the hill."[4] The two births are presented allegorically—each boy emerges from a lower space—the sea, the hold—and hits his head upon something hard. Poe writes, for the first of these births,

> Upon his first attaining any degree of consciousness, he [Augustus] found himself beneath the surface, whirling round and round with inconceivable rapidity, and with a rope wrapped in three or four folds tightly about his neck. In an instant afterwards he felt himself going rapidly upward, when, his head striking violently against a hard substance, he again relapsed into insensibility. (P 1:63)

The rope is presumably the umbilical cord, and the "hard substance" upon which he hits his head presumably his mother's pelvic bone.

That this incident is repeated for Arthur tends to confirm this reading. Poe writes of Pym emerging from the hold,

> Still I struggled forward by slow degrees, dreading every moment that I should swoon among the narrow and intricate windings of the lumber, in which event I had nothing but death to expect as the result. At length, upon making a push forward with all the energy I could command, I struck my forehead violently against the sharp corner of an iron-bound crate. (P 1:74)

Intimating the possibility of a still birth in utero, Poe goes on to describe his successful birth, including the moment of hitting his head against his mother's pelvic bone. That Poe should be inclined to be thinking of his birth in Boston is assured by the gift that he had received from his mother, a painting she had made, titled "Boston Harbour: Morning, 1808," on the back of which Eliza had written "For my little son Edgar, who should ever love Boston, the place of his birth, and where his mother found her *best*, and *most sympathetic* friends" (PL 3–4) [cf. Chapter 2, Kim, on the significance of Boston].

In the first few chapters of the novel, Pym's adventures are fairly launched—and so, too, are the lives of Henry and Edgar. Poe appeals to "the many and the few"—the many who enjoyed a nautical adventure story and the few who cared about the author and his family. And we may conjecture that Poe was enjoying his own virtuosity, the artistry that permitted him to tell two stories simultaneously. With the biblical narrative, he would actually be telling three stories at the same time—a matter, we may imagine, for Poe at the time, of some pride. The births may be suggested later with "the brig's straining" (P 1:103) and a vessel's "violent straining" (P 1:106). A later journal entry, about the *Jane Guy*'s arrival at the island of Tsalal, is dated "January 19" (P 1:167), the date of Poe's birth—and the subsequent reference to the native cry of "*Anamoo-moo!*" (P 1:168) is an allusion to the southern of the two islands of New Zealand in Benjamin Morrell's *A Narrative of Four Voyages*: "*Tavi Poënammoo*"—that is, to Poe himself.[5]

Charleston, 1811

We do not know if Poe remembered his mother's performing at the Charleston Theatre as the bride Christine in the play *Tekeli*, originally scheduled for March 22, 1811, and then presented on March 23, 1811.

After all, he had been at the time two years, two months old. But he probably recovered this performance when he consulted the *Charleston Courier* during his stay at Fort Moultrie, South Carolina, in late 1827 and most of 1828. Commenting on Poe's finding the poem "The Mourner," a source for "Annabel Lee," in the *Charleston Courier* of December 4, 1807, T. O. Mabbott notes, "It is not at all improbable that he glanced through a file when stationed near Charleston, or even had a copy of the paper" (M 1:471). The performance of *Tekeli* is evident in the climax of *Pym*, with the appearance of the white "shrouded human figure" as the white birds cry "*Tekeli-li!*":

> March 22. The darkness had materially increased, relieved only by the glare of the water thrown back from the white curtain before us. Many gigantic and pallidly white birds flew continuously now from beyond the veil, and their scream was the eternal *Tekeli-li!* as they retreated from our vision. Hereupon Nu-Nu stirred in the bottom of the boat; but upon touching him, we found his spirit departed. And now we rushed into the embraces of the cataract, where a chasm threw itself open to receive us. But there arose in our pathway a shrouded human figure, very far larger in its proportions than any dweller among men. And the hue of the skin of the figure was of the perfect whiteness of the snow. (P 1:205–206)

Malcolm Cowley termed this "the finest passage in all his [Poe's] works."[6] It brings together both the personal narrative and the biblical narrative, as will be discussed later. Poe must have planned this extraordinary passage from the start.

Richmond, 1815

Poe writes, as Pym, in the first chapter of the novel that Pym's wealthy "maternal grandfather"—really Poe's foster father John Allan—"sent me, at six years of age, to the school of old Mr. Ricketts" (P 1:57) in New Bedford, Massachusetts. In fact, Edgar was sent at the age of six to the school of William Ewing, in Richmond, Virginia (PL 23).[7] Ewing later wrote to John Allan in England, "I trust Edgar continues to do well and to like his school as much as he used to when he was in Richmond. He is a charming boy and it will give me great pleasure to hear how he is, and where you have sent him to school, and also what he is reading" (PL 35). Poe's later boyhood in Richmond is more fully represented in *Pym*.

London, 1815–1820

Young Edgar was with his foster parents John and Frances Allan in England from 1815 to 1820. Presumably, it was at one of their residences in London that he first read Daniel Defoe's *Robinson Crusoe*. Poe's *Pym* echoes Defoe's classic sea novel *Robinson Crusoe*, frequently mentioned in *Pym*'s reviews. (For Pollin's comment on *Robinson Crusoe* in the reviews of *Pym*, see P 1:216.) Critically, Poe wrote in a review of *Robinson Crusoe* in the January 1836 issue of the *Southern Literary Messenger*, "How fondly do we recur, in memory, to those enchanted days of our boyhood when we first learned to grow serious over Robinson Crusoe!—when we first found the spirit of wild adventure enkindling within us, as, by the dim fire light, we labored out, line by line, the marvelous import of those pages, and hung breathless and trembling with eagerness over their absorbing—over their enchaining interest! Alas! The days of desolate islands are no more" (P 5:98). Certainly, the adult Poe would have had the literary marketplace in mind as he undertook his novel, but he would also have recalled his boyhood affection for Defoe's boldly verisimilar work—probably read in one of his later years in London.

Liverpool, 1820

Of note is that Poe frequently mentioned in *Pym* vessels from Liverpool (P 1:65, 102, 147, 149). The phrase regarding the ship *Penguin*, "coppered and copper-fastened" (P 1:62), was observed by Burton R. Pollin in Hart's novel *Miriam Coffin* (P 1:223); however, young Edgar would probably have encountered the phrase with a more personal connection in June 1820 in Liverpool, where he and his foster parents were to take the ship *Martha* back to the USA. Eleven-year-old Edgar would likely have read the *Liverpool Mercury* of June 9, 1820, which referred to their ship the *Martha* as "coppered and copper-fastened." This newspaper also discussed the return of Queen Caroline from Italy at the death of George III–and it was Princess Caroline whom Poe memorialized in "The Purloined Letter."[8]

Richmond, 1820–1825

Poe's later boyhood in Richmond figures importantly in *Pym*. Detail about the protagonist's "maternal grandfather" suggests John Allan specifically. Pym writes, "I expected to inherit the most of his property at his death" (P 1:57), and, when he acknowledges his wish to join Augustus on the *Grampus*, "my grandfather, from whom I expected much, vowed to cut me off with a shilling if I should ever broach the subject to him again" (P 1:66). John Allan became very rich indeed with his inheritance from William Galt in 1825 (PL 63–64). He then bought "Moldavia" and lived with his family in the large house at the corner of Main and Fifth streets. Money was a matter of frequent conflict between Allan and Poe, as their letters reveal. At John Allan's death in 1834, Edgar received nothing.[9]

"Mr. E. Ronald's academy on the hill" (P 1:57) may well have been the school of Joseph H. Clarke, at Broad and Fifth, which Edgar attended when he was eleven, in 1820 (PL 47–48).[10] The nautical escapade of Pym and Augustus is probably drawn from Edgar's boating adventures on the James River with Ebenezer Burling (P 1:218). (Whether Henry Poe, who visited his brother twice in Richmond [the second time in 1825] [PL 65], also went boating with Edgar we do not know.) And Pym's memorable disguise as a dead man on board the *Grampus*, shocking the mutineers (P 1:108–113), recalls Edgar's disguise as a ghost, shocking the whist players at the Franklin and Second streets home of Charles Ellis, his foster father's business partner (H 1:26).[11]

Charlottesville, 1826

Poe attended the University of Virginia in Charlottesville in 1826, and he later set his 1844 "A Tale of the Ragged Mountains" in what he termed "the chain of wild and dreary hills that lie westward and southward of Charlottesville, and are there dignified by the title of the Ragged Mountains" (M 3:942). He suggested this famous topographical feature earlier, in *Pym*, obliquely, stating with regard to Captain Cook's exploration of the South Seas, "The northern edge of this expanse [of ice] was ragged and broken" and mentioning, three lines later, "gigantic ranges of ice mountains" (P 1:159). Perhaps his J. N. Reynolds source, *Address on the Subject of a Surveying and Exploring Expedition to the Pacific Ocean and South Seas*, which Poe reviewed in the January 1837 *Southern Literary Messenger*, prompted the association—especially its reference to "chains of mountains." (For the relevant Reynolds text, see P 1:308–309; for the review, see P 5:354–358). Poe was less oblique a few pages later when he referred to the voyage of the *Jane Guy*: "Our passage to the south again looked doubtful, as nothing was to be seen in the direction of the pole but one apparently limitless floe, backed by absolute mountains of ragged ice" (P 1:164). As he describes fictional discovery, Poe also intimates his actual life.[12]

Richmond, 1827

Aided by Augustus, Pym surreptitiously sails from Richmond in June 1827 (P 1:66) as a stowaway on the *Grampus*. This departure seems an echo of Edgar's actually traveling by coal vessel from Richmond, perhaps partway with Ebenezer Burling, in March 1827, probably stopping by Baltimore to see his brother, and then voyaging up the coast to Boston (M 1:538–539; PL 78). Annotating the relevant passage in the novel, Pollin suggests, "There are autobiographical overtones here of the flight of Poe to Boston from the Allan home in 1827, first sojourning in Baltimore, then in Boston in April" (P 1:226). The threatening grand-father and the deceptive Pym (P 1:66–67) reflect John Allan and Edgar, but Poe does not convey in his novel the hurt that is evident in his letters of the time to John Allan (O 1:10–13).

Charleston, 1827–1828

In Boston, Poe published his first book, *Tamerlane*. But by the time it appeared, in June or July 1827, he had joined the Army. He was stationed at Fort Independence, near Boston, and then, in November, voyaged to Fort Moultrie, Sullivan's Island, in Charleston Harbor. As earlier suggested, Poe would probably have sought Charleston newspapers with information about his mother's performances in that city. He was to write in an 1835 letter to Beverly Tucker, "In speaking of my mother you have touched a string to which my heart fully responds" (O 1:116). And in an 1845 review, he stated, "The writer of this article is himself the son of an actress—has invariably made it his boast—and no earl was ever prouder of his earldom than he of the descent from a woman who, although well-born, hesitated not to consecrate to the drama her brief career of genius and of beauty" (H 12:186).

Given the resemblance of "Annabel Lee" to the poem "The Mourner," appearing in the *Charleston Courier* on December 4, 1807, Mabbott thought it "not at all improbable" that Poe saw a file while staying at Fort Moultrie, or even owned a copy (M 1:471). The listing of Poe's mother's planned performance, as the bride Christine, in the play *Tekeli*, in the *Charleston Courier* on March 22, 1811, and then, after a rain cancellation, on March 23, 1811, anticipates Pym's final journal entry, the remarkable passage concerning the white "shrouded human figure" appearing on March 22, surrounded by birds crying "*Tekeli-li!*" (P 1:205–206). Recovering the performance, Poe offers not only a moment in his mother's "brief career of genius and of beauty," but also a moment in the Book of Revelation, as will be elaborated—he has created a beautiful union of the biographical and the apocalyptic to which the entire novel has been building.

Poe sailed with his company for Fortress Monroe, Old Point Comfort, Virginia, in December 1828 and was discharged from the army in April 1829 (PL 87–90).

Baltimore, 1829–1830

While Poe lived in Baltimore before attending West Point, he certainly saw his brother Henry, as well as his aunt Maria Clemm and cousin Virginia. Henry had published two of Edgar's poems under his own name in 1827, and Edgar had appropriated some of Henry's adventures and even called himself "Henri Le Rennet" in 1827;[13] we may be reminded of the "intimate communion" that "had resulted in a partial interchange of character" (P 1:65) between Pym and Augustus. Henry had also published a story, "Recollections," in 1827, which concludes with the discovery of "my *long-sought Brother*."[14] In *Pym*, the resemblance of a penguin to a "human figure" (P 1:151) and the penguin's "spirit of reflection" (P 1:153) suggests that the ship *Penguin* at the beginning and that implied by the "shrouded human figure" (P 1:206) at the end intimate facing mirrors (like those of Too-wit [P 1:169]), infinitely reflecting that which is at the center—the death of the brother-like Augustus on August 1 (P 1:142). Also, if we recall Augustus's excessive drinking in the first chapter of *Pym*—"He was drunk—beastly drunk—he could no longer either stand, speak, or see" (P 1:59)—we may note the resonance with Henry, who, Edgar wrote in August 1829, was "entirely given up to drink & unable to help himself, much less me" (O 1:43). Still, in November or December 1829 Edgar wrote to John Neal that "There can be no tie more strong than that of brother for brother" (O 1:47).

West Point, 1830–1831

At West Point, in late November 1830, Cadet Poe proposed that he and several classmates draw straws to determine who would exchange candles and a blanket for brandy at the local tavern, and Thomas W. Gibson (who left the reminiscence) drew the short straw. While the drawing of straws calls to mind the drawing of straws in *Pym* (P 1:134–35), it is a subsequent portion of the incident that is even more suggestive of the novel: carrying, along with the bottle of brandy, a slaughtered gander, Gibson returns to Poe with bloody shirt, hands, and face, and Poe devises the hoax that the bloodied student will return to the barracks and claim to have killed a professor (throwing the bird in as if it were the professor's head). Pym's hoax of the mutineers on the *Grampus*, when he was disguised as the corpse of Hartman Rogers, also involved his face being "splotched…with blood" (P 1:109).[15] Common to both the actual incident and the imagined one is a shocking hoax involving a bloody face and a dead man.

Baltimore, 1831–1835

Edgar returned to Baltimore from West Point by May 1831, living in the Wilks Street household that included Maria Clemm, Henry, and Virginia (PL 118). Having published *Al Aaraaf, Tamerlane, and Other Poems* in 1829, he published *Poems* in 1831. Given the poverty of Maria Clemm's household, Edgar and Henry probably shared the same room, perhaps the same bed. We may call to mind that at the beginning of *Pym*, the narrator writes of himself and Augustus, "We occupied the same bed" (P 1:57). Clearly, Poe would have witnessed Henry's illness and death. Allen and Mabbott write, "Edgar must have spent much of his time nursing his elder brother for whom he had gone into debt."[16] In 1831, in Baltimore, Edgar would have seen his brother Henry die on August 1 (PL 122). In the novel, Pym observes the death of the Henry-like Augustus on August 1 (P 1:142).

Augustus's death is at the precise center of *Pym*. It appears in the thirteenth chapter of twenty-five chapters, eleven paragraphs into twenty-two paragraphs, one week into a two-week period. With the mirror-like *Penguin* at the beginning and end, Poe represented his infinite memory of the death of his brother Henry. With *Pym*, seven years before the publication of "The Raven," Poe embodied what he termed in "The

Philosophy of Composition" (his essay on the creation of "The Raven") *"Mournful and Never-Ending Remembrance"* (L2 70). It is the death of his brother in Baltimore on August 1, a death never-endingly remembered by Poe, that is the moment that *Arthur Gordon Pym* honors.

And John Allan is not forgotten, for Pym's stating that "my grandfather...vowed to cut me off with a shilling" resonates with Allan's reportedly having written to Poe about his relationship with "an unnamed lady" from Baltimore [probably Mary Starr], "if he [Poe] married any such person he would cut him off without a shilling."[17] (See also "Three Sundays in a Week" [M 1:653].)

Poe shifted in 1831 from poetry to fiction, and several early short stories of his, written in Baltimore, have significant connections to *Pym*. His August 13, 1831, story "A Dream," about the consequences of the crucifixion of Christ (see M 2:6–9), anticipates a description of the apocalyptic landslide on Tsalal. Such phrasing in "A Dream" as "a muttered groan," "the day of retribution had come," and "in utter darkness" (P 2:8) finds parallels in such phrasing in *Pym* as "I heard a deep groan," "the day of universal dissolution was at hand," and "in utter darkness" (P 1:182). Furthermore, the purportedly comic retelling of Pompey's siege of Jerusalem and the offering to the twelve tribes of Israel forbidden meat in the June 9, 1832, story "A Tale of Jerusalem" (M 2:43–48), drawn from Horatio Smith's 1828 *Zillah, a Tale of the Holy City* (M 2:41–42), finds a correspondence in *Pym* as a dozen men from the *Jane Guy*, in the native chief's tent, surrounded by natives inside and outside the tent, are offered "the palpitating entrails of a species of unknown animal, probably one of the slim-legged hogs which we had observed in our approach to the village" (P 1:175). Poe allegorized in *Pym* what he had originally described literally. Additionally, the presentation of the "Flying Dutchman" in Poe's award-winning October 19, 1833, story "MS. Found in a Bottle" (M 2:135–146) anticipates Poe's account of the "Flying Dutchman" in Chapter 10 of *Pym* (P 1:122–126). The idea of a hole at the South Pole is evident in both works. And, notably, as Pollin mentions, an earlier issue of the newspaper in which "MS. Found in a Bottle" appeared, the *Baltimore Saturday Visiter*, featured an article titled *"Black Teeth,"* perhaps a prompt for the black teeth of Tsalalian native Nu-Nu (P 1:205; for Pollin's comment, see P 1:353). Finally, the conclusion of Poe's March 1835 short story "Berenice," written in Baltimore between 1833 and 1835—the narrator's finding the "thirty-two small, white, and ivory-looking substances" that he had removed from his disinterred—and still living—beloved (M 2:219)—resonates with the similarly horrifying "clotted and liver-like substance" in the beak of the seagull in *Pym* (P 1:125) and the *Jane Guy*'s "shore-party [that] consisted of thirty-two persons in all" "armed to the teeth" (P 1:180).[18]

Of note in Poe's criticism in Baltimore in 1835 is his mention of Samuel Taylor Coleridge in the April 1835 *Messenger* (P 5:6) and J. N. Reynolds in the June 1835 and August 1835 issues of the *Southern Literary Messenger* (P 5:20, 30), for both writers are of significance in *Pym*.[19]

Richmond, 1835–1837

The Richmond of Poe's *Southern Literary Messenger* period is not so much an under-current in *Pym* since it is mentioned explicitly in the "Preface" (P 1:55–56). With regard to Poe's one novel, his encoded life has yielded to his encoding life. Briefly, I'll mention some of his reading of this period and his writings as they relate to *Pym*.

Poe moved to Richmond from Baltimore in August 1835 to assist with the editing of Thomas W. White's monthly *Southern Literary Messenger*. His submitted book of tales was rejected by the Harpers, but he was encouraged to write a longer work—by James Kirke Paulding in March 1836 and by Harper and Brothers themselves in June 1836 (PL 195, 212–213). The Harpers argued against the "learned and mystical," but Poe had written in the February 1836 *Messenger*, in a review of Henry F. Chorley's *Conti the Discarded*, about "the *Art Novels*—the Kunstromanen," "books which, in the guise of Romance, labor to the sole end of reasoning men into admiration and study of the beautiful, by a tissue of *bizarre* fiction, partly allegorical, and partly metaphysical" (P 5:119).[20] Since *Pym* is a double allegory, we may infer that Poe was working within the Art Novel subgenre—which, he wrote, was "so mad—or perhaps so profound" (P 5:119).

We know that at this time Poe was still thinking about his lost mother—it was in December 1835 that he wrote the letter to Beverly Tucker, referring to his mother as "a string to which my heart fully responds" (O 1:116). And he was also thinking about an author's embedding his life in his work. After all, in the January 1836 *Messenger*, Poe offered a review of Francis Lieber's *Reminiscence of an Intercourse with Mr. Niebuhr* (P 5:95–98), in which he commented on Lieber's translation of Niebuhr's "Essay on the Allegory in the First Canto of Dante," "This Essay, we think, will prove of deeper interest to readers of Italian than even Mr. Lieber has anticipated" (P 5:96). Critically, Niebuhr asserts there about Dante, "Everything must be explained by his life, and the peculiarities connected therewith."[21] Poe's biographical allegory in *Pym* would be blended with a biblical allegory, to be discussed. For now, I will mention Poe's February 1835 *Messenger* essay "Palaestine" (P 5:106–107) and his reading in the *Norfolk American Beacon* and the *Norfolk and Portsmouth Herald* of February 18 and 19, 1836, respectively, the account by William Wiseman and J. Mann about the wreck of the Norfolk vessel *Ariel* and their survival from it.[22]

Poe elaborates on the technique of verisimilitude in fiction, which he uses to such compelling effect in *Pym*, in his January 1836 *Messenger* review of *Robinson Crusoe* (P 5:98–99) and his September 1836 *Messenger* review of *Sheppard Lee* (P 5:282–286). And he continues to write about Coleridge in the June 1836 *Messenger* (P 5:211–213) and Reynolds in the December 1835, August 1836, and January 1837 issues of the *Messenger* (P 5:58–59, 253–256, 354–358). Relevantly, he also reviews a dictionary, highlighting the importance of etymology, in the August 1836 *Messenger* (P 5:249–250), and Washington Irving's *Astoria*, from which he borrowed in *Pym*, in the January 1837 *Messenger* (P 5:345–354).

Furthermore, in the same February 1836 issue of the *Messenger* in which he reviewed Chorley's *Conti the Discarded* and wrote "Palaestine," Poe reviewed also Morris Mattson's *Paul Ulrich*, arguing for its plagiarism from Alain René Le Sage's *Gil Blas* (which had been translated into English by Tobias Smollett). (We know that Poe had a copy of *Gil Blas* as early as 1826, while at the University of Virginia [O 1:60].) Poe focuses in the *Messenger* on the descent into the robbers' cavern (P 5:111)—precisely the passage that suggests the *Grampus* hold section of *Pym*. Poe does not plagiarize, but he lightly alludes. In *Gil Blas*, the robbers take the eponymous hero through a hidden "trap-door," descending far below (with mention of an "old negro" and a female "cook"); he vows to escape, proceeds through "all the windings of this new labyrinth," but is stopped by a "cursed iron grate" at the "trap-door."[23] In *Pym*, the similarly eponymous hero is taken through a hidden "trapdoor" (P 1:69), descending into the ship's hold; he resolves to escape, proceeds "amid the narrow and intricate windings of the lumber" (P 1:74), but is stopped by the weight of "chain-cable" on that "trapdoor" (P 1:76).

His friend Augustus has not rescued him because of a mutiny led by the "black cook" (P 1:86).

Finally, Poe reviewed Peregrine Prolix's (Philip H. Nicklin's) 1835 *Letters Descriptive of the Virginia Springs* in the August 1836 *Messenger*, selecting a passage on the Red Sulphur Springs, including mention of an unusual reservoir: "The reservoir is about six feet long, five wide, and four and a half deep; and a beautiful red and mysterious substance covers the bottom, which extending some distance up the sides, sheds through the transparency of the water its own lovely hue" (P 5:259). Here may be suggested the multicolored water on the island of Tsalal in *Pym*, as L. Moffitt Cecil has noted. He also observes that a piece in the 1835 *Messenger*, "Visit to the Virginia Springs during the Summer of 1834," mentions "the lilac and peach blossom sediment" of the water at Red Sulphur Springs and "the sediment ... of a blue or rich dark purple color" at Blue Sulphur Springs.[24] Poe wrote in his novel about the water, "It was *not* colourless, nor was it of any one uniform colour—presenting to the eye, as it flowed, every possible shade of purple, like the hues of a changeable silk" (P 1:171–172). It is even possible that Poe saw the colored water during his visits to White Sulphur Springs in the summers of 1812, 1813, and 1814.[25]

Nearly four chapters of Poe's *Pym* appeared in the January and February 1837 issues of the *Southern Literary Messenger*. And sometime in January or February, Poe—having been let go from the *Messenger* for his drinking—moved with his wife Virginia and his mother-in-law Maria Clemm to New York City.

New York City, 1837–1838

There is no under-current in *Pym* of Poe's first stay in New York City, either, because the preface to the novel, imagined to be by Pym himself, concludes explicitly, "New-York, July, 1838" (P 1:56). And again, there are links between Poe's novel and his reading and writing of the time.

Poe relied on Reynolds's April 21, 1838 *New-York Mirror* narrative, "Leaves from an Unpublished Journal," for Pym's climb up the Tsalalian cliff (P 1:183–85). Notably, this piece concludes with the appearance in Antarctic waters of the ship the *Penguin*.[26] Poe also relied on passages from Benjamin Morrell's *A Narrative of Four Voyages*, J. L. Stephens's *Incidents of Travel in Egypt, Arabia Petraea, and the Holy Land*, and Alexander Keith's *Evidence of The Truth of the Christian Religion*.[27] Poe reviewed the Stephens text in the *New-York Review* in October 1837, agreeing with the belief in the "*literal* fulfillment of prophecy," but disagreeing with biblical translations (H 10:1–25).[28]

Poe left New York City for Philadelphia by July 1838; Harper & Brothers published *The Narrative of Arthur Gordon Pym* on July 30, 1838 (PL 248).

THE NARRATIVE OF THE FALL OF JERUSALEM

Even as Poe conveyed covertly a narrative about his life in *Pym*, he also intimated a narrative about the Fall of Jerusalem. Poe wrote in the April 1835 *Southern Literary Messenger*, "Coleridge's Table Talk is highly interesting, as every authentic fragment of his sentiments and opinions must be" (P 5:6). Coleridge considers there the theme of the destruction of Jerusalem "the only subject now remaining for an epic poem," but he could not write that poem. He adds later, "In the destruction of Jerusalem no genius or skill could possibly preserve the interest for the hero from being merged in the interest for the event. The fact is, the event itself is too sublime and overwhelming."[29] Here, then, was an opportunity for Poe to prove that he possessed the genius and skill to accomplish what Coleridge could not. And when he quoted in the June 1836 *Messenger* from *Letters, Conversations and Recollections of S. T. Coleridge*, he selected a passage that mentioned "what still appears to me [Coleridge] the only fit subject remaining for an epic poem—Jerusalem besieged and destroyed by Titus" (P 5:212). Poe's encounter with the story of the wreck of the Norfolk vessel the *Ariel* in February 1836 provided the nascent novelist with the solution to Coleridge's problem: the wreck of a vessel named the *Ariel* could represent allegorically the destruction of Jerusalem—for Jerusalem is called "Ariel" in the Bible: "Woe to Ariel, to Ariel, the city where David dwelt!" (Isaiah 29:1–2).

Poe offered his narrative of the Fall of Jerusalem with three sections: the crucifixion of Christ (the significance of which is a part of the Fall of Jerusalem), the Fall of Jerusalem itself, and the coming of the New Jerusalem.

Jerusalem 33 A.D.

Poe refers in Chapter 9 of *Pym* to "the blessed sun" (P 1:117); he suggests specifically Jesus' carrying the cross in Chapter 14 when he writes of "A heavy cross sea" (P 1:149). This inference is borne out by subsequent details regarding the crucifixion itself. Details of the crucifixion of Christ (at Golgotha, outside the walls of Jerusalem)—including the drawing of lots (Matthew 27:35; Mark 15:24; Luke 23:34; and John 19:23–24), Christ's asking "Eli, Eli, lama sabachtani?" (Matthew 27:46; Mark 15:34; "Father, Father, why has thou forsaken me?"), and the offering of vinegar (Matthew 27:48; Mark 15:36; Luke 23:36; John 19:29–30)—find their correspondences in Poe's *Pym*. Chapter 12 features the drawing of lots (P 1:133–135), Chapter 19 refers to "cross questioning" (P 1:176), Chapters 18 and 19 include the native cries *"Lama-Lama!"* (P 1:168, 174–175), and Chapter 13 describes the application of "a little of the vinegar from the olives" to the wounds of the dying Augustus (P 1:141). Following the crucifixion is the series of catastrophes in Jerusalem. The New Testament states about the time after the Crucifixion, "And, behold, the vail of the temple was rent in twain from the top to the bottom, and the earth did quake, and the rocks rent" (Matthew 27:51; see also Mark 15:38; Luke 23:45). After the landslide on Tsalal, Pym reports, "I was suddenly aware of a concussion resembling nothing I had ever before experienced, and which impressed me with a vague conception, if indeed I then thought of anything, that the whole foundations of the solid globe were suddenly rent asunder, and that the day of universal dissolution was at hand" (P 1:181–182). As earlier noted, phrasing here—not only "the day of universal dissolution was at hand," but also "in utter darkness" and "I heard a deep groan" (P 1:182)—recalls Poe's earlier treatment of the events following the Crucifixion in the 1831 short story "A Dream" (M 2:8).

Jerusalem, 65 B.C.

The second part of the narrative of biblical times is the actual Fall of Jerusalem in 70 A.D. But Poe begins by using an earlier instance of the Fall of Jerusalem.

Prompted by Coleridge's comments on the theme of the Destruction of Jerusalem, Poe would naturally have thought of his 1832 work, "A Tale of Jerusalem," which relied on Horatio Smith's *Zillah*. However, the siege of Jerusalem that is Poe's original here is that of Pompey in 65 B.C. Poe's tale concerns the Romans' lowering over the wall, near the Gate of Benjamin, a basket with a forbidden hog to the deceived Jews (M 2:43–48). Poe allegorizes this story in the Tsalal section of

Pym: twelve shipmates (the twelve tribes of Israel) are surrounded by many natives (the Romans), inside and outside the chief's tent, and are provided with "the palpitating entrails of a species of unknown animal, probably one of the slim-legged hogs which we had observed in our approach to the village" (P 1:175). The twelve shipmates cannot eat the objectionable food. Relying on a supposedly comic incident from an early siege of Jerusalem, Poe anticipates a later siege of Jerusalem, the one that Coleridge had in mind, that of Titus in 70 A.D.

Jerusalem, 70 A.D.

Prophecies of Jesus have been considered to anticipate the destruction of Jerusalem by Titus. (See, for instance, Matthew 24:1–8; Mark 13:1–8; Luke 19:41–44, 21:5–7). Poe recounted the destruction of Jerusalem by Titus in two different allegories in *Pym*. He was certainly thinking in January and February 1836 about the destruction of Jerusalem inasmuch as his February 1836 *Southern Literary Messenger* essay "Palaestine" concludes with Titus's destruction of that city (P 5:107; see also Pollin's comment on the Charles Anthon source, P 5:130–131). And then the Norfolk newspapers of February 18 and 19, 1836, reported the wreck of the Norfolk vessel the *Ariel*.

First, as mentioned earlier, Poe rendered the destruction of "Ariel, the city where David dwelt" (Isaiah 29:1) through the allegorical wreck of the sailboat *Ariel* in Chapter 1 of his novel. The boat is at the wharf of "Pankey & Co." (P 1:58)—probably a hint of the significance of the boat's name—"the key to it all." This covert representation of the Fall of Jerusalem is repeated at the end of the novel. That is, the wreck of the natives' canoe by the same ship that destroyed the *Ariel* in the beginning, the *Penguin*, intimates the repetition of the allegorical destruction of the city. (See P 1:205–206.) (We may recall that the "shrouded human figure" [P 1:206] recalls the penguin, whose "resemblance to a human figure is very striking" [P 1:151], and that the bird the penguin recalls the ship *Penguin*.)

Second, Poe offers in *Pym* another allegorical rendering of the Fall of Jerusalem. He inverts a prophecy of the peace of Jerusalem, Isaiah 33:20: "Look upon Zion, the city of our solemnities: thine eyes shall see Jerusalem a quiet habitation, a tabernacle that shall not be taken down; not one of the *stakes* thereof shall ever be removed, neither shall any of the *cords* thereof be broken" (emphasis added). Explaining the man-made landslide on Tsalal, Poe writes, as Pym, that the use of stakes and cords made the disaster possible:

> In several spots along the top of the eastern ridge of the gorge (we were now on the western) might be seen *stakes* of wood driven into the earth. . . . *stakes* similar to those we saw standing had been inserted, at not more than a yard apart, for the length of perhaps three hundred feet, and ranging at about ten feet back from the edge of the gulf. Strong *cords* of grape vine were attached to the *stakes* still remaining on the hill, and it was evident that such *cords* had also been attached to each of the other *stakes*. . . . There can be no doubt that, by the continuous line of *stakes*, a partial rupture of the soil had been brought about, probably to the depth of one or two feet, when, by means of a savage pulling at the end of each of the *cords* (these *cords* being attached to the tops of the *stakes*, and extending back from the edge of the cliff), a vast leverage power was obtained, capable of hurling the whole face of the hill, upon a given signal, into the bosom of the abyss below. (P 1:184–185; emphasis added)

So, twice with the wreck of the *Ariel* and once with the use of stakes and cords, Poe told the story of Titus's destruction of Jerusalem allegorically. He encoded the fulfillment of Christ's prophecy. With *The Narrative of Arthur Gordon Pym*, Poe achieved what Coleridge had conceded he could not.

The Prophesied New Jerusalem, at the End of Time

Fittingly enough, Poe followed his renderings of the Fall of Jerusalem with the prophecy of the coming of the New Jerusalem. We have already seen that the climactic white "shrouded human figure" suggests, lit-erally—by way of "the resemblance to a human figure" of a penguin (P 1:151)—the ship the *Penguin*.

We have also seen that this ship the *Penguin*, appearing at the begin-ning and end of the novel, also suggests—by way of "the spirit of reflec-tion" of the penguin (P 1:153)—facing mirrors, which infinitely reflect that which is at the center, the death of Augustus, who represents Poe's brother Henry. By way of the association of the appearance of the "shrouded human figure," with birds crying "*Tekeli-li!*" on March 22, with the March 22 scheduled performance of Poe's mother as the bride

Christine in the play *Tekeli*, we also have the maternal significance of that figure. We have the literal and the personal significance of the climactic image; what remains to be identified is its biblical significance. And for this we must return to the word "penguin."

Poe commented in his review of Richardson's dictionary, "The etymology is placed distinctly by itself for the convenience of hasty reference" (P 5:250). Here, we have a hint of why Poe chose to rely on the name "penguin." The "shrouded human figure" has sometimes been linked with the Vision of the Seven Candlesticks in the Book of Revelation, concerning the appearance of "one like unto the Son of man," Christ, whose "head and his hairs were white like wool, as white as snow" (Isaiah 1:13–14).[30] The Welsh etymology for "penguin," according to Samuel Johnson and Noah Webster, is "white" (for "guin") and "head" (for "pen"). The "shrouded human figure," which is the ship the *Penguin*, intimates the white head of Christ in the Vision of the Seven Candlesticks—who prophesies the coming of the "new Jerusalem" (Revelation 3:12). And the "shrouded human figure," conveying, in part, the white figure in the play *Tekeli*—Poe's mother Eliza Poe— embodies the union that occurs according to Christian eschatology: that of Christ (she is named, after all, Christine) and the church, his bride (Christine is, after all, a bride).

Having re-ordered place in Poe's novel, we may now return to the literal narrative, the adventures of Arthur Gordon Pym from Nantucket to the Antarctic sea, with a heightened sense of the stories beneath the stories, the places beneath the places. And the narratives all coalesce around one theme—that of loss and recovery. The sailboat the *Ariel* is lost—Poe's mother and brother are lost—Jerusalem is lost: the braiding of the three narratives makes sense in that they all concern loss. Yet with the intimation of the coming of the New Jerusalem, the fulfillment of Christian eschatology, Poe's volume anticipates the recovery of lost loved ones and of the lost holy city. *The Narrative of Arthur Gordon Pym* is a novel—an Art Novel—of great mourning and of the effort to work through that mourning. It may well be Poe's greatest literary achievement. Where may we see another such novel—one written with the complexity of a double allegory? The answer that comes readily to my mind is Nathaniel Hawthorne's 1850 classic *The Scarlet Letter*. But that's another story—or, rather, that's another three stories.[31]

NOTES

1. For my summative interpretive essay on *Pym*, see "Introduction," *The Narrative of Arthur Gordon Pym of Nantucket*, by Edgar Allan Poe (New York: Penguin, 1999), ix–xxix. For my other publications on *Pym*, see "The Secret of *Arthur Gordon Pym*: The Text and the Source," *Studies in American Fiction* 8 (1980): 203–218; "The Hidden Journey of *Arthur Gordon Pym*," *Studies in the American Renaissance 1982*, ed. Joel Myerson (Charlottesville: University Press of Virginia, 1982), 29–51; "Early Illustrations of *Pym*'s 'Shrouded Human Figure,'" *Scope of the Fantastic—Culture, Biography, Themes, Children's Literature*, ed. Robert A. Collins and Howard D. Pearce (Westport, CT: Greenwood Press, 1985), 155–170; "The '*Very* Profound Under-Current' of *Arthur Gordon Pym*," *Studies in the American Renaissance 1987*, ed. Joel Myerson (Charlottesville: University Press of Virginia, 1987), 143–175; "Poe's *Pym*-Esque 'A Tale of the Ragged Mountains,'" *Poe and His Times: The Artist and His Milieu*, ed. Benjamin Franklin Fisher IV (Baltimore: The Edgar Allan Poe Society, 1990), 167–177; "Readers Write: Nineteenth-Century Annotations in Copies of the First American Edition of Poe's *The Narrative of Arthur Gordon Pym*," *Nineteenth-Century Literature* 55, no. 3 (2000): 399–408. I also edited the first scholarly book on *Pym*, *Poe's Pym: Critical Explorations* (Durham, NC: Duke University Press, 1992).

2. Richard Kopley, *Edgar Allan Poe and the Dupin Mysteries* (New York: Palgrave Macmillan, 2008), esp. 77–85.

3. See *The Poe Log: A Documentary Life of Edgar Allan Poe, 1809–1849*, ed. Dwight Thomas and David K. Jackson. (New York: G. K. Hall & Co., 1987), xxxvii, 3 (hereafter cited as PL in text).

4. Richard Wilbur noted the anagram in his "Introduction," *The Narrative of Arthur Gordon Pym*, by Edgar Allan Poe (Boston: David R. Godine, 1973), vii–xxv. See especially pp. x–xi. For the passage from *Pym*, see *Collected Writings of Edgar Allan Poe: vol. 1, The Imaginary Voyages* (New York: Gordian, 1994), 57 (hereafter cited in text as P).

5. Benjamin Morrell, *A Narrative of Four Voyages* (1832; Reprint. Upper Saddle River, NJ: Gregg Press, 1970), 365.

6. Malcolm Cowley, "Aidgarpo," *The New Republic*, November 5, 1945, 610.

7. See also P 1:218; Mary E. Phillips, *Edgar Allan Poe—The Man*, 2 vols. (Chicago: John C. Winston, 1926), 1: 117–119; Hervey Allen, *Israfel: The Life and Times of Edgar Allan Poe*, 2 vols. (New York: George H. Doran, 1926), 1: 57–58; and Marie Bonaparte, *The Life and Works of Edgar Allan Poe A Psycho-Analytic Interpretation* (London: Imago, 1949), 296.

8. Kopley, *Edgar Allan Poe and the Dupin Mysteries*, 69. For the Princess Caroline connection, see *Edgar Allan Poe and the Dupin Mysteries*, 65–76.

9. Kenneth Silverman, *Edgar Allan Poe—Mournful and Never-Ending Remembrance* (New York: HarperCollins, 1991), 98–99.

10. See P 1:218.

11. For the Ellis address, see Thomas H. Ellis, "Edgar Allan Poe," *Richmond Standard*, May 7, 1881, 2.

12. For a treatment of the relationship of *Pym* and "A Tale of the Ragged Mountains," see my aforementioned "Poe's *Pym*-Esque 'A Tale of the Ragged Mountains.'"

13. Hervey Allen and Thomas Ollive Mabbott, *Poe's Brother: The Poems of William Henry Leonard Poe* (New York: George H. Doran, 1926), 92. The poems were "The Happiest Day" and "Dreams." See also pages 24–25 and 30.

14. Ibid., 67.

15. Thomas W. Gibson, "Poe at West Point," *Harper's New Monthly Magazine* (November 1867), 754–756 (see especially 755).

16. Allen and Mabbott, 35.

17. George E. Woodberry, *The Life of Edgar Allan Poe*, 2 vols. (Boston: Houghton Mifflin, 1909), 1: 90, 96.

18. See John Limon, *The Place of Fiction in the Time of Science: A Disciplinary History of American Writing* (New York: Cambridge University Press, 1990), 116.

19. Poe may also have written of Coleridge in the July 16, 1835, issue of the *Baltimore American* (PL 162).

20. For scholarly comment on Poe's remarks on the Art Novel, see James L. Machor, *Reading Fiction in Antebellum America: Informed Response and Reception Histories, 1820–1865* (Baltimore: Johns Hopkins University Press, 2011), 114.

21. Francis Lieber, *Reminiscences of an Intercourse with Mr. Niebuhr the Historian, During a Residence with Him in Rome, in the Years 1822 and 1823* (Philadelphia: Carey, Lea, and Blanchard, 1835), 190–191.

22. For further information on Poe's encountering the Wiseman/Mann account in the Norfolk newspapers, see "The 'Very Profound Under-Current' of *Arthur Gordon Pym*," 143–145, 160–162.

23. Alain René Le Sage, *The Adventures of Gil Blas of Santillane*, trans. Tobias Smollett, vol. 1 (New York: Henry Durrell, 1824). Hathitrust. For the "trap-door," see 1:38–39; for the descent with mention of the "old negro" and the female "cook," see 1:39–40; and for the determination to escape, see 1:51–52. For "all the windings of this new labyrinth" and the "cursed iron grate," see 1:52.

24. L. Moffitt Cecil, "Poe's Tsalal and the Virginia Springs," *Nineteenth-Century Fiction* 19, no. 4 (1965): 398–402. The colored water of Tsalal may well have been indebted to a natural source and a literary one. I have noted that "the singular character of the water" (P 1:171) may have been shaped by "the singular character of the city [of Petra]" in J. L. Stephens's *Incidents of Travel in Egypt, Arabia Petraea and the Holy Land*, 2 vols. (New York: Harper and Brothers, 1837)—a city that was also multicolored. The destroyed city of Petra hints at the destroyed city of Jerusalem. See "'*Very* Profound,'" 166, n. 34.

25. George E. Woodberry, *Edgar Allan Poe* (Boston: Houghton Mifflin, 1885), 15–16. It is unlikely that Poe went to White Sulphur Springs during the summer of 1815 (PL 18) since the Allans were traveling to England then. The Didier source cited in PL mistakenly maintains that the Allans went to England in the summer of 1816. See Memoir, *The Life and Poems of Edgar Allan Poe* (New York: W. J. Widdleton, 1877), 28–29.

26. Kopley, "The Secret of *Arthur Gordon Pym*," 211–215.

27. Alexander Keith, *Evidence of the Truth of the Christian Religion, Derived from the Literal Fulfillment of Prophecy; Particularly as Illustrated by the History of the Jews, and by Discoveries of Recent Travellers* (New York: J. & J. Harper, 1832). For Poe's use of Morrell, Stephens, and Keith, see Pollin's notes and J. V. Ridgely's "The Growth of the Text" (P 1:29–36, esp. 32–36).

28. With regard to the translations, Poe had the assistance of classicist Charles Anthon—see PL 244–245 and H 17:42–43 for Anthon's June 1, 1837, letter to Poe.

29. Samuel Taylor Coleridge, *Specimens of the Table Talk of the Late Samuel Taylor Coleridge*, comp. Hartley N. Coleridge, 2 vols. (New-York: Harper & Brothers, 1835), 2:26, 135. Much of the argument here was first elaborated in "The '*Very* Profound Under-Current' of *Arthur Gordon Pym*."

30. See William Mentzel Forrest, *Biblical Allusions in Poe* (New York: Macmillan, 1928), 157; Sidney Kaplan, "Introduction," *The Narrative of Arthur Gordon Pym* (New York: Hill and Wang, 1960), xxii; Richard Wilbur, "Introduction," *The Narrative of Arthur Gordon Pym* (Boston: Godine, 1973), xxiv; and Harold Beaver, "Commentary," *The Narrative of Arthur Gordon Pym of Nantucket* (1975; New York: Penguin, 1986), 268.

31. The three stories are the literal story involving Reverend Arthur Dimmesdale and Hester Prynne in 1640s Boston, the historical one involving John Wheelwright and Anne Hutchinson in 1630s Boston, and the biblical one involving Adam and Eve in the Garden of Eden. For the argument, see my chapter "A Novel by Ebenezer Wheelwright," *The Threads of "The Scarlet Letter": A Study of Hawthorne's Transformative Art* (Newark: University of Delaware Press, 2003), 64–96.

CHAPTER 10

Poe's German Soulscape: Influenced by Angst or Anxiety of Influence?

Sonya Isaak

Many readers regard Edgar A. Poe as the king of horror and Gothic fiction. The country most readily associated with this tradition is Germany, which comes as no surprise given that both the German Romantic movement and the proto-romantic *Sturm und Drang* (or "Storm and Stress") period helped to shape and influence Gothic fiction.

Poe both took from Germany and contributed to it. The country that inspired Poe would readily welcome the author whose works abound with references and allusions to German writers, German landscapes, and Gothic elements. In a recent publication on Poe translations, Marius Littschwager explores the history of Poe's critical reception in Germany.[1]

The German readership first became familiar with Poe through a translation of "The Gold-Bug" ("Der Goldkäfer"), which explains why he was regarded initially as a writer of narratives, rather than as a poet.[2] According to Littschwager, while the first German translation of "The Raven" was printed in 1853, it took thirty years for the first collection of Poe's poetry to be published in German. The first Poe translations reached German readers in magazine and newspaper form in the middle

S. Isaak (✉)
University of Heidelberg, Heidelberg, Germany

© The Author(s) 2018
P. E. Phillips (ed.), *Poe and Place*,
Geocriticism and Spatial Literary Studies,
https://doi.org/10.1007/978-3-319-96788-2_10

215

of the nineteenth century, but new translations continue to appear. A year before the Poe bicentennial in 2009, a new and updated critical German-language edition of his collected works was published, reflecting Poe's lasting popularity and influence in Germany.[3] In 2017, Andreas Nohl published the first book of a five-volume German translation based on Charles Baudelaire's Poe translations, underscoring the French poet's role in assuring the American writer's lasting impact in most European countries.[4]

While earlier German renditions distorted Poe's language in an awkward, antiquated translation style characteristic of much of the nineteenth century, perpetuating his reception as a bizarre or "uncanny-strange" writer, this image gradually changed, with more psychological interpretations and translations of his works conjuring up a "new vision" of a more complex and modern Poe.[5] Recent German scholarship regards Poe as an author of many genres and recognizes his unique skills as a wordsmith, making him a staple in the canon of foreign literature in Germany. The abundance of volumes of his collected works in the German language attests to his prominence and continued reception.[6]

Both Poe's tales and literary criticism suggest that he was familiar with contemporary German literature. William Crisman even goes so far as to call him "America's first scientific literary critic," discussing in detail Poe's comparison of Nathaniel Hawthorne to the German writer Ludwig Tieck and the history of critical investigations into Poe's charge of plagiarism.[7] Poe accuses Hawthorne of plagiarizing from Tieck, but his charge is unfounded since he did not provide concrete textual evidence. Crisman explores the history of these parallels, contending that the stories that struck Poe as suspiciously similar were likely to have been Hawthorne's "Young Goodman Brown" and Tieck's "Die Freunde" (*The Friends*).[8]

Yet, despite an undeniable familiarity with German sources, Poe's relationship to the German tradition remains ambivalent. Toward the beginning of his writing career, Poe capitalized on what he must have considered the popular appeal of German horror, by adding the subtitle, "A Tale in Imitation of the German," to his title, "Metzengerstein," when it was republished in the *Southern Literary Messenger* in 1836. Scholars disagree about whether the story was intended as pure parody of what was commonly considered to be the German Gothic, or whether it constitutes an exercise in mastering the craft of writing this genre. In *Poe's Fiction: Romantic Irony in the Gothic Tales*, G. R. Thompson differentiates between German "supernatural Gothic" and the "explained" and "ambiguous" forms developed by American writers. Moreover, in his discussion of "Metzengerstein," Thompson argues that this "carefully flawed tale is a paradigm for Poe's subsequent Gothic hoaxes" since it reveals Poe's "power to touch the unseen, unconscious life, to render forcefully certain dark psychological states, to suggest the demoniac in mankind and in nature and yet at the same time to bring a cool rationality, an ironic skepticism, and even mockery to bear on all that he examines."[9] Poe's contribution to the construction of this more "ambiguous" manifestation of the Gothic characteristic of American authors is significant in that he was both reproducing and mocking what he probably considered to be the leading notions of the German Gothic. A shrewd salesman, Poe knew how to present himself to his readership, using the Gothic epithet to his advantage to increase the marketability of the story.

Yet, despite this apparent initial interest in the Germanic and many instances of influence of both the German language and literature in his work, Poe became ever more reluctant to identify himself with Germany, famously declaring four years later in his *Preface* to the *Tales of the Grotesque and Arabesque* (1840) that, "[i]f in many of my productions terror has been the thesis, I maintain that terror is not of Germany, but of the soul."[10] He further stated that he "deduced this terror only from its legitimate sources, and urged it only to its legitimate results."[11] Over time, Poe's anti-German position grew even stronger, resulting in the writer's total deprecation of German literature in a public statement in 1846, when he professed, "I am not ashamed to say that I prefer even Voltaire to Goethe; and hold Macaulay to possess more of the true critical spirit than Augustus William and Frederick Schlegel combined."[12]

Despite such vehement rejections of the German spirit, allusions to German writers pervade Poe's writing even after this statement. This mysterious ambivalence and apparent rejection of a tradition that clearly guided him is puzzling. A hoaxer by nature, Poe nonetheless wanted his reading public to believe that he had mastered the language, interspersing quotations and Germanic names throughout his writing. Unfortunately, as Thomas S. Hansen and Burton Pollin confirm in *The German Face of Edgar Allan Poe*, Poe's command of the language was insufficient to read literary texts in the original, much less to write flawless German sentences. In "The Man of the Crowd," for instance, Poe makes what appears to be an unintentional grammatical error in his first sentence that is strong enough to make it incomprehensible to a German native[13]: "It was well said of a certain German book that '*er lasst sich nicht lesen*'—it does not permit itself to be read." The German noun *Buch* is neuter (calling for the article *es*) and not *er*. This is only one of many examples of his erroneous use of German.

Thomas Dunn English, a former supporter of Poe, with whom he had a falling out after the latter's slandering words in the caustic *Literati of New York City*, exposed Poe's linguistic ignorance after the latter had labeled him a *Windbeutel*, which is German for "windbag": "He professes to know every language and to be proficient in every science and art under the sun [...]. His frequent quotations from languages of which he is totally ignorant and his consequent blunders expose him to ridicule; while his cool plagiarisms from known or forgotten writers excite the public amazement."[14]

According to Hansen and Pollin, Poe seems to have had no formal training in German. Though he attended one class at the University of Virginia with a renowned German Professor by the name of Blaettermann, it is unlikely that German was taught or spoken in the class.[15] Poe's limited knowledge of German is further substantiated by prolific mistakes in his citations and erroneous or contrived use of the language, as exemplified by his choice of the exaggerated title and name *Metzengerstein*, which would make any German smirk. According to Patrick Labriola, Poe likely gained access to German literature (and especially to E. T. A. Hoffmann's writings) through different sources, including Gillis's translation of *The Devil's Elixirs*, Sir Walter Scott's essay on *Hoffmann's use of the supernatural*, and Carlyle's publication of *The German Romance*.[16] These and other readings of his own in English translation form the basis of his knowledge of the "Germanic." Moreover, as an editor of prominent journals, Poe was exposed to many texts, a number of which were influenced by European writers, and he lived in Philadelphia from 1837 to 1844, which was home to the greatest number of German immigrants at the time.[17] Poe frequently alludes to Immanuel Kant and August Wilhelm Schlegel in his work. As Margaret Alterton demonstrates, Poe was significantly influenced by August Wilhelm Schlegel in regard to his ideas on unity.[18] Yet while Poe playfully alludes to Kant, the extent of his debt to the German philosopher remains contentious. For Glen Omans, Poe's frequent disparaging references to Kant in tales like "Bon Bon" and "How to Write a Blackwood Article" are deliberate attempts to conceal the seminal impact that Kant's works—especially *The Critique of Judgment*—actually had on Poe's own aesthetic theories.[19]

Poe's ambivalent rapport with Kant is emblematic of his relationship with Germany at large. Despite sprinklings of German words, places, or writers throughout his works, Poe, the master of *angst*, seems to have been haunted by a specious "anxiety of influence," in other words, by a need he sensed to defend himself from accusations of "Germanisms." Why would Poe, who bent over backwards to feign knowledge of German that he did not have, want to distance himself from a Gothic literary tradition that seemed so akin to the nature of his works?

One answer lies in the supposed link of the Transcendentalists, whom Poe claimed to despise, and German literature and philosophy. The word *German* was charged with pejorative connotations, often synonymous with "mystical" and "transcendental." It appears that its meaning changed over time, as it was increasingly affiliated with the transcendental Bostonian school as Poe's career evolved. This might explain why while at first Poe seemed to identify readily with the label, gradually he would sense the budding need to defend himself from charges of "Germanism," of which he was often accused. One might speculate also that these defensive statements served as a cover to conceal the German *angst* that haunted him to the extent that it became the underlying essence of his writing. In other words, Germany was so much a part of him that he had to revolt against it. Perhaps to appear original as an American author, Poe felt that he had to distance himself from traces of German influence. This contentious relationship to all things "German" reflects Poe's unconscious quest for his own identity as an American writer. Perhaps while he could not help his affinity to the German soul, Poe felt that for an emerging author of what was still an Anglo-Saxon world, British sources might be seen as more respectable than the more "barbaric" German Gothic ones.

In her discussion of *angst*, Susan Bernstein cites *Romanticism and the Gothic*, whose author, Michael Gamer, asserts that Romanticism partially defines itself by differentiating itself from the Gothic. In this relationship, Gamer argues:

> While gothic's contentious reception constituted it as a conspicuously "low" form against which romantic writers could oppose themselves, its immense popularity, economic promise, and sensational subject matter made this opposition a complex and ultimately conflicted and duplicitous

endeavor. It is no accident that a considerable amount of early-nineteenth-century writing explicitly denies (or otherwise deflects) its association with the gothic at its moments of closest kinship. If my primary interest is with these moments of adjacency and overlapping, it is because within them the gothic perpetually haunts, as an aesthetic to be rejected, romanticism's construction of high literary culture.[20]

This perspective suggests that Poe, like his contemporaries, might have avoided any unnecessary association with the Gothic, despite "moments of closest kinship," since it was considered to be a "lower" form, unlike "high-brow" Romanticism.

Let us recall that the Gothic genre draws its name from the Goths, a Germanic people.[21] According to the *Norton* guide,

In the context of the Romantic period; the Gothic is [...] a type of imitation medievalism [that] featured accounts of terrifying experiences in ancient castles...experiences connected with subterranean dungeons, secret passageways, flickering lamps, screams...graveyards and the rest. By extension, it came to designate the macabre, mysterious, fantastic, supernatural, and again, the terrifying, especially the pleasurably terrifying [...].[22]

Before he wrote *The Castle of Otranto* (1784), widely considered to be the first Gothic novel, Horace Walpole (1717–1797) remodeled his estate on Strawberry Hill in London according to "Gothick style, adding towers [...] arched doors and ornaments—medieval style."[23] His novel makes use of typically Gothic elements like "a haunted castle, a Byronic villain by the name of Manfred who preceded Byron's *Manfred*, mysterious deaths and supernatural happenings."[24]

In *The Literature of Terror: Volume 1: The Gothic Tradition*, David Punter explores the rise of different literary realms of the Gothic. In the German tradition of Gothic fiction, the *Schauerroman* ("shudder novel") is analogous to the British Gothic novel. However, the German *Schauerromane* differ in that they are more pessimistic and complex, often dealing with secret societies.

A genre innovator, Poe extends the boundaries of what one might call Germanic Gothicism, focusing less on description than on the psychological disintegration of the soul. (Thompson would refer to this as Poe's "authentic American Gothic.")[25] Poe is careful to identify himself with the English rather than the German Gothic tradition, expressing his indebtedness to Ann Radcliffe in *The Oval Portrait* by dropping her name. One might even argue that he takes pride in being affiliated with such British Romantics as Coleridge or Byron, yet he distances himself from the German tradition despite an undeniable "kinship." This would also help to explain Poe's need to attack Hawthorne when the author he otherwise admired drew on German sources such as Tieck. Ironically, exposing Hawthorne is analogous to exposing himself since Poe, too, would use German sources.

To understand Poe's German dilemma, it is appropriate to trace the influence of the German spirit on Poe. First, we will explore how Poe's Gothic is rooted in the German tradition by tracing some general parallels. Then, we will illustrate Poe's use of the German Lenore saga throughout his oeuvre, demonstrating his underlying, profound affinity to Germanic sources.

Poe's first published tale, "Metzengerstein," which, as stated earlier, he would enhance with the subtitle, "A tale in imitation of the German," caters to all the expectations of a German Gothic tale. It is set in Hungary, which, as Mabbott correctly observes, was at the time part of the Holy Roman Empire and thus considered to be Germanic. This tale concerns the fall of two feuding German aristocratic families whose decaying castles are reminiscent of Walpole's castle of Otranto and who are exposed to supernatural influences and a prophecy, which ultimately lead to their demise. Poe heavily used all of these typically German Gothic components for his tale, exaggerating to the extent that some might read the work as a mere parody. However, Mabbott seems to agree with Quinn in his annotations, suggesting that the tale is "no mere burlesque," but rather "a powerful story of evil passions in a young man's soul," and remarking on the superiority of Poe's "use of the Gothic material" to "Walpole's absurd treatment." "The tale is hardly a burlesque at all, unless in reverse, but Poe and his early readers may have found the characters' names funny." He also cites Ed Winfield Parks, who claimed that "'Metzengerstein' [...] started as an imitation of the Gothic romances but [...] gathered such momentum that it became a powerful allegory, with evil leading to its own self-destruction."[26] In "Metzengerstein," the evil Baron Frederick von Metzengerstein is carried away by a satanic horse, which springs out of a tapestry and comes alive, presumably turning into his archenemy Count Wilhelm von Berlifitzing, who wants to avenge the death of his family. The story implies that it was Frederick von Metzengerstein who set fire to the castle of the rival family, resulting in the extinction of the family line. This image of a horse that serves the devil recurs elsewhere in German literature such as Goethe's famous ballad *Erlkönig* and also appears in the Lenore saga. In Poe's tales, Gothic architecture, decaying palazzi, and catacombs reminiscent of Romantic ruins abound. The fall of an aristocratic family and its ominous, deteriorating mansion is perfectly exemplified by "The Fall of the House of Usher," in which the "house of Usher" refers to both the family and the mansion itself. In "Ligeia," Poe's narrator meets his beloved in "some large, old, decaying city near the Rhine," a river in Germany.[27] Her family is well known and presumably aristocratic, all typical Gothic ingredients. The supernatural or magical is also an essential element of this tale, which recounts the narrator's second wife Rowena's transformation into Ligeia. Thompson discusses Poe's "Ligeia," exploring whether or not the narrator witnesses an attempt at reincarnation or whether the transformation is merely imagined due to the influence of opium.[28] He then inserts "Ligeia" into a framework of development of Gothic fiction from Germany to England and then to America, discussing typical characteristics of each type of "Gothic." While for European Gothic writers, the purely "terrible" stood in stark opposition to the thoroughly "explained," the American Gothic relied on a more ambiguous explanation of the supernatural. As mentioned previously, for Thompson, Poe exemplified the authentic American Gothic. In this American expression of the Gothic, an apparently supernatural tale relies on the psychological insights of a despairing mind that cannot ascertain anything with complete certainty, which is analogous to the unreliability of Poe's narrators. Poe referred to "Ligeia" and some of his other tales as *Phantasy Pieces*, alluding to the German Romantic writer by whom he was often inspired, E. T. A Hoffmann, who had published "Phantasiestücke."

Poe's use of the *Doppelgänger* motif constitutes another example of Germanic (and specifically of Hoffmanian) influence. "William Wilson" is clearly inspired by Hoffman's "The Devil's Elixirs" (1815). According to Patrick Labriola, while Poe claims to have borrowed the motif of the double in "William Wilson" from an article by Washington Irving, it is evident that "he drew extensively on German literature for his short stories and sketches." Labriola demonstrates countless parallels between "William Wilson" and Hoffmann's "The Devil's Elixirs," pointing out that the *Doppelgänger* motif is unique to German literature.[29] Now let us turn to Poe's use of the Lenore myth to acquire a deeper understanding of his relationship with Germany. Poe's frequent use of the motif of the romantic legend of the death of a beautiful maiden named "Lenore" gives us insight into his German Gothic heritage. The story of Lenore, also known by other names such as *Leonore*, *Elleanor*, *Ellenore* or *Helen*, or *Wilhelm and Helen*, recounts the gory tale of a beautiful young maiden who loses her betrothed in a battle. Unable to cope with his loss, she curses God, expressing a fond desire to be reunited with her beloved at any cost. Soon thereafter, while she is preparing for bed, a *revenant figure*, a ghost with the appearance of her lover, appears, knocking at her chamber door and wanting to take her away with him on horseback to what he claims is their wedding bed (recall the parallel to the horse in *Metzengerstein*). Lenore is both skeptical and reluctant about leaving in the middle of the night, but she finally agrees. Followed by ravens, they ride through obscure, nocturnal landscapes and arrive finally at the so-called wedding bed, which turns out to be a graveyard. The funeral rites having been read, Lenore joins her lover in the grave. Much like the Gothic tradition itself, the Lenore legend had its origins in Scotland or England, but then travelled to Germany and continental Europe before returning to the Anglo-Saxon realm.[30] As in Poe's "The Raven," the lyrical subject's deceased wife, or lover, shares the name, "Lenore," which alludes to this saga, recounted by the German poet Gottfried August Bürger in his "Lenore" ballad of 1773. Killis Campbell argues that Poe's heroine is a namesake of the heroine in the famous German ballad. Scholar Marti Lee underlines the lasting impact of Bürger's poem:

> Lenore had tremendous influence on the literature of the late eighteenth- and early [n]ineteenth-centuries, and in fact, today's popular horror books and movies are still feeling the reverberations. [...] In short, Bürger's achievement, while minor in itself, helped father an international movement that led directly to the massive popularity of Gothic works then and now. [...] As the Gothic novel borrowed many of its original conventions from the German ballads, as popularized by "Lenore," we can fairly say that Bürger is one of the most influential founding fathers of the Gothic and horror genres.[31]

Though hardly remembered today, Bürger's 1773 poem was one of the key ballads of German Gothic Proto-Romanticism, *Sturm und*

Drang, and, like Goethe's "Erlkönig," which followed in 1782, it was to have a profound influence on Romanticism. It seems that for Poe, using the "Lenore" motif constituted a deliberate attempt both to belong to and nonetheless to challenge the German literary heritage. His recurrent use of the name *Lenore* in his poems and tales demonstrates that, to some extent, he must have sensed a strong bond with this German tradition. However, his revision or deliberate use of variants of the name may suggest also that he may have wanted to make the reader aware of differences between his Lenore figures and those of his predecessors or contemporaries (Fig. 10.1).

Thomas O. Mabbott acknowledges in a footnote that Poe was aware of Bürger's ballad since the latter casually mentioned it in a review in the *Southern Literary Messenger* of October 1836. However, Mabbott then proceeds to argue that the ballad did not serve as a model for Poe's own "Lenore" since, "[i]n his reviews[,] Poe expresses no admiration for Bürger's ballad, nor even indicates that he knew its theme."[32] In reviews that appeared in that same issue of the *Southern Literary Messenger*, Poe mentioned that both Mrs. Hemans and Sir Walter Scott admired Bürger's ballad. Scott even wrote an adaptation of it with the title "William and Helen," which Poe must have known since he reviewed some of Scott's works. Bürger's version recounts the story of Lenore, who, as Mabbott states, "refusing to be reconciled to the loss of her lover Wilhelm in the Crusades, uttered such impious words as led his ghost to come and carry her off to his grave." Mabbott concludes, however, that Poe's version is not comparable to that of Bürger: "What has this precious pair [Scott's Wilhelm and Lenore] to do with [Poe's] Guy De Vere and his gentle sweetheart?"[33]

Mabbott's idea, however, begs the question whether Poe's lack of discussion of Bürger's poem is enough evidence to justify this conclusion. It is just as easy to assume that Poe was so familiar with the Bürger poem, which was, after all, one of the key texts that inspired Romanticism, that he saw no need to prove that he was familiar with its contents. It is also possible that he deliberately refrained from expressing his admiration to avoid steering attention away from his own version of the legend. After all, Poe does mention the text in his reviews and, at the very least, knew of its existence and that some of his contemporaries admired Bürger's poem. Mabbott's assumption may be correct, but it remains an assumption. Instead of taking Mabbott's words at face value, one could assume

Fig. 10.1 Johann David Schubert "Lenore" (ca. 1800). Illustration to Bürger's ballad, "Lenore." Ink drawing (Wiki Commons)

also that the opposite is true, namely, that Poe was intimately familiar with Bürger's poem and that his "Lenore" is an adaptation of the original, well-known theme.

This influence then could serve as the point of departure for an analysis raising the question as to what extent Poe's version constitutes a continuation of the German Gothic heritage or represents a revision thereof. One must keep in mind that for Poe, "Lenore" is not simply a poem. *Lenore* is also the absent subject, the lost lover of "The Raven," and the name *Lenore* recurs in other forms throughout Poe's work.[34]

After all, various English translations existed at the time, and the poem's title would have been attractive to Poe if he were to use it as a title for his own poem and if he were to use the name in different permutations.[35] One could argue that Poe was indeed familiar with the source text, and, using this as a point of departure, suggest its use as a tool to explore Poe's engagement with the German Gothic.

COMPARISON OF BÜRGER'S *LENORE* TO POE'S *LENORE*

Before attempting to compare Bürger's "Lenore" (in William Taylor's translation) and Poe's "Lenore,"[36] we might want to consider why the Lenore saga appealed to Poe. Certainly, Poe's life was marked by the death of several young, beautiful women with whom he had an emotional bond (except his aunt, Maria Clemm). We know that Poe used the name "Helen," a version of Lenore, to refer to both Jane Stannard Helen and Sarah Helen Whitman. We might speculate that his life influenced his aesthetic ideal since, for Poe, the most "poetical" of subjects was the death of a young and beautiful woman.

The Lenore saga appealed to Poe, who used the name *Lenore* and many related permutations throughout his works. In addition to a poem he wrote titled "Lenore," Poe's poem "To Helen" and his tale "Eleanor" offer variants of the name and subject matter in their titles. Moreover, one might argue that Poe's recurrent and alliterative use of the consonant "L" throughout the corpus of his works is also reminiscent of Lenore: AnabeLLe Lee, to HeLen, Ligeia, ELLeanor, MadeLeine, Ulalume, and MoreLLA. Poe seems to have had a penchant for female names that contained a sonorous "L."

In comparing Bürger's and Poe's "Lenore," one notices immediately that both poems bear the same title and deal with the Gothic romantic subject of the death of a beautiful maiden who finds her deathbed where her funeral rights are read and where she is buried. Both poems employ a similar tone, which is wrought with sarcasm and reprimanding didacticism. Both poems feature evil lovers. In the case of Bürger, William is egotistical, returning as a revenant to steal his bride; in the case of Poe's "Lenore," Guy de Vere is more of a modern anti-hero, who is indifferent to his lover's death. A moralistic undertone is inherent in both poems. In Bürger's ballad, this is particularly strong. Lenore is punished by death for having committed *hubris* by challenging God to bring back her beloved. There are also some direct intertextual parallels: Bürger's "Rabenhaar" becomes Poe's "Raven hair." "Raven hair" appears in the earliest version of Poe's "Lenore."[37]

Of course, the poems also differ in some respects. Poe did not write "Lenore" in ballad form and, as innovative as he is, his poem includes an element of comic relief. While the Romantics embraced death, Poe deliberately shattered commonplace expectations of the Gothic genre by introducing an indifferent lover who does not shed a tear at the death-bed of his beloved, but whose name, Guy de Vere, alludes ironically to the Latin *veritas* (truth). One would expect him to be a true lover, but instead he is hypocritical. While Bürger's Lenore is punished for her sin, Poe's Lenore is portrayed as a victim of her illness, a young and beautiful woman who died prematurely, and Guy de Vere is depicted as a cold-hearted lover.

COMPARISON OF BÜRGER'S *LENORE* TO *THE RAVEN*

One of the leading genres of Romanticism was the romance, texts with a novelesque character, like the ballad, a poem that recounted a story. Ballads were also very popular and dealt with Romantic or Gothic themes like the sublime, awe, or with the death of a young and beautiful maiden. When one thinks of Bürger's "Lenore" another comparison that comes to mind is Poe's "Raven."

One of the prominent features of Bürger's ballad that one can find also in Poe's balladic "The Raven" is the revenant figure (the lover who has risen from the dead—a typical Romantic subject). In Poe's version, a raven replaced the revenant, perhaps providing comic relief. Both texts are ballads that rhyme and feature a predominating "o" sound and the use of dialogue. In Bürger's version, Lenore speaks with both her mother and Wilhelm. In "The Raven," the speaker converses with a raven in what might be considered to be a tragicomic, self-deprecating monologue. In both poems, the menace comes from without. The speaker in "The Raven" is inside and afraid of sounds outside just as Lenore in Bürger's ballad is afraid of the danger that lurks outside. Finally, in both cases, death, or the memory of death, comes from the exterior, answering the melancholy calls of the protagonists, yet shattering the safety of their inner worlds.

Of course, we still find some important differences. Poe's introduction of a raven into the Romantic setting of a Lenore-cycle poem challenges the unquestionable, sublime, or supernatural context so characteristic of Romanticism. Indeed, Poe's ballad is sarcastic to the point that it fringes upon being a parody. In sum, Poe's novelties include figures that provide comic relief. For example, in the "Lenore" poem, the name of the lover Guy de Vere alludes to "veritas," suggesting that he is true, yet he proves to be indifferent when he does not sob for his dead bride. In "The Raven," a talking raven seems to mock the protagonist's sorrow. Death is embodied by a revenant figure in Bürger's poem while in Poe's version an anticlimactic raven serves as its substitute, giving Poe's ballad a modern touch. The raven itself is no menace, but the attribution of meaning on the part of the speaker to the raven's meaninglessly uttered "Nevermore" makes the poem haunting. Thus, affinities between these ballads abound, and Poe's version reads as a psychological rendition of the Bürgian model. Bürger's title becomes the name of the deceased heroine in Poe's poem, and the object of the desperate speaker's desire.

CONCLUSION

It appears, then, that given so many parallels, Mabbott's contention that Poe was unfamiliar with Bürger's text is questionable. If Poe did not use Bürger's original as a model, then why did he mention it in the first place? If Poe intended to write a poem called "Lenore," then presumably he would have read every poem he could find with that title. One might also ask what other reasons might have prompted Poe's recurring use of variants of this theme and of this name in his writing. According to Mabbott, Poe's *Lenore*, the heroine's name, changed only after Poe reworked an earlier poem into its new 1842 version. In the earlier 1836 version, the soon-to-be "Lenore" was "Helen."[38] Apparently, in 1848, Poe gave Sarah Helen Whitman a copy of the *Broadway Journal* in which he had written "Helen, Ellen, Elenore, Lenore," suggesting that all of these were variants of the same name. As mentioned earlier, Poe even referred to Jane Stannard as "Helen," evoking a mysterious, biographical connection he had with the symbolic meaning of the name.[39] Etymologically, the name "Lenore" and its variants mean "light," prompting the reader to reflect on the symbolic meaning of this attribution. Was Poe, then, suggesting that his Lenores or Helens served as guiding lights in his life?

As for the literary implications of drawing upon various versions of *Lenore*, was Poe using a name that meant "light" to enlighten his readers by reshaping outdated notions of German Gothic Romanticism or was he passing on the torch of his predecessors? It was no coincidence that Poe considered the death of a young and beautiful woman to be the most Romantic and tragic of subjects. He famously proclaimed in "The Philosophy of Composition": "When it most closely allies itself to *Beauty*: the death, then, of a beautiful woman is, unquestionably, the most poetical topic in the world—and equally is it beyond doubt that the lips best suited for such topic are those of a bereaved lover."[40] Perhaps it was Poe's anxiety of Germanic influence that spawned his own angst, making him the master of Gothic horror. The country and culture with which he feared most to be identified do not fear him, but rather delight to this day in the angst that his writing instills.

Notes

1. Marius Littschwager, "Poe in Germany: A Panoramic and Historical View of His Works Translated into German Language," in *Translated Poe*, ed. Emron Esplin and Margarida Vale de Gato (Bethlehem, PA: Lehigh University Press, 2014), 55–64.
2. Littschwager, 64.
3. Edgar Allan Poe, *Werke in vier Bänden: Vier Bände im Schuber.* Berlin: Suhrkamp Verlag, 2008. Kuno Schuhmann and Hans Dieter Müller (Editors), Arno Schmidt, Hans Wollschläger, Richard Kruse, Friedrich Polakovics and Ursula Wernicke (Translators).
4. Edgar Allan Poe, *Unheimliche Geschichten*, Charles Baudelaire, Herausgeber, Andreas Nohl Übersetzter, München: DTV: 2017.
5. Littschwager, 59.
6. In addition to the more recent German collections mentioned above Littschwager counts five.
7. William Crisman, *Poe as Comparatist: Hawthorne and "the German Tieck" (Once More). ATQ (Special Issue)*, 16, no. 1 (March 2002): 53–64.

8. Crisman, *Poe as Comparatist: Hawthorne and "the German Tieck" (Once More)*, 57.

9. G. R. Thompson cited in Scott Peeples, *The Afterlife of Edgar Allan Poe* (Rochester, NY: Camden House, 2004), 82.

10. See http://www.eapoe.org/works/misc/tgap.htm.

11. See http://www.eapoe.org/works/misc/tgap.htm.

12. Cited in Thomas S. Hansen and Burton Pollin, *The German Face of Edgar Allan Poe: A Study of Literary References in His Works* (Columbia, SC: Camden House, 1995), 34.

13. Poe uses the same German quotation twice for emphasis, both at the beginning and at the end of his tale. As Mabbott points out in a footnote, the same German can also be found in *suggestion 46* of Poe's "Fifty Suggestions." The exact source for this German sentence has not been found yet, possibly because of the blatant mistake. After my own first reading of the text, I was tempted to believe that Poe's mistake was deliberate to underline the analogy book/man. My interpretation was that the man in the "Man of the Crowd" was so puzzling that one might not understand him even if one tried. However, as Mabbott further speculates, the sentence invited two further interpretations. The beginning of his story Poe constitutes as a literal translation: "It does not permit itself to be read." In other words, the book is so shocking that it is difficult for any reader to cope with the shock. Additionally, this source may have another, hidden meaning. For instance, perhaps the book in question was no longer available. In any case, the cryptic German sentence arouses any reader's curiosity, especially thanks to its conspicuous, repeated use. It is highly suggestive in that the foreignness seems to bear a hidden, underlying meaning that transcends the tale itself.

14. James A. Harrison, "Chapter 9," *Life and Letters of Edgar Allan Poe* (New York: Thomas W. Crowell and Co., 1903), Vol. II, 238. See https://www.eapoe.org/papers/misc1900/jah03209.htm.

15. Hansen and Pollin, 21.

16. See Patrick Labriola, "Edgar Allan Poe and E. T. A. Hoffman: The Double in 'William Wilson' and 'The Devil's Elixirs,'" *International Fiction Review* (2002): 69–77. Also, in his survey of Poe translations in Germany, Littschwager argues that similarities between Poe and Hoffmann facilitated Poe's reception in Germany, since Hoffmann's fantastic tales "provided Poe's stories a space in which they could flourish." See Littschwager, 56.

17. For details on German immigration to Philadelphia, see http://philadelphiaencyclopedia.org/archive/immigration-1790-1860/.

18. Margaret Alterton, "Chapter 3," *Origins of Poe's Critical Theory* (Iowa City: University of Iowa, 1925), 68–94. See https://www.eapoe.org/papers/misc1921/maopct00.htm.

19. Omans, Glen A. "'Intellect, Taste, and the Moral Sense': Poe's Debt to Immanuel Kant." *Studies in the American Renaissance*, 1980, 123–168.
20. Cited in Susan Bernstein, "Bells and Spells: Gothic Repetition and Romantic Redundancy," *Differences: A Journal of Feminist Cultural Studies* 21, no. 3 (2010): 55.
21. For a definition, see http://www.etymonline.com/index.php?term=gothic. The Goths were a "Germanic people who lived in Eastern Europe c. 100 C. E." The term "Gothic" also meant "Germanic, Teutonic" (1640s). While in the seventeenth century it was used to describe the "art style that emerged in northern Europe in the Middle Ages," in the early nineteenth century "Gothic" referred to "the literary style that used northern European medieval settings to suggest horror and mystery."
22. See http://www.wwnorton.com/college/english/nael/romantic/topic_2/welcome.htm.
23. See http://www.wwnorton.com/college/english/nael/romantic/topic_2/welcome.htm.
24. See http://www.wwnorton.com/college/english/nael/romantic/topic_2/welcome.htm.
25. David Punter, *The Literature of Terror: The Gothic Tradition* (New York: Routledge, 2013). See also G. R. Thompson, "'Proper Evidences of Madness': American Gothic and the Interpretation of 'Ligeia.'" *ESQ*, 18(1972): 30–49.
26. See Mabbott, http://www.eapoe.org/works/mabbott/tom2t010.htm. Mabbott refers to Edd Winfield Parks (M, 1964, 24).
27. Thomas Ollive Mabbott (E. A. Poe), "Ligeia," *The Collected Works of Edgar Allan Poe—Vol. II: Tales and Sketches* (1978), 310.
28. See E. R. Thompson, "'Proper Evidences of Madness': American Gothic and the Interpretation of 'Ligeia,'" *ESQ: A Journal of the American Renaissance* 66 (1972): 30–49.
29. See Patrick Labriola, "Edgar Allan Poe and E. T. A. Hoffman: The Double in 'William Wilson' and 'The Devil's Elixirs,'" *International Fiction Review* (2002): 69–77.
30. A Scottish ballad titled *Sweet William's Ghost*, which can be found in a collection of Percy's *Reliques*, and an English Ballad called the "Suffolk Miracle" offer very similar versions of the previous story. A *Low German Volkslied* based on the Scottish ballad inspired the German poet Gottfried August Bürger to write his famous *Lenore* ballad, which uses the same legend as its theme. Poe wrote a brief poem titled "Lenore," which initially bore the title "A Paean," and which he reworked several times in the course of his career.
31. See Killis Campbell, cited in a footnote in Thomas Olive Mabbott, *Edgar Allan Poe: Complete Poems* (Cambridge, MA: Harvard University Press,

1969), 331. See also Marti Lee, "The Germanic Invasion: Bürger's Ballads and Their Influence on English Writers," at http://personal.georgiasouthern.edu/~dougt/german.htm.

32. See http://www.eapoe.org/works/mabbott/tom1p078.htm.

33. See http://www.eapoe.org/works/mabbott/tom1p078.htm, 332.

34. His use of variants of the name just might demonstrate his desire to challenge the established romantic notions.

35. The first is William Taylor's 1790 translation, which I use as the basis for my comparative analysis since it is most akin to the original. The full text of this translation appears in the Appendix to this chapter. Gottfried August Bürger, "Lenora" Trans. William Taylor of Norwich. *Monthly Magazine and British Register 2* (March 1796): 135–137. Another noteworthy rendition is W. R. Spencer's *Leonora*, translated from the German of Gottfried August Bürger by W. R. Spencer, with Designs by the Right Honourable Lady Diana Beauclerc (London: Edwards and Harley, 1796). Poe, who reviewed Sir Walter Scott's work, was certainly familiar with the latter's Bürgian rendition: *William and Helen*, translated from the German of Gottfried August Bürger by Sir Walter Scott. (Edinburgh: Murdell and Son, 1796). See https://babel.hathitrust.org/cgi/pt?id=uc 1.31175035211369;view=1up;seq=7.

36. See https://archive.org/stream/earliestenglish00emergoog/earliestenglish00emergoog_djvu.txt.

37. The use of variants of the name just might demonstrate Poe's desire to challenge established romantic notions. The early poem was still titled "A Paean," and Poe changed it later to "yellow hair."

38. The earlier version was called "A Paean."

39. See http://www.eapoe.org/works/mabbott/tom1p078.htm.

40. See http://www.eapoe.org/works/essays/philcomp.htm.

Appendix

Gottfried August Bürger, "Lenora." Trans. William Taylor of Norwich. *Monthly Magazine and British Register 2* (March 1796): 135–137.

L E N O R A.
A BALLAD, FROM BÜRGER.

> At break of day, with frightful dreams
>   Lenora struggled sore:
> My William, art thou slaine, say'd she,
>   Or dost thou love no more?

He went abroade with Richard's host,
  The Paynim foes to quell;
But he no word to her had writt,
  An he were sick or well.

With sowne of trump, and beat of drum,
  His felow-soldyers come;
Their helmes bydeckt with oaken boughs,
  They seeke their long'd-for home.

And ev'ry roade, an ev'ry lane
  Was full of old and young,
To gaze at the rejoicing band,
  To hail with gladsome toung.

"Thank God!" their wives and children saide,
  "Welcome!" the brides did saye:
But greete or kiss Lenora gave
  To none upon that daye.

She askte of all the passing traine,
  For him she wisht to see:
But none of all the passing traine
  Could tell if lived hee.

And when the soldyers all were bye,
  She tore her raven haire,
And cast herself upon the growne
  In furious despaire.

Her mother ran and lyfte her up,
  And clasped in her arme,
"My child, my child, what dost thou ail?
  God shield thy life from harm!"

"O mother, mother! William's gone!
  What's all besyde to me?
There is no mercye, sure, above!
  All, all were spar'd but hee!"

"Kneel downe, thy paternoster saye,
　　'Twill calm they troubled spright;
The Lord is wyse, the Lord is good;
　　What hee hath done is right."

"O mother, mother! say not so;
　　Most cruel is my fate:
I prayde, and prayde; but watte avayl'd?
　　'Tis now, alas! Too late."

"Our Heavenly Father, if we praye,
　　Will help a suff'ring childe:
Go take the holy sacrament;
　　So shall they grief grow milde."

"O mother, what I feel within,
　　No sacrament can staye;
No sacrament can teche the dead
　　To bear the light of daye."

"May be, among the heathen folk
　　Thy William false doth prove,
And puts away his faith and troth,
　　And takes another love.

Then wherefore sorrow for his loss?
　　Thy moans are all in vain:
And when his soul and body parte,
　　His falsehode brings him paine."

"O mother, mother! Gone is gone:
　　My hope is all forlorn;
The grave mie onlye safeguarde is—
　　O, had I ne'er been borne!

Go out, go out, my lampe of life;
　　In grislie darkness die:
There is no mercye, sure, above!
　　For ever let me lie."

"Almighty God! O do not judge
　　My poor unhappy childe;

She knows not what her lips pronounce,
    Her anguish makes her wilde.

My girl, forget thine earthly woe,
    And think on God and bliss;
For so, at least, shall not thy soule
    Its heavenly bridegroom miss."

"O mother, mother! what is blisse,
    And what the fiend is celle?
With him'tis heaven any where,
    Without my William, helle.

"Go out, go out, my lamp of life;
    In endless darkness die:
Without him I must loathe the earth,
    Without him scorne the skye."

And so despaire did rave and rage
    Athwarte her boiling veins;
Against the Providence of God
    She hurdle her impious strains.

She bet her breaste, and wrung her hands,
    And rollde her tearlesse eye,
From rise of morne, till the pale stars
    Again did freeke the skye.

When harke! abroade she hearde the trampe
    Of nimble-hoofed steed;
She hearde a knighte with clank alighte,
    And climb the staire in speede.

And soon she herde a tinkling hande,
    That twirled at the pin;
And thro' her door, that open'd not,
    These words were breathed in.

"What ho! what ho! thy dore undoe;
    Art watching or asleepe?
My love, dost yet remember mee,
    And dost thou laugh or weep?"

"Ah! William here so late at night!
    Oh! I have watche and wak'd:
Whence dost thou come? For thy return
    My hearte has sorely ak'd."

"At midnight only we may ride;
    I come o'er land and sea:
I mounted late, but soone I go;
    Aryse, and come with me."

"O William, enter first my bowre,
    And give me one embrace:
The blasts athwarte the hawthorne hiss;
    Awayte a little space."

"Tho' blasts athwarte the hawthorn hiss,
    I may not harboure here;
My spurre is sharpe, my courser pawes,
    My houre of flighte is nere.

All as thou lyest upon thy couch,
    Aryse, and mount behinde;
To-night we'le ride a thousand miles,
    The bridal bed to finde."

"How, ride to-night a thousand miles?
    Thy love thou dost bemocke:
Eleven is the stroke that still
    Rings on within the clocke."

"Looke up; the moone is bright, and we
    Outstride the earthlie men:
I'll take thee to the bridal bed,
    And night shall end but then."

"And where is, then, thy house and home;
    And where thy bridal bed?"
"Tis narrow, silent, chilly, dark;
    Far hence I rest my head."

"And is there any room for mee,
    Wherein that I may creepe?"

"There room enough for thee and mee,
    Wherein that we may sleepe.

All as thou ly'st upon thy couch,
    Aryse, no longer stop;
The wedding guests thy coming waite,
    The chamber dore is ope."

All in her sarke, as there she lay,
    Upon his horse she sprung;
And with her lilly hands so pale
    About her William clung.

And hurry-skurry forth they go,
    Unheeding wet or dry;
And horse and rider snort and blow,
    And sparkling pebbles fly.

How swift the flood, the mead, the wood,
    Aright, aleft, are gone!
The bridges thunder as they pass,
    But earthly sowne is none.

Tramp, tramp, across the land they speede;
    Splash, splash, across the see:
"hurrah! the dead can ride apace;
    Dost feare to ride with mee?

The moone is bryghte, and blue the nyghte;
    Dost quake the blast to stem?
Dost shudder, mayde, to seeke the dead?"
    "No, no, but what of them?

How glumlie sownes yon dirgye song!
    Night-ravens flappe the wing,
What knell doth slowlie toll ding-dong?
    The psalmes of death who sing?

It creeps, the swarthie funeral traine,
    The corse is onn the beere;
Like croke of todes from lonely moores,
    The chaunte doth meet the eere."

"Go, bear her corse when midnight's past,
    With song, and tear, and wayle;
I've gott my wife, I take her home,
    My bowre of wedlocke hayl.

Lead forth, O clarke, the chaunting quire,
    To swell our nuptial song:
Come, preaste, and reade the blessing soone;
    For bed, for bed we long."

They heede his calle, and husht the sowne;
    The biere was seene no more;
And followde him ore feeld and flood
    Yet faster than before.

Halloo! halloo! away they goe,
    Unheeding wet or drye;
And horse and rider snort and blowe,
    And sparkling pebbles flye.

How swifte the hill, how swifte the dale,
    Aright, aleft, are gone!
By hedge and tree, by thorpe and towne,
    They gallop, gallop on.

Tramp, tramp, across the land they speede;
    Splash, splash, acrosse the see:
"Hurrah! the dead can ride apace;
    Dost fear to ride with me?

Look up, look up, and airy crewe
    In roundel daunces reele:
The moone is bryghte, and blue the nyghte,
    Mayst dimlie see them wheele.

Come to, some to, ye gostlie crew,
    Come to, and follow mee,
And daunce for us the wedding daunce,
    When we in bed shall be."

And brush, brush, brush, the gostlie crew
    Come wheeling ore their heads,

All rustling like the wither'd leaves
  That wyde the whirlwind spreads.

Halloo! halloo! away they go,
  Unheeding wet or dry;
And horse and rider snort and blowe,
  And sparkling pebbles flye.

And all that in the moonshyne lay,
  Behynde them fled afar;
And backwarde scudded overhead
  The sky and every star.

Tramp, tramp, across the lande they speede;
  Splash, splash, across the see:
"Hurrah! the dead can ride apace;
  Dost fear to ride with me?

I weene the cock prepares to crowe;
  The sand will soone be runne:
I snuffe the earlye morning aire;
  Downe, downe! our worke is done.

The dead, the dead can ryde apace;
  Oure wed-bed here is fit:
Our race is ridde, oure journey ore,
  Our endlesse union knit."

And lo! an yren-grated grate
  Soon biggens to their viewe:
He crackte his whyppe; the clangynge boltes,
  The doores asunder stewe.

They pass, and'twas on graves they trode;
  "'Tis hither we are bounde:"
And many a tombstone gostlie white
  Lay inn the moonshyne round.

And when hee from his steede alytte,
  His armour, black as cinder,
Did moulder, moulder all awaye,
  As were it made of tinder.

His head became a naked skull;
    Nor haire nor eyne had hee:
His body grew a skeleton,
    Whilome so blythe of blee.

And att his dry and boney heele
    No spur was left to be;
And inn his witherde hande you might
    The scythe and hour-glasse see.

And lo! his steede did thin to smoke,
    And charnel fires outbreathe;
And pal'd, and bleach'd, then vanish'd quite
    The mayde from underneathe.

And hollow howlings hung in aire,
    And shrekes from vaults arose.
Then knew the mayde she mighte no more
    Her living eyes unclose.

But onwarde to the judgement seat,
    Thro' myste and moonlight dreare,
The gostlie crewe their flyghte persewe,
    And hollowe inn her eare:--

"Be patient; tho' thyne herte should breke,
    Arrayne not Heven's decree;
Thou nowe art of thie bodie refte,
    Thie soule forgiven bee!"

PART IV

Imagining Spaces

CHAPTER 11

"Demon of Space": Poe in St. Petersburg

Alexandra Urakova

In 1841, Edgar A. Poe wrote an autobiographical note for the upcoming anthology, *The Poets and Poetry of America* (1842), edited by Rufus Griswold. In this note, he claims that he left the University of Virginia because his foster father had refused to pay his debts of honor and "ran away from home without a dollar on a quixotic expedition to join the Greeks, then struggling for liberty." He failed in reaching Greece, but he did make his way to St. Petersburg (H 1:343). While Greece was suggested by Byronic fashion, the sudden change in Poe's imaginary route was not so obvious: one may only wonder why Poe chose the Russian capital as his only destination on the other side of the Atlantic. Thomas Ollive Mabbott suggests that William Poe "probably did visit Russia" in 1827 and therefore Edgar "adopted the sailor's yarns of his brother as adventures of his own" (M 1969, 515). To make the story plausible, he furnished it with real-life details, such as using the name of the actual American consul in St. Petersburg, Henry Middleton. We learn that Poe "got into many difficulties, but was extricated by the kindness of Mr. Middleton, the American consul at St. P." and with the help of the latter safely returned home in 1829 (H 1:343). Henry Middleton, a planter

A. Urakova (✉)
A.M. Gorky Institute of World Literature, Russian Academy of Sciences, Moscow, Russia

© The Author(s) 2018
P. E. Phillips (ed.), *Poe and Place*,
Geocriticism and Spatial Literary Studies,
https://doi.org/10.1007/978-3-319-96788-2_11

from Charleston, South Carolina, was indeed consul in Russia from 1820 to 1830, and he likely would have sympathized with and rendered aid to a Virginian-born compatriot. Moreover, albeit coincidentally, Poe was serving in the military under the name of Edgar A. Perry at Ft. Moultrie, in Middleton's native South Carolina, when his imaginary double supposedly got into trouble in St. Petersburg.

There could be literary explanations for Poe's choice as well. Byron's Don Juan travels from Greece to Russia through Turkey. He is warmly received at the Russian court but becomes ill as the result of the fierce Russian cold and flees to England. In Poe's time, Russia had the reputation of being a country known for its cold climate and despotic government. It is not surprising, however, that Poe, like Don Juan, got into "many difficulties," albeit of different nature. Besides, we should not forget that Russia already had a place in Poe's imagination: three years before sketching the autobiographical note, he had sent his alter ego, William Wilson, and his haunting double, to Moscow: "Years flew, while I experienced no relief. Villain! – at Rome, with how untimely, yet with how spectral an officiousness, stepped he in between me and my ambition! At Vienna, too—at Berlin—and at Moscow" (M 1979, 2:445)! These and other conjectures notwithstanding, Poe's choice of St. Petersburg remains an obscure, mysterious fact in his biography, which partly explains the endurance of this self-created legend that fueled the popular imagination.

This chapter consists of two parts. The first describes the persistence and growth of the autobiographical myth and the influence it exerted on Russian poetry and fiction. The second highlights the typological parallels and affinities between Poe's cityscape in "The Man of the Crowd," on the one hand, and Gogol's and Dostoevsky's fictional St. Petersburg on the other, claiming that St. Petersburg was indeed the right place for Poe. Thus, the chapter centers on and yet departs from the well-studied subject of Poe's reception in Russia,[1] inviting readers to think of Poe's "underground" or "undercurrent" presence in Russian culture[2] in terms of *place*.

"While I Was Drinking with Edgar Poe"

It is well known that Poe's autobiographical legend survived him and became part of his afterlife in biographies that not only picked up the story but also attempted to fill in its gaps. Rufus Griswold, in his infamous "Memoir," overtly used the autobiographical note to slander Poe's reputation. Griswold writes:

He soon after left the country with the Quixotic intention of joining the Greeks, then in the midst of their struggle with the Turks. He never reached his destination, and we know but little of his adventures in Europe for nearly a year. By the end of this time, he had made his way to St. Petersburg, and our Minister, in that capital, the late Mr. Henry Middleton, of South Carolina, was summoned one morning to save him from penalties incurred in a drunken debauch. Through Mr. Middleton's kindness, he was set at liberty and enabled to return to this country.[3]

The "many difficulties" in Poe's note became "penalties incurred in a drunken debauch" in line with Griswold's general representation of Poe as a hopeless alcoholic and debaucher.

In the "Obituary of Edgar A. Poe," John M. Daniel, the editor of *The Examiner* and Poe's acquaintance, offers a different interpretation of the story:

On Mr. Allan's refusal to pay some of his gambling debts, he broke with him and went off at a tangent to join the Greeks — those being the times of Bozzaris and the Greek Revolution. When he reached St. Petersburg, however, he found both money and enthusiasm exhausted, and he got into a quarrel with the Russian authorities — whether about liberty or lucre is not known. At any rate he found himself nearly adding some knowledge of the knout and Siberia to his already extensive knowledge of men and manners, and was glad enough to accept the intervention of the American consul, Henry Middleton, and his aid to get home.[4]

Here, instead of the drunken debaucher, Poe had a trouble with Russian authorities for reasons unknown and luckily escaped "the knout and Siberia." The comment is as exaggerated as it is absurd: Poe never would have been exposed to the *knout* (a lash) because he was a gentleman and, above all, a foreigner. However, it reflects a stereotypical vision of Russia as a barbaric country and Siberia as the *ultima thule* of all possible evils and mischiefs. Charles Baudelaire, who in 1852 used Daniel's obituary as his only biographical source, apparently accepted Daniel's exaggeration at face value and repeated his statement almost verbatim, leaving out "the knout" but keeping Siberia: "It is said that the situation was so bad that Poe was about to add Siberia to his precocious knowledge of men and things."[5]

Predictably, Poe's alleged visit to St. Petersburg impressed his Russian readers. The popular interest in the legend, however, increased with the growth of Poe's popularity only later in the century since "the Poe cult in

France, boosted by Baudelaire's translations, was not paralleled in Russia in the 1850s and 1860s."[6] Joan Delaney gives a curious example of an early biography published in a respectable magazine *Sin otechestva* of 1856 in "which the whole episode is relegated to Vienna and Poe's difficulties blamed on the strictness of the *Austrian* laws."[7] Other than that, the biography closely follows Baudelaire. While the biographer cited by Grossman seemed cautious about introducing the author, who had become a *persona non grata* in Russia during his visit, Poe's later Russian proponents became excited and enthusiastic about the fact that he actually could have travelled to St. Petersburg. They were hoping that solid evidence of this visit would be found either in the USA or in Russia. Poe's translator and biographer Nikolai Shelgunov (1824–1891), for example, writes in 1872:

> By the way, as is known, Poe was in St. Petersburg where he became involved in a story that cast a shade on his reputation; in order to avoid criminal persecution and get back home, he had to turn to American council for help. The account of Edgar Poe's life, his youth, his adventures in Russia, and the publication of his correspondence have long been promised by American magazines, but this promise has not yet been fulfilled.[8]

Shelgunov closely translates the cited fragment from Baudelaire where it says that "the life of Edgar Poe, his adventures in Russia and his correspondence have been promised by American magazines for a long time and have never appeared."[9] It is noteworthy, however, that he changes Baudelaire's "never appeared" to a more optimistic "not yet fulfilled" ("do sih por ne ispolneno"), leaving the story open-ended.

The anecdote assumed the status of a literary myth by the turn of the century, starting from the 1880–1890s, when Poe had become a "soul mate" and a darling of the Russian Symbolist poets,[10] who, under the influence of Baudelaire and the French Symbolists, felt a mystical connection to the American *poète maudit*. Russian literary historian Alexander Lavrov provides ample evidence of this legend's perseverance during the period. Not only did Russian translators and biographers repeat the scarce facts provided by Baudelaire, but they also attempted to explain the nature of the "difficulties" he encountered in St. Petersburg. In the foreword to his translation of "The Raven" (the first one in the history of its Russian translations), Sergey Andreevsky writes that Poe was detained because he had no passport and that was illegal according to the Russian law. Another author hints at some scandal with police that Poe contrived. The most exotic interpretation belongs to Zinayda Vengerova, a well-known writer, translator, critic, and connoisseur of nineteenth-century literature. In a short note signed by Z.V. in a prestigious 1898 *Encyclopedic Dictionary*, we read:

> Expelled from univ. for the outrage behavior, P. quarreled with Allan who did not pay his debts and headed to Europe aiming to fight against Turkey with the Greek. His dwellings in Europe, with no money and friends, were full of adventures and ended in Petersburg where P. was loitering in pubs and leading a life of a vagabond and a beggar. He was found by American priest Middleton who helped him return to America where P. made peace with Allan and entered the military academy at the expense of the latter.[11]

This note, remarkably dense with inaccuracies, from Middleton turning into a priest to Poe making peace with John Allan on his "return," exemplifies how the legend could trace its way back to such seemingly reliable sources as an encyclopedia. Vengerova's negligence is surprising given that most turn-of-the-century Poe biographers in Russia knew John Ingram's work. However, as Lavrov has persuasively shown, the myth-making mechanism continued to function despite the exposure of the legend in biographical essays, in which truth and fiction coexisted, even in the pages of the same magazine. Thus, *Istorichesky vestnik* published two brief notes about Poe, one in 1897 and the other ten years later: while the first one stuck to the true biographical data, the second one reproduced the familiar narrative about Poe's debauches and problems with police in St. Petersburg.[12] Even Konstantin Bal'mont, a renowned Symbolist poet and Poe's translator, who, in Grossman's words, "came close to duplicating in Russia Baudelaire's service towards Poe,"[13] was reluctant to dismiss the myth, despite his familiarity with Ingram's biography. He allowed for the possibility that both versions of the story might have been true and famously proclaimed: "If a legend that may be called *Poe on the Nevsky Prospect* is only a legend, all of us who love him should be happy that it exists."[14] Symbolists who claimed to be able to catch a glimpse of the mystical and the spiritual behind the everyday routine welcomed an alternative reality—"ideal series of events which run parallel with the real ones," to quote from the motto to "The Mystery of Marie Rogêt." Thus, they favored the story of Poe's St. Petersburg trip regardless of its accuracy and made Poe's fictitious presence in the ghostly St. Petersburg almost tangibly felt.

One of the most ardent and devoted admirers of Poe, a minor Symbolist poet, Vladimir Pyast,[15] even "discovered" tangible, material evidence of Poe's visit to Russia's capital. In his memoir, "Encounters," written after October Revolution and published in 1929, he mentions a police archive in Kazanskaya area of St. Petersburg set to fire in 1917 by either revolutionaries or Zarist secret agents. It contained "a thing of fantastic value for the history of the world literature—a document proving the truth of the fact that has become a legend in the twentieth century: a record of arrest of an American citizen Edgar Allen Poe at the beginning of the 1830s."[16] Pyast confuses dates: neither Poe nor Middleton could have been in St. Petersburg in the early 1830s. Yet the idea of the destroyed archive adds a dramatic touch to Poe's "St. Petersburg story." By that time, the myth had long been debunked, but the turmoil of the October Revolution—during which many archives were destroyed—unexpectedly gave it a new life. Indeed, how could anyone be sure whether some valuable evidence had perished among many other documents consumed in the flames of Revolution?

Poe-inspired images and pre-revolutionary chaos converged in the famous novel by a major Symbolist author, Andrey Bely, entitled *Petersburg* (1913), which is particularly relevant for our discussion. In this novel, Bely places a Poesque red domino on the streets of the Russian capital: a haunting image in the haunted city. The domino that the main character, a terrorist Nikolai Appolonovich Ableykov, wears, together with a black mask, perfectly fits in the phantomlike, surreal cityscape of the novel. Allusions to "The Masque of the Red Death" are emphasized by such epithets as "a jester" and "a buffoon" attributed to Ableykov. When the character puts on a domino and a mask for the first time and looks at himself in the mirror, he sees "an unknown, pale, languishing—demon of space."[17] Bely's "demon of space" [*demon prostran-stva*], an inversion of *genius loci*, may also be an allusion to Poe's "Imp of the Perverse," known to Russian readers as "demon de la perversité" in Baudelaire's translation (in fact, "perversity" pervades both Ableykov's behavior and the pre-revolutionary life in St. Petersburg). It is tempting to suggest that in this way Bely was inscribing Poe into the fictional topography of his novel, making him—via recognizable symbolic attributes—a "demon" or a "genius" of the city.

The red domino Gothicizes Bely's Petersburg, which was captured after the defeat in the Russian-Japanese war and in the wake of the October Revolution; it is not only a symbol of death and ghostly masquerade but also "an emblem of the chaos that was leading Russia to ruin."[18] Bely thus uses Poesque language to describe the restless life of the city facing new challenges and changes. The image of the domino was running through the entire work of the author, haunting his imagination. In his memories, he recalls an episode when, going through a personal drama in 1906, he habitually wore a lacy black mask in his St. Petersburg apartment. He writes about an irresistible desire to appear in front of his lover "in a domino of the color of blaze [zveta plameni], black mask, and with a sword in [his] hand."[19] The red domino assumes a metafictional status in Bely's work, merging the boundaries between the real and the fictional. In the city haunted by the Masque of the Red Death as represented in Bely's novel, the conspiracy plot that Pyast would invent later in the century—the evidence of Poe's trip to Russia kept in police archives and destined to be destroyed amidst the revolutionary chaos—was highly plausible.

Other famous early twentieth-century allusions to Poe, beyond the Symbolist movement, belong to Osip Mandelstam's poetry and are closely intertwined with the image of St. Petersburg. This is evident, for example, in his poem entitled "Solominka" or "Straw" (1916). The poem is addressed to Salomeya Nikolaevna Andronikova, a star of Petersburgian literary salons and an object of Mandelstam's veneration. Salomeya's nickname was Solomka or Solominka ("straw" in Russian), hence the poem's title. The first part of the poem describes Solominka lying sleepless in a "giant bedroom" amid the "solemn satin" while the "twelve months are singing of the death hour."[20] The chamber is situated right above the black Nieva; under the breath of December, it feels as if "the heavy Nieva were in the room." Critics have pointed out allusions to both "Ligeia" and "The Raven" in the dense poetical language of the poem such as December, velvet/satin, insomnia, and melancholia.[21] The giant bedroom, with its high ceilings and heavy bed, is reminiscent of Rowena's chamber. So too is the inclusion of a sarcophagus in the second part of the poem: "In my blood there is Ligeia of December / Whose blessed love sleeps in the sarcophagus." Allusions to both texts in the second part of the poem become explicit:

I've learned you, blessed words:
Lenore, Solominka, Ligeia, Seraphita.
In the giant chamber, there is heavy Nieva
And the blue blood is streaming from out the granite. [2: 1–4]

All these allusions, however, are inseparable from the images associated with St. Petersburg. The image of Nieva, black and heavy, dominates the poem; it adds more restlessness and gloom to the Poesque chamber, even transforming and overtaking it (Nieva under/in the room). At the same time, December, one of the coldest and windiest months in St. Petersburg, becomes Poe's "bleak December"; the poet feels "Ligeia of December" in his blood: "The Raven" and "Ligeia" merge in his imagination. In the same poetic series entitled "Tristia" (1916), Mandelstam refers to St. Petersburg as to Petropolis, the kingdom of Proserpine and the city of death.[22] Mandelstam's city on the Nieva as Poe's city in the sea where "the melancholy waters lie" evokes motives of death, doom, repentance, and oblivion; it is disturbing, apocalyptic, and bleak. Allusions to Poe naturally fit into Mandelstam's cityscape, as if Poe had provided the Russian poet with an obscure poetic language for describing St. Petersburg. Mandelstam was certainly familiar with the legend of Poe's visit to Russia given that the story was popular and widespread. As in the case with Bely's *Petersburg*, Poe was present in his imaginary Petropolis, indirectly yet tangibly. Allusions to Poe served as a secret code that added a mystical, surreal dimension to St. Petersburg plunging in the historical abyss.[23]

In the Soviet era, Poe's personal cult diminished, but his autobiographical myth survived and continued to stir popular imagination as a missed opportunity. A famous Russian Formalist and writer, Yuri Tynyanov (1894–1943), designed to write a short story about Poe meeting Alexander Pushkin on the Nevsky Prospect in the 1930s. Tynyanov's Poe and Pushkin are antipodes, but they are antipodes precisely because they are counterparts. Many Russians would see Poe as a national genius of the same stature and stance as Pushkin—the central figure of the nineteenth-century poetical canon in the USA. It is ironic that Tynyanov's story has never been written, as if the non-written story replicates the non-visit. However, it does exist in the form of an oral record:

> Pushkin enters a restaurant on Nevsky Prospect. There he sees a young man with a large forehead and a strange look, his eyes glaring and somber. The man is drinking vodka and murmuring English verses. Pushkin feels an irresistible desire to come and shake his hand. But the young man gives him a scornful look and mutters through his teeth: You have bluish fingernails betraying your race.[24]

Nikolai Hardjiev who recorded the germ of the story draws a parallel between Tynyanov's ending and Vladimir Mayakovsky's observation in his book "My Discovery of America" (1925–1926). A famous avant-garde poet claims that "no decent hotel in New York would have allowed Pushkin to stay because he had curly hair and African bluish finger-nails."[25] Tynyanov's anecdote thus radically breaks with the Symbolist, turn-of-the-century tradition of presenting Poe as an angel or a "Lucifer"[26] hovering above the mortals. Poe in the story is an American gentleman, a Southerner, and a racist. Pushkin, like Alexander Dumas, was of African descent and was proud of it (in *Eugene Onegin*, he speaks of his desire to live "beneath the sky of [his] Africa"[27]). The encounter of Poe and Pushkin, both social equals, yet one a white Southerner and the other a mixed-raced Russian, perhaps could have been dramatic and equivocal. To my knowledge, Tynyanov is the only Russian writer who addressed (or rather intended to address) the question of Poe's alleged racism in the open.

At the same time, Tynyanov's portrait of Poe is stereotypical and therefore graphic and recognizable. Poe has a strange look and a glaring eye; drinking in solitude betrays him as a misanthrope. Vodka is a source of inspiration for Poe since he is both drinking and murmuring verses; it explicitly refers to the infamous drunken debauch that, according to Griswold, was the cause of his "difficulties" in St. Petersburg. Poe's drink-ing habits were well known to Russian readers and were often invoked, for example, in such famous lines from Boris Pasternak's poem "About these verses" (1917): "While I was smoking with Byron, // While I was drinking with Edgar Poe."[28] In Tynyanov's story, Poe's somber, melancholic demeanor and misanthropic attitude are counterpoised by Pushkin's natural gregariousness, another cultural stereotype familiar to Russian readers.

The encounter of Poe and Pushkin is mentioned, albeit in passing, in the novel *Time, Forward!* (1932), belonging to the pen of Tynyanov's contemporary, a well-known Russian and Soviet writer, Valentin Kataev (1897–1986). The novel's American character, a tourist called Ray Roupe, makes "a subtle compliment" to his host Nalbandov by saying that "certain of Pushkin's poems had a kinship with the stories of Edgar Poe, which is, of course, paradoxical but quite explicable [...] When still a youth, Edgar Poe had travelled to St. Petersburg on a boat. They say that in one of the taverns he had met Pushkin. They talked all night over a bottle of wine, and the great American poet made a gift of the plot of his remarkable poem *The Bronze Horseman* to the great Russian poet."[29] In Kataev's version of the story, as told by Roupe, Poe and Pushkin meet in "one of the taverns" of St. Petersburg and peacefully drink together. What is particularly remarkable about this paragraph is the mention of *The Bronze Horseman* (1833), Pushkin's famous narrative poem that belongs to the so-called "Petersburg text" continued in the work of Gogol, Dostoevsky, and Bely. Roupe's idea is not altogether far-fetched if we consider that St. Petersburg in Pushkin's poem is an uncanny, gloomy, and ghostly city captured during and after the flood. It is a city with a monument of the despotic founder at its heart, whom the character Evgeny believes to be responsible for the death of his sweetheart. In Evgeny's delirium, the Bronze Horseman comes to life and gallops after him; Evgeny runs away hearing the clatter of the bronze hooves.

Allusions to *The Bronze Horseman* in relation to Poe reappear in a 1966 story, "The Precious Burden" ("Dragozenni Gruz"), by Leonid Borisov, a minor Russian and Soviet writer. A comic story dedicated entirely to Poe's visit to St. Petersburg gives its own version of the legend: Poe is delegated to the Russian capital by an American magazine; however, his visit takes place only in 1847, after Virginia's death. At first, Poe is portrayed as a dark genius whose "Ulalume" calms the sea storm; yet when in St. Petersburg, he gets drunk, swears in Russian, and is arrested after kicking a dog. Poe never meets Pushkin during his trip, but sitting on a bench in front of the Bronze Horseman on a moon night, he has the same hallucination as Pushkin's Evgeny: "the horseman on the granite said something loudly to the horse and the horse clattered along; Edgar frightfully raised from the bench."[30] Hinting at Poe's *delirium tremens* or madness, Borisov makes him, albeit in one episode, change places with Pushkin's character. In Borisov's story, Poe finds a niche for himself in the Gothicized Petersburg of *The Bronze Horseman* and becomes part of "Petersburg text" at large. Regardless of its modest place in the history of Russian literature, "The Precious Burden" seems a logical outcome of the Poe legend: the autobiographical myth gets at once a fictional and a metafictional dimension.

Indeed, if Pushkin's poems had any kinship with Poe's stories, *The Bronze Horseman* would undoubtedly head the list. The kinship is even more evident between Poe and two other nineteenth-century Russian writers, Nikolai Gogol and Fyodor Dostoevsky, both of whom he would have had no chance to meet during his alleged trip: Gogol moved to St. Petersburg in December 1828 while Dostoevsky was only

6 years of age in 1827. The second part of this chapter will consider what made Poe's own city imagery consonant with the fictional St. Petersburg in the work of these two authors.

"THE MOST ABSTRACT AND PREMEDIATED CITY IN THE WORLD"

A famous motto to "The Mystery of Marie Rogêt" from Novalis about "ideal series of events which run parallel with the real ones" (M 1979, 2:723) is appropriate to the discussion of Poe's kinship with Gogol and Dostoevsky. In this case, however, we are dealing with two series of "real" biographical events, on the one hand, and "ideal" or fictional events, on the other. Both Gogol and Dostoevsky can be seen, to a certain extent and yet somewhat uncannily, as Poe's doubles. Poe and Nikolai Gogol were born in the same year, 1809. Influenced by German Romanticism, both worked in the genres of grotesque and arabesque. Both were haunted by the image of premature entombment, Poe in his art and Gogol in his life; Gogol's death, like Poe's, remains wrapped in mystery. Fyodor Dostoevsky, an avid gambler, had a passionate temper and a somewhat perverse, intemperate character. Like Poe, he spent most of his life engaged in journalist hackwork, pressed to write hastily under financial circumstances. It is not surprising that he took interest in Poe and published three of his tales in his journal *Time* [*Vremya*] in 1861. To Dostoevsky belongs perhaps the most accurate and original nineteenth-century commentary on the nature of Poe's work that goes against the contemporary Romantic opinion of Poe as ethereal dreamer and *poète maudit*.[31]

Literary interconnections between Poe, Gogol, and early Dostoevsky are striking given that there was no question of mutual awareness or influence, at least in the case of Poe and Gogol. They were connected primarily via Hoffman and other German Romantics, whereas Poe and Dostoevsky were devoted readers of Dickens. The parallels between the authors find explanation in the phenomenon of cultural transfer, dissemination of ideas that were in the air. Poe's "The Man of the Crowd" (1840), a story best known for its representation of the urban life pertaining to modernity and introducing the figure of the *flâneur* to the literary scene, invites important comparisons with Gogol's *Petersburg Tales* (his 1835 "Nevsky Prospect" in particular), on the one hand, and with Dostoevsky's "The Landlady" (1847), on the other.

A comparative reading of "The Man of the Crowd" and "Nevsky Prospect" might well be a subject of a special study[32] since even the plot lines of the tales run in parallel. "Nevsky Prospect" concerns a failed heterosexual romance. Two young men, Piskarev and his companion, Lieutenant Pirogov, follow two mysterious women, a brunette and a blond, on Nevsky Prospect. Piskarev, a Romantic artist seeking ideal love, takes a prostitute for the incarnation of heavenly beauty and commits suicide after he fails to persuade her to quit her profession and marry him. Pirogov, a vulgar, down-to-earth officer in search of an easy love affair, discovers that his stranger is a silly but virtuous wife of a German tinsmith; he attempts to seduce her but gets flogged by her drunken husband and his fellow artisans. Gogol's plot of pursuing a woman, which is common in the European "city mysteries" genre, is counterpoised by the apparently sexless yet homoerotic tension of Poe's story, which ends in epistemological disappointment and frustration. When the narrator of "The Man of the Crowd" sees an old man on a London street, he feels "a craving desire to keep the man in view—to know more of him" (M 1978, 2:511),[33] but this desire remains unsatisfied. As Leland S. Person persuasively has suggested, "The Man of the Crowd" "derives its energy and its plot, after all, from the provocation of male desire, from the pursuit of one man by another, from the close encounter—face-to-face—between men."[34] One may speculate that while Gogol's tale reflects a stereotypical nineteenth-century binary vision of women's social functions (prostitute vs. housewife), Poe's homosocial intrigue, for obvious reasons, remains obscure, like "a book that does not permits itself to be read" (507).

Yet, perhaps, the most striking detail that brings "Nevsky Prospect" and "The Man of the Crowd" together is the opening panoramic description of the city crowd in both stories as well as the alternation of detachment and engagement. In "The Man of the Crowd," the narrator describes the city crowd as he observes it one evening through the smoky panes of the bow window of the London coffeehouse. As Tatiana Senkevitch nicely put it, "the tentative flâneur in Gogol's story is the narrator who navigates the city with the characters and comments critically on the signs of its conspicuous progress."[35] Both observers focus on the principal thoroughfares of the cities, an unnamed main street of London and Nevsky Prospect.

The descriptions of the crowd in Poe and Gogol are similar in that they "dehumanize" the crowd, presenting it as a succession of grotesque, surreal images. The Londoners marching in front of the narrator of "The Man of the Crowd" uncannily resemble manikins or automatons, the aspect of the narrative that was emphasized by Walter Benjamin.[36] The narrator's gaze not only dehumanizes but also commodifies the crowd. As Robert Byer observed, the setting itself "might be likened to, though it inverts, the window gazing and endless appetency that define the perspective of the commodity shopper."[37] This perspective is even more evident in the ironic framework of "Nevsky Prospect." Gogol's discourse closely imitates window gazing in that it metonymically reduces the crowd to a display of overcoats, hats, pretty eyes, smiles, whiskies, mustaches, and noses. "One displays a foppish frock coat with the best of beavers, another a wonderful Greek nose, the third is the bearer of superb side-whiskers, the fourth of a pair of pretty eyes and an astonishing little hat, the fifth of a signet ring with a talisman on his smart pinkie, the sixth of a little foot in a charming bootie, the seventh of an astonishment-arousing necktie, the eighth of an amazement-inspiring mustache."[38] In this way, the narrator captures the spirit of the avenue that "served as a showcase for the wonders of the new consumer economy that modern mass production was just beginning to open up."[39] Both authors are particularly concerned with the nightlife of the city when the light of gas lamps lends "a wondrous, enticing light to all things"[40] or throws "over every thing [sic] a fitful and garish lustre" (Poe: 511). The gas illumination, another sign of modern urbanity, produces illusive and hallucinatory effects in these two tales, blurring the boundary between reality and daydreaming.

Poe's London and Gogol's St. Petersburg convey a modern idea of the city, consumerist and uncanny, elusive and grotesque, dense with desire, eroticism, and delusion. It is not surprising that both authors are often considered precursors of new literary and cultural trends and modern sensibility at large. Benjamin interprets "The Man of the Crowd" in the context of modernity, the spirit of which will be fully manifested in Baudelaire's work. Marshall Berman states that, in "Nevsky Prospect," "Gogol seems to be inventing the twentieth century out of his own head," from Joyce's *Ulysses* and Doblin's *Alexanderplatz, Berlin* to the cinema montage of Eisenstein and Dziga Vertov."[41]

There is no evidence of Dostoevsky being familiar with Poe at the time when he wrote "The Landlady," although he could have read a detailed account of "The Man of the Crowd" in the 1846 issue of *Revue de Des Mondes*.[42] The plots of the stories are different, yet there is an episode at the beginning of "The Landlady" that is reminiscent of "The

Man of the Crowd." Ordynov, the main character of Dostoevsky's story, restlessly rambles in St. Petersburg without any evident purpose. In his heart, there is "a sort of intoxication, like the ecstasy of a hungry man who has meet and drink before him after a long fast": "He stared about at everything like a *flâneur*. But even now, inconsistent as ever, he was reading significance in the picture that lay so brightly before him, as though between the lines of a book. Everything struck him; he did not miss a single impression and looked with thoughtful eyes in the faces of the passing people."[43] In the same passage, Dostoevsky compares Ordynov with an "invalid, who for the first time gets joyfully up from his sickly bed" (7).

Olga Voltchek observes that Dostoevsky's metaphor of illness and recovery directly parallels the opening of "The Man of the Crowd."[44] The convalescent narrator finds himself "in one of those happy moods which are so precisely the converse of ennui—moods of the keenest appetency, when the film from the mental vision departs—*achlus os prin epeen*—and the intellect, electrified, surpasses as greatly its everyday condition" (507). The same can be said about the book metaphor that is equally important in both texts: Ordynov is reading faces "as though between the lines of a book"; Poe's narrator reads newspapers and then turns his attention to the crowd. The old man disturbs him as the only "book" that remains "unread." The old man's behavior is eccentric, but so is the behavior of his pursuer who follows him on London streets. In "The Landlady," an eccentric looking stranger restlessly stalking backward and forward is Ordynov himself; he even attracts attention of the pedestrians by his own strange looks and conversation: "He saw that they took him for a madman or a very original, eccentric character, which was, indeed, perfectly correct" (7). He is both the one who observes and the one who attracts attention of the passersby. Thus, like Poe, Dostoevsky shows that a modern *flâneur* in a modern city is an unsocial eccentric simultaneously being part of the crowd and standing outside of it.

All three authors were "painters of modern life,"[45] sharing similar attitudes toward the changing cityscape. However, I would suggest that the congeniality of their fictional cities, London and St. Petersburg (often called a second London due to its bleakness and fog), is more complex. Gogol and Dostoevsky were bearing on Petersburg myth that allotted St. Petersburg with its surreal, uncanny, and ghostly character in Russian collective consciousness from the very beginning of its history. Founded by Peter the Great on the banks of the Nieva, the city appeared, like a phantom, amid the swamps. Moreover, unlike other Russian towns, it was built in strict accordance with the given architectural design; it was the incarnation of the emperor's idea of a European capital—the theme reflected in Pushkin's previously mentioned poem, *The Bronze Horseman*. St. Petersburg is therefore "the most abstract and premediated city in the world"[46] in Dostoevsky's sharp definition. Elaborating on the myth, Gogol and Dostoevsky add a touch of unreality to the otherwise specific topography and description of the city based on immediate experience and knowledge.

Poe's London, partly imagined, partly based on childhood memories, partly plagiarized from Dickens,[47] is by itself a phantasmagoric, artificial construct. Its description lacks the spontaneity of actual impression and contact. Benjamin says: "In his description Poe did not aim at any direct observation."[48] Poe's representation of London with an unnamed thoroughfare in the center and crowds marked by "uniformity"[49] is both detailed and generalized, abstract and concrete. Poe invents a city he scarcely knew and makes it appear both lifelike and grotesque. Hypothetically, Poe's London could have been any other European capital, either Paris as in Dupin circle or St. Petersburg that he visited in his imagination. It is tempting to suggest that Poe's fictional London shares its "abstract and premediated" character with the mythologized and fictionalized Russian capital since the preconceived *idea* of the city presides over the actual urban imagery in Poe's story.

In another early story of Dostoevsky, "White Nights" (1848), the narrator speaks of "strange places in Petersburg." The life of the people living in these places "is a mixture of something purely fantastic, something fervently ideal, and at the same time something [...] frightfully prosaic and ordinary, not to say incredibly vulgar."[50] The same idea runs through his later novel *A Raw Youth* (1875). The character speaks of the ambience in a small restaurant on the canal as being "so vulgar and prosaic that it almost borders on the fantastic."[51] In the same novel, the narrator walking in St. Petersburg feels that even "the air [he] breathed, was from another planet."[52] Dostoevsky's Petersburg has accurate topography. It is graphic and realistic, but it also "borders on the fantastic," in his own words, being at once canny and uncanny, real and hallucinatory, familiar and strange, prosaic and nightmarish.

Commenting on Poe's tales in 1861, Dostoevsky observes a particular property of Poe's genius: "You will so clearly see all the details of the form of the existence presented to you, that finally you will be convinced, as it were, of its possibility, its actuality, whereas this existence is either almost wholly impossible or has never occurred on earth."[53] For Dostoevsky, Poe, being a true American, makes fantastic, nonexistent, or "almost wholly impossible" things appear lifelike and concrete. Analyzing Dostoevsky's vision of Poe, Stephen Rachman argues that "Dostoevsky's concern lies in that Poe's imaginings may or may not pertain to any reality and yet they have the effect of inducing in the reader a conviction of an utterly concrete reality."[54] The word "concern" seems to be important in this comment. Admiring Poe's art (although privileging Hoffman over Poe), Dostoevsky seems to take it with a slant of uneasiness. Poe's utterly concrete, yet nonexistent, alternative reality is disturbing but so is Petersburg in his own (or in Gogol's) work that only "pretends" to be real but deep down is "fantastic" or "preconceived."

In his slanderous and fictitious account of Poe's life, Griswold portrayed him as a madman wandering through the streets of American cities: "He walked the streets, in madness or melancholy, with lips moving in indistinct curses, or with eyes upturned in passionate prayers [...] with drenched garments and arms wildly beating the winds and rains...[.]"[55] In the memoir of Dostoevsky, his daughter Lubov' Fyodorovna remembers him "wandering in the darkest and remotest streets of St. Petersburg. While walking, he talked to himself and gesticulated so that the pedestrians would turn round at him. Friends who met him thought that he was mad."[56] Although these two texts were written with different purposes,[57] these descriptions evince striking similarities. Both Poe and Dostoevsky restlessly walk the city streets. Both talk to themselves and look like madmen. Both pay no attention to the weather (wind and rain) or distance (darkest and remotest streets). Both bear an uncanny similarity to Poe's famous wanderer, the Man of the Crowd, and to any of Dostoevsky's lunatic Petersburg dwellers. Eventually, both contribute to popular images of Poe and Dostoevsky as two literary eccentrics, mad and haunted geniuses of American and Russian literature, respectively.

Yet while Dostoevsky and Gogol are closely associated with St. Petersburg, it is, indeed, hard to "place" Poe in any particular American city, whether Boston, Richmond, Baltimore, Philadelphia, or New York. Not only did he move from one American city to another, but he also placed his fictional characters in London and Paris and his virtual double in St. Petersburg. Thus, St. Petersburg might as well have a claim on Poe. There are certain qualities of Poe's art—his obsession with melancholia and death, the hyper-reality of his fantastic images, the spirit of conspiracy and mystification, or the uncanny premeditation of his designs—that make him feel at home in Russia's most haunted, strange, ghost-like, and fictitious city. Congenial with major Russian geniuses and inspiring generations of Russian readers, Poe is a true *genius loci* or "demon of space" of St. Petersburg.

NOTES

1. On this subject, see Joan Delaney Grossman, *Edgar Allan Poe in Russia: A Study in Legend and Literary Influence* (Würzburg: Jal-Verlag), 1983; Eloise M. Boyle, "Poe in Russia," in *Poe Abroad: Influence, Reputation, Affinities*, ed. Lois Davis Vines (Iowa: University of Iowa Press, 2002), 19–25; Elvira Osipova, "The History of Poe Translations in Russia," in *Translated Poe*, ed. Emron Esplin and Margarida Vale de Gato (Bethlehem: Lehigh University Press, 2014), 65–73; Александр Николюкин, *Литературные связи России и США* [Alexander Nikoliukin, *Literary Ties Between Russian and USA*] (М.: Наука, 1981), 376–346. This essay is much indebted to the recent chapter devoted to Poe's St. Petersburg legend in the circle of Russian symbolists: Александр Лавров, "Эдгар По в Петербурге: контуры легенды," in Александр Лавров, *Символисты и другие: Статьи. Разыскания. Публикации* [Alexander Lavrov, "Edgar Poe in St. Petersburg: the Contours of a Legend"] (М.: Новое литературное обозрение, 2015), 54–59.

2. Russian famous Symbolist poet, Alexander Blok, called Poe "the underground stream of Russia" (podzemnoe techenie v Rossii); see Александр Блок. *Собр. соч. в 8 т.* Т. VII [Alexander Blok, *Collected Works* in 8 vols. Vol. 7] (М., Л.: Худ. лит, 1963), 81.

3. Rufus Griswold Wilmot, "Memoir of the Author," in *The Works of the Late Edgar Allan Poe*, 3 vols. (New York: J. S. Redfield, 1850–1853, III), vii.

4. John M. Daniel, "Review of Poe's Works," in *The Southern Literary Messenger* (1850). Qtd. in Charles Baudelaire, *Edgar Allan Poe: Sa vie et ses ouvrages*, trans. and ed. William Thomas Bandy (Toronto: University of Toronto Press, 1973), 63.

5. Baudelaire, *Edgar Allan Poe: Sa vie et ses ouvrages*, 48.

6. Osipova, 66.

7. Grossman, 30.

8. Н. В. Шелгунов, "Эдгар По" [N.V. Shelgunov, "Edgar Poe"], *Дело*, no. 5 (1874): 278.

9. Baudelaire, *Edgar Allan Poe: Sa vie et ses ouvrages*, 96.

10. See Grossman, 64–98; Boyle, 20–23; Osipova, 67–69.

11. Лавров [Lavrov], 189–191.
12. Лавров [Lavrov], 193.
13. Grossman, 73.
14. Константин Бальмонт, "Очерк жизни Эдгара По" [Konstantin Bal'mont, "Essay About the Life of Edgar Poe"] (1911). In По Э.А. *Очерк жизни Эдгара По. Стихотворения. Рассказы* [Edgar Allan Poe, *Selected Works*] (М.: Терра, 1996), 23.
15. His own poetical works have allusions to "Ligeia" and "The Fall of the House of Usher," the two most loved tales among Russian symbolists.
16. Владимир Пяст. *Встречи* [Vladimir Pyast, *Encounters*] (М.: Новое литературное обозрение, 1997), 189.
17. Andrey Bely, *Petersburg* (1913). The English translation is quoted from Judith Wermuth, *The Red Jester: Andrey Bely's Petersburg as a Novel of the European Modern* (Münster: LIT Verlag, 2012), 89.
18. Qtd. in Judith Wermuth, *The Red Jester*, 100.
19. Андрей Белый, *Начало века* [Andrey Bely, *The Beginning of the Century*] (М.: Худ. лит., 1990), 85.
20. Osip Mandelstam, "Solominka" (translation mine). See the original in: Осип Мандельштам, *Стихотворения, переводы, очерки, статьи* [Osip Mandelstam, *Poems, Translations, Sketches, Essays*] (Тбилиси: Мерани, 1990), 107.
21. See Лада Панова, "'Уворованная соломинка': К литературным прототипам любовного лирики Осипа Мандельштама" [Lada Panova, "'A stolen straw': On the Literary Prototypes of Osip Mandelstam's Love Poetry"], *Вопросы литературы* 5 (2009): 143–148; Stuart Goldberg, "The Poetics of Return in Osip Mandel'stam's 'Solominka,'" *Russian Literature* 45 (1991): 137.
22. Osip Mandelstam, "We Will Die in Transparent Petropolis" [В Петрополе прозрачном мы умрем…], translation mine. See the original in Осип Мандельштам, *Стихотворения, переводы, очерки, статьи* [Osip Mandelstam, *Poems, Translations, Sketches, Essays*], 104.
23. I think along the same lines with Lavrov, who suggested in broader terms that Poe and St. Petersburg were perceived as congenial by the Russian readers: "…American writer ('mad Edgar') and mythopoetical Petersburg were like two individuals attracted by each other, feeling a deep kinship and the shared essence of their natures" Лавров [Lavrov] (Lavrov, 197).
24. Н.И. Харджиев, "О том, как Пушкин встретился с Эдгаром По," in *Воспоминания о Ю. Тынянове: Портреты и встречи* [N.I. Hardziev, "About Pushkin Meeting Edgar Poe"] (М.: Советский писатель, 1983), 260.
25. Ibid.

26. That's how Bal'mont called him in his essay, "The Genius of Discovery" (1901). Константин Бальмонт. "Гений открытия" [Konstantin Bal'mont, "The Genius of Discovery"]. In Э.А. По. *Рассказы* [Edgar Allan Poe, *Tales*] (СПб.: Кристалл, 2000), 8.

27. Alexander Pushkin, *Eugene Onegin*, trans. Vladimir Nabokov (Princeton: Princeton University Press, 1990), 117.

28. Борис Пастернак, "Про эти стихи," in Борис Пастернак. *Услышать будущего зов': стихотворения, поэмы, переводы, проза* [Boris Pasternak, *"To hear the call of the future": Poems, Translations, Fiction*] (М.: Школа Пресс, 1995), 814.

29. Valentin Kataev, *Time, Forward!* trans. Charles Malamuth (Evanston: Northwestern University Press, 1961), 228.

30. Леонид Борисов, Драгоценный груз [Leonid Borisov, "The Precious Burden"], in Леонид Борисов. *Эллинский секрет*. Сост. Брандис, В. Дмитревский [Leonid Borisov, *Hellenic Secret*, ed. E. Brandis and V. Dmitrievsky] (Л.: Лениздат, 1966), 371.

31. As I have argued, both "The Man of the Crowd" and "The Portrait" elaborate on a traditional folkloric figure of the Wandering Jew, a popular image of contemporary European fiction, by placing a malicious, demonic old man on the mean streets of the modern city. See my essay, "'Breaking the Law of Silence': Rereading Poe's 'The Man of the Crowd' and Gogol's 'The Portrait,'" in *Poe's Pervasive Influence*, ed. Barbara Cantalupo (Bethlehem, PA: Lehigh University Press, 2012), 63–75.

32. See, for example, Ivan Delazari, "'The Man of the Crowd' along 'Nevsky Avenue': Urban Expositions and Musical Developments in Nikolai Gogol and Edgar Allan Poe," in *Urban Dimensions of American Civilization*, ed. M. D. Dinn, J. B. Fernández, L. Hepner, and N. P. Zemlayanski (Orlando and Moscow: University of Central Florida and RSUH, 2015), 35–43.

33. Poe, Edgar Allan, "Man of the Crowd" in Poe, Edgar Allan. *Collected Works of Edgar Allan Poe*, ed. Thomas Ollive Mabbott, vol. 2 (Cambridge MA: Belknap Press of Harvard University Press), 501.

34. Leland S. Person, "Queer Poe: The Tell-Tale Heart of his Fiction," *Poe Studies: History, Theory, Interpretation* 41 (2008): 13.

35. Tatiana Senkevitch, "The Phantasmagoria of the City: Gogol's and Sadovnikov's Nevsky Prospect, St. Petersburg," in *The Flâneur Abroad: Historical and International Perspectives*, ed. Richard Wrigley (Cambridge: Cambridge Scholars Publishing, 2014), 186.

36. Walter Benjamin, "The Paris of the Second Empire in Baudelaire," in *Charles Baudelaire: A Lyric Poet in the Era of High Capitalism*, trans. Harry Zohn (Brooklyn: Verso Classics, 1997), 52.

37. Robert H. Byer, "Mysteries of the City: A Reading of Poe's 'The Man of the Crowd,'" in *Ideology and Classic American Literature*, ed. Sacvan Berkovitch and Myra Jehlen (New York: Cambridge University Press, 1986), 221–246.

38. Nikolai Gogol, "Nevsky Prospect" in *The Collected Tales by Nikolai Gogol*, trans. and annot. Richard Pevear and Larissa Volokhonsky (First Vintage Classic Edition, 1999), 138.

39. Marshall Berman, *All that is Solid Melts into the Air: The Experience of Modernity* (New York: Penguin, 1988), 194.

40. Ibid., 138.

41. Ibid., 198.

42. This evidence is given by Olga Voltchek. See Ольга Волчек, "Топология города и повествовательные маски у По, Бодлера, Достоевского" [Olga Voltchek, "City Topology and Narrative Masks in Poe, Baudelaire, and Dostoevsky"], in *По, Бодлер, Достоевский: Блеск и нищета национального гения*. Под. ред. Сергея Фокина и Александры Ураковой [*Poe, Baudelaire, Dostoevsky: Splendors and Miseries of National Genius*, ed. Sergey Fokine and Alexandra Urakova] (М.: Новое литературное обозрение, 2017), 68–97.

43. Fyodor Dostoevsky, "The Landlady," trans. Constance Garnett (New York: Digireads.com, 2011), 6–7. The references will be to this edition and noted parenthetically.

44. Voltchek, 79–80.

45. Paraphrasing the title of Baudelaire's famous essay, "The Painter of Modern Life" (1863).

46. Fyodor Dostoevsky, *Notes from Underground*. Qtd. in Frank, Joseph, *Dostoevsky, A Writer in His Time* (Princeton: Princeton University Press, 2009), 428.

47. See Stephen D. Rachman, "'Es lässt sich nicht schreiben': Plagiarism and 'The Man of the Crowd,'" in *American Face of Edgar Allan Poe*, ed. Shawn Rosenheim and Stephen Rachman (Baltimore: The Johns Hopkins University Press, 1999), 49–91.

48. Benjamin, "The Paris of the Second Empire in Baudelaire," 52.

49. The anonymous *Blackwood's* reviewer complains of inaccurate topography of London in the tale: "American Library," *Blackwood's Magazine*, November 1847, 585.

50. Fyodor Dostoevsky, "The White Nights," in *The Best Short Stories by Fyodor Dostoevsky*, trans. David Magarshack (New York: Modern Library, 2014), 18.

51. Fyodor Dostoevsky, *A Raw Youth*, trans. Constance Garnett (Honolulu: University Press of the Pacific, 2001), 175.

52. Fyodor Dostoevsky, *A Raw Youth*, 212.

53. Qtd. in Grossman, 33.

54. See Stephen Rachman, "Violence and Voice: Hearing Poe's Sociopaths" Стивен Рэкмен, "Слушая социопатов По: Преступление, наказание, голос," пер. А.Ураковой [Stephen Rachman, "Hearing Poe's Sociopaths: Crime, Punishment, and Voice," trans. Alexandra Urakova], in *По, Бодлер, Достоевский* [*Poe, Baudelaire, Dostoevsky: Splendors and Miseries of National Genius*], 117–131.

55. Rufus W. Griswold, "Death of Edgar A. Poe," *New-York Daily Tribune* (October 9, 1849): 2, cols. 3–4.

56. Любовь Ф. Достоевская. *Достоевский в изображении его дочери Л. Достоевской*. Перев. с немецкого Л.Я. Круковской [Liubov Dostoevskaya, *Dostoevsky as Represented by his Daughter, L. Dostoevskaya*, trans. from German by L. Ya. Krukovskaya] (Санкт-Петербург: Государственное издательство, 1922), 78. The book was written in French and originally published in German in 1920.

57. Dostoevskaya's memories, unlike Griswold's obituary, were not written to slander her father; however, based mainly on the stories of her mother since her father died when she was 11, they are considered unreliable and biased.

CHAPTER 12

Poe, Egypt, and "Egyptomania"

Emily James Hansen

When considering Edgar A. Poe as a writer and poet, we often place him in the gothic tradition as many of his best-known fictional works focus on the supernatural, the macabre, and the mysterious. In rare instances, we contemplate Poe from outside this tradition, or space, such as when we consider his prose poem on the material universe, *Eureka*, or his reviews and critical writings, such as "The Philosophy of Composition" and "The Rationale of the Verse." However, this chapter aims to focus on another place—Egypt—and its role in Poe's works. While Poe never visited Egypt, he lived during a time of profound interest in Egypt—a phenomenon known as "Egyptomania." Indeed, Poe spent five years (1815–1820) in London (including a brief spell in Scotland), a location that plays a significant role in the history of Egyptology and the early years of Poe.

Elliott Colla writes in *Conflicted Antiquities: Egyptology, Egyptomania, Egyptian Modernity* that "Egyptology's object, the artifact, came into being somewhere between Egypt and London, and…this ushered in a new form of power linking archaeology, Egyptology, print culture, literature, and the arts with colonial and national politics."[1] Egyptomania was closely intertwined with national identity, politics, and colonialism

E. J. Hansen (✉)
Middle Tennessee State University, Murfreesboro, TN, USA

© The Author(s) 2018
P. E. Phillips (ed.), *Poe and Place*,
Geocriticism and Spatial Literary Studies,
https://doi.org/10.1007/978-3-319-96788-2_12

265

during its infancy. This is evident in early nineteenth-century London, where the Egyptian Sculpture Room of the British Museum served as "a national space," which "displays an arrangement that attests to the culture refinement of the English nation and to the reach of the British Empire."[2] This is not unique to England; ancient Egypt is intertwined within American identity, and according to Scott Trafton, there exists a close "relationship between modern America and ancient Egypt...based on family ties: mirror images, twinned and inseparable."[3] A great obelisk stands in Washington, DC, just as obelisks once stood in Egypt. The Great Seal of the United States, currently emblazoned on the reverse side of the one-dollar bill, also features an unfinished, thirteen-step pyramid underneath the Eye of Providence.[4] America made strides to be more closely associated with the grandeur of ancient Egypt, and as J. Gerald Kennedy writes in *Strange Nation: Literary Nationalism and Cultural Conflict in the Age of Poe*, "More than any other writer of that epoch, Poe trafficked in the grotesque and had an uncanny ability to discern what was truly strange about the American nation."[5] Indeed, both "The Fall of the House of Usher" and "William Wilson" feature elements of doubling, while "The Murders in the Rue Morgue" takes doubling one gruesome step further in the form of an ape who mirrors the actions of his owner to a bloody end. "The Black Cat" incorporates doubling, too, for as soon as the narrator kills his black cat Pluto in a fit of perversion and madness, he adopts another black cat with strikingly similar features (including a missing eye). These strange fascinations (premature burial, Egyptomania, resurrection, doubling, the Other, the grotesque, the macabre, the mysterious, and so on) color Poe's prose and poetry. However, Poe simultaneously rejected nationalism and embraced the strangeness of society through his myriad works on perverseness, doubling, and explorations of the "Other"; Poe's various writings direct readers' attention to the strangeness of antebellum America's overt fascination with Egypt.

Historical context is key when attempting to uncover the significance of place, especially that of ancient Egypt, in Poe's work. During the early nineteenth century, Egypt experienced a surge in popularity and interest thanks to the frequent discoveries and excavations that were cataloged in numerous books and newspapers. Indeed, Poe was surrounded by Egypt's influence as he "delivered a lecture on the state of American poetry" in the Egyptian Saloon of Odd Fellows Hall in Baltimore in 1844.[6] The Saloon itself was no doubt a product of Egyptomania.

Egypt's mysterious nature, and the generalized mystery of the "Orient," captivated the imagination of not only Poe but also the general public. As Edward Said notes, "Orientalism is a style of thought based upon an ontological and epistemological distinction made between 'the Orient' and (most of the time) 'the Occident,'" or the West and East, and much of the study of the "Orient" during Poe's time would have been rooted in subjugation as European scholars and explorers sought to both understand the mysteries of the Orient and to craft their identity in stark contrast to it.[7] Egypt's intriguing specter certainly would have captivated Poe, too, who enjoyed both the crafting and unravelling of mystery and suspense in his work. Perhaps he felt called to defend Egypt against its destruction in the name of European exploration. After all, as the adage goes, "archaeology is a destructive process." It is also plausible that the ancient Egyptian concepts of death and the afterlife gave Poe a semblance of hope; he wrote about resurrection in several works. Poe experienced profound loss throughout his life, including the untimely deaths of his biological mother, his foster mother, and his wife. Indeed, a recurring theme in a number of Poe's poems and prose is the untimely death of a beautiful woman but, in at least two works, "Ligeia" and "The Fall of the House of Usher," the beautiful women who suffer untimely deaths are subsequently resurrected. Their resurrections are more grim than gleeful, to be sure. Yet, it is worth noting that, as his wife, Virginia, slowly succumbed to her illness, Poe wrote "Some Words with a Mummy" (1845) in which the mummy is resurrected and, in which, the narrator himself desires to be embalmed and resurrected at a later date. His frequent use of resurrection—perverse or otherwise—reveals his desire to be reunited with loved ones.

Looking at Egypt through Poe's works reveals another often overlooked aspect of the author and his genius. In examining his works and Egypt's place in relation to his works, we discover something new not only about Poe but also about *us*. Poe was conscious of place and identity; he includes the line "by a Bostonian" in his first book of poetry not only to establish his identity as someone born in Boston but also to associate himself with a particular place and, according to Arthur Hobson Quinn, to "[make] the most of his fragile connections with his birthplace."[8] The places Poe lived and visited colored his poetry and prose; his childhood school in Stoke Newington, England, was immortalized in "William Wilson,"[9] and Sullivan's Island, SC, where Poe was briefly stationed in 1827, makes an appearance in "The Gold-Bug." Place was significant to him, and Egypt was significant to America in the nineteenth century. Although he never lived in or visited Egypt, Poe seemed interested in preserving this place creatively in his works. In the nineteenth century, Egypt was on the verge of being destroyed for the sake of scientific discovery. Egypt's people, it seemed, were doomed to disappear among the ruins.

Egypt intrigued the young republic in the early nineteenth century—but this intrigue was not limited solely to the USA. England and France, too, were swept up in Egyptomania. With each discovery, drawing, and report, the obsession with understanding the mysteries of the pyramids and cryptic hieroglyphics grew. As Bob Brier and Jean-Pierre Houdin note, "prior to the eighteenth century...practically no one outside of Egypt had seen the pyramids."[10] Indeed, "[t]he earliest report directly connected to the Great Pyramid is an account by the famous Greek Historian Herodotus."[11] In antebellum America, there was a flood of sketches and reports regarding the myriad excavations taking place up and down the Nile.

Cryptography, the practice of writing and analyzing symbols and codes, may have fostered Poe's interest in Egypt as he even employed a coded message in "The Gold-Bug." One of the most prominent cryptographers of Poe's day was Jean-François Champollion. Between 1841 and 1849, Poe mentions Champollion by name in such works as "A Chapter on Autography—Part I" (1841), "The Literati of New York City—Part IV" (1846), *Eureka: An Essay on the Material and Spiritual Universe* (1848), and "Mellonta Tauta" (1849). Scholars such as John T. Irwin have noted the calculated reasoning of C. August Dupin as having been modeled on Champollion.[12] Yet, Poe's interest in Egypt seems to have extended beyond a casual interest in cryptography and the many ongoing attempts to decipher the ancient texts. Poe, in fact, incorporates other aspects of Egypt in his works that reveal interests beyond hieroglyphics. He used the events in Egypt as a means to satirize and chastise vulgar practices in his own society, calling attention to the destruction of Egypt and its artifacts at the hands of Egyptologists themselves. Poe did not write "Some Words with a Mummy" out of spite, but rather out of disbelief. Ligeia's reincarnation in a room full of Egyptian sarcophagi is equally significant, and "The Fall of the House of Usher" employs the Osiris and Isis myth. The narrator's misfortunes in "The Black Cat" might have been prevented had he not killed Pluto the cat, a highly revered creature in ancient Egypt.[13]

WHY EGYPT? EGYPTOMANIA AND POE IN CONTEXT

An understanding of the cultural and aesthetic landscape of nineteenth-century Europe and America helps us to put Poe's incorporation of and contributions to this contemporary craze into perspective, yielding a better appreciation of the importance of Egypt in the popular imagination. In brief, "Egyptomania" is a unique fascination with the "mysteries" of Egypt, including mummies, hieroglyphs, mythology, architecture, culture, and fashion that heavily influenced art, architecture, literature, and science in Europe and America. That influence emerged in Poe's time and persists in our own. We can trace the beginning of Egyptomania to Napoléon's failed conquest of Egypt in the late eighteenth century. As part of his campaign, he commissioned a group of *savants* to catalog their findings in Egypt, an effort that was published as the *Description de l'Égypte* in an impressive 21+volumes.[14] These *savants* consisted of artists, engineers, architects, and scientists. According to Jason Thompson, "There was more to the French expedition than its army and navy, for it was accompanied by 151 civilians who were constituted into the Commissions of Sciences and Arts."[15] The *Description de l'Égypte* did more to catalog Egypt than anyone could have anticipated. In some cases, these sketches provide the only historical record of some structures long since destroyed.

In the mid-1800s, there was a lack of legislation and safeguards that prevented people from excavating and removing Egypt's relics. These relics often were either gifted or sold to museums in Europe or put into private collections (though most often these collections were eventually gifted or sold to museums across the world). Excavation techniques ranged from the delicate to the disastrous: for example, in the late 1830s, explorers used dynamite to blast a hole in the Great Pyramid at Giza while looking for treasure. In 1858, Auguste Mariette was appointed as director of antiquities in Egypt, and protections were finally put into place.[16]

THE BRITISH MUSEUM: A TREASURE TROVE OF INSPIRATION

Greek, Roman, and Egyptian artifacts were the British Museum's primary contents in the early nineteenth century. These artifacts were largely acquired from the bequests of private collections owned by wealthy benefactors such as Sir Hans Sloane. Ancient artifacts were relatively easily acquired, and there were few protections for the antiquities themselves. Relics were acquired even with the knowledge of the governing bodies—but often without. In some cases, precious antiquities removed from Egypt were gifted to other nations as gestures of goodwill and friendship. Two obelisks known as Cleopatra's Needles, which currently reside in New York and London, and the Luxor Obelisk, currently residing in Paris, were gifts from the Khedives (equivalent to an English viceroy), who ruled Egypt shortly after France and Britain departed.[17]

The London Needle was presented as a gift to Britain in 1819 while Poe was living with the Allan family in London. However, the obelisk did not actually arrive in London until decades later. When the British Government declined to fund the transfer of the obelisk, a wealthy British surgeon and amateur Egyptologist, coincidentally named William Wilson (no known relation to Poe's *William Wilson*), personally funded the move.[18] Today, these ancient Egyptian obelisks are still standing and can be admired in the City of Westminster's Victoria Embankment (London), the Place de la Concorde (Paris), and Central Park, west of the Metropolitan Museum of Art (New York) (Figs. 12.1, 12.2, and 12.3).[19]

Fig. 12.1   Cleopatra's Needle, London (Photo by Adrian Pingstone)

Fig. 12.2 Luxor Obelisk, Paris (Photo by Nathaniel Hansen)

Fig. 12.3 Cleopatra's Needle, New York City (Photo by Philip Edward Phillips)

Although Napoléon's conquests in Egypt were not so advantageous for the general himself (as he failed to conquer Egypt), they have proved fruitful for humanity and Western culture. The precious relics found there are preserved for generations in museums. While his troops and *savants* were in Rosetta cataloging their findings for their *Descriptions*, they discovered a large broken stone slate with three distinct sets of glyphs. The Rosetta Stone was a unique find, although it was unclear to what extent at the time of its discovery. The stone was the key to understanding Egyptian hieroglyphs as the stone's message was written in three scripts: two versions of ancient Egyptian (hieroglyphic and demotic) and ancient Greek. This artifact was not in France's possession long before the British took control of the area and seized it as a spoil of war.

The sting of losing the Rosetta Stone failed to quash France's enthusiasm for the Egyptian mysteries. Both Neoclassicism and Neo-Egyptian style were incredibly popular during Napoléon's reign and during the period immediately following. Susan Punzel Conner writes in *The Age of Napoleon*, that "[a]rchitecture was, in fact, a tool of politics." This explains why Napoléon still commissioned art and statues to commemorate the battles that France had won in Egypt, among his other conquests.[20] The idea of architecture as politics extends beyond Napoléon; we see it when France gifted the Statue of Liberty to the United States, and it offers one reason why France, Britain, and the United States proudly display their matching obelisks. In the nineteenth century, France embraced Egypt as a symbol of hope and discovery at the same time they struggled to bring the French Revolution to a close. Napoléon had failed in his Egyptian conquest, at least militarily. The *savants* and their work, however, laid the cornerstone for a budding interest in Egypt that fueled the fires for what became modern Egyptology: "The discovery, or rediscovery, of ancient Egypt in the first half of the nineteenth century was a momentous event in intellectual history," though born out of politics rather than academia.[21]

The Rosetta Stone is arguably the most popular antiquity in the British Museum today, with a crushing queue of visitors eager to see the stone up close. However, it was not received with the same fervor when it first arrived in London on a French frigate (aptly named the *L'Egyptienne*) in 1802. By the time Thomas Young and Jean-François Champollion began working on deciphering the text, however, the masses came around. The stone provided a gateway to understanding the ancient civilization; until its discovery, scholars struggled to decipher

Egyptian hieroglyphs. Once the ancient Greek text was translated, scholars determined that the hieroglyphs were phonetic depictions of words—they represented *sounds* rather than *letters*. No one could have anticipated what that broken slate of cryptic text would mean for the British, nor was there any indication of the craze that this stone would spark for the better part of a century—a craze that has lost some of its original fervor but none of its relevance.

The Rosetta Stone would become the cornerstone of British nationalism and instrumental in a trans-Atlantic interest in Egypt. Deborah Ann Logan writes, "That the Rosetta Stone and Parthenon friezes continue to be associated with the British Museum as part of England's national identity offers an eloquent case in point" that artifacts are part of nationalism and museums play a strong supporting role in collecting, curating, and broadcasting that identity.[22] Though Europe had an interest in Egypt prior to the Rosetta Stone's discovery, after it was put on display in 1802 there was an immediate surge in the use and appreciation of Egyptian style, culminating in the architectural movement known as the Egyptian Revival. Buildings, fashion, and even advertising witnessed a stark uptick in Egyptian and "Oriental" elements.

At the same time that England became keenly interested in Egypt with the acquisition of the Rosetta Stone, Poe lived only a short walk from the British Museum. In October 1815, Poe's foster father, John Allan, wrote a letter to Charles Ellis giving his family's current address as "No. 47 Southampton Row, Russel [sic] Square," a mere five-minute walk from the British Museum.[23] While there is nothing to prove that Poe, in fact, visited the British Museum, we can speculate that he might have wandered through its vast corridors and immersed himself in its rich history. There is speculation that Poe's interest in both classical and Egyptian history was fostered by the immense collection at the British Museum. As Harry Lee Poe suggests, "The recently acquired Rosetta Stone may have sparked Poe's lifelong interest in cryptography which played the central role in *The Gold-Bug*. The collection of mummies may have been the origin of his comic tale *A Few Words with a Mummy* [sic]."[24] Even if he did not actually visit the British Museum, Poe must have been aware of the collections as he demonstrated his awareness of cultural climates and current events in various writings.

Regardless, because of the growing popular interest in Egypt during Poe's stay in London, he may have walked past the Egyptian Hall in Piccadilly Square, which stood from 1812 until it was demolished in the early twentieth century. He likely would have heard the news in 1819 that England was gifted one of the obelisks known as Cleopatra's Needle (although the obelisk was not erected until 1878, well after Poe's death). Although Poe never visited Egypt, Egypt surrounded him in London.

Unraveling Egypt in Poe's Works

There are numerous references to Egypt, pharaohs, and mummies in Poe's works, and these may simply be colorful flourishes in his poetry and prose. Other references seem more deliberate and not just mere ornamentation. Poe's inclusion of Egyptian elements and allusions is a deliberate stylistic choice that appears in multiple works.

As a burgeoning nation, the United States sought ways to align itself with other empires and, in Poe's day, one of those empires was ancient Egypt. Scott Trafton focuses much of his work, *Egypt Land: Race and Nineteenth-Century American Egyptomania*, on *why* America was so keen and willing to incorporate Egypt into its culture. He notes that some of the cultural landmarks central to America's image are distinctly Egyptian: the Washington Monument, an obelisk, is the tallest structure in the nation's capital, and in the main reading room of the Library of Congress, figures representing Egypt and America appear next to one another.[25] However, the rise of Egyptology also served to justify slavery for some, such as Samuel George Morton, at a time of increasing racial tensions. "From their earliest appearances in nineteenth-century America," according to Trafton, "images and discourses of and about ancient or Pharaonic Egypt were scandalously radicalized."[26] While Poe does not explicitly address race and racism in his works, he does include Jupiter in his tale, "The Gold-Bug," a freed slave who remains a loyal servant to Legrand. His decision to include a freed Southern slave likely would have been a controversial choice in 1843.

While Poe dabbled in provocative topics, he also understood the need to appeal to his audience to ensure his survival as a writer. "Since he [Poe] could not support himself by writing poetry," Terence Whalen argues, "he had to adapt his talents to the unstable and perhaps unfathomable tastes of a distant mass audience. Some of his most extravagant tales were, by his own admission, composed 'to supply a particular demand.'"[27] To sustain himself financially as a "Magazinist," Poe engaged in a multiplicity of genres, including satire, elegy, and horror. His tales "Ligeia," "The Fall of the House of Usher," "Some Words with a Mummy," "The Gold-Bug," and "The Black Cat," as well as other works of prose and prose fiction, display his incorporation of trends in popular culture, especially with a focus on the emerging interest in Egypt. For Poe, tapping into this cultural consciousness was another way to attempt to secure a foothold in the literary marketplace, as evidenced by the myriad genres in which he wrote.

Perhaps Poe saved the larger and more overt references for pieces in which Egypt factored heavily in terms of agency, and in which the removal of the Egyptian motif would alter the "effect" of the story, perhaps significantly. In other cases, however, Egyptian motifs simply add a colorful flourish to the scenery. G. R. Thompson argues that in "The Gold-Bug," for example, "Poe was capitalizing on the contemporary popularity of puzzles and cryptograms in mass-market publications," likely because of the translations of the Rosetta Stone that Thomas Young and Jean-François Champollion had very recently worked on—and the many that came afterward in the attempt to fully decode and understand hieroglyphics.[28] More than this, the transmigration of souls in "Ligeia," among other works, draws upon Egyptian mythology and practice. While transmigration does appear in other cultures, it certainly factored heavily in Egyptian mythology.

Three tales, in particular, exemplify Poe's fascination with and artistic incorporation of Egypt. These are "Ligeia," "The Fall of the House of Usher," and "Some Words with a Mummy." While Poe does reference Egypt in other works—such as "The Black Cat," "The Assignation," and "The Colloquy of Monos and Una," among others—these three tales are especially significant in their treatment and use of Egypt. Poe offers commentary on Egyptomania and satirizes prominent Egyptologists, incorporates Egyptian mythology and resurrection motifs in his works, reveals the commonality of Egyptian and antebellum attitudes toward death, and explores the balance between racial tension and a fascination with ancient Egypt during his time.

We can make some informed speculation about Poe's interest in Egypt because he uses it in a variety of ways. Much like a budding Egyptologist might decorate his house with relics in the nineteenth century, Poe scatters artifacts throughout his stories. His use of Egypt in "Ligeia" highlights Egypt's mystifying nature and the interest in magic and alchemy. To convey his message in "Some Words with a Mummy," Poe uses Egypt and the mummy to entertain the reader, while castigating two prominent Egyptologists, George Gliddon and James Silk

Buckingham, and satirizing the harmful aspects of the scientific (or pseudoscientific) interest in Egypt. In some works, Egypt is a backdrop, relegated to tchotchkes in the gothic setting, or a passing reference to a cultural figure, but the country is sometimes a major part of the story, aiding in a character's transformation or serving as an allegory for larger issues that Poe wanted to address. Poe wields Egypt carefully, unlike the many other who were, at the time of his writing, pillaging its ancient tombs and landmarks.

"Some Words with a Mummy" (1845)

Poe's tale, "Some Words with a Mummy," published in the *American Review: A Whig Journal*, in 1845, functions both as a satire of Egyptomania and as a social commentary on Egyptomaniacs. In this tale, the narrator is summoned in the middle of the night to a dinner party hosted by Doctor Ponnonner, whose principal entertainment for the evening is the unwrapping of a mummy he acquired for that very purpose. Ponnonner writes in his letter to the narrator, "At last, by long persevering diplomacy, I have gained the assent of the Directors of the City Museum, to my examination of the Mummy...to unswathe it and open it, if desirable" (M, 1178). The sarcophagus was displayed in a museum for eight years, and Ponnonner remarks how fortunate they were to have a perfectly preserved relic to explore: "We had now, therefore, the complete Mummy at our disposal; and to those who are aware how very rarely the unransacked antique reaches our shores, it will be evident, at once, that we had great reason to congratulate ourselves upon our good fortune" (M, 1179). The party breaks through the sarcophagus to find the red-hued body, which they almost immediately defile: "...on scraping the surface [of the skin] with a steel instrument, and throwing into the fire some of the powder thus obtained, the flavor of camphor and other sweet-scented gums became apparent" (M, 1180–1181). As they reanimate the body, the mummy (whose name "Allamistakeo" the group easily deciphers from the sarcophagus) rebukes the group for their treatment of his body. After offering apologies, the group speaks with the mummy, asking questions about history before shifting to a discussion of their technological advances. In response to their inquiries and observations, the mummy claims that the technological feats of his day were equivalent, or greater, than those of the present day. The group grows incredulous and finally proffers "cough drops" as an example of a modern technology that surpasses those of the mummy's day; they revel in their victory.

Once the reanimated mummy begins to lecture the group that unwrapped him, Poe's own voice can be heard from behind the mummy's words. In this tale, Poe describes a real-life scenario. In the early nineteenth century, affluent citizens would sometimes invite guests over to examine a mummy using crude, rudimentary scientific methods under the guise of a party. They unwrapped mummies simply for pleasure—because they *could*. No rationale for the scientific experiment is offered, save for Gliddon whose explanation is as misguided as Gliddon himself. In this tale, Poe satirizes the practice of unwrapping a mummy and discloses the grotesque and callous treatment of the previously interred body after remarking how fortunate they were to have such a perfect and "unransacked antique." The dinner party does not actually discover anything worth noting because scientific discovery is not their primary objective. As the mummy chastises the group for its deplorable handling of his body, buried deep in the text is Poe's voice, chastising the public about its own mishandling of precious artifacts and the Egyptologists for doing so little to protect Egypt. The mummy scolds Buckingham and Gliddon for their mishandling of an antiquity and serves as Poe's vehicle for commenting on the behavior of these Egyptologists, who have become glorified celebrities instead of serious scientists.

In this work, the dinner party guests behave almost as if they desire to learn something new from their scientific exploration; yet the crowd demonstrates indifference at moments when the mummy imparts wisdom. The mummy "challenges Anglo-Saxon progress, equality and democracy, and American mechanical superiority."[29] Yet, the group fails to note this as they are not, in fact, prepared to learn anything. For Trafton, "Mummy" is "a story in which the figure of ancient Egypt is placed at anxious odds with the inhabitants of the nineteenth century and one in which Egypt is seen as a marker of the absolute, the eternal, and an authority to which *all* questions—social, scientific, trivial, and profound—can be referred."[30] While the mummy represents authority, an historical figure who attempts to explain contemporary, antebellum America by discussing the past, the group does not quite understand the significance of his words, nor do they know how to comprehend what the mummy reveals to them. They cannot see past themselves.

"The Fall of the House of Usher" (1839)

Much like in "Some Words with a Mummy," the narrator of "The Fall of the House of Usher" receives a letter summoning him to visit an old friend. The old friend, Roderick Usher, is unwell and desperate to see the narrator. Arriving at the house, the narrator remarks on the condition of the exterior of the home, observing "a barely perceptible fissure, which, extending from the roof of the building in front, made its way down the wall in a zigzag direction" until it disappeared into the tarn below (M, 400). Roderick's sister, Madeline, is also unwell and suffering from a mysterious malady that results in periodic catatonic states. The narrator and Roderick pass the time by reading and playing music until one evening when Madeline suddenly dies. She is temporarily interred in the family tomb before her subsequent burial. Roderick's condition seems to improve until one stormy evening when Roderick confesses that he has been tormented by strange sounds coming from within the house and asserts, "*We have put her living in the tomb!*" (M, 416). Suddenly, the "lofty and enshrouded figure of the lady Madeline of Usher" appears and falls upon her brother. As they are reunited, the house, the symbol of the remaining Usher family, splits in two and falls into the tarn.

The Egyptian aspects of "Usher" may not be clear upon first glance because they are subtly woven into the text. The books listed in the Usher library focus primarily on journeys to the underworld, and some include prayers for the dead. If Usher's library contains texts that prepare the reader for the afterlife, this attitude toward death is not unlike the approach ancient Egyptians took—that death is a natural progression and one must be prepared. Indeed, Egyptians spent much of their life on this preparation, saving funds for burial and gathering materials needed in their tombs to aid them in the afterlife. Death was not a fearful end, just inevitable. Many of the attitudes toward death in the nineteenth century were similar to Egyptian sentiment until the American Civil War (1861–1865) changed that perception. Drew Gilpin Faust writes in *The Republic of Suffering: Death and the American Civil War* that "Civil War soldiers were, in fact, better prepared to die that to kill, for they lived in a culture that offered many lessons in how life should end."[31] Much like the ancient Egyptians, antebellum Americans did not fear death. The Civil War resulted in a dramatic shift in death customs due to the number and rate of occurring casualties. The horror of so many violent deaths left an indelible mark on the public.

Barton Levi St. Armand notes that in regard to "Usher," Poe's "Gothic frame is supported by a basically Egyptian foundation" and, more importantly, that "in resurrecting the Egyptian mode as part of the dramatic stage setting of his tale, Poe also revived the pattern of initiation ritual which underlaid the symbols of the Egyptian Mysteries, the Mysteries of Isis and Osiris, as they were understood by his own age."[32] Roderick and Madeline appear as antebellum counterparts to the mythological Osiris and Isis, respectively, in their enactment of resurrection.

St. Armand asserts that Madeline and Roderick are doubles of Osiris and Isis, and that "Usher" plays on the resurrection myth in a gothic fashion. E. A. Wallis Budge explains in *Osiris and the Egyptian Resurrection* that in mythology Osiris and Isis are brother and sister as well as husband and wife. Osiris's brother, Set (or Typhon), tricks Osiris into climbing into a wooden box and is thrown into the Nile. After Isis recovers her husband's body, Set breaks Osiris's body into many pieces and scatters them across the country. Isis takes it upon herself to gather the pieces of his body and thus Osiris is "returned from the Other World."[33]

In "Usher," Poe alludes to a parallel between Roderick and Madeline, and Osiris and Isis. The "very ancient" Usher family had been in decline for some time. Critics such as G. R. Thompson have noted that "the Usher family is extremely inbred and has been so for generations."[34] This may explain why Roderick and Madeline look nearly identical. Although Roderick and Madeline are brother and sister, they live as husband and wife in a ceremonial sense, much like many Egyptian pharaohs, who customarily married siblings and co-ruled (Cleopatra was one such pharaoh to marry and co-rule with her brothers).

The earliest reference to Isis in Poe's tale occurs when the narrator first approaches the House of Usher. He is uneasy, feeling "an utter depression of soul" to which nothing can compare save "the hideous dropping off the veil" (M, 397). The "dropping off the veil," interestingly, may refer to the goddess Isis and her priests. Thompson explains that Poe is alluding to a tradition in ancient Egypt, in which "the priests of Isis who peered beneath the veil of the goddess to see her actual face were driven mad."[35] Although the narrator may be uneasy that he either is, or eventually will be, mad, Roderick is the one who will feel the effects of peering beneath the veil. Once his sister Madeline has died and is seemingly resurrected, Roderick goes mad when she appears before him. Roderick's fractured mind is emblematic of a split consciousness: by putting Madeline alive in the tomb, Roderick becomes both Osiris and Set, and he sets in motion the actions leading to his demise. Thus, while Isis brings Osiris back from the dead, Madeline and Roderick appear to subvert this initiation ritual in "Usher."

According to Thompson, Poe's story is "an appellation which seemed to include, in the minds of the peasantry who used it, both the family and the family mansion."[36] It refers not only to the physical building but also to the family that has inhabited it for years. The Egyptians built pyramids as monuments for a dynasty or a particular pharaoh, and they also served to house the dead. The pyramids represented a family or pharaoh just as the House of Usher is a monument to the Usher family. Moreover, the crumbling mansion resembles a ruin, much like an Egyptian pyramid as it would have appeared in the nineteenth century: that is, as a crumbling façade representing a family that once lived there.

"Ligeia" (1838)

"Ligeia," is another of Poe's tales that features Egyptian elements, though much more subtly than in "Some Words with a Mummy." While "Mummy" is a satire of Egyptomania and a social commentary on early nineteenth-century America, "Ligeia" is a supernatural story centered on resurrection. The story incorporates Egyptian motifs not only in the physical descriptions of the narrator's abbey but also in the dénouement of the tale in which Lady Rowena seems to metamorphose into Ligeia through transmigration.

The narrator cannot recall for certain how and when he came to know the enigmatic Ligeia but he can readily recall her beauty, and especially her face, in exquisite detail. Ligeia captivates him, and they soon marry. The narrator is impressed by her immense knowledge; she is well-versed in mathematical science and multilingual. However, as with Madeline in "Usher," Ligeia suddenly becomes ill and dies. After her death, the narrator buys an abbey in England and remarries to the Lady Rowena. Within their second month of marriage, Lady Rowena falls ill and dies as well. One evening, after her death, the narrator observes Lady Rowena as she appears to be reviving. All through the night, Lady Rowena had evidenced signs of returning to life, only to die again. Finally, she seems to stir once more, and as her shroud falls from her face, the narrator marvels to see that Lady Rowena has transformed into Ligeia.

As the transformation takes place, the narrator's eyes turn to the "sarcophagi in the angles of the room," an Egyptian receptacle for the body (M, 326). Poe acknowledges an Egyptian symbol at a key moment in the story. By having the narrator's eyes gaze upon the sarcophagi at the beginning of Rowena's transformation into Ligeia, Poe reminds readers of the ancient Egyptian belief that the soul can embody any living object. E. A. Wallis Budge describes the transmigration of souls in *Osiris and the Egyptian Resurrection*, noting that "[t]he Egyptians believed in the transmigration of souls, and their priests composed a series of Chapters, the recital of which enabled the souls of the dead to take any form they pleased.... It could remain in [its chosen form] so long as it pleased, presumably without losing its identity, and it could pass from one form to another at pleasure."[37] At the moment of Lady Rowena's death, Ligeia not only takes over Rowena's body, but she also retains her own identity. Rowena is no more while Ligeia is fully realized. The quotation attributed to Joseph Glanville at the tale's start remarks that weak-willed people die. That Ligeia can be resurrected demonstrates her desire and ultimately her power to live.

The narrator's abbey, decorated in Egyptian and occult style, provides the perfect setting for this transmigration, for Ligeia to demonstrate the strength of her will. The bridal chamber is a five-sided room, a pentagon, and "[i]n each of the angles of the chamber stood on end a gigantic sarcophagus of black granite, from the tombs of the kings over against Luxor, with their aged lids full of immemorial sculpture" (M, 322). The entire room is decorated with symbols and relics from different styles, among others, Gothic, Druidic, and Indian. It is the Egyptian relics, though, that are most relevant to Ligeia's transformation.

The narrator's description of Ligeia's face is covered in some 800 words, roughly ten percent of the story as a whole. He makes a point of identifying her features as decidedly Eastern, with a graceful Hebrew nose and large eyes that were "far larger than the ordinary eyes of our own race" (M, 313). Poe implies that Ligeia is learned in alchemy as well, "a forbidden knowledge considered akin to witchcraft," which the Egyptians practiced (M, 306). Shortly before her transformation within the magical and Egyptian-styled bridal chamber, the narrator claims to see fall within Rowena's goblet of wine "as if from some invisible spring in the atmosphere of the room, three or four large drops of a brilliant and ruby colored fluid" (M, 325). As alchemy is thought to allow transmutation of an object into another (such as turning metals into gold), Ligeia employs her knowledge of alchemy to revivify herself.

MOB MENTALITY AND RACIAL TENSIONS: HISTORY REPEATS ITSELF

In "Some Words with a Mummy," Poe's scathing and satirical characterization of Gliddon and Buckingham is indicative of his feelings toward those who ransacked Egypt through archeological excavations that did more to destroy than to preserve Egypt. For every artifact placed in a museum during the early nineteenth century, there were likely other ones that were destroyed in their place. Poe's treatment of these historical figures also speaks to his views on the excavation and destruction of Egypt. While these experts were literally unraveling Egypt (Gliddon actually unwrapped mummies during public lectures), Poe preserves Egypt in his writing, only figuratively unwrapping the ancient country's mysteries. His castigation of rudimentary "science for science's sake" for its potential to destroy, rather than preserve through inquiry and curiosity, is apparent not only in "Mummy" but also in his early poem, "Sonnet—to Science." In the last few lines of that poem, Poe laments that science has driven out the mythical creatures and stripped away their traditional mystery. Science threatens creativity and imagination and Poe fears science's potential impact ("dull realities") on poetry. Just as archeology has the power to destroy as it uncovers truth, so does science. Thus, for Poe, science for the sake of science had dangerous potential. Of course, Poe wrote *Eureka: A Prose Poem*, a predominantly scientific work, only a few years after publishing "Mummy," but even Poe's scientific text is purely theoretical and seeks to explain mysteries (in this case, the universe) without simultaneously doing irreparable harm. Poe's disdain for "science for science's sake" coincides with his fear of another danger—the mob.

As in "Ligeia," "Some Words with a Mummy" reveals Poe's disgust for the mob, the general public who is incapable of drawing meaningful conclusions. Worse, they are incapable of making significant changes to society. The mob in "Mummy" attempts to decimate a corpse for both entertainment and a futile attempt at scientific discovery. Their mishandling of the body displays their ignorance of anything historical and sacred. They also do not attempt to learn anything noteworthy from the reanimated mummy and likely would have thrown away the corpse when finished with it. Poe's contempt for the public in "Mummy" indicates his attitude that the mob is blind to its own actions and disrespectful of the past, even when trying to manipulate it to answer futile questions.

Trafton argues that "[t]he group intends to remove the mummy from its case, unwrap it, characterize it, analyze it, and dissect it. Interestingly enough, the specific motivations for performing these tests are left conspicuously unspecified."[38] The host and his guests have no clear goal in mind, and nothing to gain, when unwrapping the mummy. Trafton further argues that Poe uses the historical figure of George Gliddon, a prominent, contemporary Egyptologist, to represent "not the under-educated enthusiasm of the narrator, nor the specialized but only partly related knowledge of the other men, but precisely the point at which American Egyptology could be said in 1845 to have come into its own."[39] While the dinner party removes layers of wrappings to uncover historical truth, they do not know how to apply or understand it—and it seems that is never their intent in the first place. The group desecrates and rewrites history by destroying the physical evidence of ancient Egypt: the mummy. This work perfectly illustrates that there were few protections at the time to keep Egypt safe.

Although he lived in an era of great social reform, Poe felt and expressed deep skepticism about human progress and whether social reform could actually *do* anything.[40] Some of his reservations about democracy are chronicled in his tales dealing with the "mob," such as "Mummy" and "The Man of the Crowd." Ernest Marchand explains that, in Poe's day, "[t]he great staples of thought and discussion…were democracy, social reform, and progress," and he doubted the sincerity of reformers.[41] Although Poe lived during a time of great social reform, he was afraid of the consequences, reasoning that democracy hands power to "the obtuse in intellect" and is therefore dangerous.[42] The mob mentality in "Mummy" prevents the group from regarding the past as sacred. The mob is looking forward, not backward, which is clear in the group members' conversations with the mummy as they share their great and forward-thinking achievements.

Coupled with the mob mentality are the racial anxieties in antebellum America, which Poe explores in both "Mummy" and "Ligeia." Scholars and Egyptologists debated the race of the mummies in the nineteenth century. Some, including Gliddon, were convinced that the Egyptians were white, especially since the bulk of Egyptian (re)discoveries were made during the period of slavery in the United States. Those who favored slavery certainly would have wanted to quash any arguments that the Egyptians were not white. The idea that a population revered and worshiped a powerful black pharaoh displeased many Egyptologists. Some emphasized hieroglyphics in which slaves appeared to labor under the pharaoh in order to counteract such impressions.[43] A satirical article appeared in *The North Star*, an anti-slavery African American newspaper in 1850, which sums up the sentiment: "We were assured, therefore, by the learned doctors, that the Thebans were not Africans, but a nobler race," or a race that was "white."[44] One such "learned doctor" was George Gliddon, who, along with his mentor Samuel George Morton, tried to downplay the fact that most ancient Egyptians were not, in fact, white—or the kind of "white" that they imagined.[45] For Gliddon, the people responsible for building great empires, such as Egypt, were unmistakably white. Gliddon argued in one work co-written with Dr. Josiah Nott that the Egyptians had black slaves—not asking why one race would enslave their own, they suppose that the Egyptians were, in fact, a different race altogether.[46]

Perhaps Poe was speaking through the narrator of "Mummy" when he remarked, "The truth is, I am heartily sick of this life and of the nineteenth century in general. I am convinced that everything is going wrong" (M, 1195). Although Poe does not call out racism and slavery explicitly in "Mummy," Count Allamistakeo does dismiss nearly every "achievement" of the nineteenth century, including ideas on the origins of man. In "The Gold-Bug," the freed slave Jupiter is portrayed as extremely loyal to Legrand. As Poe spent most of his childhood in Richmond, Virginia, he regularly encountered slaves and slaveholders. Poe's writing seems to refute the popular attitudes regarding slavery held by his contemporaries.

CONCLUSION

What can we learn about Poe's use of Egypt and by studying this particular aspect of his work and interests? In short, history repeats itself. To understand where we are going, we must look at where we have been. While examining Egyptomania in Poe's works, it becomes possible to understand more than what was happening in Poe's time. We can draw meaningful parallels to the present. We are still unraveling mysteries of the universe and trying to learn about the world around us while attempting to preserve it. We are still struggling with race and racism. When engaging with "Mummy," we find an often-neglected story that is still poignant some 170 years later, when racial tensions are still high, when the earth is being pillaged in the name of science and advancement, when the mob mentality is as strong as ever.

With such thematic complexities in "Ligeia," "The Fall of the House of Usher," and "Some Words with a Mummy," it is easy to overlook Egyptian motifs in the works. But, to overlook this aspect of his writing is to ignore a large part of our own history. Poe never visited Egypt; he would have had to be satisfied with visiting the British Museum as a child or attending a lecture from a prominent Egyptologist, such as George Gliddon. Yet, Poe makes great use of Egypt in his works. This recurring theme prompts a deeper discussion on the significance of Egypt during the nineteenth century, including how racial tensions may have influenced public perception of ancient Egypt.

In the mid-nineteenth century, scholars and amateur Egyptologists were just beginning to explore and understand ancient Egypt. For Poe to write about Egypt with such authority indicates that he went to great lengths to gather information on Egypt, as his formal education would have centered on Greek and Roman history. Poe wields Egypt in an informed way that indicates his audience's interest in the subject as well as his own. He chastises the fictional proxies of Gliddon and Buckingham for their mistreatment of the mummy, and questions popular nineteenth-century theories on racial origin. Poe also makes a case for scientific exploration without destruction. In "Ligeia," "The Fall of the House of Usher," and "Some Words with a Mummy," Poe uses Egypt to talk about difficult subjects and offer his position. Examining Poe's inclusion of Egyptian themes allows modern readers to gain a broader understanding of the nineteenth century as well as reassess Poe's attitudes toward race and science. Much as Poe did during his time, we have to be willing to peer beneath the veil and hope that we will not go mad.

NOTES

1. Elliott Colla, *Conflicted Antiquities: Egyptology, Egyptomania, Egyptian Modernity* (Durham: Duke University Press, 2007), 16–17.
2. Ibid., 5.
3. Scott Trafton, *Egypt Land: Race and Nineteenth-Century American Egyptomania* (Durham: Duke University Press, 2004), 2.
4. U.S. Department of State, Bureau of Public Affairs. *The Great Seal of the United States* (Washington, DC: U.S. Department of State, Bureau of Public Affairs, 2003), 3.
5. J. Gerald Kennedy, *Strange Nation: Literary Nationalism and Cultural Conflict in the Age of Poe* (New York: Oxford University Press, 2016), xi.

6. Michael J. Collins, *The Drama of the American Short Story, 1800–1865* (Ann Arbor: University of Michigan Press, 2016), 77.

7. For a discussion of the origins and significance of "Orientalism," see Edward W. Said's seminal study, *Orientalism* (London: Routledge & Kegan Paul, 1978).

8. Arthur Hobson Quinn, *Edgar Allan Poe: A Critical Biography* (Baltimore: Johns Hopkins University Press, 1941), 119.

9. The narrator of "William Wilson" travels to Egypt among other locations such as Paris, Naples, and Rome.

10. Bob Brier and Jean-Pierre Houdin, *The Secret of the Great Pyramid: How One Man's Obsession Led to the Solution of Ancient Egypt's Greatest Mystery* (New York: HarperCollins, 2008), 9.

11. Ibid., 117.

12. John T. Irwin, *American Hieroglyphics: The Symbol of the Egyptian Hieroglyphics in the American Renaissance* (Baltimore: Johns Hopkins University Press, 1980), 44.

13. It was extremely bad form to harm or kill a cat in ancient Egypt, and the punishment was severe. In ancient Egypt, cats were revered as the living embodiment of Bastet, the cat goddess, and were even mummified and buried with their owners. In "The Black Cat," Poe could have drawn from ancient tradition when he alluded to the narrator's misfortunes resulting from his perverse killing of Pluto.

14. The official number of volumes varies from 21–29 depending on the text consulted.

15. Jason Thompson, *Wonderful Things: A History of Egyptology 1: From Antiquity to 1881* (Cairo: American University in Cairo Press, 2015), 98.

16. Thompson, *Wonderful Things*, 228.

17. Ibid., 280–281.

18. Thompson, *Wonderful Things*, 280.

19. The London obelisk was offered to the British as early as 1801 but did not reach the UK until 1878. The New York obelisk was offered to the United States in 1877 and finally arrived in 1880. These obelisks were taken from Alexandria while the Paris obelisk stood outside the Luxor temple until 1833 when it was moved to Paris. Champollion was influential in the acquisition of the Paris obelisk. See Jason Thompson's *Wonderful Things: A History of Egyptology 1: From Antiquity to 1881* for more information about the obelisks.

20. Susan Punzel Conner, *The Age of Napoleon* (Westport: Greenwood Press, 2004), 55.

21. Thompson, *Wonderful Things*, 97.

22. Deborah Ann Logan, *Harriet Martineau, Victorian Imperialism, and the Civilizing Mission* (New York: Routledge, 2016), 206.

23. Quinn, *Edgar Allan Poe*, 67.
24. Harry Lee Poe, "Edgar Allan Poe: London's claim on Baltimore's greatest poet," *Baltimore Post Examiner*, June 25, 2015, accessed December 30, 2015, http://baltimorepostexaminer.com/edgar-allan-poe-londons-claim-on-baltimores-greatest-poet/2015/06/25.
25. Trafton, *Egypt Land*, 2.
26. Ibid., 49.
27. Terence Whalen, *Edgar Allan Poe and the Masses: The Political Economy of Literature in Antebellum America* (Princeton: Princeton University Press, 1999), 7.
28. G. R. Thompson, ed., *The Selected Writings of Edgar Allan Poe. A Norton Critical Edition* (New York: W. W. Norton & Company, 2004), 321.
29. Kennedy, 399.
30. Trafton, 133.
31. Drew Gilpin Faust, *The Republic of Suffering: Death and the American Civil War* (New York: Vintage Books, 2008), 6.
32. Barton Levi St. Armand, "The 'Mysteries' of Edgar Poe: The Quest for a Monomyth in Gothic Literature." In *Modern Critical Interpretations: The Tales of Poe*, edited by Harold Bloom (New York: Chelsea House, 1987), 30–32.
33. E. A. Wallis Budge, *Osiris and the Egyptian Resurrection*, vol. 1 (New York: Dover,1973), 1–17.
34. Ibid., 200.
35. Thompson, *The Selected Writings of Edgar Allan Poe*, 199.
36. Ibid., 201.
37. Budge, *Osiris and the Egyptian Resurrection*, 139.
38. Trafton, *Egypt Land*, 133.
39. Ibid., 134.
40. Quinn, *Edgar Allan Poe*, 468.
41. Ernest Marchand, "Poe as Social Critic," *American Literature* 6, no. 1 (1934), 30–34.
42. Ibid., 41.
43. Trafton, *Egypt Land*, 49.
44. Ibid., 45.
45. It is worth noting that Cleopatra VII was actually Macedonian Greek as Egypt was ruled by both Greece and Rome for a time.
46. J. C. Nott, and George R. Gliddon, *Types of Mankind: or Ethnological Researches, Based upon the Ancient Monuments, Paintings, Sculptures, and Crania of Races, and upon Their Natural, Geographical, Philological, and Biblical History* (Philadelphia: Lippincott and Grambo, 1854; Repr., Miami: Mnemosyne, 1969).

CHAPTER 13

Poe, Paris, and "The Murders in the Rue Morgue"

Philip Edward Phillips and George Poe

> *Ai-je besoin d'avertir à propos de la rue Morgue [...] qu'Edgar Poe n'est jamais venu à Paris?[1]*
> Do I need to point out apropos of the Rue Morgue [...] that Edgar Poe never came to Paris?

Prior to Charles Baudelaire's rhetorical query, E. D. Forgues, the first French literary critic to write about Edgar A. Poe—a full decade before Baudelaire would do so in his initial volume of translated tales—had called into question Poe's use of the "unfamiliar terrain of Paris," concluding that doing so, in fact, "increased 'vraisemblance' for [Poe's] American readers."[2] Poe scholar Burton Pollin rightly concluded, in turn, that "Forgues admires Poe's inventive daring and accepts it as

P. E. Phillips (✉)
Middle Tennessee State University, Murfreesboro, TN, USA

G. Poe
The University of the South, Sewanee, TN, USA

© The Author(s) 2018
P. E. Phillips (ed.), *Poe and Place*,
Geocriticism and Spatial Literary Studies,
https://doi.org/10.1007/978-3-319-96788-2_13

no detriment."[3] Although Poe's famous detective tales, "The Murders in the Rue Morgue" (1841), "The Mystery of Marie Rogêt" (1842), and "The Purloined Letter" (1845)—all featuring the brilliant C. Auguste Dupin—are set in Paris, Poe never actually set foot in France. Nevertheless, to this day, the French consider *Edgar Poe* to be almost one of their own. Poe owes his place in both the French literary pantheon and France's popular imagination largely to Baudelaire's masterful translations of his works and his biographical essay, "*Edgar Allan Poe: sa vie et ses ouvrages*" ["Edgar Allan Poe: His Life and Works"], published in the *Revue de Paris* for March/April 1852, which introduced the American writer to a broader European audience and, eventually, to the world.

In a letter dated November 30, 1846 to editor Evert Augustus Duyckinck, Poe excitedly relates the news that his work had reached France. He recounts that his aunt and mother-in-law Mrs. Maria Clemm "mentioned [...] that some of the Parisian papers had been speaking about [...] 'Murders in the Rue Morgue,'" and that it was "spoken of in the Paris 'Charivari,' soon after the first issue of the tale in Graham's Mag:—April 1841."[4] Although he quickly moves the letter toward other concerns after his abrupt opening, Poe's statement about being recognized in Paris expresses his belief that he was being read in France,[5] and connects him to the legendary setting of his ratiocinative tales featuring C. Auguste Dupin.

This chapter traces two major facets of Poe's relationship with France. First, the circulation of Poe's work in Paris led to its fateful encounter with the poet Baudelaire. Seeing himself as Poe's French "double,"[6] Baudelaire was the first to establish the rich reputation and distinction of writer and genius that Poe gained in France after his death. Although he never visited Paris during his lifetime, Poe's connection to the place is well documented through the efforts of Baudelaire. What remains underappreciated, as the second concern of this chapter, is Poe's lifelong engagement with France. Through youthful linguistic pursuits and in his subsequent language studies at both the University of Virginia and West Point, his ongoing interest in French literature, and his various uses of French phrases and quotations in literary works such as "The Murders in Rue Morgue"—which is credited for establishing the genre of detective fiction—Poe engaged with France and its culture long before Baudelaire ever encountered his work.

BAUDELAIRE'S POE

Baudelaire is best known to readers worldwide as the author of *Les Fleurs du mal* [*The Flowers of Evil*] (1857), arguably the first major work of modern poetry. Baudelaire believed that he had discovered his "double" in the American writer, whose works and aesthetic theories influenced his own writings and thought. Indeed, this doubling was so intense that, in his authoritative critical biography of Baudelaire, Claude Pichois refers to him as "the French Edgar Allan Poe."[7] Because of Baudelaire's famous biographical essay on Poe and his translations of his works, beginning with the publication of *Histoires extraordinaires* in 1856,[8] Poe's literary influence subsequently extended to other French authors, such as Stéphane Mallarmé and Paul Valéry, and played a vital role in the emergence of the Symbolist Movement in Europe. In an age during which Poe's works were maligned, misunderstood, and unappreciated in the United States, Baudelaire's translations of the American author were being celebrated, studied, and enjoyed (Fig. 13.1).

There have been periodic attempts, however, to place Poe physically on the European continent. One such legend, perpetuated by Poe's infamous literary executor, Rufus Wilmot Griswold, concerns the period of 1827–1829, between Poe's departure from the University of Virginia and his appointment to West Point, when he disappeared for a time, supposedly to help the Greeks fight the Turks, and later found himself in difficulty with the Russian authorities of St. Petersburg. Baudelaire tells the same Byronic story (originally concocted by Poe)[9] in his 1852 essay about "Poe's sad life, which had not been recounted earlier in Forgue's article."[10] According to Lois Davis Vines, this article (as well as later iterations of it), which "contain[ed] both an analysis of Poe's works and biographical material (including several errors), became the source of information for future French authors and was widely translated around the world."[11] Another myth, reawakened recently, places Poe on the continent, specifically in Paris and with strong republican sentiments in the early 1830s, visiting none other than the famous French author of *The Three Musketeers*, Alexandre Dumas.[12]

Despite Poe's recognition in antebellum America as an acerbic literary critic (the "Tomahawk Man"), as a popular writer of tales in the 1830s and 1840s, and eventually as the celebrated author of "The Raven" in 1845, his popular reception was an amalgamation of both positive and negative impressions. Poe's contentious, if one-sided, Longfellow Wars,

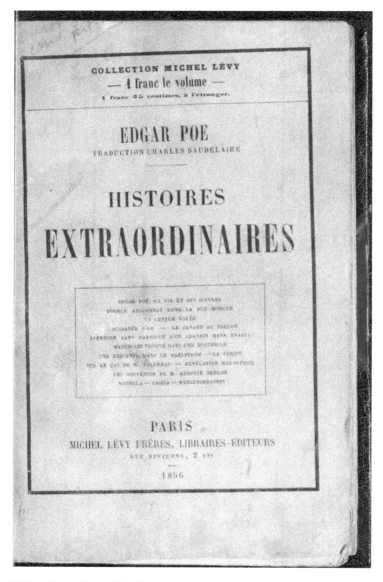

Fig. 13.1   Edgar Poe, *Histoires extraordinaires*, traduction Charles Baudelaire, Paris, 1856. W. T. Bandy Center for Baudelaire and Modern French Studies, Jean and Alexander Heard Library, Vanderbilt University

his disputes with the literary establishment of New England, whose members he termed "Frogpondians,"[13] and his reactions in print in the aftermath of his appearance at the Boston Lyceum[14] did much to diminish his already tenuous reputation in his final years. Griswold's misrepresentations, forgeries, and malicious slanders were accepted as accurate accounts of Poe's life and character for over a century. Fortunately, Baudelaire's influential 1852 article "inaugurated his [Baudelaire's] campaign to make of the American writer a great man for France."[15] Four years later, Baudelaire modified this article and used it as the preface to his translations of Poe.[16] Baudelaire's preface is arguably the most widely known study of an American author. It was reprinted often and translated into almost every language. Baudelaire's representation of Poe "neutralized, so far as Europe was concerned, the effect of Griswold's vindictive *Memoir*," which had so negatively influenced American readers.[17] It established in its place a passionate defense of Poe that guaranteed him a legitimate connection to the pantheon of France's greatest writers.

In the classic study, *The French Face of Edgar Poe*, Patrick F. Quinn acknowledges the extraordinary influence of Poe in France, but he questions the French appreciation of Poe, thinking it to be misguided.[18] Quinn could not believe that Poe was included in the pantheon of French writers preserved in Gallimard's prestigious Pléiade editions,[19] nor could he believe the high esteem in which Poe was held throughout Europe. Initial inquiries led him to believe it all to be a "grand hoax" perpetrated by Baudelaire, "the man who, on the subject of Poe, had led France and most of Europe up the garden."[20] Quinn's scholarly investigations, however, led him to different conclusions. Comparing Baudelaire's translations to Poe's original texts, Quinn asserted that "by participating in the French response to Poe it becomes possible to bring a new and enlarged understanding" to him.[21] Concerning the question of whether the French poet improved upon Poe's original texts in his translations, Quinn concludes that in some specific cases Baudelaire did strengthen Poe's syntax and diction, but that in other cases he did not, especially those passages that included expressions that would have been particularly difficult for a non-native speaker of English: "It would be mistaken to conclude that his translations as a whole represent a decided improvement on their originals. [...] Baudelaire did not melt down these stories, remove their dross, and recast them in the pure gold of his French. He could have done so, perhaps. But his admiration for Poe's work was too intense, his identification with the man too complete, to allow him to contemplate such an experiment in literary metallurgy."[22]

Theories regarding his travels aside, Poe's observed unfamiliarity with Paris was no doubt first detected in the Dupin tales themselves, and scholars such as Forgues and Baudelaire have contributed to such sentiments. According to W. T. Bandy, France was the first European country to show an interest in Poe,[23] and much attention has been paid to the French fascination with Poe. Indeed, prior to Baudelaire's efforts to establish Poe's reputation in France, some scattered translations of the writer's work had appeared in France as early as 1844, including an imitation of "William Wilson" published in a Parisian newspaper. Baudelaire chanced in 1847 "to see some of these translations and was deeply affected by them, recognizing in their author a kindred spirit."[24] He immediately procured a copy of Poe's *Tales*, most likely the Wiley & Putnam edition of London, from which he translated "Mesmeric Revelation" for the July 1848 issue of *La Liberté de penser* (Fig. 13.2).[25]

Originally published in New York in 1845, Poe's *Tales* was reprinted in this 1846 London edition, which was readily available in Paris.[26] Unable initially to obtain a copy of the 1850 Redfield edition of *The Works of the Late Edgar Allan Poe*, edited by Griswold, Baudelaire secured a copy of the 1852 *Tales and Sketches*, a pirated edition published in Routledge's New Cheap Series. He used this version when translating several of Poe's tales. According to W. T. Bandy, this volume contained numerous misprints that caused Baudelaire to make some strange errors (Fig. 13.3).[27]

According to Pichois, Baudelaire was exploring various philosophical systems during the years 1847–1848 to confirm for himself the existence of some kind of unity or harmony that would come to inform his own poetry. In the introduction to his translation of "Mesmeric Revelation," Baudelaire expresses an admiration for Balzac, who attempted to combine the ideas of diverse philosophers to create his own unifying vision, and he notes that Poe too was also haunted by the idea of unity. Baudelaire's unorthodox artistic and philosophical curiosity led him to Poe, and his profound identification of himself with Poe compelled Baudelaire to read and translate him. Poe was not entirely unknown in France when Baudelaire began his translations; a French version of "The Black Cat" had appeared in *La Démocratie pacifique* at the end of January 1847. Nevertheless, Baudelaire's growing admiration for Poe as a reactionary, a mystic, a visionary, and a creator of fantastic tales in which nothing is left to chance—as well as his understanding of him as a genius imprisoned within an unsympathetic, unappreciative, and puritanical American culture—is clear.

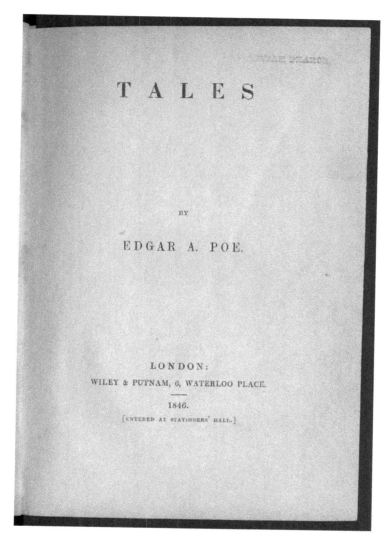

Fig. 13.2 *Tales* by Edgar A. Poe, London, 1846. W. T. Bandy Center for Baudelaire and Modern French Studies, Jean and Alexander Heard Library, Vanderbilt University

Fig. 13.3 *Tales and Sketches* by Edgar A. Poe, London, 1852. W. T. Bandy Center for Baudelaire and Modern French Studies, Jean and Alexander Heard Library, Vanderbilt University

According to Elizabeth Duquette, Baudelaire argued, in his preface to *Histoires extraordinaires* (1856), that Poe was simply born in the wrong place at the wrong time (Poe was "an overlooked genius") and that "unsophisticated and shallow, the adolescent United States was constitutionally incapable of nurturing an author of Poe's complexity."[28] Poe was for Baudelaire his other self, his artistic mirror image or double, and he would stop at nothing to locate people who knew or knew about Poe. In his critical biography, Pichois recounts Baudelaire going to a hotel on one occasion and interrogating an American writer who knew Poe but did not have a good opinion of him. Baudelaire dismissed the man with disgust, saying "He's just a Yankee!"[29] Baudelaire's obsession with Poe (and his rejection of negative opinions of his "double") led him to dedicate the most vital years of his life to the production of his own translations of Poe's works, which would introduce Poe not only to France but also to the rest of Europe.[30]

While much attention has been paid to the story of Baudelaire's admiration for Poe's genius and of his translations of Poe's prose works for French-speaking audiences, less attention has been paid to Poe's attraction to—and actual knowledge of—things French, as evidenced in his literary life and portrayed in his ratiocinative tales set in Paris. Therefore, it is productive to examine what Poe actually did know, or likely knew, about the French language and the specific geographic setting of "The Murders in the Rue Morgue," published in *Graham's Magazine* in 1841 as the first tale of the Parisian trilogy.

Poe's French

If one subscribes to a commonly held belief that a country and its culture are best known through the language of the nation in question, then it is appropriate to conclude that Poe knew something about France. As funny as it may sound, Poe's first exposure to spoken French may have been from the mouth of a French-speaking parrot that his guardian mother, Frances Allan, procured soon after the Allan family arrived in Britain in 1815 for their five-year stay there (PL 34). The young Edgar studied writing, spelling, geography, and the Catechism of the Church of England, along with a little church history, under the tutelage of the Misses Dubourg during his initial years in London (PL 30). Then, from 1818 to 1820, Poe was a boarding student at the Manor House School in Stoke Newington where he studied Latin, history, math, dance, and French (Chapter 4, J. Gerald Kennedy, on young Edgar's studies in England). Based on the information available from the Manor House School, William Elijah Hunter wrote in an 1878 issue of *The Athenaeum* that when Poe left the school, "he was able to speak the French language, construe any easy Latin author, and was far better acquainted with history and literature than many boys of a more advanced age who had had greater advantages than he had had."[31] Upon the Allan family's return to Richmond in the fall of 1820, Edgar studied at Joseph H. Clarke's Academy. The Academy publicized a curriculum of English, French, Latin, Greek, geography, arithmetic, geometry, and astronomy (PL 41–42). A schoolmate from the Clarke Academy, John T. L. Preston, later recalled that "Poe was among the first" in Latin and "that [he] was also a very fine French scholar" (PL 53). At the age of fourteen, Edgar was enrolled at William Burke's "Seminary" for boys, where he continued his study of French, with some additional instruction in Italian. One classmate, Andrew Johnson, later recounted that "Poe was a much more advanced scholar than any of us" (PL 58).

Around this time, Poe's connection to France strengthened during his interactions with a major historical figure; he had an encounter with none other than celebrated Revolutionary War hero, the marquis de La Fayette. During his tour of the United States in 1824, La Fayette learned of the death of Quartermaster General David Poe, Sr., affectionately known as "General Poe" (also Poe's paternal grandfather). The two men had been friends, prompting La Fayette to recollect that, "when I was here, […] out of his own very limited means [he] supplied me with five hundred dollars to aid in clothing my troops, and [his] wife, with her own hands, cut five hundred pairs of pantaloons, and superintended the making of them for the use of my men."[32] During his tour of the United States, La Fayette paid his respects to David Poe's widow in Baltimore. Furthermore, fifteen-year-old Poe was a member of the "Junior Morgan Riflemen" and was selected by the French general as a bodyguard during his formal reception later in Richmond.[33]

At the age of seventeen, Poe was in the second class to matriculate at the newly established University of Virginia, where he enrolled in the School of Ancient Languages (Latin, Greek, and Hebrew) under Professor George Long and in the School of Modern Languages (French, Spanish, Italian, German, and the English language "in its

Anglo-Saxon form") under Professor George Blaettermann.[34] Library records confirm that Poe checked out books by Voltaire (PL 72), indicating his ability to appreciate great French writing in the original.[35] At Mr. Jefferson's University, as it is known to its students to this day, Poe and eight of his classmates were listed as "students who excelled in Senior French class."[36] Later, at West Point, Poe ranked third among the eighty-seven cadets of his class taking the midterm exam in French (PL 112). It is clear that Poe was well trained in French and, in today's equivalent terms, would have held the comparative competency of an undergraduate French major. He possessed the linguistic tools necessary for reading and communicating in French with some proficiency, though without having attained a mastery of the language.

Throughout his career, Poe liked to give the impression to his Anglophonic audience that he was writing in near-bilingual ink. The betrayals of such a projection were already identifiable, however, in Poe's misguided usage of diacritical markings; his surprising grave accent on Isidore Musèt's last name in "The Murders in the Rue Morgue" (similar to circumflex accents on Marie Rogêt's last name or the "Rue Dunôt" in "The Purloined Letter") brought Jacques Barzun to quip that "the French have had their revenge by dressing him up as Edgar Poë" (Fig. 13.4).[37]

Throughout "Rue Morgue," Poe reveals his lack of knowledge of French patterns of capitalization: R̲ue throughout the trilogy, M̲adame L'Espanaye, F̲aubourg St. Germain (normally Saint-Germain), or Quartier St. Roch (normally Saint-Roch), "a neighboring M̲aison de Santé," T̲héâtre des Variétés, Gazette des T̲ribunaux, among other superfluous capitalizations. One notices other linguistic betrayals as well: Poe's unhesitating application of his own meaning to the obscure French word "*ferrade*," which according to him is a "peculiar" type of window shutter (PT 419–420) rather than a branding ceremony for Provençal livestock; his preciously placed French adjective in contiguity with an English noun ("some *recherché* movement" [PT 398]); or his narrator's pedantic assertion, in reference to Dupin's many whims, that "there is no English equivalent" for "*Je les ménageais*" (PT 413)—"I knew how to deal with them" would work just fine. And in "[t]he next day's paper," the Rue Morgue case is referred to as a "most extraordinary and frightful affair," with the narrator adding in parentheses: "The word '*affaire*' has not yet, in France, that levity of import it conveys upon us" (PT 406)—a puzzlingly strong lexical conviction for our "French major's" narrator.

Fig. 13.4   *rue Edgar Poë*, Paris, France. Photo by George Poe

Baudelaire would not only translate the tale in 1856 for his initial volume of Poe's tales, but also edit an important portion of the un-French "Frenchness" that Poe attempted to paint across his "Rue Morgue" canvas. Despite these sociolingual incongruities, Baudelaire was attracted to Poe as an artist for whom works of literature were not the products of frenzied inspiration but rather of calculated design. This echoes what Forgues had written about Poe in the October 1846 issue of *Revue des deux mondes*, in which he stated that Poe is a "logician, a pursuer of abstract truth" and a "lover of the most eccentric hypotheses and the strictest calculations."[38]

Jacques Barzun pointed to Poe's tenuous hold on the finer points of French usage, speaking to the linguistic awkwardness at the very level of "Rue Morgue's" title: "[Poe] certainly never visited Paris. Else in the title of 'The Murders in the Rue Morgue' he would not have gained compression at the expense of idiom: the only possible phrase is *rue de la Morgue*."[39] On the other hand, Poe was capable of weaving simple word-play into his writing, like the sprightly coded surname "Le Bon" (even if "Lebon" would be the more common surnominal spelling) for the Parisian police inspector's prime suspect who ends up being innocent. In sum, although Poe's active French had its shortcomings, his passive linguistic skills, sharpened throughout his formative years, were adequate for reading almost any French texts he encountered.

POE'S READING IN FRENCH AND ABOUT FRANCE

The process of building up his French cultural and literary baggage through eclectic reading was an important ingredient of Poe's writing formula for his Dupin trilogy. In "The Geography of the Imagination," Guy Davenport argues that "Poe's imagination was perfectly at home in geographies he had no knowledge of except what his imagination appropriated from other writers. We might assume, in ignorance, that he knew Paris like a Parisian."[40] Poe traveled there intertextually through reading and then let his imagination take over as guide. The Goncourt brothers (Edmond [de] and Jules [de]), famous for their journal on nineteenth-century literary and artistic culture and probably upon encountering Poe in Baudelaire's first translated volume, commented upon the novelty of such an approach, writing as early as 1856 that "Poe was a new kind of man writing a new kind of literature"[41]—a literature seizing also on all the fertile possibilities of the urban setting. As Benjamin F. Fisher observes, "[l]ike Charles Dickens in England, Poe may be one of the first American writers to put city locale to effective uses, a natural tendency in a writer who spent most of his life in or near cities."[42] Baudelaire—the French champion of the "modern" urban setting and of Poe—praised the city's literary potentialities: "Parisian life is rich in poetic and marvelous subjects. The marvelous envelopes and saturates us like the atmosphere."[43] Through his reading, Poe would have sensed the richness alluded to and would have no doubt been drawn to the effective ambience of France's capital.

Taking cues from "The Purloined Letter," one might also look to the two books that Poe reviewed in his first issue of *Graham's Magazine* as review editor—reviews lying in proximity to the publication, in the very same pages, of Poe's "Rue Morgue." The initial work reviewed was "*Night and Morning*": *A Novel by the Author of "Pelham"* (Edward Lytton Bulwer), wherein Poe, who usually wrote positively about Bulwer, had a strong, negative reaction to *Night and Morning*.[44] However, Bulwer's novel *Pelham* would prove to be arguably the most important documentary source for establishing the Parisian setting of "Rue Morgue." The second work that Poe criticized in the April 1841 issue of *Graham's Magazine* exemplifies a type of study that was being translated from French to English at the time: *Sketches of Conspicuous Living Characters of France* (Philadelphia: Lea & Blanchard, 1841), translated by Robert M. Walsh from the original—*Galerie des contemporains illustres par un homme de rien*, by Louis de Loménie and published only several months earlier in France.[45] This book is listed in the *Catalogue of the Mercantile Library of Philadelphia* of the period—a library that Poe probably frequented with regularity during his years in Philadelphia. Poe's review of the translated book offered him the opportunity to show off his knowledge of French. He applauds the fifteen biographical sketches, "originally published in weekly numbers at Paris, by some one [*sic*] who styles himself '*un homme de rien*'—the better to conceal the fact that he is really *un homme de beaucoup*."[46] Poe offers some general comments about the profiles presented of contemporary French political figures (including a certain André Dupin, perhaps a real-life candidate for the created surname of his Parisian detective),[47] military heroes like Soult, and various Romantic writers of the day.[48] Poe prefers the sketches of "Thiers, Hugo, Sand, Arago, and Bèranger [*sic*, for the inverted accent]."[49] Poe does look down his nose at Walsh's translating efforts, despite the latter's apparent experience as an established Philadelphian translator of French. In fact, during Poe's second year in the City of Brotherly Love (1839), Walsh had translated a biography of the *Cardinal de Cheverus, Archevêque de Bordeaux*, penned by the Révérend M. Dubourg. There are other possibilities for Poe's attraction to the surname "Dubourg" for the laundress and character witness in "The Murders in the Rue Morgue," as well as for the name of the street—which did not exist at the time—where the sailor's missing orangutan was supposedly being kept (e.g., the Dubourg sisters who were Poe's first instructors in London). Whatever the case, an intertextual borrowing should not be ruled out, in keeping with Guy Davenport's theory of Poe the "appropriator."[50] In spite of Poe's authoritative voice when writing about French litterateurs, much of his knowledge of them and their work was likely second hand, coming from just such documentary sources as these *Sketches* or, in the case of earlier French writers, from anthologies like *La Manière de bien penser* (1687) by Père Dominique Bouhours. Indeed, Edgar C.

Knowlton, Jr., has made an excellent case for "Poe's dependence on *La Manière*" for French and other European literary references.[51] Also, through literary parlor talk, Poe would have been able to absorb comments about—and opinions of—contemporary French Romantics, as well as about earlier French writers.

POE AND PERIODICALS

Although determined as a young man to devote his life to poetry, Poe engaged in the production of periodical literature throughout his working career, adapting himself successfully to its demands by transforming himself into what he later termed a "magazinist" (CL 1: 470). As Poe once remarked, to be a successful writer "you must be *read*" (CL 1: 85). In antebellum America, this meant publishing one's work in newspapers and periodicals. At the *Southern Literary Messenger*, for example, Poe adapted to the new print culture by developing expertise as a reviewer, a writer of tales, an editor, and, briefly, a magazine proprietor. Scott Peeples observes that the term "Magazinist" is appropriate for Poe because "[a]lmost everything he wrote appeared in a magazine before it appeared in a book."[52] Bruce I. Weiner argues that Poe "never relinquished the idea that art has nothing to do ultimately with commerce, but the marketplace forced him to become more and more pragmatic."[53] Thus, because of his daily work, Poe maintained stacks of journals and newspapers in his personal library.[54] As Jonathan Elmer has observed, "[o]ne of Poe's regular tasks was to produce editorial miscellanies, much of them culled from his extensive reading in competing journals."[55]

As a "magazinist," Poe must have been aware of French journalism, having no doubt encountered it in such American publishing capitals as Philadelphia and New York, in order to speak so highly of it in his review of the *Sketches*, referring to Paris as "that hot-bed of journalism, and Paradise of journalists."[56] Moreover, Parisian journalism—so highly regarded by Poe—plays an integral role in his detective trilogy. Such is the case in "Rue Morgue" with the *Gazette des tribunaux* (PT 404–405), which certainly existed at the time, despite there being no "evening edition."[57] Another journal afforded a place in "Rue Morgue" was *Le Monde*, even if not founded until 1944 and never "a paper devoted to the shipping interest" (PT 425). Finally, there is *Le Musée* (PT 404), an imagined review that would appear to have specialized in the arts, no doubt having sprung from Poe's lure toward the *vraisemblable*.

Four Textual Influences Informing Poe's "Rue Morgue"

In "The Murders in the Rue Morgue," there are at least four major reading influences to consider: *Pelham, or the Adventures of a Gentleman* by Edward Lytton Bulwer (often referred to as Bulwer-Lytton), first published by Henry Colburn in London in 1828 and soon thereafter by J. Harper of New York, with no international copyright laws to slow things down; *Le Règne animal distribué d'après son organisation* [*The Animal Kingdom Distributed According to Its Organization*] by the famous nineteenth-century French anatomist, Georges Cuvier, which was published in Paris in 1817 by Jean-François-Pierre Deterville and later translated into English in an abridged school version by the Philadelphian scientist Henry McMurtrie; *Memoirs of Vidocq, Principal Agent of the French Police Until 1827*, which first appeared in French in 1829, penned by the famous French detective Eugène-François Vidocq himself, and which was almost immediately translated into English in London, though an American edition published by Carey & Hart of Baltimore would not appear until 1834 when Poe was still in Baltimore and most likely would have encountered the Vidocq tales there; and Richard Kopley's recently revealed "series of pieces that appeared in May–December of 1838 in a long-neglected newspaper, *The Philadelphia Saturday News and Literary Gazette*."[58]

Poe and *Pelham, or the Adventures of a Gentleman*

The most influential reading on such a list, as Richard Kopley, Burton Pollin, Stuart Levine and Susan Levine, and others have stressed, is Bulwer's *Pelham*,[59] a paragon of nineteenth-century British dandyism. It is the best suspect of the four in our intertextual sleuthing for Parisian cultural traces. In such an inquiry, one must try to determine how much of "Rue Morgue" was dependent upon "geographical imagination," and how much was grounded in Parisian reality. And in the latter case, how much did Poe glean from *Pelham*, a relatively reliable source?

Bulwer obviously knew Paris and its culture well, having resided there for a time, and was able to portray the city dependably, such that Poe was right to take *Pelham* seriously for documentary purposes. For example, noticeable references abound, such as Galignani's *rive droite* bookstore, which would have been popular among Anglophones living in Paris. Concerning the "Rue Morgue," Baudelaire noted its created nature, as Poe would say, for "effect."[60] The same is true of the "Lamartine" alleyway, which did not become a Parisian street until 1848, following the poet Lamartine's fiery republican speech in front of the Hôtel de Ville that February. This was also the case for Poe's rue Dubourg, which was first used as a Parisian street name in 1897 to mark a private throughway among the dwellings referred to as "la cité Dubourg," in Paris's northeast sector.[61] Poe's geographic liberties are not to be found in *Pelham*; rather, Bulwer seems intent upon showing off his generally accurate knowledge of French and Paris.

The two major geographical foci of Poe's Paris are the old faubourg Saint-Germain area, where Dupin and his narrating guest reside "au troisième" in the then no-longer fashionable *rive gauche* outskirts of the city which had lost their noble glimmer following the French Revolution, and the mid-city *rive droite* area around the Palais-Royal where Poe places the murders. These are the same two areas negotiated by Henry Pelham, between his own "Hôtel de —, Rue de Rivoli"[62]— "the streets usually known to, and tenanted by the English"[63]—and the faubourg Saint-Germain address of his Parisian acquaintance, Mr. Thornton, which Pelham prefers because "there, you are among the French, the fossilized remains of the old regime [where] the houses have an air of desolate, yet venerable grandeur."[64] Such a gothic description would have likely captured Poe's imagination, offering a symmetrical balance of "effect" on the *rive gauche*, in parallel with his imagined "Street of the Morgue" on the *rive droite*. Unlike Bulwer, however, Poe does not mention the Seine or a bridge for passing from one bank to the other. If Poe had a contemporary map of Paris available, he must not have consulted it very carefully. Otherwise, he would not have suggested such a long trek between the two focalized areas of his tale.[65]

Jocelyn Fiorina has helped to pinpoint the likely name of the "miserable thoroughfare" where the murders took place, which Poe might have been able to decipher on a mid-city map. But marked no doubt with such small and quasi-illegible characters, Poe instead opted to create his more "effective" appellation. "There are two rues Saint-Roch," writes Fiorina. "There is the one that we call the rue Saint-Roch today and that used to be called la rue Neuve Saint-Roch in 1832 [to the west of the église Saint-Roch, whose main entrance is from the rue Saint-Honoré].

Between this rue Neuve Saint-Roch and la rue Richelieu, there is a little side street [to the east side of the église Saint-Roch] named, in fact, the passage Saint-Roch, which was sometimes referred to as the rue Saint-Roch. The passage Saint-Roch […] is the street of the double murder!" (Fig. 13.5).[66]

Fig. 13.5 *passage Saint-Roch*, Paris, France. Photo by George Poe

Geography aside, Poe also appears to have been attentive to Bulwer's literary references. Bulwer employs an epigraph from Molière's *Bourgeois Gentilhomme* at the outset of Chapter XLVIII of his *Pelham*[67]—a brief exchange between Monsieur Jourdain and his dance teacher. Poe, who likely would have read *Le Bourgeois Gentilhomme* at the University of Virginia, would in turn choose to slip in Monsieur Jourdain's comical line about needing to put on, in the presence of his fleecing music teacher, his "stylish"—actually ridiculous—new "robe de chambre pour mieux entendre la musique" ["his bathrobe in order to better hear the music"] (PT 412). Stuart Levine and Susan Levine also mention references to "Crébillon,"[68] though Pelham refers to Thornton's concierge who was reading one of the libertine novels of Crébillon fils (junior).[69] Poe's reference is to Crébillon père (senior), tragic playwright and author of *Xerxès* (Poe leaves off the grave accent from the name of Crébillon père's tragic hero, see PT 402) and of *Atrée et Thyeste,* from which he would later quote in concluding "The Purloined Letter." Such tragedies would have been common reading assignments for a "French major" of the first half of the nineteenth century, but probably not an erotic novel by Crébillon fils.

The most striking literary commonality between *Pelham* and "The Murders in the Rue Morgue" can be found in Poe's decision to conclude his tale with Dupin offering a critical assessment of the Parisian Prefect of Police's methods, ending with the very same quotation from Jean-Jacques Rousseau's *La Nouvelle Héloïse* that Bulwer has his character Vincent analyze in the latter's lengthy discussion of French literature with madame d'Anville: "de nier ce qui est, et d'expliquer ce qui n'est pas" ["to deny that which is, and to explain that which is not"].[70] This rather pretentiously bookish Chapter XXIV of *Pelham* nevertheless demonstrates Bulwer's superiority over Poe in French literary background and language proficiency; indeed, Bulwer uses French words and phraseology on just about every page, and usually with general accuracy, while his young protagonist is in Paris. Once again, Poe was wise to pay attention to Bulwer's writing.

Finally, well before "Jack l'orang-outan" came to the Jardin des Plantes in 1836, through the efforts of the menagerie's superintendent Geoffroy Saint-Hilaire, Bulwer already had featured a big monkey referred to as "Jocko" in his 1828 novel—a "most hideous animal"[71] who at first enjoys a post-restaurant soirée with guests in Vincent's Parisian apartment but eventually becomes rambunctious, even aggressive. Vincent and Pelham therefore banish "Monsieur Jocko" to a back passageway where he attacks the landlady of the building. "There he sat … showing his sharp, white teeth, and uttering the most menacing and diabolical sounds."[72] Similarly, Poe's sailor describes having seen through the window his orangutan "[g]nashing its teeth, and flashing fire from its eyes" (PT 430), and several witnesses report having heard an agitatedly "shrill voice" that turns out to be the menacing sounds of the orangutan (PT 407–10). The landlady in *Pelham* is finally rescued from her dangerous predicament when one of the guests lands a mortal blow to the head of the monkey with a poker. Bulwer's scenario is obviously meant to entertain, whereas Poe nudges his own encounter of ape versus human victim(s) in a darker direction that only Dupin is capable of comprehending.

Poe and Georges Cuvier

Among his many pursuits, Poe had a special interest in natural history. While stationed, in 1827–1828, as an enlisted soldier at Fort Moultrie, South Carolina (the geographical inspiration for "The Gold-Bug"), Poe enjoyed meeting a celebrated local conchologist. A decade later, he would write the preface and introduction to a curious volume entitled *The Conchologist's First Book* (Philadelphia: Haswell, Barrington, & Haswell, 1839) that would carry his name as the principal author, even though Philadelphian Thomas Wyatt did most of the writing, with translational assistance from fellow Philadelphian Henry McMurtrie for some of the material in French from Georges Cuvier's *Le Règne animal*. Poe also claims to have provided some of the translations from Cuvier's French.[73] *Le Règne animal* offered some important information about the orangutans of Borneo and Sumatra, and though fixed in their non-human identity, they were nevertheless, Cuvier had to admit to his evolutionist adversary Geoffroy Saint-Hilaire, quite capable of mimicking human behavior. It was upon reading the "passage from Cuvier" (PT 424), as provided by Dupin, that the narrator "understood the full horrors of the murder at once" (PT 424). Some four years after Cuvier's death, there would appear in Paris, as mentioned earlier, "Jack l'orang-outan" that a French maritime captain had brought back from Sumatra in 1836 and sold to Saint-Hilaire's menagerie at the Jardin des Plantes for 3500 francs.[74] Stendhal, Mérimée, and others wrote about the celebrated ape in the contemporary Parisian press. The suggestive connections between a human-mimicking orangutan brought back from the East Indian isles to France by a French sailor—and eventually sold to Paris's Jardin des Plantes for a handsome sum—and Poe's "fully lathered" ape, of similar origin and ultimately sold as well to the Jardin des Plantes for "a very large sum" (PT 431), "attempting the operation of shaving" (PT 428–429) are striking indeed.

Poe and *Memoirs of Vidocq, Principal Agent of the French Police Until 1827*

Eugène-François Vidocq was a criminal in his early years. In and out of prison, he learned much about how criminals think and act. He decided to sell such insider information to the Parisian police and, after some detective spying, was asked to head up the Sûreté nationale service under Napoléon, where he served in such a capacity until his first resignation in 1827. He was later rehired by the new *préfet de police* under Louis-Philippe, Henri Gisquet, who was perhaps Poe's "G–, the Prefect of Police" (PT 412). He resigned again in 1832 and started his own private detective agency, where he was reported to have often outsmarted the official police. In his *Mémoires,* Vidocq recalled some of the most celebrated cases having occurred between 1809 and 1827. But in Philadelphia, between September 1838 and May 1839, William Burton's *Gentleman's Magazine* would feature under the cryptic authorship of "J. M. B." a monthly Vidocq story not included in the earlier translated *Memoirs of Vidocq* (Philadelphia and Baltimore: Carey & Hart, 1834).[75] The very first story in the *Gentleman's Magazine* series, under the rubric of "Unpublished Passages in the Life of Vidocq," was that of "Marie Laurent," whose maiden name was Marie Dupin—yet another surnominal possibility for Poe's detective?—an "amiable and well-disposed" girl who would marry "such a worthless man as Antoine Laurent."[76]

Poe would have been following these "unpublished" tales while he was in Philadelphia. Within a month after the ninth and final "J. M. B." story appeared, William Burton announced that Poe would be joining his magazine. Remaining in the position for less than a year, Poe then rejoined George Graham when the latter purchased *Burton's.* And, as mentioned earlier, Poe's own first detective tale—which he chose to anchor in Vidocq's principal setting of Paris—was published in the April 1841 issue of *Graham's Magazine*, with Poe as review editor. As for influential detective reading informing "The Murders in the Rue Morgue," the Vidocq material surely deserves one's close attention.

Poe and *The Philadelphia Saturday News and Literary Gazette*

Poe scholar Richard Kopley has done some skillful journalistic detective work of his own in drawing several compelling links between the "Rue Morgue," which correspondence suggests began to take shape in Poe's mind as early as 1839, and certain publications having appeared in *The Philadelphia Saturday News* of Poe's newly adopted city during the final eight months of 1838. The first piece of May 1838 was entitled "Orang Outang" and described an orangutan in the London Zoo that amazed visitors by its "prodigious" strength and its "unusual activity."[77] Then, later that summer, there was a chilling article about a certain Edward Coleman of New York City who had slit his wife's throat with a razor in a violent fit of jealousy. Kopley makes a convincing hypothetical argument for "Poe's conflation of the murderous Edward Coleman and the orangutan of the London Zoo in 'Rue Morgue.'"[78]

Kopley also draws attention to a piece in a September issue of *The Philadelphia Saturday News* entitled "A Mischievous Ape" and notes that "[t]he story relates the escape of a 'large ape' […] in New York City" that "'seized hold of the hair of a child' and 'nearly took his scalp off,'" as would happen to the poor Madame L'Espanaye.[79] In October and November, there were "two pieces concerning a Parisian morgue" as well as "a reprint of a story from the *Gazette des Tribunaux*."[80] Finally, a December issue mentioned the Théâtre des Variétés, where the cobbler Chantilly would have done better to appear, according to Dupin, rather than attempting the role of Xerxès in Crébillon's high-minded tragedy (PT 402).[81] Though other significant influences inform the composition of "The Murders in the Rue Morgue," these telltale echoes from *The Philadelphia Saturday News* were likely circulating in Poe's mind, joining others, and shaping the mosaic that is "The Murders in the Rue Morgue." After all, as Kopley notes, Poe would theorize that "[t]o originate is carefully, patiently, and understandingly to combine."[82]

CONCLUSION

The narrator of "The Murders in the Rue Morgue" expresses his early impression of Dupin, saying: "I was astonished … at the vast extent of his reading; and, above all, […] by the wild fervor, and the vivid freshness of his imagination" (PT 400). Dumas, in his Italian version of the story, connects Poe the writer so tightly to Dupin the character that he inserts "Edgar Poë" directly into his reworking of the tale as a replacement for Dupin. Similarly, in asserting the relationship between Poe and his detective, it seems reasonable to attribute a healthy creative portion of the tale to Poe's own "vast reading," in both English and French, of journals, magazines, novels, and probably maps, though his whim, "fervor," and "vivid imagination" are equally—and perhaps even more—important compositional ingredients. Jacques Cabau, in his introduction to the French Gallimard edition of Poe's *Aventures d'Arthur Gordon Pym*, sees the recipe slanted in the other direction: "Poe prefers that reality exceed by just a little the fictional."[83] Whatever the exact formulaic balance between Poe's poetic imagination and his constructed French baggage—or as Dupin puts it, between the ingeniously inspired "creative" and the more intellectually anchored "resolvent" (PT 402)—we are reminded of Pollin's earlier summary of Forgues's 1846 introduction of Poe to the French: "Forgues admires Poe's inventive daring and accepts it as no detriment."[84] The "Frenchness" of "The Murders in the Rue Morgue" seems to have been sufficiently *vraisemblable* to assure the tale's long-standing success on Gallic soil, just as has been the case throughout the Anglophone world and, indeed, the world at large.

It is through the inseparably tangled nature of Poe and Baudelaire's correlative lives and artistic visions, two figures from opposite sides of the Atlantic, that Poe gained an international reputation. Poe's worldwide fame owes much to Baudelaire's influential biographical essay and his widely admired translations of Poe's prose works. The inclusion of those translations in the early numbers of the Pléiade editions has permanently afforded Poe, via Baudelaire, a special place in the hearts and minds of French readers. The appropriation of Poe in modern popular culture, and what most readers "know" about Poe, has been filtered through the various representations—and misrepresentations—of his life and works by admirers and critics alike. Poe's "creative" treatment of Parisian landmarks and culture also serves to conflate reality and mythic effect. Poe set his Dupin trilogy in Paris, contributing to the idea that he had perhaps been to France and causing some readers even to wonder whether he may actually have been French. It is possible that a work like "The Murders in the Rue Morgue" encouraged these theories. Despite the fact that he was not French and had not traveled there himself, Poe was influenced by French literature and language. Poe's actual connections to France, French literature, and the French language remain less known and appreciated. It is fortunate that his obvious familiarity with

French linguistics, along with his interest in volumes of French literature and philosophy, has been recorded. More fortunate still are the ways in which these influences provided the alchemic materials necessary to create narratives set in a place of such significance to him and to his double, Baudelaire.[85]

NOTES

1. Charles Baudelaire, "Edgar Poe: sa vie et ses oeuvres," in *Histoires extraordinaires par Edgar Poe*, trans. and ed. Charles Baudelaire (Paris: Michel Lévy Frères, 1856), 11. Unless otherwise indicated, all translations from French to English in this chapter belong to George Poe.
2. Burton R. Pollin, *Insights and Outlooks: Essays on Great Writers* (New York: Gordian Press, 1986), 107. Pollin's insights concerning Forgues's appreciation of Poe can be traced to E. D. Forgues, "Études sur le roman anglais et américain: Les Contes d'Edgar A. Poe," *Revue des deux mondes* (October 15, 1846): 341–366.
3. Pollin, *Insights and Outlooks*, 107.
4. Arthur Hobson Quinn, *Edgar Allan Poe: A Critical Biography* (Baltimore and London: The Johns Hopkins University Press, 1998), 516.
5. Quinn states that "Poe's reference to the *Charivari* was probably an error, but it is true that the first important analytical criticism of the *Tales* of 1845 came in 1846 from France and a translation [signed by A. B.] of 'The Gold-Bug' entitled 'Le Scarabée d'or' was published in 1845" (ibid.). According to Baudelaire scholar W. T. Bandy, the translation by A. B. (Alphonse Borghers, pseudonym of Amédée Pichot) of "Le Scarabée d'or," which was published in *Revue britannique, Sixième Série*, XXX (November 1845), 168–212, was "the first translation of Poe in which he is properly credited with authorship." See W. T. Bandy, "Introduction," in *Edgar Allan Poe: sa vie et ses ouvrages*, by Charles Baudelaire, ed. W. T. Bandy (Toronto and Buffalo: University of Toronto Press, 1973), xiii.
6. Concerning the undeniable "affinity" that existed between Baudelaire and Poe, at least from Baudelaire's perspective, W. T. Bandy writes that the French poet believed "what Poe contributed was not a stock of new ideas and principles, but rather the welcome confirmation of ideas and principles he had already arrived at" (Bandy, "Introduction," xlii). In a famous letter to the art critic, Théophile Thoré, Baudelaire responds to the charge that he was imitating Edgar Poe: "Eh bien! On m'accuse, moi, d'imiter Edgar Poe! Savez-vous pourquoi j'ai si patiemment traduit Poe? Parce qu'il me ressemblait." ["Well! One accuses me of imitating Edgar

Poe! Do you know why I have so patiently translated Poe? It's because he resembled me so."] Bandy identifies this as "the definitive and most striking statement by Baudelaire of his feeling toward Poe" (ibid.), that is to say, that Baudelaire regarded Poe as his mirror image.

7. Claude Pichois, *Baudelaire*, additional research by Jean Ziegler, trans. by Graham Robb (London: Hamish Hamilton, 1989), 125.

8. Edgar Poe, *Histoires extraordinaires*, trans. Charles Baudelaire (Paris: Michel Lévy Frères, 1856). The rest of Baudelaire's translations of Poe's prose *oeuvres* were published as *Nouvelles Histoires extraordinaires* (1857), *Aventures d'Arthur Gordon Pym* (1858), *Eureka* (1864), and *Histoires grotesques et sérieuses* (1865).

9. Poe sometimes supplied fabricated details to romanticize his image or to underscore his precocity. Such is the case with the February 25, 1843, issue of the *Saturday Museum* of Philadelphia that included a biography of Poe (largely based on details supplied by Poe), which states that Poe had traveled to Greece and St. Petersburg. The same biography was reprinted in the issue of March 4, 1843. See Arthur Hobson Quinn, *Edgar Allan Poe: A Critical Biography* (1941; repr., Baltimore and London: Johns Hopkins University Press, 1997), 370–373. Poe supplied the same false information to James Russell Lowell, whose biographical sketch of Poe appeared in the February 27, 1845, issue of *Graham's Magazine*. These intentional fabrications on Poe's part, combined with the malicious falsehoods and slander of Griswold's infamous "Memoir," posed significant challenges (to say the least) to later biographers and has contributed to misunderstandings about Poe's life and writings that persist until this day.

10. Lois Davis Vines, "Charles Baudelaire," in *Poe Abroad: Influence, Reception, Affinities*, ed. Lois Davis Vines (Iowa City: University of Iowa Press, 1999), 167.

11. Ibid.

12. The "recent reawakening" refers to the fascinating discovery of Jocelyn Fiorina, a respected electrical engineer teaching and researching in Paris, though with an advanced degree from Rome, who stumbled upon an unknown text in Italy in 2013 attributed to Alexandre Dumas from the days of his self-imposed exile in Naples (while fleeing France's Second Empire), where Dumas maintained his *L'Indipendente* literary journal between 1860 and 1864. A local assistant likely helped to translate Dumas's French manuscript into "L'Assassinio della strada S. Rocco," with a serial appearance in *L'Indipendente* running between December 28, 1860, and January 8, 1861. But where was the French manuscript that would have predated Dumas's publication in Italian—the tale of "Edgar Poë," who takes over the role of Dupin while visiting a Parisian

narrator acquaintance in 1832? Fiorina first translated his Italian discovery back into the purported French of Dumas. He later discovered the first 20% of his French translation actually in Dumas's hand, hiding next to Poe's original manuscript of "The Murders in the Rue Morgue" in the Rare Book Collection of the Free Library of Philadelphia! Though Dumas artfully reworks the scenario of Poe's tale, some passages appear to have been taken directly from Baudelaire's translation of 1856. Again, without international copyright laws, such "borrowings" were not uncommon. The first two "translations" of "The Murders in the Rue Morgue" into French were anonymous adaptations (Adolphe Borghers was later identified as the author of the first adaptation [also see note 5, above] and E. D. Forgues of the second). The reconstitution of the original French version of Dumas's "L'Assassinio della strada S. Rocco" is amazing in and of itself, but Fiorina, less convincingly, allows for the possibility of the text actually reflecting a true Poe visit to Paris in 1832, when he might have stayed with Dumas, upon a letter of introduction from James Fenimore Cooper. This is where we must rejoin Baudelaire, Forgues, and others in the conviction that no such visit to Paris ever took place. See Fiorina's discovery: Alexandre Dumas, *L'Assassinat de la rue Saint-Roch*, ed. Jocelyn Fiorina (Paris: Fayard, Éditions Mille et Une Nuits, 2015).

13. Paul Lewis, "Poe's Quarrel with Boston Writers," in the Boston Public Library's exhibition, *The Raven and the Frog Pond: Edgar Allan Poe and the City of Boston* (December 17, 2009–March 31, 2012).

14. See Philip Edward Phillips, "Poe's 1845 Boston Lyceum Appearance Reconsidered," in *Deciphering Poe*, ed. Alexandra Urakova (Bethlehem, PA: Lehigh University Press, 2013), 41–52.

15. W. T. Bandy, "New Light on Baudelaire and Poe," *Yale French Studies*, no. 10 (1952): 66.

16. Bandy refutes earlier biographers of Baudelaire by demonstrating that Baudelaire did not base his essay upon Griswold's *Memoir* but rather upon an unsigned review in the Redfield edition by John M. Daniel, published in *The Southern Literary Messenger*. According to the review, Daniel disliked Poe as a man, but he called him "the greatest genius of the day" and predicted that "no other American has half the chances of remembrance in the history of literature." Bandy demonstrates that over half of Baudelaire's essay is a word-for-word translation of a review by John M. Daniel's (published in the *Messenger*), although Bandy notes that Baudelaire "does not hesitate, upon occasion, to interject a few lines of personal comment, usually Poe's mistreatment at the hands of his countrymen, and also to omit words, phrases and sentences in order to soften Daniel's aspersions" (ibid., 67). Bandy notes also that Baudelaire

drew upon an obituary of Poe by John R. Thompson (also published in the *Messenger*), for certain details concerning Poe's physical appearance and manners (ibid., 67). See also the Introduction to Bandy's edition of Baudelaire's *Edgar Allan Poe: sa vie et ses ouvrages* (Toronto: University of Toronto Press, 1973).

17. Bandy, "New Light on Baudelaire and Poe," 65.
18. Patrick F. Quinn, *The French Face of Edgar Poe* (Carbondale and Edwardsville: Southern Illinois University Press, 1957), 3.
19. Ibid., 4.
20. Ibid., 5
21. Ibid.
22. Ibid., 134.
23. Bandy, "New Light on Baudelaire and Poe," 65. Although France was the first continental European country to show an interest in Poe and Baudelaire's translations served as the base texts for most European and South American translators of Poe, especially during the second half of the nineteenth century, Emron Esplin and Margarida Vale de Gato point out that in South America, in 1847, "an anonymous author published three articles in the biweekly Peruvian newspaper *El instructor peruano* that offered lengthy summaries of Poe's stories 'The Colloquy of Monos and Una,' 'The Conversation of Eiros and Charmion,' and 'The Black Cat.'" Although these three summaries may not be translations per se, Esplin and Vale de Gato remark that "they [do] demonstrate that someone in Peru was reading Poe and offering his work to a Spanish-speaking audience almost a decade before" Baudelaire's 1856 *Histoires exrtaordinaires*, which is "typically credited for introducing Poe to Spanish America." See Emron Esplin and Margarida Vale de Gato, "Introduction: Poe in/and Translation," in *Translated Poe*, eds. Emron Esplin and Margarida Vale de Gato (Bethlehem, PA: Lehigh University Press, 2014), specifically xiii–xiv.
24. Bandy, "New Light on Baudelaire and Poe," 65.
25. The original edition was issued by Wiley & Putnam in New York in 1845. The only difference between the British and American versions is the title page. According to Bandy, this edition was the first collection of Poe's tales to reach France, and it was the only work by Poe that Baudelaire owned when he wrote his 1852 essay. See W. T. Bandy, *Baudelaire: An Exhibition Commemorating the Centennial of Les Fleurs du Mal* (Madison: Memorial Library, University of Wisconsin, 1957), 20.
26. Most of the early translations of Poe's *Tales* were based on British editions, which are identical to the American ones except for the title page, and available in Paris. During this same year, several of Poe's tales were translated, or adapted, into French. See Philip Edward Phillips,

Baudelaire's Poe: Selections from the W.T. Bandy Collection, Jean and Alexander Heard Library, Vanderbilt University, permanent online exhibition available at http://exhibits.library.vanderbilt.edu/BaudelairePoe/.

27. Phillips, *Baudelaire's Poe*.

28. Elizabeth Duquette, "'The Tongue of an Archangel': Poe, Baudelaire, Benjamin," *Translation and Literature* 12, no. 1 (2003): 21.

29. Pichois, 146.

30. Pichois, 144–145. Baudelaire's translations of Poe, which did not begin to appear until the summer of 1848, represented Baudelaire's largest and most sustained literary activity until shortly before his death in 1867. In total, Baudelaire's translations of Poe's prose fiction—and *Eureka*—over the course of eighteen years filled five volumes. As Esplin and Vale de Gato correctly observe, the volumes that introduced much of the world to Poe's fiction should be regarded not only as translations but also as "significant parts of Baudelaire's literary *corpus*—as parts of a body of work that reached its zenith with the publication of *Les Fleurs du Mal* in 1857, the year *after* Baudelaire released his highly influential *Histoires extraordinaires*," *Translated Poe*, eds. Emron Esplin and Margarida Vale de Gato, xiv.

31. William Elijah Hunter, "Poe and His English Schoolmaster," *Athenaeum* (October 19, 1878): 496–497.

32. Quinn, *Edgar Allan Poe*, 18.

33. Ibid., 18, 88.

34. Charles W. Kent, "Poe's Student Days at the University of Virginia," *Bookman* 13, no. 5 (1901): 432.

35. Poe was manifestly interested in spoken French as well. Borrowing records from the university's nascent library "indicate that Edgar Allan Poe consulted [Nicolas Dufief's early nineteenth-century *Nature Displayed in her Mode of Teaching Language to Man*] during his short time at the University of Virginia in 1826" (Marcus Tomalin, *The French Language and British Literature, 1756–1830* [London and New York: Routledge, 2016], 74). "[Dufief] outlined an approach for teaching French that was *not* based on rote memorisation of grammatical rules." […] "The Class will have made such rapid progress in the acquisition of the true French pronunciation," Dufief boasts, "that many of them would almost equal the well-bred French in the purity of accent" (Tomalin, *Nature Displayed*, 74–76). Poe would have no doubt been intrigued by such a "modern" approach to language learning.

36. Kent, "Poe's Student Days," 432.

37. Jacques Barzun, "A Note on the Inadequacy of Poe as a Proofreader and of His Editors as French Scholars," *The Romanic Review* 61 (1970): 26.

38. Lois Davis Vines, "Poe in France," in *Poe Abroad*, ed. Lois Davis Vines, 10.

39. Jacques Barzun, "A Note on the Inadequacy of Poe as a Proofreader and of His Editors as French Scholars," *The Romanic Review* 61 (1970): 26.
40. Guy Davenport, "The Geography of the Imagination," in *The Geography of the Imagination: Forty Essays* (San Francisco: North Point Press, 1981), 9.
41. Ibid., 9.
42. Benjamin F. Fisher, *The Cambridge Introduction to Edgar Allan Poe* (Cambridge: Cambridge University Press, 2008), 21.
43. Charles Baudelaire, "Salon de 1846: De l'héroisme de la vie modern," in *Curiosités esthétiques* (Paris: Michel Lévy Frères, 1868), 198.
44. Edgar Allan Poe, "Review of New Books," in *Graham's Magazine* 18, no. 4 (April 1841): 197–202.
45. Ibid., 202–203.
46. Ibid., 202.
47. T. O. Mabbott also suggested with understandable conviction, apropos of the initial part of Dupin's name, that "'C. Auguste' (for César Auguste) [...] was obviously taken from that of Monsieur C. Auguste Dubouchet, a friend [of Poe] who was seeking a position as a teacher of French" in 1840. *The Collected Works of Edgar Allan Poe—Vol. II: Tales and Sketches*, ed. and annotated Thomas Ollive Mabbott (Cambridge, MA: The Belknap Press of Harvard University Press, 1978), 524.
48. These writers included Chateaubriand, Lamartine, Hugo, and George Sand, to whom Poe refers as Madame Dudevant, perhaps not knowing that, via her maiden name of Aurore Dupin, she too could have provided nominal inspiration for his detective.
49. Poe, "Review of New Books," 202.
50. Davenport, "The Geography of the Imagination," 3–15.
51. Edgar C. Knowlton, Jr., "Poe's Debt to Father Bouhours," *Poe Studies* 4, no. 2 (1971): 27.
52. Scott Peeples, "Teaching Poe the Magazinist," in *Approaches to Teaching Poe's Prose and Poetry*, eds. Jeffery Andrew Weinstock and Tony Magistrale (New York: Modern Language Association, 2008), 27.
53. Bruce I. Weiner, *The Most Noble of Professions: Poe and the Poverty of Authorship* (lecture, Baltimore, MD: The Edgar Allan Poe Society of Baltimore, October 5, 1986), 15.
54. William Gowans, who spent time with Poe in New York during the year before the latter moved to Philadelphia, maintained that Poe "had a library made up of newspapers, magazines bound and unbound, with what books had been presented to him." Roger E. Stoddard, "Put a Resolute Heart to a Steep Hill," in *William Gowans, Antiquary and Bookseller* (New York: Book Arts Press, 1988), 26.
55. Jonathan Elmer, *Reading at the Social Limit: Affect, Mass Culture, and Edgar Allan Poe* (Stanford: Stanford University Press, 1995), 5.

56. Poe, "Review of New Books," 202.
57. Pollin, *Insights and Outlooks*, 106.
58. Richard Kopley, *Edgar Allan Poe and the Dupin Mysteries* (New York: Palgrave, 2008), 29–44.
59. Ibid., 27–29. And see endnote 5, 96–97, in which Kopley reveals: "I first encountered Poe's borrowings for 'Rue Morgue' from Bulwer's *Pelham* when I examined the markings of Palmer C. Holt in an edition of Bulwer's novels." See also Burton Pollin's inquiry entitled "Bulwer-Lytton's Influence on Poe's Works and Ideas, Especially for an Author's 'Preconceived Design,'" *The Edgar Allan Poe Review* 1, no. 1 (2000): 5–12. As for Stuart Levine and Susan Levine, see their anthology, *The Short Fiction of Edgar Allan Poe: An Annotated Edition* (1976; repr., Urbana and Chicago: University of Illinois Press, 1990), 53.
60. Claude Richard explained in an interview for *The Iowa Review*: "*Effect….* That's Poe's word. It's the most frequently used of all Poe's critical words." "An Interview with Claude Richard," *The Iowa Review* 12, no. 4 (1981): 19–20.
61. Stuart Levine and Susan Levine conjecture mistakenly about this northeastern area of Paris, suggesting that there was perhaps another Saint-Germain location close to the cité Dubourg and that, since Dupin tells the sailor that the ape is being kept "in the Rue Dubourg, just by" (PT 427), this sector could well have been Dupin's neighborhood. But any street known as "Dubourg" would have been a pure fabrication in 1841 (Pollin misses this anachronism as well). The faubourg Saint-Germain was indeed where Bulwer knew it to be, as an extension beyond the old Saint-Germain abbey church—an area that would have been the tony outskirts of Paris in the late seventeenth and the eighteenth centuries, having become increasingly neglected during the nineteenth century. See Poe's *Thirty-Two Stories*, eds. Stuart Levine and Susan Levine (Indianapolis and Cambridge: Hackette, 2000), 136–137; the Levines use the same map and key on pages 176–177 that appeared in their earlier volume, *The Short Fiction of Edgar Allan Poe* (see note 56 above).
62. Edward Lytton Bulwer, *Pelham, or Adventures of a Gentleman* (New York: A. L. Burt, 1902), 47.
63. Ibid., 87.
64. Ibid.
65. See Poe's description of the walk: "It was late in the afternoon when we reached it [the Rue Morgue] … this quarter is at a great distance from that in which we resided" (PT 413). It would have been about twenty minutes away by foot, with a quick crossing of the Pont Royal bridge from their residential neighborhood and a stroll in front of the Palais des Tuileries (still extant at the time) right to the Église Saint-Roch and to

Madame L'Espanaye's address along "one of those miserable thorough-fares between the Rue Richelieu and the Rue St. Roch" (PT 413).

66. Dumas, *L'Assassinat de la rue Saint-Roch*, ed. Fiorina, 169. Alexandre Dumas, in his reworked version of the story that appeared in Italian in 1860–1861, tidied things up geographically, actually naming his adaptation of the tale "L'Assassinio della strada S. Rocco."

67. Bulwer, *Pelham*, 177.

68. Poe, *The Short Fiction of Edgar Allan Poe*, eds. Stuart Levine and Susan Levine, 153.

69. Bulwer, *Pelham*, 177.

70. Ibid., 94.

71. Ibid., 81.

72. Ibid., 82–83.

73. See endnote 7 on page XXX of Elise Lemire's Chapter 7 ("'The Murders in the Rue Morgue': Amalgamation Discourses and the Race Riots of 1838 in Poe's Philadelphia," in *Romancing the Shadow: Poe and Race*, eds. J. Gerald Kennedy and Liliane Weissberg [Oxford: Oxford University Press, 2001]): "I [Poe] wrote it, in conjunction with Professor Thomas Wyatt, and Professor McMurtrie of Pha.—my name being put to work, as best known and most likely to aid its circulation. I wrote the Preface and Introduction, and translated from Cuvier, the accounts of the animals etc." (qtd. in D. Thomas, "Poe in Philadelphia," 950).

74. Jean-Charles Cozic, *L'Orang-outan du capitaine Van Iseghem* (Nantes: Éditions Joca Seria, 2014), 28.

75. See Leroy Lad Panek, *Before Sherlock Holmes: How Magazines and Newspapers Invented the Detective Story* (Jefferson, NC and London: MacFarland, 2011), 38–40.

76. J. M. B., "Marie Laurent," *The Gentleman's Magazine* 3, no. 3 (September 1838): 174.

77. Kopley, *Edgar Allan Poe*, 32.

78. Ibid., 34.

79. Ibid., 35–36.

80. Ibid., 36.

81. Ibid., 38.

82. Ibid., 41. With Poe's quotation coming from *Collected Writings of Edgar Allan Poe*, vol. 3, ed. Burton R. Pollin (New York: Gordian Press, 1986), 137.

83. Jacques Cabau, introduction to *Aventures d'Arthur Gordon Pym*, by Edgar Allan Poe, trans. Charles Baudelaire and ed. Jacques Cabau (Paris: Gallimard, 1975), 7.

84. Pollin, *Insights and Outlooks*, 107.

85. The authors gratefully acknowledge the assistance of Yvonne Boyer, Bill Engel, and Amy Harris-Aber for their valuable contributions to this chapter.

CHAPTER 14

"Un muerto vivo": Poe and Argentina

Emron Esplin

Edgar A. Poe's relationship with Argentina, unlike his connections with most of the other places in this collected volume, is completely post-mortem. Poe's narrators, characters, and poetic personae never mention Argentina, and his lack of interaction with Argentina (and with South America in general) reveals a blind spot in Poe's global engagement. Poe was certainly aware of the southern hemisphere, but when he turned his attention and his pen toward the most southern latitudes, he focused on Antarctica rather than on Argentina or any other place at the southern tip of the American continent. For Poe, Argentina was not a place, but Argentina was and is a place for Poe. Put another way, the absence of Argentina in Poe's literary corpus merely underscores, through a jux-taposition of opposites, the ubiquitous presence of that same corpus in Argentina's literary history.

Argentine writers with competing aesthetics and from disparate lit-erary movements have claimed Poe as an important influence on their work from the late nineteenth century—about two decades after Charles Baudelaire's French translations of Poe introduced Poe's work to many Argentine readers—to the early years of the twenty-first, and Poe's Argentine reputation has continued to grow to the point where he has

E. Esplin (✉)
Brigham Young University, Provo, UT, USA

P. E. Phillips (ed.), *Poe and Place*,
Geocriticism and Spatial Literary Studies,
https://doi.org/10.1007/978-3-319-96788-2_14

become a central figure in Argentina's literary history and an important part of the nation's literary polysystem.[1] In the place-oriented terminology of geographer Edward Relph, Poe's Argentine advocates have moved him from a position of oblivious "outsideness" to one of "existential insideness."[2] Rather than crossing literal city "walls," "town limit signs," or "national frontiers,"[3] Poe's texts have crossed their literary equivalents in Argentina—the metaphorical walls and borders created by both highbrow and popular culture canons—to become a part of this literary tradition. Poe's current standing as "existential insider" in Argentina manifests itself in the holdings of both national and local libraries that include hundreds of Poe titles in translation, in the vast variety of Poe editions in Spanish available in local bookstores both large and small, in his presence in Argentina's secondary schools, and in the significant amount of "hits" Poe's name generates when searched for on the websites of Argentina's largest newspapers.[4] One of these newspaper articles, a brief 2008 piece entitled "El regreso de un muerto vivo" in which contemporary author and journalist Jorge Fernández Díaz celebrates a recent re-release of Julio Cortázar's translations of Poe's short stories, demonstrates Poe's centrality to Argentina's literary history by posing this question: "¿Cómo concebir la literatura breve argentina de los siglos XIX y XX sin la presencia de este padre omnipresente, en cuya obra se inspiraron genios de la novela y el cuento?" ["How can we conceive Argentine short fiction from the nineteenth and twentieth centuries without the presence of this omnipresent father, in whose work geniuses of the novel and the short story found inspiration?"].[5]

Fernández Díaz's piece shows an Argentine culture saturated with Poe to the point where Poe's actual works reach his Argentine audience after that audience has already ingested Poe via popular culture. Yet, Poe's own prose still affects his Argentine audience's foreign and domestic reading habits. Fernández Díaz claims that Argentines born near 1960 first came to Poe via cinema while watching Vincent Price and Peter Lorre in Roger Corman's Poe cycle.[6] He notes that he was then introduced to Poe's fiction (through Julio Cortázar's translations) by a school teacher and that when he finished reading all of Poe's tales, he and his peers "[p]ara seguir leyendo a Poe [...] compra[ron] libros de Henry James, Lovecraft, Kafka, Bradbury y Stephen King. Y después le[yeron] a Quiroga, Lugones, Bioy, Borges, Mujica Lainez y al propio Cortázar" ["[t]o continue reading Poe, bought books by Henry James, Lovecraft, Kafka, Bradbury, and Stephen King. And later [they] read Quiroga,

Lugones, Bioy, Borges, Mujica Lainez, and Cortázar's own work"].[7] Using his own place-based metaphor, Fernández Díaz states that "[t]odos los corredores daban al gran patio de Edgar Allan Poe" ["all passages led to the great patio of Edgar Allan Poe"], and he closes his article by juxtaposing Poe with his character, M. Valdemar: "Algunos escritores, cuando los despertamos después del paso de los años, se deshacen en cenizas y se nos caen de las manos. Estaban muertos y no lo sabíamos. Poe está vivo y vuelve de su tumba una y otra vez para vengarnos" ["Some writers, when we wake them after the passing of the years, disintegrate into ashes and fall from our hands. They were dead and we did not know it. Poe is alive and returns from his tomb again and again to avenge us"].[8] Some dead writers may deteriorate in Argentina in a fashion similar to Valdemar's instantaneous rotting, but Poe, still alive and fresh, continually leaves his crypt to find his Argentine reader.

Among these readers, of course, we also encounter Argentina's writers, and Poe's texts strike important cords with this nation's most significant authors of the twentieth century, who, in turn, rewrite Poe into Argentina's literary history. Translation studies scholar André Lefevere claims that "[r]ewritings tend to play at least as important a part in the establishment of canonized works of literature as those works do themselves."[9] For Lefevere, any type of literary interpretation or commentary is a rewriting,[10] and he notes the specific power wielded by literary critics, literary historians, anthologizers, and translators as rewriters of texts.[11] Following this line of argument, Poe's prominent position in Argentine letters and his popularity in Argentine society certainly originate in the ways his works call out to his Argentine readers, but his success in Argentina depends not only on the genius contained within Poe's source texts, but also on how Poe's Argentine advocates have recreated and retooled that genius for an Argentine audience. The very availability of Poe's works in Argentina depends on a long history of Argentine and other rewritings of Poe that keep his literary corpus alive and rescue his works from oblivion.[12]

Just as Poe was fortunate enough to have Charles Baudelaire, Stéphane Mallarmé, and Paul Valéry respond to, openly support, and rewrite his work in nineteenth- and early twentieth-century France, he was also privileged enough to serve as a primary influence on Spanish American *modernismo* and to receive the advocacy of four of Argentina's most important twentieth-century writers—Leopoldo Lugones, Horacio Quiroga, Jorge Luis Borges, and Julio Cortázar.[13] Each of these authors responded to and rewrote Poe through his own serious, sustained, and complex literary relationship with Poe's corpus of works—Lugones as a poet, fiction writer, and literary critic; Quiroga as a literary critic and a writer of short fiction; Borges as a translator, anthologizer, literary critic, and fiction writer; and Cortázar as a translator and author of fiction. Between them, these twentieth-century staples of Argentina's literary canon rewrote Poe in every way that Lefevere analyzes.[14] Due to the length constraints of a short essay and to the fact that I have recently examined Poe's literary relationships with Borges and Cortázar elsewhere, this study begins with a brief examination of Poe, the *modernistas*, and Lugones; it continues with a reading of Poe and Quiroga; and it concludes with a gloss on Borges's and Cortázar's multifaceted interactions with Poe.[15] These four writers' combined engagement with Poe plants him squarely within Argentina's literary tradition, carving out a permanent and vital home for this "muerto vivo" ["living dead man"] and his works in a place that Poe never knew.[16]

POE, NINETEENTH-CENTURY ARGENTINA, AND THE *MODERNISTAS*

In the early pages of *Edgar Allan Poe in Hispanic Literature*, John Eugene Englekirk demonstrates that Poe's work began to appear in Argentina and throughout Spanish America in the late 1860s through Charles Baudelaire's French translations, Spanish peninsular translations based on Baudelaire's French versions, and, probably, through editions of Poe in English that made their way south.[17] One of the first Argentine translations of Poe appeared during this same time period when Ricardo Gutiérrez translated Poe's poem "Ulalume" as "Eleonora" for *El Correo del Domingo* in June of 1865.[18] The brief and anonymous essay entitled "Edgardo Poe" that introduces Gutiérrez's translation supports the basic argument that Baudelaire (via his French renditions or through Spanish translations from his French) brought Poe to Argentina by commenting on the popularity of *Historias extraordinarias*—the Hispanicized and often reused title of Baudelaire's celebrated *Histoires extraordinaires*.[19] The first Argentine collection of Poe's stories, Carlos Olivera's 1884 *Novelas y cuentos*, reiterates Baudelaire's importance to Poe's early reception in Argentina while also demonstrating Poe's presence in English. Olivera explicitly states on his title page that the tales in this collection have been "traducidos directamente del inglés" ["translated directly from English"], but he also praises Baudelaire's translations and offers his own Spanish translation of Baudelaire's "Edgar Poe, sa vie et ses oeuvres" as "Edgar Poe. Su vida y sus obras" to introduce the thirteen Poe stories in the collection.[20] Finally, Borges notes later, and with more irony than Englekirk or Olivera, that the "americano" ["American"] who "nace en Boston" ["is born in Boston"] and "muere en Baltimore" ["dies in Baltimore"] then "llega" ["arrives"] on the Argentine literary scene "porque Baudelaire lo tradujo" ["because Baudelaire translated him"].[21]

These traces of Poe in Argentina increased significantly by the end of the nineteenth and into the first two decades of the twentieth century as the Spanish American *modernistas* adopted Poe as their poet-prophet and spread his literature—especially his poetry—and his aesthetics throughout Spanish-speaking America.[22] Englekirk claims that "[a]lmost all of the followers of Modernism were directly or indirectly influenced by Poe[,]"[23] he notes the *modernistas'* proclivity for Poe's poetry over his fiction,[24] and he dedicates almost half of the pages of his lengthy study of Poe's influence in the Spanish-speaking world to paired readings between Poe and individual *modernistas*—including a chapter on Argentine's most important *modernista*, Leopoldo Lugones.[25] Lugones kept Poe, his works, and his aesthetics on the mind of Argentine readers via commentary on Poe and, more significantly, through his own literature that consistently recalls Poe. An example of the former type of rewriting appeared in the prologue that Lugones wrote for a collection of poems—*Castalia Bárbara*—published by his colleague Ricardo Jaimes Freyre in 1920. In this piece, Lugones argues that "[t]odo poema" ["every poem"] contains "tres elementos internos" ["three internal elements"] and "tres external externos" ["three external elements"], and he claims that "hasta hoy" ["up until today"] Poe's poetry best combines these six elements—"la idea, el sentimiento y la proporción" ["idea, emotion and proportion"] and "la perspectiva, la metáfora y el ritmo" ["perspective, metaphor and rhythm"].[26] Englekirk details how Lugones's own poetry and short fiction, with few exceptions, consistently remain "Poesque" although some volumes demonstrate direct influence while others simply remind the reader of Poe.[27] In both cases, Lugones rewrites Poe and keeps his image alive in Argentine letters.

The tales Lugones published in his 1906 collection *Las fuerzas extrañas* [*Strange Forces*], for example, do not openly repeat characters, settings, or plots from Poe's fiction. Instead, they create similar effects of both awe and horror for the narrators and characters within and the readers of the stories, evoking Poe's own pseudoscientific tales and fantastic narratives. The reader of *Las fuerzas extrañas* often feels, especially while reading "La fuerza Omega" ["The Omega Force"],"La metamúsica" ["Metamusic"], and "El origen del Diluvio" ["Origins of the Flood"], the way the Poe reader feels while reading "The Facts in the Case of M. Valdemar" (M 1233–1244).[28] She willfully suspends her disbelief in the experiments these stories describe due to the narrators' reliance on scientific or pseudoscientific jargon only to be left in a space by the stories' horrific finales in which neither the narrators nor the reader herself can really explain what has happened. Similarly, the narrators of Lugones's "Un fenómeno inexplicable" ["An Inexplicable Phenomenon"] and Poe's "The Black Cat" both confront haunting situations that they try to explain away via logic and science but ultimately must accept as real. In the former, the narrator tries to prove to his host that the host is not (as the host fears) haunted by a monkey who is his double, only to trace the man's shadow and reveal the monkey's form.[29] In the latter, the narrator seeks to explain how a charred image of his hanged cat appears in the one standing wall of his burned house, only to have another one-eyed, enormous black cat drive him toward murder and then cry out his crime (M 849–860). The science or pseudoscience within each of these tales creates the most visible difference between Poe and Lugones since Poe's scientific explanations can become almost comical while Lugones's use of science, although now dated, feels more real. Englekirk captures both sides of this juxtaposition when he claims that "[a]fter reading" *Las fuerzas extrañas*, "one is convinced that here is an author who best exemplifies the spirit of Poe in a science-conscious generation of a century later."[30]

Poe's influence on and affinities with Lugones as both a poet and a fiction writer serve as a valuable bridge that evokes Poe's influence on the poetry of the *modernistas* while foreshadowing his connections to Argentine fiction throughout the twentieth century. Poe's Argentine presence also serves as a type of touchstone post-Lugones as Argentina's most important fiction writers disparately wield Poe in battles of competing poetics and/or personal worldviews. Claiming Poe as an influence allowed Quiroga—whose earliest writings could be defined as *modernista*, who cut his literary teeth alongside the *modernistas*, and who considered Lugones a friend and a mentor—to share the muse of his contemporaries even though he put that inspiration to different uses.[31]

Engaging Poe allowed Borges—whose early works challenged and even mocked Lugones, who only praised Lugones long after the earlier writer's death, and who openly disparaged Quiroga—simultaneously to alter Poe's image and critique his rivals for misunderstanding their own literary idol.[32] Finally, translating Poe's prose and writing Poesque fiction allowed Cortázar, a leading voice in the so-called Latin American Boom (a movement whose fiction revealed both Borges and Poe as essential precursors), to maintain a respectful literary relationship with Borges although his political views differed widely from those held by Borges. In short, Poe influenced Quiroga, Borges, and Cortázar, and each of these writers, in turn, influenced Poe by using and/or altering his image, reputation, and literary corpus to carve out their own places within Argentine's literary landscape.

POE AND QUIROGA

Several literary critics in both English and Spanish have examined Horacio Quiroga's disciple-like relationship with Poe.[33] From the early Poe parodies Quiroga wrote as a young man in both Uruguay and Argentina to the seasoned stories of madness, revenge, and horror that he published during a three-decade-long career in Argentina, Quiroga openly and directly approached Poe more than any other significant literary figure from Spanish America. Even Quiroga's jungle tales often continue his conversation with Poe. Quiroga's friends and his biographers consistently reveal that he did not shy away from comparisons to Poe. For example, Quiroga's friend and fellow writer, Ezequiel Martínez García, suggested that even toward the end of his life Quiroga still "[r]ecordaba casi literalmente [...] todos los cuentos de Poe, uno de sus ídolos" ["remembered almost literally [...] all of the stories of Poe, one of his idols"], and prominent Latin Americanist, Emir Rodríguez Monegal, named Poe as one of Quiroga's primary influences and claimed that Quiroga "[n]o temió las influencias—ningún escritor fuerte las teme" ["did not fear influences, no strong writer fears them"].[34] Quiroga's willingness to identify with both Poe's persona and his work forged a strong connection between the two writers that reveals itself in almost any literary criticism of serious length that deals with Quiroga, to the point where critics and readers often describe Quiroga as the Latin American Poe, the Spanish-speaking Poe, or, as Luis Alberto de Cuenca suggests, "una reincarnación hispánica del mismísimo Edgar Allan Poe" ["a Hispanic reincarnation of the selfsame Edgar Allan Poe"].[35] Read out of context, these comparisons might appear to sell Quiroga short by casting him as an imitator of Poe, but read within the context of Argentine, Río de la Plata, and Spanish American literature during the first third of the twentieth century and with a knowledge of Quiroga's career, such sayings are certainly accolades.

Out of the many literary conversations Quiroga created with Poe, his portrayals of revenge probably serve as the best examples of how he rewrote Poe and how his works matured as he continued writing. Quiroga's depictions of revenge also demonstrate several of the other Poe-related themes Quiroga approached in his own corpus of fiction. Quiroga showed a specific proclivity for Poe's "The Cask of Amontillado," and, as Caroline Egan suggests, his four tales—"El tonel de Amontillado" ["The Cask of Amontillado"] from 1901, "El crimen del otro" ["The Other Crime"] from 1904, "La lengua" ["The Tongue"] from 1906, and "Una bofetada" ["A Slap in the Face"] from 1916[36]—rewrote Poe's tale in different ways over an extended time period.[37] These four rewritings shift from a type of reply in the first two tales that relies so wholly on Poe's titles, plotlines, and/or characters that these pieces are often described in terms of parody to a complex yet subtle response in the latter two stories in which Quiroga masters the theme of Poe's "Cask"—revenge—without mimicking his predecessor.

In the midst of his rewritings of "Cask," Quiroga also approached revenge in both his lesser-known works and his most highly proclaimed fiction without directly alluding back to Poe's famous story. As examples of the former, Quiroga published six novellas in the magazines of Buenos Aires under the pseudonym S. Fragoso Lima between 1908 and 1913. Two of these novellas—"Las fieras cómplices" ["Beasts in Collusion"] and "Un mono que asesinó" ["A Murderous Monkey"]—deliver revenge narratives that can be read alongside Poe's use of revenge but without direct connections to his stories.[38] "Las fieras cómplices" foreshadows the logging camp setting that Quiroga creates in "Una bofetada," but in this narrative, an honest and compassionate foreman named Longhi takes revenge on Alves, the corrupt owner of a logging company who has tortured Longhi and a peon named Guaycurú who looks up to him. Alves tortures Longhi by placing him over an empty well that has been converted into a makeshift bomb connected to a slow-burning fuse, and he torments Guaycurú by repeatedly forcing his body into a massive hill of vicious ants.[39] Just as the jungle provides the methods of torture, it also delivers the tool of vengeance—a young puma that Longhi trains and then unleashes on Alves in the novella's conclusion.[40] Like "Una bofetada," this novella shows the reason why the avenger seeks revenge, but unlike both "Una bofetada" and "Cask," Longhi's vengeance in "Las fieras cómplices" seems justified since Quiroga depicts Alves as a despicable tyrant who continually abuses his workers both financially and physically. This sense of justice that the reader can share with Longhi reminds her more of the dénouements Poe offers in "Metzengerstein"—in which one fiery death justifies another (M 25, 29)—or in "The Black Cat," where the narrator who has hanged his cat faces the hangman's noose for having killed his wife (M 852, 859), than it reminds her of "Cask."

Similarly, "Un mono que asesinó" mixes various Poesque themes— from the revenge Poe portrays in several of his narratives, to the metempsychosis he depicts in "Ligeia" (M 310–334), "Morella" (M 229–237), or "Metzengerstein" (M 18–31), to the horror he creates when an orangutan mimics human behavior in "The Murders in the Rue Morgue" (M 527–574)—into a complex revenge plot. In this tale, the soul of an ancient Brahman priest or teacher takes revenge on the distant progeny of the peasant who murdered him by taking over the human body of that posterity—a twentieth-century Argentine named Guillermo Boox— and trapping Boox's soul within the body of the gibbon ape in which the priest's soul had been residing.[41] By combining revenge, metempsychosis, and animal violence in "El mono que asesinó," Quiroga most closely recalls "Metzengerstein," a story in which a horse with a human's soul exacts revenge on the man and the family line that have made him suffer. However, Quiroga's novella stretches the initial victim's thirst for revenge for over 3000 years, suggesting even more than Poe's tale that the need for vengeance never dies. This novella also demonstrates how Quiroga receives a double dosage of Poe (one dose from the nineteenth-century US source himself and another from Quiroga's contemporary, Lugones) and simultaneously rewrites both Poe and Lugones since "El mono que asesinó" clearly converses with two of Lugones's Poe-like stories—"Yzur" and "El fenómeno inexplicable"—in which primates feature prominently in the stories' fantastic and/or horrific plots.[42]

One of Quiroga's most famous stories, "La gallina degollada" ["The Decapitated Chicken"], also examines revenge in ways that differ from Poe's revenge plots. This horrific 1909 tale culminates when four brothers described as "idiotas" ["idiots"] kill their healthy and spoiled younger sister by mimicking the family servant's decapitation of a chicken, which the boys had observed earlier in the day.[43] A knowledge of Quiroga's literary relationship with Poe might tempt the reader to interpret this act of violence as a personalized revenge, but the story obviates this reading by openly noting that the boys have extremely limited mental capacities and that "[t]enían, en cambio, cierta facultad imitativa; pero no se pudo obtener nada más" ["they possessed a certain imitative faculty, but nothing more"].[44] The brothers' capacity to imitate the actions of the servant evoke Poe's orangutan from "The Murders in the Rue Morgue," whose imitation of the mundane act of shaving leads to an equally gruesome death for a Parisian mother and daughter. Although the boys are human, the story shows how their parents increasingly animalize and neglect them to the point where they each blame the other for their sons' illness and think of the boys as "monstruos" ["monsters"].[45] The boys' aping of the servant does reveal a revenge plot, but one in which the brothers are the tools of nature rather than the seekers of vengeance. The narrator mentions that the servant learned the technique she uses to bleed the newly decapitated chicken from Berta, the boys' mother, who, in turn, learned the method from her mother—showing that the boys literally copy their mother when killing their sister.[46] Their actions also repeat the brutality with which their parents have treated them and, more pointedly, how their parents have treated one another. Nature takes its revenge on these parents for their obsession with having a healthy child, their negligence toward and abuse of their four sons once that healthy child arrives, and their caustic treatment of one another. Quiroga depersonalizes or universalizes revenge in this story in a way that it quite distinct from Poe's revenge tales while simultaneously and paradoxically re-personalizing that revenge by having the very children whom the parents have treated like animals fulfill that role, robbing the parents of their sound daughter due to the circumstances in which the boys find her rather than due to any hatred on their part. Yet, this revenge tale creates a horrifying effect that feels familiar to the reader of Poe's revenge tales and horror stories.[47]

The previous analysis demonstrates that Quiroga openly accepted Poe's influence but that he was also more than a Poe follower. Quiroga's literary criticism supports the same conclusion and further spreads Poe's influence in a somewhat more prescriptive fashion. Between 1925 and 1927, Quiroga published three "how to"-type guides for aspiring story writers in the popular magazines of Buenos Aires, and two of the three articles prescribe Poe's writing methods. In the first essay, "El manual del perfecto cuentista," Quiroga's thoughts on knowing the end of a story before writing the beginning and on the necessity of understanding "adónde se va" ["where you are going"] clearly grow out of the ideas Poe shared about effect in "The Philosophy of Composition."[48] In the third piece, "Decálogo del perfecto cuentista," Quiroga offers ten brief pieces of advice for story writers. The first rule directly names Poe and demonstrates how Quiroga embraced, rather than feared, the influence of his precursors, "Cree en un maestro—Poe, Maupassant, Kipling, Chejov—como en Dios mismo" ["Believe in a master—Poe, Maupassant, Kipling, Chekhov—as in God himself"], and the fifth rule echoes Quiroga's thoughts on the beginning and ending of stories that he shared in his earlier essay.[49] In 1928, Quiroga published another magazine article in which he defended the short story as a brief, direct, and effective genre—recalling, again, Poe's thoughts on the brevity and directness of tales as stated in "The Philosophy of Composition" and in his second review of Hawthorne's *Twice-Told Tales*—and in which he again named Poe as an exemplary story writer.[50] Through each of these articles, Quiroga both reveals Poe's influence and further spreads that influence by making Poe's poetics his own and recommending those poetics to other authors as rules for successful writing.

Both Quiroga's creative and prescriptive rewritings of Poe exerted a strong influence on Quiroga's contemporaries and on younger writers in Argentina and the Río de la Plata region. Englekirk describes Quiroga's prominence in the region by the early 1930s and notes how Quiroga's reputation also circulates Poe:

> he is esteemed as the most outstanding short-story writer of the Río de la Plata country and as one of the great authors of Hispanic-American literature. Many of the younger prose writers have been inspired and guided by Quiroga's genius. They must have sensed the Poesque spirit that has motivated their master's pen and, in turn, succumbed in some degree to the ever fresh inspiration of Poe himself.[51]

Quiroga's work wields its own influence while also disseminating Poe's. In short, Quiroga kept and still keeps Poe alive in Argentina.

POE, BORGES, AND CORTÁZAR

Of all Argentine writers, Jorge Luis Borges maintained the longest and most complex relationship with Poe. Borges was a reader and re-reader of Poe from his youth until his death; he consistently referred to Poe in literary criticism, lectures, interviews, and collaborative projects from the 1920s into the 1980s; he translated "The Purloined Letter" and "The Facts in the Case of M. Valdemar" with Adolfo Bioy Casares; and he wrote fiction that conversed with Poe's works throughout his long career. Most visibly, he seriously engaged the analytic detective genre for several years—reviewing detective novel after detective novel in the pages of *Sur* and *El Hogar*, writing detective story "parodies" with Bioy Casares and rewriting Poe's Dupin tales in three of his own detective stories.[52] In sum, Borges alone rewrote Poe in each and every way that Lefevere suggests later authors rewrite their predecessors to canonize and sustain them. While John T. Irwin has written extensively on Borges, Poe, and detective fiction, I have examined Borges's literary criticism on Poe, his Poe translations, and other connections between his and Poe's fiction beyond the detective genre; however, few scholars have analyzed Borges's work with Poe as an anthologizer.[53]

Poe's works appear in all sorts of anthologies in Argentina, and Borges was one of the first Argentine anthologizers of Poe. In the early 1940s, Borges and Bioy Casares published their translations of "Valdemar" and "The Purloined Letter" in two major Spanish-language anthologies—*Antología de la literatura fantástica* and *Los mejores cuentos policiales*, respectively.[54] The former anthology places Poe among the early masters of fantastic fiction, and the latter claims Poe as the inventor of the detective genre. Both anthologies deliver and re-deliver these interpretations of Poe as a significant literary figure, along with the particular pieces of Poe's fiction, to generations of Argentines and other Spanish-language readers throughout the globe as both collections have seen multiple reprintings and remain actively in print into the second decade of the twenty-first century. Borges also included Poe compilations in two lengthy collections or "libraries" that he assembled during the last years of his life. In 1985, Borges published *La carta robada*, a collection of five Poe stories in Spanish translation, as a part of the "Biblioteca de Babel" series that he released with three separate publishers in the 1970s and 1980s, and in 1986, he published a Poe book entitled *Cuentos* that contains Spanish translations of eight Poe stories and one essay and makes up the fortieth volume of a seventy-two book set that Borges published with Hyspámerica as his "Biblioteca Personal."[55] Each of these collections places Poe squarely within Borges's canon of texts that readers should read and reread. Borges even continues to anthologize Poe after Borges's own death as contemporary publishers put out volumes such as the 1999 collection from Santillana—*Cuentos memorables según Jorge Luis Borges*—that prints a Spanish translation of Poe's "The Gold-Bug" alongside translations of eleven other stories by authors whom the book's editors suggest Borges admired.[56]

Like Borges, Julio Cortázar also rewrote Poe in multiple ways, but while Borges only translated two full Poe stories, Cortázar translated the bulk of Poe's prose canon. Cortázar's 1956 *Obras en prosa* contains his translations of all of Poe's tales, *Eureka*, *Pym*, and a large selection of Poe's literary criticism in two lengthy volumes, and these translations have remained in print in various ways up until today—most popularly through Alianza's continual reprinting of the stories as *Cuentos* in two volumes and most recently through Jorge Volpi and Fernando Iwasaki's "commented edition" of Cortázar's translations of the tales.[57] Before Cortázar's Poe translations, Argentine readers either came to Poe in fragments via the works of various Spanish-language translators, or they came to a more complete Poe in French or English. Volpi and Iwasaki's introduction to *Cuentos completos: Edición comentada* makes abundantly clear that after Cortázar's translations Spanish-language readers from the Americas and the Iberian Peninsula usually come to Poe via Cortázar, and Fernández Díaz's previously cited "El regreso de un muerto vivo" suggests the same for Poe's Argentine readers of the same time period.[58]

Focusing on the theme of the double might be the most succinct way to demonstrate Cortázar's intricate relationship with Poe. Cortázar suggested that Baudelaire was literally Poe's double, his translations of Poe always open with "William Wilson" (Poe's most famous story of doubling), and he continually wrestled with doubling in his most well-known short fiction.[59] Finally, Cortázar's first published story, "Casa tomada" ["House Taken Over"], although not a story of doubling itself, doubles Poe's "The Fall of the House of Usher" in twentieth-century Argentina.[60] The backstory of this tale's initial publication might be even more representative of Poe's Argentine presence than the story proper. "Casa tomada" first appeared in *Los anales de Buenos Aires* in 1946, a journal that Borges founded and edited during its first two years.[61] Many years later, Borges remained proud of the fact that he had played a part in the initial stages of Cortázar's literary career.[62] Through the publication of "Casa tomada," one Argentine Poe reader and rewriter supported another. This support not only launched Cortázar's career, but as I have argued elsewhere, it also established a long-term relationship of mutual respect between Cortázar and Borges regardless of their disparate political opinions.[63] Cortázar's rewriting of "Usher" as "Casa tomada" brought Cortázar and Borges into one another's spheres and initiated a long-lasting connection between the two of them while each of their literary efforts continued to disseminate Poe.

CONCLUSION

I would like to return to "Usher" to bring my argument full circle. Fernández Díaz's claim that Poe is "un muerto vivo" ["a living dead man"] in twenty-first-century Argentina certainly makes sense, but his choice of Poe stories to drive this point home might miss the mark. Poe's character M. Valdemar surely could qualify as "un muerto vivo" for the seven-month mesmeric limbo in which his body remains intact while his tongue suggests that he is, in fact, dead. Fernández Díaz, however, defines Poe against his character and his story by claiming that *other* authors disintegrate like Valdemar while "Poe está vivo y vuelve de su tumba una y otra vez para vengarnos" ["Poe is alive and returns from his tomb again and again to avenge us"].[64] I suggest, instead, that we can draw a clearer comparison between Poe's continued presence in Argentina and his character, Madeline Usher, who does, indeed, return from her tomb alive.

Madeline's return from the grave allows us to play with the somewhat strange construction—"para vengarnos"—that Fernández Díaz uses when describing Poe's Argentine return. "Vengar" ["to avenge or to take revenge"] can function as a transitive verb with a direct object as it does in Fernández Díaz's claim, but it is much more common in Spanish to use "vengarse" ["to avenge oneself"] as a pronominal verb in which the subject acts upon itself, rather than upon a direct object. If used in the pronominal form, the phrase "para vengarse" would beg the question "¿de quién" ["of whom"], and in this case, the clearest answer would be "de nosotros" ["of us"]. So while "vengarnos" literally means "to avenge us," it can leave the reader with the strange feeling that Fernández Díaz *could* also mean that Poe avenges himself of us or takes his revenge on us—the exact opposite of Fernández Díaz's literal meaning. This misreading recalls the differences that often become visible when reading Poe versus watching adaptations of his work. Poe's "Usher," for example, ends in what appears to be both a mad and terrified embrace as Madeline and Roderick Usher die together before their house sinks into the tarn that surrounds it (M 416–417). In Roger Corman's *House of Usher* (one of the Poe films starring Vincent Price in the very Corman cycle that introduced Poe to Fernández Díaz), Madeline returns and strangles Roderick, and both characters die as their house burns down before it sinks into the tarn.[65] Poe's tale allows for interpretations that do and do not include revenge while the film openly shows Madeline taking vengeance on her twin. Through the likes of Lugones, Quiroga, Borges, and Cortázar, Poe—like Madeline—returns from the grave to embrace and avenge his Argentine readers or to grasp them and take his revenge upon them. In either case, this "muerto vivo" and his Argentine advocates stake out what appears to be a permanent abode for Poe in Argentine literary history and popular culture.

Notes

1. Itamar Even-Zohar claims that "translated literature" is "an integral system" and "a most active system" within "any literary polysystem." His descriptions of what happens when "translated literature maintains a central position in the literary polysystem" and "participates actively in shaping the center of the polysystem" to create a "situation" in which "no clear-cut distinction is maintained between 'original' and 'translated' writings" certainly apply to Poe's presence in Argentina. Even-Zohar, "The Position of Translated Literature Within the Literary Polysystem," in *The Translation Studies Reader*, ed. Lawrence Venuti, 3rd ed. (New York: Routledge, 2012), 163.

2. Edward Relph's groundbreaking *Place and Placelessness* (London: Pion Limited, 1976), 49–55, theorizes place, describing various relationships to place through different types of "insideness" and "outsidenss" that create fruitful comparisons with the work of Even-Zohar. Relph has no particular term for an unaware or oblivious outsideness similar to Poe's lack of engagement with Argentina. However, his description of "existential insideness" as "[t]he most fundamental form of insideness … experienced without deliberate and selfconscious reflection … the insideness that most people experience when they are at home and in their own town or region, when they know the place and its people and are known and accepted there" describes a person's relationship to place in terms that resonate with Even-Zohar's discussions of what happens when a translated work becomes a part of a particular literary polysystem.

3. Ibid., 49.
4. Argentina's National Library holds over 300 books of Poe translations, anthologies that include one or more of Poe's works, or books about Poe. The consortium of city libraries in Buenos Aires holds nearly 200 Poe books, and the association of city libraries in Córdoba holds just over 100. Argentine bookstores typically carry several editions of Poe's fiction, poetry, and/or literary criticism—from deluxe, hardback editions to small, inexpensive "libros del bosillo" or pocket books. The Web sites of various Argentine secondary schools list Poe as assigned reading, and Argentina's national education portal "educ.ar" contains a 4000-word entry on Poe at http://www.educ.ar/sitios/educar/recursos/ver?id=91494. Finally, searches for "Edgar Allan Poe" on the Web sites of the prominent Argentina newspapers *La Nación* and *Clarín* bring up 367 and 736 hits, respectively.
5. Jorge Fernández Díaz, "El regreso de un muerto vivo," *La Nación*, December 13, 2008, http://www.lanacion.com.ar/1078949-el-regreso-de-un-muerto-vivo. This article, two others on Poe, and a reprint of Cortázar's translation of Poe's "Von Kempelen and His Discovery" formed a Saturday section of *La Nación* that celebrated Poe's bicentennial and announced the release of Jorge Volpi and Fernando Iwasaki's commented edition of Cortázar's Poe translations. Unless otherwise noted, all translations from Spanish to English are my own.
6. Ibid.
7. Ibid.
8. Ibid.
9. André Lefevere, "Why Waste Our Time on Rewrites: The Trouble with Interpretation and the Role of Rewriting in an Alternative Paradigm," in *The Manipulation of Literature: Studies in Literary Translation*, ed. Theo Hermans (New York: St. Martin's Press, 1985), 231.
10. Ibid., 217.
11. Ibid., 233; Lefevere, "Mother Courage's Cucumbers: Text, System and Refraction in a Theory of Literature," in *The Translation Studies Reader*, ed. Lawrence Venuti, 3rd ed., (New York: Routledge, 2012), 205; Lefevere, *Translating Literature: Practice and Theory in a Comparative Literature Context* (New York: Modern Language Association of America, 1992), 6–7.
12. Lefevere notes that rewriting, in essence, keeps texts alive. He argues that "[i]f a work of literature is not rewritten in one way or another, it is not likely to survive its date of publication by many years or even many months," *Translating Literature*, 14.
13. Quiroga was born in Uruguay and spent most of his life there until his early 20s. He then left his home country for Argentina and never

returned. He wrote the vast majority of his work while living in Argentina, and his writings were heavily influential in both Argentina and Uruguay. Both nations claim Quiroga as a part of their national literary traditions, and one can comfortably analyze Quiroga as a significant part of one, the other, or both. John Eurgene Englekirk avoids this tension by simply referring to Quiroga as a "*cuentista rioplatense*" ["storyteller from Río de la Plata"], *Edgar Allan Poe in Hispanic Literature* (New York: Instituto de las Españas en los Estados Unidos, 1934), 340.

14. The multiplicity of the rewritings of Poe in Argentina—the sheer number of authors, critics, and translators who have engaged his works there, and the fact that some of Argentina's most important writers have rewritten Poe in more than one way—has certainly enhanced Poe's Argentine presence and his longevity in Argentine letters and popular culture. Lefevere claims that "[n]o one form of rewriting alone can establish or disestablish, make or break the reputation of a writer and/or a work inside the receiving culture," "Why Waste Our Time on Rewrites?" 235.

15. For detailed analyses of the literary relationship between Borges and Poe, see my recent monograph *Borges's Poe: The Influence and Reinvention of Edgar Allan Poe in Spanish America* (Athens: University of Georgia Press, 2016) and John T. Irwin's seminal *The Mystery to a Solution: Poe, Borges, and the Analytic Detective Story* (Baltimore: The Johns Hopkins University Press, 1994). For more on Cortázar and Poe, see my "'William Wilson' as a Microcosm of Julio Cortázar's Poe Translations: Horror in the Doubling of the Human Will" in *Translated Poe*, ed. Emron Esplin and Margarida Vale de Gato (Bethlehem, PA: Lehigh University Press, 2014), 251–260 and "Epilogue: Commemorative Reframing," in *Borges's Poe*, 152–165.

16. I pull the description of Poe as a "muerto vivo" in this sentence and in my title from the title of Fernández Díaz's previously cited article "El regreso de un muerto vivo."

17. Englekirk, 20–21.

18. Ricardo Gutiérrez, trans., "Eleonora" by Edgar Allan Poe, *El Correo del Domingo* (Buenos Aires), June 18, 1865, 396–397. This translation, regardless of its confusing title, is a translation of "Ulalume," not a Hispanicized title shift for Poe's poem "Lenore," and not a translation of Poe's tale "Eleonora." I would like to thank Juan Pablo Canala from Argentina's National Library for making me aware of this translation which is not available in Englekirk's bibliography nor in the two supplementary bibliographies published by Heliodoro Valle and Woodbridge, respectively. Rafael Heliodoro Valle, "Fichas para la bibliografía de Poe en Hispánoamerica," *Revista Iberoamericana* 16 (1950): 199–214; Hensley C. Woodbridge, "Poe in Spanish America: A Bibliographical Supplement,"

Poe Newsletter 2 (1969): 18–19. Canala is currently searching for three Poe translations that purportedly appeared in the nineteenth-century Argentine newspaper, *El Nacional* between 1856 and 1860.

19. "Edgardo Poe," *El Correo del Domingo* (Buenos Aires), June 18, 1865, 396.

20. Carlos Obligado, trans., *Novelas y cuentos* by Edgar Allan Poe (Paris: Librería Española Garnier y Hermanos, 1884), i, 9–42.

21. Jorge Luis Borges and Osvaldo Ferrari, "Dialogo sobre el Modernismo y Rubén Darío," in *Libro de diálogos* (Buenos Aires: Editorial Sudamericana, 1986), 119. Borges makes similar claims about Poe's French arrival in Argentina in "Sobre los clásicos," *Sur* 85 (October 1941): 12; and in the prologue to *Prólogos con un prólogo de prólogos*, in *Obras completas* (Buenos Aires, Emecé Editores, 2007), 4: 13.

22. In 1888, Nicaraguan poet Rubén Darío initiated the transnational literary movement that would come to be known as *modernismo* with the publication of his now famous book *Azul*. *Modernismo* primarily valued beauty and art for art's sake, and it quickly became the dominant aesthetic in Spanish American letters. For the first time, a Spanish American literary aesthetic gained global notoriety as *modernismo* also spread back across the Atlantic to influence writers on the Iberian Peninsula. *Modernismo* was certainly the most significant Spanish American literary movement before the so-called Boom of the middle to late twentieth century.

23. Englekirk, 146.

24. Ibid., 34, 97.

25. Ibid., 278–304.

26. Leopoldo Lugones, "Prologue," in *Castalia Bárbara y otros poemas* by Ricardo Jaimes Freyre (Mexico City: Cultura, 1920), V–XXI.

27. Englekirk, 278–304.

28. Lugones, "La fuerza Omega," "La metamúsica," and "El origen del Diluvio," in *Las fuerzas extrañas* (Buenos Aires: Editorial Huemul, 1966), 25–37, 79–91, 93–100; Lugones, "The Omega Force," "Metamusic," and "Origins of the Flood," in *Strange Forces: The Fantastic Tales of Leopoldo Lugones*, trans., Gilbert Alter-Gilbert (Pittsburgh: Latin American Literary Review Press, 2001), 69–79, 57–68, 80–86.

29. Lugones, "Un fenómeno inexplicable," in *Las fuerzas extrañas*, 53–62; Lugones, "An Inexplicable Phenomenon," in *Strange Forces*, 35–43.

30. Englekirk, 294.

31. Quiroga first experienced the jungle—a space that became central to his writing and his life—when he traveled to Misiones as Lugones's photographer.

32. See Borges, "Leopoldo Lugones, *Romancero*," in *El tamaño de mi esperanza* (Madrid: Alianza Editores, 2002), 105–108, for a biting critique

of Lugones. See Borges and Betina Edelberg, *Leopoldo Lugones* in *Obras completas en colaboración* (Buenos Aires: Emecé, 1979), 455–508, for a more charitable appraisal of Lugones and his work. Borges criticized Quiroga at various times. One of his harshest critiques of Quiroga came in a conversation with Fernando Sorrentino in which he called Quiroga "un escritor muy mediocre" ["a very mediocre writer"] and opined that "[e]l estilo de Quiroga me parece deplorable, su imaginación me parece pobre" ["Quiroga's style seems deplorable to me, his imagination seems poor to me"]. Sorrentino, *Siete conversaciones con Jorge Luis Borges* (Buenos Aires: Casa Pardo, 1973), 76–77.

33. See, for example: Englekirk's chapter on Quiroga in *Edgar Allan Poe in Hispanic Literature*, 340–368; Mary G. Berg, "Horacio Quiroga," in *Poe Abroad*, ed. Lois Davis Vines (Iowa City: University of Iowa Press, 1999), 239–243; and Margo Clantz, "Poe en Quiroga," in *Aproximaciones a Horacio Quiroga*, ed. Angel Flores (Caracas: Monte Avila, 1976), 93–118.

34. Ezequiel Martínez Estrada, *El hermano Quiroga* (Montevideo: Arca, 1966), 73; Emir Rodríguez Monegal made this claim in at least two different places: Rodríguez Monegal, *La objetividad de Horacio Quiroga* (Montevideo: Número, 1950), 23; and Rodríguez Monegal, *Las raices de Horacio Quiroga* (Montevideo: Alfa, 1961), 164.

35. Luis Alberto de Cuenca, "Prólogo," in *El devorador de hombres y otras novelas cortas* by Horacio Quiroga (Palencia: Menoscuarto, 2013), 8.

36. Horacio Quiroga, "El tonel de Amontillado," in *Todos los cuentos* (Madrid: Allca, 1997), 813; Ibid., "El crimen del otro," 871–879; Ibid., "La lengua," 471–472; Ibid., "Una bofetada," 204–211. "El crimen del otro" has been translated as "The Other Crime" by Jennifer A. Mattson, *The Literary Review* 38, no. 1 (1994): 145–156 although the "The Crime of the Other" or "The Other's Crime" better captures the possessive within Quiroga's title. Margaret Sayers Peden included "A Slap in the Face" as her translation of "Una bofetada," in *The Decapitated Chicken and Other Stories* (Madison: University of Wisconsin Press, 2004), 63–72. "El tonel de Amontillado" and "La lengua" are not currently available in English.

37. Caroline Egan, "Revivification and Revision: Horacio Quiroga's Reading of Poe," *The Comparatist* 35 (2011): 239–248.

38. Quiroga, "Las fieras cómplices," in *El devorador de hombres y otras novelas cortas* (Palencia: Menoscuarto, 2013), 13–58; Ibid., "El mono que asesinó," in *El devorador de hombres y otras novelas cortas*, 61–105; and J David Danielson offers his translation of "Las fieras cómplices" as "Beasts in Collusion," in *The Exile and Other Stories* by Horacio Quiroga (Austin: University of Texas Press, 1987), 3–33. To my knowledge, "El mono que asesinó" is not available in English translation.

39. Quiroga, "Las fieras cómplices," 42–45; Ibid., "Beasts in Collusion," 23–24.

40. Ibid., "Las fieras cómplices," 55–57; Ibid., "Beasts in Collusion," 31–32.
41. Quiroga, "El mono que asesinó," 100–102.
42. I have already discussed the haunting monkey in "El fenómeno inexplicable." Lugones's "Yzur" concerns a man's obsession with trying to prove that his chimpanzee can talk. The chimpanzee finally speaks to its master while on its deathbed. Lugones, "Yzur," in *Las fuerzas extrañas*, 117–126.
43. Quiroga, "La gallina degollada," in *Todos los cuentos*, 94–95; Ibid., "The Decapitated Chicken," in *The Decapitated Chicken and Other Stories*, trans. Margaret Sayers Peden, 54–56.
44. Ibid., "La gallina degollada," 91; Ibid., "The Decapitated Chicken," 51.
45. Ibid., "La gallina degollada," 94; Ibid., "The Decapitated Chicken," 55.
46. Ibid., "La gallina degollada," 94; Ibid., "The Decapitated Chicken," 54.
47. Several other Quiroga stories continue this conversation between Quiroga and Poe about revenge, including Quiroga's masterful tale "Juan Darién," in *Todos los cuentos*, 590–601.
48. Quiroga, "El manual del perfecto cuentista," in *Todos los cuentos*, 1189–1191.
49. Ibid., "Decálogo del perfecto cuentista," 1194–1195. Quiroga's third rule in this article almost perfectly describes his own relationship with Poe—a relationship that begins with imitation but changes as Quiroga finds his own voice. He states: "[r]esiste cuanto pueda a la imitación, pero imita si el influjo es demasiado fuerte. Más que ninguna otra cosa, el desarrollo de la personalidad es una larga paciencia" ["resist imitation as much as you can, but imitate if the influence is too strong. More than any other thing, the development of a personality requires endless patience"].
50. Ibid., "La retórica del cuento," in *Todos los cuentos*, 1195–1196.
51. Englekirk, 368.
52. For a fascinating interpretation of Borges's doubling of Poe's Dupin stories, see Irwin's *The Mystery to a Solution*.
53. See my *Borges's Poe*, 99, for a brief discussion of Borges as Poe anthologizer.
54. Jorge Luis Borges, Adolfo Bioy Casares, and Silvina Ocampo, eds., *Antología de la literatura fantástica* (Buenos Aires: Sudamericana, 1940); Borges and Bioy Casares, eds. *Los mejores cuentos policiales* (Buenos Aires: Emecé, 1943).
55. Jorge Luis Borges, dir., *La carta robada* (Madrid: Ediciones Siruela, 1985); Ibid., *Cuentos* (Barcelona: Hyspamérica Ediciones Argentina, 1986). The former volume contains translations of Poe's "The Purloined Letter," "MS. Found in a Bottle," "The Facts in the Case of M. Valdemar," "The Man of the Crowd," and "The Pit and the Pendulum." The second volume includes different translations of those same five stories plus translations

of "A Descent into the Maelström," "The Murders in the Rue Morgue," "The Cask of Amontillado," and "The Philosophy of Composition." The only translations connected to Borges are the Borges/Bioy Casares translations of "Valdemar" and "The Purloined Letter" in *La carta robada*. Both books contain original prologues about Poe written by Borges.

56. *Cuentos memorables según Jorge Luis Borges* (Buenos Aires: Santanilla, 1999).

57. Julio Cortázar, trans., *Obras en prosa* by Edgar Allan Poe, 2 vols. (Madrid: Revista de Occidente; Río Piedras: Editorial Universitaria Universidad de Puerto Rico, 1956); Ibid., *Cuentos* by Edgar Allan Poe, 2 vols. (Madrid: Alianza Editorial, 1970–2012); Ibid., *Cuentos completos: Edición comentada* by Edgar Allan Poe, eds. Jorge Volpi and Fernando Iwasaki (Madrid: Páginas de Espuma, 2008).

58. Volpi and Iwasaki, "Poe & cía," in *Cuentos completos: Edición comentada*, 13–14; Fernández Díaz, "El regreso de un muerto vivo."

59. For Cortázar's thoughts on Baudelaire as Poe's double, see Ernesto González Bermajo, *Conversaciones con Cortázar* (Barcelona: Editora y Distribuidora Hispano Americana, 1978), 35–36. For examples of Cortázar's use of the double in short fiction, see, among many other titles, "Lejana" and "Axolotl," in *La autopista del sur y otros cuentos* (New York: Penguin Books, 1996), 7–15, 43–48.

60. Cortázar, "Casa tomada," in *La autopista del sur y otros cuentos*, 1–6; Ibid., "House Taken Over," in *Blow-up and Other Stories*, trans. Paul Blackburn (New York: Pantheon Books, 1985), 10–16. Several critics have offered parallel readings of "Usher" and "Casa tomada." For two very different comparative readings of these stories, see Valentín Pérez Venzalá, "Incesto y espacialización del psiquismo en 'Casa tomada' de Cortázar," *Espéculo: Revista de Estudios Literarios* 10 (1998): np, http://www.ucm.es/info/especulo/numero10/cort_poe.html; and Daniel Bautista, "Popular Culture in the Houses of Poe and Cortázar," *Intertexts* 14, no. 1 (2010): 1–20.

61. Cortázar, "Casa tomada," *Los anales de Buenos Aires* 1, no. 11 (1946): 13–18.

62. See Borges, "Prólogo a Julio Cortázar, *Cuentos*," in *Obras completas* (Buenos Aires: Emecé Editores, 2007) 4: 551–252.

63. Esplin, *Borges's Poe*, 157.

64. Fernández Díaz, "El regreso de un muerto vivo."

65. Roger Corman, *House of Usher* (1960; MGM, 2001), DVD.

PART V

Coda: Space as Place

CHAPTER 15

"Finding His Way Home": Tracing Poe's Solutions in *Eureka*

Harry Lee Poe

For most of his life, Edgar Allan Poe and all the other people on Earth lived in an unimaginably large universe whose age stood beyond comprehension. This universe of infinite size and eternal duration represented the apex of intellectual speculation, and its definition involved such great minds as Aristotle, Bacon, and Newton. During 1847–1848, however, Edgar Allan Poe created a much smaller, much younger universe. Today, Poe's explanation for the material universe goes by the name The Big Bang Theory.[1] In order to make such a universe work, however, Poe also needed to envision and combine the interrelated phenomena that we now call the unified field, Relativity Theory, Chaos Theory, the nuclear forces, and fine-tuning into a theory of everything.[2] A critical piece of this unity of effect came as early as 1841 in his short story "A Succession of Sundays," when Poe took the position that no place or time had

---

This essay was originally presented as a paper at the International Edgar Allan Poe Conference in New York City in February 2015 as "Poe's Big Ideas: The Science of *Eureka* in the 21st Century".

H. L. Poe (✉)
Union University, Jackson, TN, USA

© The Author(s) 2018
P. E. Phillips (ed.), *Poe and Place*,
Geocriticism and Spatial Literary Studies,
https://doi.org/10.1007/978-3-319-96788-2_15

preference over any other, which is a foundational aspect of Einstein's ideas about relativity.[3]

Technically speaking, Poe's ideas about the nature of the universe are not called science because when he developed the logic of the universe, the scientific world did not have the vocabulary or the observational instruments and techniques needed to express them in mathematical form. Darwin, born the same year as Poe, had the same problem with his ideas because the necessary scientific work related to heredity had not yet been undertaken.[4] Except for the single year during which Poe inhabited his new universe before his death in 1849, Poe's cosmos went largely uninhabited for over a century until the scientific community accepted Poe's conclusions about how the universe works.[5] It was a place that would not be noticed until twentieth-century science began to discover what Poe had realized.

Poe had always been interested in science, but scientific questions about the material universe did not motivate his study. With the death of his wife to tuberculosis in January 1847, however, Poe set out to understand how a universe of such powerful love and beauty could end in misery and suffering. If a loving God exists, then why did Virginia Poe die? Poe intended to solve one of the greatest questions of human existence. He had grappled with the problem of justice at least as early as 1841 when he wrote the first detective story, but he brought the question to cosmic proportions when he wrote *Eureka*, the book he considered his masterpiece.

Before he could settle the problem of suffering, Poe first had to understand what kind of place this universe really is. The kind of universe that exists predetermines the possible answers to the problem of suffering. When the Buddha asked the same question, he began with a universe that only exists as an illusion. Poe, on the other hand, took the material world seriously. When David Hume dealt with these questions in the eighteenth century, he assumed a universe of eternal duration in which eventually everything would happen by accident, including the appearance of life.[6] Poe's finite universe had a beginning, and the nature of his universe sets limits on possible answers to his questions.

When Poe, ever the lover of classical forms and allusions, began to write his conclusions, he gave his work with a classical name, *Eureka*, and modeled his discussion of cosmology and God on the greatest work of its kind in antiquity, Plato's *Timaeus*. Plato began his somewhat pessimistic cosmology with a tale set thousands of years before his own time: the story of the destruction of the lost continent of Atlantis. Poe, by contrast, began his cosmology with a story set a thousand years in the future. In contrast to Plato's dreary tale of doom, Poe's tale is a lighthearted romp through the failure of Western epistemology until 1848 when a poet set everyone on the right track. Poe thought his ideas would achieve universal acceptance, but he also thought that other writers would appreciate his criticism of their work and improve their writing. Neither would be the case.

More than 165 years after its publication, *Eureka* remains one of Edgar Allan Poe's most obscure and least understood works about which critical opinion cannot agree.[7] The great divide begins with how one reads the title. Poe gave the work two different titles! The title page of the first edition gives the title as *Eureka: A Prose Poem*. All things being equal, the title page should settle the question. But all things are not equal. Poe gave the title again on the first page of the text as *Eureka: An Essay on the Material and Spiritual Universe*. Jerome McGann has declared emphatically that Poe had no intention of making truth claims about science, philosophy, or theology in *Eureka*.[8] McGann treats *Eureka* as a prose poem, but he ignores Poe's second title without comment. In contrast, Sir Patrick Moore ignored the first title of Poe's book and only printed the second title in his 2002 edition of the book without reference or allusion to *Eureka* as a prose poem.[9] Those with only a literary background tend to see it as some odd form of poetry. Those with some scientific background recognize that Poe has not simply hit upon the idea of an expanding universe but rather has hit upon the rest of the big ideas in physics necessary to make an expanding universe work.[10]

The classical Greek title was especially apt for this book, because, as we have seen, Poe took *Eureka*'s structure from Plato's *Timeaus*.[11] The title also suggests another alternative understanding of the book. Though many people may use the Greek word *eureka* (first person singular, perfect active verb from *eurisko*) as a mere exclamation for emphasis, it does actually mean something. Familiarly, it is the word uttered by Archimedes when the displacement theory came to him in his bath. Just as the title of Poe's first mystery story means "The Murders in Mortuary Street," the title of Poe's greatest achievement is *I Have Discovered a Prose Poem*. In concluding *Eureka*, Poe declared that "*the Universe ... is but the most sublime of poems....*"[12] This reading would fit Poe's love of the puzzle, the joke, and the doppleganger, but it does not hold up with the second title at the beginning of the text. A second alternative is that Poe regards *Eureka* as both a "Book of Truths ... for the Beauty that abounds in its Truth" and "as a Poem," for he makes both claims in his Preface.[13] In his concluding remarks, Poe stated that "Poetry and Truth are one."[14] A number of studies have explored the poetic dimension of *Eureka*, but this essay explores the scientific ideas that Poe discussed in terms of the status of those ideas within the scientific community in the twenty-first century.

In addition to the possibilities of seeing *Eureka* as an essay or a prose poem, the work has a third form. Before he called *Eureka* a prose poem, Poe presented the substance of *Eureka* as a lecture on "The Universe" at the Society Library on February 3, 1848. Poe provided the outline of this lecture to two of his correspondents: George Eveleth and George Isbell. The outline appears to have been taken by Poe from his notes due to the identical phrasing of the key points, though he amplified these points in the letter to Eveleth.[15] Poe's outline contained seven points:

1. An inspection of the *universality* of Gravitation—of the fact that each particle tends not to any common point—but to every other particle—suggests perfect totality, or *absolute unity*, as the source of the phaenomenon.
   [*Empirical evidence suggests that original unity is the source of gravity.*]
2. Gravity is but the mode in which it manifested the tendency of all things to return to their original unity.
3. I show that the law of return—i.e., the law of gravity—is but a necessary result of the necessary and sole possible mode of equable irradiation of matter through a *limited* space.
   [*Gravity is the result of the expansion of matter.*]
4. Were the Universe of stars—(contradistinguished from the universe of space) unlimited, no worlds could exist.
   [*In a static, infinite universe, gravity could not develop and star systems could not exist.*]
5. I show that Unity is Nothingness.
   [*In a state of unity, attraction and repulsion disappear along with matter.*]
6. All matter, springing from Unity, sprang from, i.e., Nothingness, was *created*.
   [*Matter was created out of nothing.*]
7. All will return to Unity; i.e.—to Nothingness.
   [*Everything will return to the apophetic One.*]

Poe came to regard gravity and other phenomena of nature, not as primary causes or forces in themselves, but as effects of prior causes. In stating the general proposition of *Eureka*, Poe declared, "*In the Original Unity of the First Thing lies the Secondary Cause of All Things, with the Germ of their Inevitable Annihilation.*"[16]

Empirical Evidence Suggests That Original Unity Is the Source of Gravity

Poe believed that the entire universe of matter came from a single "primordial particle" and that in its diffusion from the normal state of *One*, it took on the abnormal condition of *Many*. Today, we call this cosmogony The Big Bang Theory, but in his own day, it was a bizarre notion that went against all that science had ever known of the heavens. For many people, Poe's vision of a finite universe that expanded from a primordial particle is the only scientific idea in *Eureka*; however, the beginning is really only the beginning. Poe has a comprehensive cosmology that deals with all levels of the organization of the universe beginning at the beginning. He thought that the very action of diffusion implies a reaction of return to Unity.[17] With these words, Poe made a huge assumption, but one that controls the rest of his essay. He assumed the concept of reaction as a result of the change from the One to the Many apparently based upon the old Newtonian idea of the "return into Unity." He returned to the concept/idea/principle/experience/force of reaction, like a refrain in a poem—in this case a prose poem, seven times in the course of this seven part work.[18]

Poe suggested that the first recourse of people in recognizing a diffusion of difference from the original homogeneity would be to imagine that God had caused the differences by a special act of creation, but he believed that such a course would not be necessary by God owing to the nature of matter itself as created. Instead of an act of the divine will in creating each element separately, Poe reasoned that the elements can be accounted for as the result of the process of dispersion "in the very first processes of mass-constitution."[19] At this point, Poe describes what twentieth-century cosmogony would regard as the result of the collapse of first-generation stars that had served as the ovens in which the elements other than hydrogen and helium were produced and dispersed as micro-recapitulations of the original Singularity.

Poe believed that an original state of unity implied a tendency of the material universe to return to unity (attraction) unless something else happened to frustrate that return. Several times in his introductory remarks to this point, he repeated the claim that the expansion implied a return. He also stressed that the initial force that caused the diffusion of the universe was not a continuing sustained force, but only an initial force that initiated the diffusion and then ceased to act upon the universe.[20]

To offset the tendency to return to a unified state (attraction), Poe suggested a repulsive force at work that prevents the reunification of the atoms of the universe. Poe believed that this repulsive force had the power to prevent a reunification of the material world until some future epoch at which point the collective power of the attractive force would overwhelm the repulsive force and "thus permit the universal subsidence into the inevitable, because original and therefore normal, *One.*"[21] Poe cited the current state of physics in his day to substantiate the view that two atoms could not be brought into contact and that science had no means to cause such a contact. Physics has advanced since Poe's day to the point that a way has been devised for causing two atoms to come into contact. It is known as nuclear fusion, and the device for carrying out the operation is known as a hydrogen bomb. The attractive and repulsive characteristics of atomic particles would not be discovered until 1906.[22]

GRAVITY AS THE MODE OF THE RETURN TO UNITY

Poe frequently stated that the return to unity was implied, but he did not explain why it was implied until he turned to the issue of gravity. He reminded his readers that the return to unity is the principle of Newtonian Gravity. Having led the reader down the garden path, he began to overturn the whole of the Newtonian and Euclidean universe. Poe suggested that the physics of his day had spoken imprecisely of the repulsive force, referring to it alternatively as heat, magnetism, and electricity. Focusing only on electricity as a situation in which the repulsive force acts, Poe explained that electricity becomes apparent when a "difference" in atoms occurs.[23] Poe recognized that some relationship exists between matter and the exertion of force/power, or what Einstein called "energy." The effort to bring together two atoms results in what Poe called "electricity," but what Nils Bohr and the twentieth-century quantum physicists would call "energy."[24] Poe discarded gravity and electricity as the primary phenomena of physics and turned to attraction and repulsion as the determinative forces so that Matter equals Attraction and Repulsion. This equation would be Poe's equivalent of Einstein's famous Energy equals Mass times the Speed of Light squared.[25]

Poe criticized the Newtonian understanding of gravity and the confirmations of it by the experiments of Maskelyne, Cavendish, and Bailly, because the theory and the experiments were all developed with respect to *"the planet on which they stand."*[26] By giving priority to the place on which the theory was developed and on which the experiments were conducted, Newton and the other philosophers (for so scientists were called in those days) committed a grave error. The everyday experience of gravity on Earth predisposes people to think of gravity as pulling people toward the center of the Earth while at the same time making it "inconceivable" that gravity could be pulling them in any other direction. This is the problem of locality and privileged place which Poe treated in a comic way in relation to time in his romantic comedy "Three Sundays in a Week" in 1841.

Having introduced the problem of locality and the functional tendency of people to think from a privileged place, Poe turned to the universe in which every particle of matter exerts force on every other particle. Instead of tending toward a point called the center, "each atom attracts—sympathizes with the most delicate movements of every other atom, and with each and with all at the same time, and forever, and according to a determinate law of which the complexity, even considered by itself solely, is utterly beyond the grasp of the imagination."[27] Laplace had claimed that he could predict with certainty every future event in the universe if he knew the starting conditions. Poe challenged this deterministic view of the universe because of the interdependent relationship of matter acting mutually to attract and repulse every other bit of matter. In order to know the influence of "one mote in a sunbeam on its neighbouring mote," Poe said that it would be necessary to count, weigh, and determine the position of all the matter in the universe at one moment.[28] Thus, Poe advocated what twentieth-century physics came to call *uncertainty* most famously in Heisenberg's Uncertainty Principle.

Poe explained, "If I venture to displace, by even the billionth of a part of an inch, the microscopical speck of dust which lies now on the point of my finger, what is the character of that act upon which I have adventured? I have done a deed which shakes the Moon in her path, which causes the Sun to be no longer the Sun, and which alters forever the destiny of the multitudinous myriads of stars that roll and glow in the majestic presence of their Creator."[29] With these words, Poe declared the fundamental characteristics of what we now know as *Chaos Theory*, expressed in its most popular form as "the Butterfly Effect." Because of the interdependence of all matter, a butterfly that flaps its wings in the Amazon jungle will create a hurricane in the Indian Ocean. Rather than the deterministic, mechanical universe of physics that had prevailed since the time of Newton, Poe conceived of what we now call an *open and indeterminate universe* in which cause and effect do not so much determine the future as describe the past. He would further expound his ideas of cause and effect, or mutual adaptation, at the end of *Eureka*.[30]

Given such a universe, Poe asked how we can account for such a scientific principle as attraction. Poe did not assume that such a principle has always existed. Instead, he asked how to account for the existence of such a principle, or from what situation such a principle as attraction might have arisen. Here, Poe began his exploration of what recent science refers to as the *Unified Force*. Poe differed, however, in how he conceived it. Contemporary science imagines an original Unified Force from which the other forces broke away. Poe conceived of an original force which caused the other forces to evolve. The sympathy, affinity, or attraction of matter throughout the universe suggested to Poe a "common paternity."[31]

Instead of gravity attracting all atoms toward a center, Poe argued that attraction does not work toward a center as such. Instead, with each atom attracting each other atom in proportion to their distance from each other, atoms inevitably congregate and form globes of atoms whose center will have the greatest attractive force. The relationship of atoms toward a center, rather than a center as such, creates the effect of gravity. The tendency is toward unity which creates a center by the very effect of attraction. Instead of any particular privileged space within the universe, Poe conceived of the expanse of the universe as relative in relation to "the primordial and irrelative *One*."[32]

Gravity Is the Result of the Irradiation or Expansion of Matter in a Limited Space

In contrast to the prevailing scientific view since Aristotle, Poe believed that the material universe was limited in size and that the diffusion of stars in space can only be understood in relation to a process of radiation from an original unity. Poe provided the example of light that travels outward from its source and diffuses as it grows farther from that source according to an established mathematical formula.[33] Poe then inserted a geometric illustration of the concept of light diffusion, one of the few graphic illustrations he ever used (Fig. 15.1). The inverse of the process of radiation Poe called "concentralisation" by which he meant "*the degree of drawing together*."[34] Assuming that the universe began from an original unity and is now returning to that unity, Poe concluded that the concentralization "proceeds *exactly as we know the force of gravitation to proceed*."[35] In order to demonstrate the proportion between "'concentralisation' and the *force* of concentralisation" (gravity), Poe proposed to establish the "proportion between 'radiation' and the *force* of radiation."[36]

Poe argued that after the initial exertion of force propelled matter outward, a second and a third pulse of force extended the universe farther with the result of creating concentric strata of matter in concentric spheres that we might picture as an onion.[37] In these pulses of force,

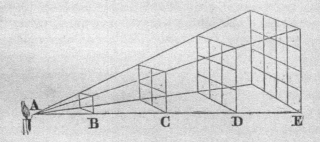

For example : at the distance B, from the luminous centre A, a certain number of particles are so diffused as to occupy the surface B. Then at double the distance—that is to say

at C—they will be so much farther diffused as to occupy four such surfaces :—at treble the distance, or at D, they will be so much farther separated as to occupy nine such surfaces :—while, at quadruple the distance, or at E, they

Fig. 15.1 Illustration from *Eureka*, 1848 (Harry Lee Poe Collection)

Poe saw the rhythmical creation of beauty.[38] The idea of an additional exertion of force to the expanding universe now forms a key element of current cosmology and is referred to as *inflation*. The most recent measurements of the rate of expansion of the universe suggest that the rate of expansion has increased, which ends the debate for now over whether the universe will implode in heat as Poe suggested or if it will continue to expand into deep freeze.

In dealing with objections to his proposal thus far, Poe put forward what we now call *fine tuning*. He explained:

> Had the force which radiated any stratum to its position, been either more or less than was needed for the purpose—that is to say, not *directly proportional* with the purpose—then to its position that stratum could not have been radiated. Had the force which, with a view to general equability of distribution, emitted the proper number of atoms for each stratum, been not *directly proportional* with the number, then the number would *not* have been the number demanded for the equable distribution.[39]

The laws of motion, the laws of gravity, and even the four fundamental forces did not exist at the moment of diffusion of matter. All the forces and principles of science have occurred as a result of the diffusion. They are an effect rather than a cause.[40] As for the charge that his idea of the diffusion of matter from the primordial particle is only a hypothesis, Poe replied that Newton's Law of Gravity was also a hypothesis without explanation about which Newton himself would not speculate.[41]

Instead of a universe of determinism and absolute certainty, Poe presented the universe as a relative space without any privileged time or place. Only the original unity of the primordial particle could serve as a reference point or privileged position, but as a Singularity it had a perfectly irrelative situation without relation. Poe declared, "My *Particle Proper* is but *Absolute Irrelation*."[42]

In a Static, Infinite Universe, Gravity Could Not Develop and Star Systems Could Not Exist

Poe said that if the force that caused the diffusion of matter had continued, then the reaction that we call gravity could never have occurred and we would have an infinite universe of unconsolidated matter.[43] In a finite, spherical universe, gravity appears and draws all matter toward all other matter, which allows for the development of stars and planets. In an infinite universe, however, the force of attraction would be of equal degree in every direction which would hold everything in a static state.[44] Instead of a static, infinite universe, Poe posited a finite, dynamic universe in which the principles of gravity and repulsion appeared almost instantaneously upon the cessation of the diffusive force which Poe attributed to Divine Volition.[45]

Under present Big Bang cosmogony, in contrast to Poe, physicists tend to believe that gravity separated from the other forces as an independent force at 10^{-39} seconds after the Big Bang and that the nuclear forces followed suit at 10^{-35} seconds. Poe imagined that the different elements (hydrogen, helium, iron, mercury, lead, etc.) were immediately caused by the diffusion rather than coming as a later consequence of his principles of attraction and repulsion. Between Poe's diffusion of matter and the current state of elements in the periodic table came the coalescence of hydrogen and helium, by the process Poe described, joined with the force of gravity as Poe described. Poe did not envision that this process would form the first-generation stars in which the other 103 elements in the periodic table were created. This feature of the coalescing of matter is another example of fine-tuning.

In explaining the nature of the finite universe with its development of stars, planets, and galaxies, Poe turned to the Nebular Hypothesis of Laplace which he elaborated in great detail from paragraph 134 through paragraph 213, comprising approximately one-third of the book. According to the Nebular Hypothesis, the Sun and its planets condensed under the effects of gravity from a huge cloud of matter. In the model of Laplace, the Sun threw off rings of matter as it cooled, and these rings formed into the planets. By contrast, the current theory posits massive disks of matter, not unlike the rings of Saturn that eventually coalesced into planets. In his exploration of a massive but finite universe, Poe carried the Nebular Hypothesis farther. Just as Newton thought our solar system was the galaxy, Laplace thought our galaxy was the universe. Poe, on the other hand, believed that the Nebular Hypothesis could account for the formation of innumerable stars and planets within innumerable galaxies in a finite universe. Poe's view became the standard view of astronomers only after observations by William Huggins beginning in 1864 and subsequent observations of Edwin Hubble in 1922.

Newton's model of the universe and the planetary orbits in our solar system had several problems that he explained by divine intervention.

Instead of attributing the solution of tangential velocity to "the finger of Deity" or "the direct and continual agency of God," Poe insisted that the universe he described contained within it the solution to all such problems.[46] He boldly asserted "that *each law of Nature is dependent at all points upon all other laws,* and that all are but consequences of one primary exercise of the Divine Volition. Such is the principle of the Cosmogony which, with all necessary deference, I here venture to suggest and to maintain."[47]

In what appears to be a digression, Poe devoted a number of pages to the contemplation of the immense size of the universe and the difficulty of having a frame of reference for comprehending such vast distances between the parts. The world of 1848 had not yet grown accustomed to imagining the enormity of the universe even though Poe's age still clung to the idea of an infinite universe. Poe took time to help his readers imagine the incomparable distances between our closest galactic neighbors, beginning with our own solar system.

LE CIEL   PL. LIII

GRAND TÉLESCOPE DE LORD ROSSE
à Parsonstown (Irlande).

Fig. 15.2 The great reflecting telescope of Lord Rosse in Ireland (Harry Lee Poe Collection)

Because of the great distances and the speed at which light travels, Poe reasoned that the stars we see in the heavens are actually the light sent from those stars ages ago. In the night sky, we see the past rather than the present. Furthermore, he pointed out that many of the stars we see have been demonstrated by Lord Rosse's reflecting telescope constructed in 1845 to be clusters of stars or galaxies (Fig. 15.2). The enormous amount of empty space was as important to Poe as the universe of galaxies. In his cosmogony, the empty space is the evidence of the theory of matter drawing together. To make his point, Poe takes his readers on an excursion across space from the Sun:

> Mercury at 37 million miles distance
> Venus at 68 million miles distance
> Earth at 95 million miles distance
> Mars at 144 million miles distance
> The asteroids at about 250 million miles distance
> Jupiter at 490 million miles distance
> Saturn at 900 million miles distance
> Uranus at 1900 million miles distance
> Neptune at 2800 million miles distance[48]

Such vast distances are difficult to fathom, so Poe as poet suggested combining the idea of distance with velocity. For instance, we might combine distance with the speed of sound at the velocity of 1100 feet of space per second. If a person on Earth could see the flash of a cannon discharging on the Moon, it would take thirteen days for the Earthling to hear the accompanying sound of the cannon fire if it were possible.[49] Poe then gave calculations for how long it would take the most advanced cannonball to travel from the Sun to the Earth or to Neptune as examples of the use of velocity to measure vast distances. Then, he turned to the speed of light. Earlier in his discussion, Poe claimed in a passing remark that light travels at a constant speed throughout the universe—167,000 miles per second, 10 million miles per minute, and 600 million miles per hour. At this rate, the light from the distant nebulae observed by Lord Rosse had taken three million years to travel to Earth.[50] Poe resorted to the use of the light year which had been introduced by Friedrich Bessel in 1838 to measure distance.[51] This vast distance illustrates the emptiness of space and the enormity of time in relation to space.

IN A STATE OF UNITY, ATTRACTION AND REPULSION DISAPPEAR ALONG WITH MATTER

Given the vastness and relative emptiness of space in relation to the diffusion of matter, Poe considered the problem of the needless amount of "mere space" in the universe. In light of what he had proposed regarding time and space, Poe concluded that "*Space and Duration are one.*"[52] Einstein would say that time and space are one, but Poe had noted the ambiguous problem with the word "time" since writing "A Succession of Sundays" in 1841 as well as the curious relationship between time and space since publishing "Dreamland" in 1844.[53] The universe required both immense time and space to accomplish the "Divine purposes" involved in the development of life and the "inevitable End" of all things. Today, this idea of the enormity of time and space in relation to the development of life is known as one of the cardinal *anthropic principles.*

Instead of a play that has no end, Poe proposed a universe for which the end is the purpose. It is not the meaningless nihilism of Nietzsche that he proposed, but a well-planned plot by God to create love (relation), beauty, and pleasure while destroying evil and sorrow by extending himself through creation and then drawing all things to himself. Poe rejected the common analogy of his time that like the Earth traveling around the Sun and the Sun traveling around the center of our galaxy that our galaxy travels around some other great center and this great center travels around an even greater and vaster center in an infinite regression. Instead, Poe continued to appeal for a finite universe in which space is curved such "that a flash of lightning itself, travelling *forever* on the circumference of this unutterable circle, would still, *forever*, be travelling in a straight line."[54] In 1979, Nigel Calder used a similar illustration in reverse to explain Einstein's universe: "If you projected an extremely powerful laser beam into space in a 'closed' universe it could eventually zoom right around behind you and singe the back of your head."[55]

Poe argued that evidence for the collapse of the universe could be found in the case of Encke's Comet whose orbit around the Sun had been degrading such that it would eventually hit the Sun. The explanation for the degrading of the orbit was that the universal ether inhibited the comet's movement. The presence of the invisible, undetectable ether was known to science because no other explanation for the decrease in the orbit made sense, given the assumptions of the science of Poe's day. Poe, however, rejected the ether of science as unfounded and illogical.[56] Newton had based his initial work on gravity and motion with the assumption of the pervasive ether, the medium through which light travels and by which gravity operates. The idea of universal ether was later overthrown as a result of the Michelson–Morley experiment in 1887. Instead of the ether of chemistry and physics, Poe proposed a spiritual ether that permeates the universe and is responsible not only for the "phænomena of electricity, heat, light, magnetism," but also for "vitality, consciousness, and thought."[57] For Poe, the entire plot of the universe is contained in the initial action and its reaction.

Poe speculated that the poetic fancy of the human race which seeks symmetry had no trouble in finding symmetry on the surface of the universe with what appeared to be the endless cycles of nature locally and from the perspective of a privileged time and space. Poe, on the other hand, saw the symmetry of the universe not on the "mere surface" but in the grand principle of symmetry by which "the end of all things" is "metaphysically involved in the thought of a beginning."[58] The principle of symmetry "finds, in this origin of all things, the *rudiment* of this end."[59] In restating how the forces of attraction and repulsion operate to create stars and then galaxies, Poe's argument proceeds to explore how the increasing mass of matter becomes what we now call *black holes*, but only in a rudimentary form that he could only call "infinitely superior spheres."[60] But this is not the end.

MATTER WAS CREATED OUT OF NOTHING

Poe finally introduced the ideas of the universe as a plot and the "reciprocity of adaptation" from his earlier essay on "The American Drama."[61] Until this section of *Eureka*, Poe had explored the physical universe of matter for its own sake, which is all that science can do. The tools of Aristotle and Bacon cannot look behind the veil. From the perspective of art, however, it occurred to Poe that creation could not end in any other way. In his original proposition on the first page of *Eureka*, Poe had declared, "*In the Original Unity of the First Thing lies the Secondary Cause of All Things, with the Germ of their Inevitable Annihilation.*"[62] Humanity could never conceive of an end to the universe because it had never conceived scientifically of its beginning, and any collateral cause for an end could never have satisfied human fancy. He drew once more from his literary theory of plot to explain that "Creation would have affected us as an imperfect *plot*

in a romance, where the *dénoûment* is awkwardly brought about by interposed incidents external and foreign to the main subject; instead of springing out of the bosom of the thesis—out of the heart of the ruling idea—instead of arising as a result of the primary proposition—as inseparable and inevitable part and parcel of the fundamental conception of the book."[63]

At this point in his discussion, however, Poe invoked the "*reciprocity of adaptation*" and declared, "With a perfectly legitimate reciprocity, we are now permitted to look at Matter, as created *solely for the sake of this influence*—solely to serve the objects of this spiritual Ether."[64] Spirit has individualized itself by the use of matter, and then, it became animate, and then, it became conscious intelligence. Matter is the means, but not the end of creation. With the return into unity, attraction and repulsion would cease; thus, matter would cease since matter is only attraction and repulsion. With the end of matter, the universe would cease to exist and "God would remain all in all."[65]

Everything Will Return to the Apophetic One

Poe concluded *Eureka* by suggesting a unity of relationship between the physical and the spiritual with a vision of a universe that pulses poetically, rhythmically from unity/nothingness into existence and then back into nothingness with "every throb of the Heart Divine."[66]

Conclusion

When Poe wrote *Eureka*, the scientific world had neither the vocabulary nor the instruments adequate to explore the ideas that swirled in his head. Without the necessary scientific work that would not begin to come until several decades after Poe's death, it was impossible for Poe to present his ideas mathematically, which would have constituted the form for a scientific hypothesis. Poe appears to have realized this dilemma, and possibly for this reason, he asked that his ideas be judged as poetry. In the twenty-first century, however, he leaves the scientific community in awe of how a French major could have conceived so many ideas essential to a theory of everything.

Notes

1. Harold Beaver declared, "At their broadest synthesis, Poe's Universe and Einstein's cohere." See, Harold Beaver, ed., *The Science Fiction of Edgar Allan Poe* (London: Penguin Books, 1976), 402. For the person inclined to regard *Eureka* as an allegory or symbolic metaphor for something other than an exploration of cosmology, Beaver's introduction and commentary provide a most helpful introduction to the major scientific issues that Poe explored and how his ideas correspond to the accepted theories of today. The Big Bang Theory had just become the accepted cosmology when Beaver's edition was published. Until the acceptance of Big Bang cosmology, Poe's ideas seemed crazy.

2. Arthur Hobson Quinn took the view that Poe's ideas anticipated the science of the twentieth century, but when Quinn wrote his biography of Poe, much of the science of the twentieth century did not yet exist. Relativity was accepted, but Big Bang cosmology and quantum mechanics were highly disputed and rejected by such giants as Einstein. Chaos theory was still unknown. See, Arthur Hobson Quinn, *Edgar Allan Poe: A Critical Biography* (New York: Cooper Square, 1969), 542–556. Quinn consulted Sir Arthur Eddington, a giant of physics in his day, about Poe's ideas. Eddington dismissed Poe's ideas as science but grudgingly conceded that someone of his mind "is likely to hit the mark sometimes" (556).

3. Edgar Allan Poe, "Three Sundays in a Week," in *Poetry and Tales* (New York: The Library of America, 1984), 480. "A Succession of Sundays" is now known as "Three Sundays in a Week."

4. Darwin's theory of natural selection lacked any scientific proposal for a mechanism to account for changes from one generation to the next. He referred to this unknown mechanism as "unknown causes." See, Charles Darwin, *The Origin of Species* (New York: Gramercy Books, 1979), 66, 236. It would be left to Gregor Mendel's study of heredity in peas in 1866 and the discovery of DNA in 1953 by Watson and Crick that Darwin's theory had a scientific mechanism to support it. See, Jimmy H. Davis and Harry L. Poe, *Chance or Dance: An Evaluation of Design* (West Conshohocken, PA: Templeton Foundation Press, 2008), 142–144.

5. I have explored *Eureka* as a work of scientific speculation aimed at resolving the relationship between the physical and the metaphysical, or science and religion, in *Evermore: Edgar Allan Poe and the Mystery of the Universe* (Waco, TX: Baylor University Press, 2012). David N. Stamos credits *Evermore* as the catalyst for his treatment of *Eureka* from a philosophy of science perspective in *Edgar Alan Poe, Eureka, and Scientific Imagination* (Albany, NY: SUNY Press, 2017).

6. David Hume, *Principle Writings on Religion* (Oxford: Oxford University Press, 1998), 86. "A finite number of particles is only susceptible of finite transpositions: And it must happen, in an eternal duration, that every possible order or position must be tried an infinite number of times."

7. The overwhelming majority of Poe scholars who have taken a position on *Eureka* as a statement about the scientific nature of the universe have rejected it as a serious attempt at scientific speculation by Poe. In 1949, Allen Tate took the view that Arthur Hobson Quinn was wrong in seeing any scientific merit in *Eureka*. See, Allen Tate, "Our Cousin, Mr. Poe," *Partisan Review* 16, no. 12 (1949): 1217. Two years later, Tate accused Quinn of trying to gather testimonials from scientists to bolster up a work [Quinn's?] in which Quinn had little confidence. See, Allen Tate, "The Angelic Imagination," in *The Recognition of Edgar Allan Poe*, ed. Eric W. Carlson (Ann Arbor, MI: Ann Arbor Paperbacks, 1970), 253. Once The Big Bang Theory came to be accepted in the 1970s, however, Tate took a different view and remarked, "I have wondered why the modern proponents of the Big Bang hypothesis of the creation have not condescended to acknowledge Poe as a forerunner." See, Allen Tate, ed., *The Complete Poetry and Selected Criticism of Edgar Allan Poe* (New York: New American Library, 1981), viii. Richard Wilbur regarded *Eureka* as Poe's "myth of the cosmos." See, Richard Wilbur, "The House of Poe," *The Recognition of Edgar Allan Poe*, 258. T. S. Eliot dismissed *Eureka* as a "cosmological fantasy" because Poe was not a qualified scientist. See, "From Poe to Valéry," *The Recognition of Edgar Allan Poe*, 218. Ben Fisher took the position that *Eureka* has too many "comic insinuation" for it to be taken seriously as science. See, Benjamin F. Fisher, *The Cambridge Introduction to Edgar Allan Poe* (Cambridge: Cambridge University Press, 2008), 99. Following close behind Fisher, Jennifer Rae Greeson reads *Eureka* as a political satire. In contrast to those who see the embryonic form of The Big Bang Theory, Greeson sees "the rise and fall of a compulsively expanding American Empire." See, Jennifer Rae Greeson, "Poe's 1848: *Eureka*, the Southern Margin, and the Expanding U[niverse] of S[tars]," *Poe and the Remapping of Antebellum Print Culture*, ed. J. Gerald Kennedy and Jerome McGann (Baton Rouge: Louisiana State University Press, 2012), 132. Julian Symons took the view that, with respect to any scientific ideas about the universe, "*Eureka* is almost valueless, but that it is vitally important as a final statement of Poe's attitude to art." See, Julian Symons, *The Tell-Tale Heart: The Life and Work of Edgar Allan Poe* (London: Faber & Faber, 1978), 200. Kenneth Silverman, citing T. S. Eliot, said that it was "a work neither of science nor of imagination, but a yes-and-no 'Prose Poem.'" See, Kenneth Silverman, *Edgar Allan Poe: Mournful and Never-Ending*

Remembrance (New York: HarperCollins, 1991), 534. Some scholars, however, have taken a more cautious position and see an element of scientific curiosity at the least in *Eureka*. Scott Peeples takes the position that *Eureka* is simultaneously a "poetic and scientific exploration of the universe" in "Perverting the American Renaissance: Poe, Democracy, Critical Theory," *Poe and the Remapping of Antebellum Print Culture*, 70. Seo-Young Jennie Chu argues that *Eureka* involves a form of intellection dubbed "hypnotic ratiocination" which forms a bridge between logic and emotion in "Hypnotic Ratiocination," *The Edgar Allan Poe Review* 6, no. 1 (Spring 2005), 5–19; N. Bryllion Fagin acknowledged that "Critics to This Day Are Baffled by It and Differ Widely on Its Value," in *The Histrionic Mr. Poe* (Baltimore: The Johns Hopkins Press, 1949), 23. For the first century after the publication of *Eureka*, most Poe scholars dismissed it as the ravings of a mad man under the influence of alcohol and drugs, because the scientific ideas differed so radically from the standard science of the day. Hervey Allen remarked, "There are irreconcilable inconsistencies of thought in its thesis, with misapplications and misapprehensions of the data of science, even at the time that it was written (1847)." And then, in an effort to excuse Poe his radical departure from the science of his day, Allen added, "It must be remembered, in considering it in connection with Poe's life and the nature of his intellect, that the man was very ill, mentally and physically, when he wrote it." See, Hervey Allen, *Israfel*, vol. 2 (New York: George H. Doran Company, 1926), 742, 743. Philip Lindsay amplified this view with his view that *Eureka* "is a maddening conglomeration of sense and nonsense, but its value to us lies in its revelation of Poe's state of mind, the semi-insane egoism that deludes itself into believing that it holds the key to the universe," riding as it does "on the wings of opium." See, Philip Lindsay, *The Haunted Man: A Portrait of Edgar Allan Poe* (New York: The Philosophical Library, 1954), 197. In an article on collecting first printings and first appearances of Poe, the internationally prominent rare book dealer, Lee Bondi referred to this book as "the lunatic/fascinating *Eureka*," See, Lee Bondi, "Collecting Edgar Allan Poe," *Firsts: The Book Collector's Magazine* 8, no. 10 (October 1998): 38.

8. Jerome McGann, *The Poet Edgar Allan Poe: Alien Angel* (Cambridge, MA: Harvard University Press, 2014), 98, 101, 102, 106, 107.

9. Edgar Allan Poe, *Eureka*, foreword by Sir Patrick Moore (London: Hesperus Press, 2002).

10. In 2003, Lasley Dameron invited me to give a lecture on Poe at the University of Memphis. Over dinner, he confessed that he had never understood *Eureka* and did not know anyone who did. The scientific narrative made no sense. Even those who know the science well must adjust

their thinking, because Poe had to invent terms and concepts that did not exist at the time and which twentieth-century science gave other names. For instance, what Poe describes as electricity, Einstein would call energy. Poe did not mean what we call electricity. Poe also preferred to speak of duration while Einstein spoke of time. In 2009, I gave a lecture on *Eureka* and Poe's concept of imagination in Philadelphia. Ed Devinney, the astrophysicist who did the initial work on binary star systems responded to the lecture. He had not read or known of *Eureka* until he read it in preparation for his response. He said that he was stunned, startled, and amazed by the power of Poe's imagination to distil the scientific data of 1848 into a premonition of twentieth-century science so different from his own day that coincided so closely to current science. See, https://www.youtube.com/watch?v=ZO5JMQMwIqA, accessed February 19, 2018.

11. Perhaps Paul Valéry recognized this relationship in his remarks about *Eureka* with the observation, "It belongs to a department of literature remarkable for its persistence and astonishing in its variety; cosmogony is one of the oldest of all literary forms." See Paul Valéry, "On Poe's 'Eureka'," *The Recognition of Edgar Allan Poe*, 110.

12. Edgar Allan Poe, *Eureka*, ed. Stuart Levine and Susan F. Levine (Chicago: University of Chicago Press, 2004), 96. For an online version of the text in which the paragraphs are numbered, see the text prepared by René van Slooten for The Eureka Project at http://www.poe-eureka.com/the-eureka-project/, [¶ 237]. Throughout this work, citations from The Eureka Project text will cite the paragraph number in brackets following the print citation of the Levine edition.

13. Ibid., 5 [¶ not numbered].

14. Ibid., 96 [¶ 237]. In *Evermore*, I argued that Poe considered the universe to be the prose poem that he discovered:

Poe proposed that … the process of creating universes might go on "forever, and forever, and forever" with "a novel Universe swelling into existence, and then subsiding into nothingness, at every throb of the Heart Divine." With this phrase we return to the question of what Poe meant by calling *Eureka* a "prose poem" in defiance of all he had written about poetic theory. The "throb of the Heart Divine" returns us to Poe's idea of poetry as the "rhythmic creation of beauty." The universe itself manifests the source of rhythmic beauty, for Poe perceived the universe as a regularly expanding and contrasting creation. The beating of the heart has long been suspected to be the origin of the use of rhythm in music and poetry. Poe interposed the beating heart in several of his works, most probably to heighten the excitement, as in "The Tell-Tale Heart" and in "The Raven." See, Harry Lee Poe, *Evermore*, 160.

David Stamos drew a startlingly similar conclusion in *Edgar Allan Poe, Eureka, and Scientific Imagination*, 72–73:

Add now an expanding and contracting Universe, over and over again, "a novel Universe swelling into existence, and then subsiding into nothingness, at every throb of the Heart Divine," a process "renewed forever, and forever, and forever," making music like a beating heart, music that can be read, and you have a poem, the rhythmical creation of beauty using words, or rather each expansion and contraction of the Universe a poem, followed by another, and so forevermore.

15. See John Ostrom, ed., *The Letters of Edgar Allan Poe*, vol. 2 (Cambridge, MA: Harvard University Press, 1948), 361–364.
16. Levine, 7 [¶ 5].
17. Ibid., 23 [¶ 45, 47, 48].
18. Ibid., 23, 26, 41, 44, 48, 68, 95 [¶ 48, 52, 91, 107, 118, 165, 236].
19. Ibid., 25 [¶ 50].
20. Ibid., 25 [¶ 51].
21. Ibid., 26 [¶ 53].
22. George Johnstone Stoney first proposed the existence of particles as components of atoms in 1874, and J. J. Thomson received the Nobel Prize in 1906 for his experimental discovery of the electron with its negative or repulsive charge. In 1909, Ernest Rutherford proposed the existence of the positively charged nucleus at the center of the atom as a result of his experimentation in bombarding metal foil with alpha particles.
23. Levine, 27 [¶ 55].
24. Ibid., 27 [¶ 56].
25. Ibid., 28–29 [¶ 58].
26. Ibid., 30–31 [¶ 62–63].
27. Ibid., 32 [¶ 68]. René van Slooten has focused on Poe's statement that the effects of gravity occur "all at the same time" to make some startling conclusions: "In Poe's view this 'sympathy' between atoms is the fundamental force upon which gravity rests. Gravity itself is not a force but an effect that is caused by the deeper 'sympathy' between fundamental particles. This 'sympathy', and thus gravity, acts instantaneous, regardless of distance. Modern physics and astronomy are based on the assumption that gravity travels with the velocity of light, although attempts to prove that have failed so far. Gravity remains the most familiar, but also the most elusive and mysterious of all physical phenomena! However, modern quantum physics has proven that a form of immediate 'sympathy' does indeed exist between paired fundamental particles." See http://www.poe-eureka.com/the-eureka-project/, footnote 19.
28. Ibid., 32 [¶ 68].

29. Ibid., 32 [¶ 68].
30. Poe had previously discussed his ideas about mutual adaptation in Edgar A. Poe, "The American Drama," *The American Review*, 2 no. 2 (1845): 121.
31. Levine., 33 [¶ 71].
32. Ibid., 35 [¶ 74].
33. Poe provided the following formula: "From a *luminous* centre, *Light* issues by radiation; and the quantities of light received upon any given plane, supposed to be shifting its position so as to be now nearer -the centre and now farther from it, will be diminished in the same proportion as the squares of the distances of the plane from the luminous body, are increased; and will be increased in the same proportion as these squares are diminished." "The expression of the law may be thus generalized: — the number of light-particles (or, if the phrase be preferred, the number of light-impressions) received upon the shifting plane, will be *inversely* proportional with the squares of the distances of the plane. Generalizing yet again, we may say that the diffusion — the scattering — the radiation, in a word — is *directly* proportional with the squares of the distances." Levine, 38 [¶ 82–83].
34. Ibid., 39 [¶ 85].
35. Ibid., 39 [¶ 85].
36. Ibid., 39 [¶ 86].
37. Ibid., 42–43 [¶ 95–98].
38. After writing *Eureka*, Poe defined poetry as the "*Rhythmical Creation of Beauty.*" See "The Poetic Principle," *Sartain's Union Magazine*, 7 no. 4 (October 1850): 234.
39. Levine, 47 [¶ 114].
40. Ibid., 48 [¶ 118].
41. Ibid., 49 [¶ 122].
42. Ibid., 51 [¶ 126].
43. Ibid., 52 [¶ 129].
44. Ibid., 52–53 [¶ 130].
45. Ibid., 53 [¶ 132].
46. Ibid., 61 [¶ 151].
47. Ibid., 62 [¶ 152].
48. Ibid., 80 [¶ 193].
49. Ibid., 81 [¶ 194].
50. Ibid., 87 [¶ 213].
51. Ibid., 86 [¶ 209].
52. Ibid., 87 [¶ 214].
53. In "A Succession of Sundays," later published as "Three Sundays in a Week," the punch line to his comic romance came with the concluding

observation that no time has preference to place and no place has preference to time. In "Dreamland," Poe linked time and space together, much
as Augustine had done, in expressing the idea that to leave the world of
space is to leave the world of time: "Out of Space—Out of Time."

54. Levine, 92 [¶ 224].
55. Nigel Calder, *Einstein's Universe* (New York: Viking Press, 1979), 129.
56. Ibid., 97–98 [¶ 239–242].
57. Ibid., 99 [¶ 243].
58. Ibid., 99 [¶ 245].
59. Ibid., 99 [¶ 245].
60. Ibid., 100 [¶ 247].
61. Ibid., 101 [¶ 249]; Edgar A. Poe, "The American Drama," *The
American Review*, 2 no. 2 (1845): 121. Poe had explored this idea in a
"Marginalia" column a year earlier in the *Democratic Review*.
62. Ibid., 7 [¶ 5].
63. Ibid., 99 [¶ 244].
64. Ibid., 101 [¶ 249].
65. Ibid., 101 [¶ 250].
66. Ibid., 103 [¶ 255].

Selected Bibliography

What follows is a highly selective list of suggested readings about Edgar A. Poe whose headings correspond chronologically to the places and concepts examined in this volume. After the first three sections devoted to biographical sources, general studies, and theoretical approaches concerning place and space, the remaining sections are devoted to the geographical, imaginary, imagined, and intuited spaces related to Poe's life and reflected in his works. All of the books and articles have been recommended for inclusion by the chapter authors. These selections are provided as a place for readers to begin their search for more information on these topics and to supplement the notes at the end of each chapter. This bibliography is by no means intended to be exhaustive.

Biography

Allen, Hervey. *Israfel: The Life and Times of Edgar Allan Poe.* 2 vols. New York: George H. Doran, 1926.

Bittner, William R. *Poe: A Biography.* Boston: Little, Brown, 1962.

Bonaparte, Marie. *The Life and Works of Edgar Allan Poe a Psycho-Analytic Interpretation.* Translated by John Rodker. London: Imago, 1949. Published in French in 1933.

Dwight, Thomas, and David K. Jackson. *The Poe Log: A Documentary Life of Edgar Allan Poe, 1809–1849.* New York: G. K. Hall, 1987.

Griswold, Rufus Wilmot. "Edgar Allan Poe." In *The Poets and Poetry of America* (First published in 1842), 387.

———. "Edgar Allan Poe." In *The Prose Writers of America* (First published in 1847), 523–524.

———. "Memoir of the Author." *The Works of the Late Edgar Allan Poe.* New York: Redfield, 1850.

Hutchisson, James M. *Poe.* Jackson: University Press of Mississippi, 2005.

Meyers, Jeffrey. *Edgar Allan Poe: Life and Legacy.* New York: Cooper Square Press, 1992.

Miller, John Carl, ed. *Poe's Helen Remembers.* Charlottesville: University Press of Virginia, 1979.

Phillips, Mary E. *Edgar Allan Poe: The Man.* 2 vols. Chicago: John C. Winston, 1926.

Quinn, Arthur Hobson. *Edgar Allan Poe: A Critical Biography.* New York and Baltimore: D. Appleton-Century Company and The Johns Hopkins University Press, 1941.

Silverman, Kenneth. *Edgar A. Poe: Mournful and Never-Ending Remembrance.* New York: HarperCollins, 1991.

Woodberry, George E. *Edgar Allan Poe.* Boston: Houghton Mifflin, 1885.

Woodberry, George E. *The Life of Edgar Allan Poe.* 2 vols. Boston: Houghton Mifflin, 1909.

GENERAL STUDIES

Cantalupo, Barbara. *Poe and the Visual Arts.* University Park, PA: The Pennsylvania State University Press, 2014.

Hayes, Kevin J. *Poe and the Printed Word.* New York: Cambridge University Press, 2004.

Machor, James L. *Reading Fiction in Antebellum America: Informed Response and Reception Histories, 1820–1865.* Baltimore: Johns Hopkins University Press, 2011.

McGann, Jerome. *The Poet Edgar Allan Poe: Alien Angel.* Cambridge, MA: Harvard University Press, 2014.

Ocker, J. W. *Poe-Land: The Hallowed Haunts of Edgar Allan Poe.* Woodstock, VT: The Countryman Press, 2015.

Peeples, Scott. "Nowhere Man: The Problem of Poe and Place." *Nexus (Publication of the Asociación Española de Estudios Anglo-Norteamericanos)* 1 (2009): 85–90.

Tane, Susan Jaffe. *Nevermore: The Edgar Allan Poe Collection of Susan Jaffe Tane.* Ithaca: Cornell University Press, 2006.

On Place and Space

Blunt, Alison, and Robyn Dowling. *Home*. London and New York: Routledge, 2006.

Casey, Edward S. *Remembering: A Phenomenological Perspective*. Bloomington and Indianapolis: Indiana University Press, 1987.

———. *The Fate of Place: A Philosophical History*. Berkeley: University of California Press, 1997.

Davenport, Guy. *The Geography of the Imagination: Forty Essays*. San Francisco: North Point Press, 1981.

Relph, Edward. *Place and Placelessnes*. London: Pion Limited, 1976.

Stanard, Mary Newton, ed. *Edgar Allan Poe Letters Till Now Unpublished in the Valentine Museum Richmond, Virginia*. Philadelphia: J. B. Lippincott, 1925.

Tally, Robert T., Jr., ed. "On Geocriticism." In *Geocritical Explorations: Space, Place, and Mapping Literary and Cultural Studies*, 1–12. New York: Palgrave Macmillan, 2011.

Tuan, Yi-Fu. *Space and Place: The Perspective of Experience*. Minneapolis: University of Minnesota Press, 1977.

———. *Landscapes of Fear*. Minneapolis: University of Minnesota Press, 1979.

———. *Cosmos & Hearth: A Cosmopolite's Viewpoint*. Minneapolis: University of Minnesota Press, 1996.

Westphal, Bertrand. "Foreword." In *Geocritical Explorations: Space, Place, and Mapping Literary and Cultural Studies*, edited by Robert T. Tally, Jr., ix–xv. New York: Palgrave Macmillan, 2011.

Geographical Places

Boston

Beidler, Philip. "Soldier Poe." *Midwest Quarterly* 53, no. 4 (2012): 329–343.

Higginson, Thomas Wentworth. *Short Studies of American Authors*. Boston: Lee and Shepard, 1880.

Kopley, Richard. "Naysayers: Poe, Hawthorne, and Melville." In *The Oxford Handbook of Transcendentalism*, edited by Joel Myerson, Sandra Harbert Petrulionis, and Laura Dassow Walls, 597–616. Oxford: Oxford University Press, 2010.

Lewis, Paul, and Dan Currie. "The Raven in the Frog Pond: Edgar Allan Poe and the City of Boston." In *Born in the U.S.A.: Birth, Commemoration, and American Public Memory*, edited by Seth C. Bruggeman, 217–239. Amherst: University of Massachusetts Press, 2012.

Phillips, Philip Edward. "Poe's 1845 Boston Lyceum Appearance Reconsidered." In *Deciphering Poe: Subtexts, Contexts, Subversive Meaning*, edited by Alexandra Urakova, 41–52. Bethlehem: Lehigh University Press, 2013a.

————. "The American Stage." In *Edgar Allan Poe in Context*, edited by Kevin J. Hayes, 118–128. Cambridge: Cambridge University Press, 2013b.

Prown, Katherine Hemple. "The Cavalier and the Syren: Edgar Allan Poe, Cornelia Wells Walter, and the Boston Lyceum Incident." *The New England Quarterly* 66, no. 1 (1993): 110–123.

Rossiter, William Sidney Rossiter. *Days and Ways in Old Boston*. Boston: H. R. Stearns, 1915.

Silcox, Heidi. "Transcendentalism". In *Edgar Allan Poe in Context*, edited by Kevin J. Hayes, 269–287. Cambridge: Cambridge University Press, 2013.

Smith, Geddeth. *The Brief Career of Eliza Poe*. London and Toronto: Associated University Presses, 1988.

Richmond

Case, Keshia A., and P. Christopher. Semtner on Behalf of the Poe Museum. *Images of America: Edgar Allan Poe in Richmond*. Richmond: Arcadia, 2009.

Dabney, Virginius. *Richmond: The Story of a City*. Garden City, NY: Doubleday, 1976.

Inge, M. Thomas, ed. *James Branch Cabell Centennial Essays*. Baton Rouge: Louisiana State University Press, 1983.

Mordecai, Samuel. *Richmond in By-Gone Days: Being Reminiscences of a Very Old Citizen*. Richmond, VA: George M. West, 1856.

London

Allen, Michael. *Poe and the British Magazine Tradition*. New York: Oxford University Press, 1969.

Caygill, Marjorie. *The Story of the British Museum*. 3rd ed. London: British Museum Press, 2002.

Nichol, Bran. "Reading and Not Reading 'The Man of the Crowd': Poe, the City, and the Gothic Text." *Philological Quarterly* 91, no. 3 (2012): 465–493.

Webb, R. K. *Modern England: From the 18th Century to the Present*. New York: Harper & Row, 1980.

Baltimore

French, John C. "Poe's Literary Baltimore." *Maryland Historical Magazine* 32, no. 2 (June 1937): 112.

Hammond, Alexander. "Edgar Allan Poe's Tales of the Folio Club: The Evolution of a Lost Book." *Poe at Work: Seven Textual Studies*, 13–43. Baltimore: Edgar Allan Poe Society, 1978.

Hewitt, John Hill. *Shadows on the Wall.* Baltimore: Turnbull Bros., 1877.

Hickman, Nathaniel, ed. *The Citizen Soldier at North Point and Fort McHenry, September 12 & 13, 1814.* Baltimore: Nathaniel Hickman, 1858.

Mabbott, Thomas Ollive, ed. *Merlin, Together with Recollections of Edgar A. Poe.* New York: Scholar's Facsimiles and Reprints, 1941.

Pearl, Matthew. "A Poe Death Dossier: Discoveries and Queries in the Death of Edgar Allan Poe" (Parts I and II). *Edgar Allan Poe Review* 7, no. 2. (2006) and 8, no. 1 (2007): 4–29, 8–31.

Powell, Michael A. *Too Much Moran: Respecting the Death of Edgar Poe.* Eugene, OR: Pacific Rim University Press, 2009.

Reilly, John E. "Robert D'Unger and His Reminiscences of Poe in Baltimore." *Maryland Historical Magazine* 88 (Spring 1993): 60–72.

Rice, Sara Sigourney, ed. *Edgar Allan Poe: A Memorial Volume.* Baltimore: Lucus, 1877.

Sherman, Stuart C. "The Library Company of Baltimore, 1795–1855." *Maryland Historical Magazine* 39, no. 1 (March 1944): 6–24.

Uhler, John Earle. "The Delphian Club: A Contribution to the Literary History of Baltimore in the Early Nineteenth Century." *Maryland Historical Magazine* XX, no. 4 (December 1925): 305–346

Walsh, John E. *Midnight Dreary: The Mysterious Death of Edgar Allan Poe.* New Brunswick, NJ: Rutgers University Press, 1998.

Philadelphia

Britt, Theron. "The Common Property of the Mob: Democracy and Identity in Poe's 'William Wilson.'" *Mississippi Quarterly* 48, no. 2 (1995): 197–210.

Cleman, John. "Irresistible Impulses: Edgar Allan Poe and the Insanity Defense." *American Literature* 63, no. 4 (1991): 623–640.

Dayan, Joan. "Poe, Persons, and Property." *American Literary History* 11, no. 3 (1999): 405–425.

Haslam, Jason. "Pits, Pendulums, and Penitentiaries." *Texas Studies in Language and Literature* 50, no. 3 (2008): 268–284.

Haspel, Paul. "Bells of Freedom and Foreboding: Liberty Bell Ideology and the Clock Motif in Edgar Allan Poe's 'The Masque of the Red Death.'" *Edgar Allan Poe Review* 13, no. 1 (2012): 46–70.

Lemay, Leo, J. A. "Poe's 'The Business Man': Its Contexts and Satire of Franklin's Autobiography." *Poe Studies/Dark Romanticism: History, Theory, Interpretation* 15, no. 2 (1982): 29–37.

Lemire, Elise. "'The Murders in the Rue Morgue': Amalgamation Discourses and the Race Riots of 1838 in Poe's Philadelphia." In *Romancing the Shadow,* ed. J. Gerald Kennedy, 177–204. Oxford: Oxford University Press, 2001.

Sloane, David E. E. "Usher's Nervous Fever: The Meaning of Medicine in Poe's 'The Fall of the House of Usher.'" In *Poe and His Times: The Artist and His Milieu*, ed. Benjamin Franklin Fisher, IV, 146–153. Baltimore: Edgar Allan Poe Society, 1990.

New York City

Kennedy, Gerald J. "Introduction." In *Poe and the Remapping of Antebellum Print Culture*, ed. J. Gerald Kennedy and Jerome McGann, 1–12. Baton Rouge: Louisiana State University Press, 2012a.
Kennedy, Gerald J. "Inventing the Literati: Poe's Remapping of Antebellum Print Culture." In *Poe and the Remapping of Antebellum Print Culture*, ed. J. Gerald Kennedy and Jerome McGann, 13–36. Baton Rouge: Louisiana State University Press, 2012b.
Lee, Maurice S. "Poe by the Numbers: Odd Man Out?" In *Poe and the Remapping of Antebellum Print Culture*, ed. J. Gerald Kennedy and Jerome McGann, 227–244. Baton Rouge: Louisiana State University Press, 2012.
Schick, Joseph. "The Origin of 'The Cask of Amontillado.'" *American Literature* 6 (March 1934): 18–21.
Scott Peeples, "'To Reproduce a City': New York Letters and the Urban American Renaissance." In *Poe and the Remapping of Antebellum Print Culture*, ed. J. Gerald Kennedy and Jerome McGann, 101–122. Baton Rouge: Louisiana State University Press, 2012.

UNKNOWN SPACES

Fantastic Spaces

Ariès, Philippe. *The Hour of Our Death: The Classic History of Western Attitudes Toward Death*. Translated by Helen Weaver. 2nd ed. New York: Vintage, 1982. Especially Chapter 10, "The Age of the Beautiful Death."
Berman, Jacob Rama. *American Arabesque: Arabs and Islam in the Nineteenth Century Imaginary*. New York: New York University Press, 2012. Especially Chapter 3, "Poe's Taste for the Arabesque."
Cantalupo, Barbara. "Preludes to *Eureka*: Poe's 'Absolute Reciprocity of Adaptation' in 'Shadow' and 'The Power of Words.'" *Poe Studies/Dark Romanticism* 29, no. 1 (June 1996): 17–21.
Dempsey, Charles. *Inventing the Renaissance Putto*. Chapel Hill, NC: University of North Carolina Press, 2001.
Engel, William E. "Echoic Effects in Poe's Poetic Double Economy—of Memory." *Connotations* 23, no. 1 (2013/2014): 26–48.

Erkkila, Betsy. "The Poetics of Whiteness: Poe and the Racial Imaginary." In *Romancing the Shadow: Poe and Race*, edited by J. Gerald Kennedy and Liliane Weissberg, 41–74. Oxford: Oxford University Press, 2001.

———. "Perverting the American Renaissance." In *Poe and the Remapping of Antebellum Print Culture*, edited by J. Gerald Kennedy and Jerome McGann, 65–100. Baton Rouge: Louisiana State University Press, 2012.

Heninger, S. K., Jr. *Touches of Sweet Harmony: Pythagorean Cosmology and Renaissance Poetics*. San Marino: The Huntington Library, 1974.

Huttar, Charles A. "Poe's Angels." In *Essays for Richard Ellmann*, edited by Susan Dick, et al., 82–84. Montréal: McGill-Queens University Press, 1989.

Martin, Therese. "The Development of Winged Angels in Early Christian Art." *Espacio, Tiempo y Forma, Serie VII, Historia del Arte* 14 (2001): 11–30.

Montgomery, Travis. "Poe's Oriental Gothic: 'Metzengerstein' (1832), 'The Visionary' (1834), 'Berenice' (1835), the Imagination, and Authorship's Perils." *Gothic Studies* 12 (2) (2010): 4–28.

———. "The Near East." In *Edgar Allan Poe in Context*, edited by Kevin J. Hayes, 53–62. Cambridge: Cambridge University Press, 2012.

Raymond, Joad. *Milton's Angels*. Oxford: Oxford University Press, 2010.

The South Seas

Kopley, Richard, ed. *Poe's* Pym: *Critical Explorations*. Durham, NC: Duke University Press, 1992.

———, ed. "Introduction." *The Narrative of Arthur Gordon Pym of Nantucket*, by Edgar Allan Poe, ix–xxix. New York: Penguin, 1999.

Limon, John. *The Place of Fiction in the Time of Science: A Disciplinary History of American Writing*. New York: Cambridge University Press, 1990.

Wilbur, Richard. "Introduction." *The Narrative of Arthur Gordon Pym*, edited by Edgar Allan Poe, vii–xxv. Boston: David R. Godine, 1973.

Poe and Germany

Crisman, William. *Poe as Comparatist: Hawthorne and 'the German Tieck' (Once More)*. ATQ. Special Issue 16, no. 1 (March 2002): 53–64.

Hansen, Thomas S., and Burton Pollin. *The German Face of Edgar Allan Poe: A Study of Literary References in His* Works. Columbia, SC: Camden House, 1995.

Littschager, Marius. "Poe in Germany: A Panoramic and Historical View of His Works. Translated into German Language." In *Translated Poe*, edited by Emron Esplin and Margarida Vale de Gato, 55–64. Bethlehem, PA: Lehigh University Press, 2014.

Omans, Glen A. "'Intellect, Taste, and the Moral Sense': Poe's Debt to Immanuel Kant." *Studies in the American Renaissance* (1980): 123–168.
Punter, David. *The Literature of Terror: The Gothic Tradition.* New York: Routledge, 2013.
Thompson, G. R. "'Proper Evidences of Madness': American Gothic and the Interpretation of 'Ligeia.'" *ESQ* 18 (1972): 30–49.

IMAGINED PLACES

Russia

Grossman, Joan Delaney. *Edgar Allan Poe in Russia: A Study in Legend and Literary Influence.* Würzburg: Jal-Verlag, 1983.
Lavrov, Alexander. "Edgar Po v Peterburge: konturi legendi" [Edgar Poe in St. Petersburg: The Contours of a Legend"]. In Lavrov, Alexander. Simvolisti i grugie: Stat'i. Rozyskanya. Publikatsii [Symbolists and Others: Essays. Inquiries. Publications], 54–59. Moscow: New Literary Observer [in Russian].
Po, Bodler, Dostoevskii: Blesk i nisheta nazionalnogo genia [Poe, Baudelaire, Dostoevsky: Splendors and Miseries of National Genius]. Edited by Sergey Fokine and Alexandra Urakova. Moscow: Novoe literaturnoe obozrenie, 2017 [in Russian].

Egypt

Irwin, John T. *American Hieroglyphics: The Symbol of the Egyptian Hieroglyphics in the American Renaissance.* Baltimore: The Johns Hopkins University Press, 1980.
Thompson, Jason. *Wonderful Things: A History of Egyptology: 1: From Antiquity to 1881.* Cairo: American University in Cairo Press, 2015.
Trafton, Scott. *Egypt Land: Race and Nineteenth-Century American Egyptomania.* Durham: Duke University Press, 2004.

France

Bandy, W. T. "New Light on Baudelaire and Poe." *Yale French Studies* 10 (1952): 65–69.
———, ed. "Introduction." In *Edgar Allan Poe: sa vie et ses ouvrages*, by Charles Baudelaire, xi–xlii. Toronto and Buffalo: University of Toronto Press, 1973.
Barzun, Jacques. "A Note on the Inadequacy of Poe as a Proofreader and of His Editors as French Scholars. *The Romanic Review* 61 (1970): 12–122.

Baudelaire, Charles. "Edgar Poe: Sa Vie et ses oeuvres." In *Histoires extraor-dinaires par Edgar Poe*, translated and edited by Charles Baudelaire. Paris: Michel Lévy Frères, 1856.

Cabot, Charles. Introduction in *Aventures d'Arthur Gordon Pym*. By Edgar Allan Poe. Translated by Charles Baudelaire. Edited by Charles Cabot. Paris: Gallimard, 1975.

Kent, Charles W. "Poe's Student Days at the University of Virginia." *Bookman* 44, no. 5 (1917): 430–440.

Kopley, Richard. *Edgar Allan Poe and the Dupin Mysteries*. New York: Palgrave, 2008.

Phillips, Philip Edward. *Baudelaire's Poe: Selections from the W. T. Bandy Collection*, Jean and Alexander Heard Library, Vanderbilt University, Permanent Online Exhibition. Available at http://exhibits.library.vanderbilt.edu/BaudelairePoe/.

Pollin, Burton R. "'Murders in the Rue Morgue': The Ingenious Web Unraveled." In *Insights and Outlooks: Essays on Great* Writers, 235–259. New York: Gordian Press, 1986.

———. "Bulwer-Lytton's Influence on Poe's Works and Ideas, Especially for an Author's 'Preconceived Design.'" *The Edgar Allan Poe Review* 1, no. 1 (2000): 5–12.

Pichois, Claude. *Baudelaire*. Additional research by Jean Ziegler, translated by Graham Robb. London: Hamish Hamilton, 1989.

Quinn, Patrick F. *The French Face of Edgar Poe*. Carbondale and Edwardsville: Southern Illinois University Press, 1957.

Vines, Lois Davis, ed. *Poe Abroad: Influence, Reception, Affinities*. Iowa City: University of Iowa Press, 1999.

Argentina

Berg, Mary G. "Horacio Quiroga." In *Poe Abroad*, edited by Lois Davis Vines, 239–243. Iowa City: University of Iowa Press, 1999.

Clantz, Margo. "Poe en Quiroga." In *Aproximaciones a Horacio Quiroga*, edited by Angel Flores, 93–118. Caracas: Monte Avila, 1976.

Esplin, Emron. "'William Wilson' as a Microcosm of Julio Cortázar's Poe Translations: Horror in the Doubling of the Human Will." In *Translated Poe*, edited by Emron Esplin and Margarida Vale de Gato, 251–260, 410–416. Bethlehem, PA: Lehigh University Press, 2014.

———. *Borges's Poe: The Influence and Reinvention of Edgar Allan Poe in Spanish America*. Athens: University of Georgia Press, 2016.

González Bermajo, Ernesto. *Conversaciones con Cortázar*. Barcelona: Editora y Distribuidora Hispano Americana, 1978.

Heliodoro Valle, Rafael. "Fichas para la bibliografía de Poe en Hispánoamerica." *Revista Iberoamericana* 16 (1950): 199–214.

Irwin, John T. *The Mystery to a Solution: Poe, Borges, and the Analytic Detective Story.* Baltimore: The Johns Hopkins University Press, 1994.

Lefevere, André. "Why Waste Our Time on Rewrites: The Trouble with Interpretation and the Role of Rewriting in an Alternative Paradigm." In *The Manipulation of Literature: Studies in Literary Translation*, edited by Theo Hermans, 215–243. New York: St. Martin's Press, 1985.

Woodbridge, Hensley C. "Poe in Spanish America: A Bibliographical Supplement." *Poe Newsletter* 2 (1969): 18–19.

INTUITED PLACES

The Universe

Greeson, Jennifer Rae Greeson. "Poe's 1848: *Eureka*, the Southern Margin, and the Expanding U[niverse] of S[tars]." *Poe and the Remapping of Antebellum Print Culture*, edited by J. Gerald Kennedy and Jerome McGann. Baton Rouge: Louisiana State University Press, 2012.

Poe, Edgar Allan. *Eureka.* Edited by Stuart Levine and Susan F. Levine. Urbana: University of Illinois Press, 2004.

Poe, Harry Lee. *Evermore: Edgar Allan Poe and the Mystery of the Universe.* Waco, TX: Baylor University Press, 2012.

Stamos, David N. *Edgar Alan Poe, "Eureka," and Scientific Imagination.* Albany, NY: SUNY Press, 2017.

INDEX

Buckingham, James Silk, 276, 278, 283, 286
Budge, E.A. Wallis, 280, 282, 288
  Osiris and the Egyptian Resurrection, 280, 282
Bulfinch, Charles, 24
Bulwer-Lytton, Edward
  Pelham, or the Adventures of a Gentleman, 304
  Rienzi, the Last of the Tribunes, 83
  "Jocko," 307
Bürger, Gottfried August, 223, 224, 227, 228, 231, 232
  "Lenore," 223–228
Burk, John Daly, 55
Burling, Ebenezer, 198, 199
Burne-Jones, Edward, 170, 172, 189
Burns, Robert, 75
Burr, C. Chauncey, 114
Butler, Frances Anne, 84
Byer, Robert, 90, 95, 255, 262
Byron, Lord, 27, 49, 78, 79, 81, 86, 221
  Childe Harold's Pilgrimage, 79
  Don Juan, 244
  Manfred, 220
  "Tamerlane," 27

C
Cabell, James Branch, 65, 67–69
Calder, Nigel, 358, 367
Calisch, Rabbi Edward N., 62
Campanella, Tommaso, 180, 191
  City of the Sun, 180
Campbell, Killis, 191, 223, 231
Canning, Geroge, 85
Cannon, James E., 62
Cantalupo, Charles, 139, 143
Carlyle, Thomas, 218
  The German Romance, 218
  "Germanic," 218
Cary, Henry, 156, 157

Casares, Adolfo Bioy, 332, 340, 341
Casey, Edward S., 190
Castronovo, Russ, 87, 88
Catholocism, 85, 117, 125
Cavendish, Henry, 351
Cecil, L. Moffitt, 205, 213
Champollion, Jean-Francois, 268, 273, 276, 287
Chaos Theory, 345, 352, 361
  "the Butterfly effect," 352
Charleston, 6, 28, 56, 57, 71, 194–196, 199, 244
  Daily Courier, 57
  Sullivan's Island, 4, 7, 71, 98, 135, 199, 267
Charlottesville
  Enlightenment, 50
  Ragged Mountains Nature Preserve, 53
  University of Virginia, 7, 50, 51, 56, 198, 204, 218, 243, 290, 291, 298, 307; Blaettermann, 218, 299
Child, Lydia Maria, 17, 149, 156
Childs, George William, 115
Chorley, Henry F., 82, 203
Chorographia, xiii
Chronology, Chronologos, 108, 111. *See also* Poe, Edgar A., work by, *Tales of the Folio Club*
Clarke, Joseph H., 48, 79, 198, 298
Clark, Lewis Gaylord, 157
Cleland, Thomas, 59
Clemm, Maria "Muddy" Poe, 8, 35, 60, 106, 118, 123, 200, 201, 205, 226, 290
Clemm, Rev. W.T.D., 113
Clemm, Virginia, 8, 106
  death of, 9
  marriage to Poe, 8
Colburn, Henry, 95, 304
Coleman, Edward, 310

Snodgrass, Joseph Evans, 111, 113,
118, 122
Soult, 302
South America, 321
South Carolina, 3, 29, 57, 71, 98,
135, 196, 244, 245, 308
Charleston, 57, 196
South Pole. *See* Poe, Edgar A., work
by, "MS found in a Bottle" and
"Narrative of Arthur Gordon
Pym"
South Seas, 198
Space
angelic, 183
"and Duration are one," 358
imaginative, 186
indeterminacy, 186
spatial independence, 91
spatio-temporality, 23
Spain, 135
Toledo, 135
Spanish America, 315, 323–325, 327,
337
modernismo, 323
Sparks, Jared, 103
Spatial, Sense of place, 145
Stage, 14, 24, 25, 31, 33, 47, 102,
128, 135, 139, 280, 334
American, 25, 26, 39, 40
Stanard, Jane Stith Craig, 61, 193
Stanard, Mary Newton, 61
Dreamer, 61
Stanard, Robert Craig, 58
Stanard, William G., 61
St. Armand, Barton Levi, 288
Starr, Mary, 202
Stephens, J.L., 205
*Incidents of Travel in Egypt, Arabia
Petraea, and the Holy Land*,
205
St. Petersburg, 243–252, 255–261,
291, 313

"character in Russian collective
consciousness," 256
Sullivan's Island, 4, 71, 98, 135, 199,
267
Charleston Harbor, 199
Fort Moultrie, 7, 199
Surgical amphitheater, 131
Symbolism, 185
French, 246
movement, 249, 291
Russian, 246, 259, 260

T
Tane, Susan Jaffe, 7, 37, 38, 40, 41,
107, 110, 120
Tekeli, 26, 195, 196, 200, 210
Temporal, 145, 175
Theater
Federal Street, 24, 25, 31
Odeon, 31
Theory, 15, 17, 53, 61, 67, 108, 135,
140, 261, 336, 347, 351, 355,
357, 360, 364
Theron, Brit, 133
Thomas, Calvin F.S., 7, 28
Thompson, G.R., 216, 276, 280
*Poe's Fiction:Romantic Irony in the
Gothic Tales*, 216
Thompson, John Ruben
*Genius and Character of Edgar
Allan Poe, The*, 61
Thoreau, Henry David, 31, 123
Tieck, Ludwig, 216
"Die Freunde," 216
Titus, 206, 208, 209
Tobacco, 125. *See also* Virginia; Allan,
John
crops, 44
export of, 43, 47
Tomc, Sandra M., 33, 34, 41
Topographia, 248, 257, 262

CPSIA information can be obtained
at www.ICGtesting.com
Printed in the USA
LVHW082017211119
638117LV00005B/8/P